TALK

For Judy—
so nice sharing
this evening with
you.

Susan Schaenz

TALK

NPR's Susan Stamberg Considers All Things

Susan Stamberg

A PERIGEE BOOK

For Joshua Collins Stamberg

Perigee Books
are published by
The Berkley Publishing Group
200 Madison Avenue
New York, NY 10016

First Perigee Edition 1994
Copyright © 1993 by Susan Stamberg
Published by arrangement with Random House, Inc.

Library of Congress Cataloging-in-Publication Data

Stamberg, Susan, date.

Talk : NPR's Susan Stamberg considers all things / Susan Stamberg.

p. cm.

"A Perigee book."

ISBN 0-399-51873-8 (acid-free paper)

1. National Public Radio (U.S.) I. Title.

[AC5.S69 `1994]   93-32928 CIP

081—dc20

Cover design by Anthony Russo
Cover photo © by Douglas Edmunds
Printed in the United States of America
1 2 3 4 5 6 7 8 9 10

This book is printed on acid-free paper.
∞

Dear Jonathon:

For the last few days I've found myself thinking of an especially balmy evening in 1981 or '82, when a number of us had been working late—some news development kept changing as we went off the air at 6:30 and needed tending, updating, until 9:30 or so. We came out into the soft air of a Washington spring to discover that the pavement in front of our building on M Street had been resurfaced, the freshly cemented squares blocked off with frail walls of string held in place by small wooden pegs. I leaned out over the string and with my forefinger traced my initials—S.S.—and the date in the wet cement. Some people I'd come outside with added their initials. We started laughing, feeling giddy and carefree and just the slightest bit sinful. As more co-workers emerged, I said, "We're playing Grauman's Chinese—come help!" Soon, even our boss, the news director, was crouched down, etching her initials into the pavement. Others stepped over the string to add handprints and shoe prints. After a while, we ran out of sidewalk and people. We called laughing good-nights to one another and went home. In the morning, I checked the pavement. All our initials, the dates, everything, had been erased. Trowels had smoothed new cement over those squares. We hadn't been able to leave our marks.

—From letter of proposal for this book

Radio is about as lasting as a butterfly's cough.

—Fred Allen

Contents

Foreword

Four months after the hardcover edition of *Talk* came out, thirty years into a career in broadcasting, and sitting in as host for *Weekend Edition*/Saturday, I had The Radio Dream: My program went on the air at 8:00 A.M. I had to be at work by 5:15. Arriving at M Street, waiting for the elevator, I peered at my watch. It was 9:30.

"WHAT HAPPENED?" I screamed in the fog of sleep. "Didn't the alarm go off? Did I take too much time in the shower? An hour and a half late! What have they done on the air? WHAT HAPPENED?"

Everyone who's ever sat in front of a microphone has had that dream, or one of its variations: the On Air light goes on and you get lockjaw; the On Air light goes on and you have no script; the On Air light goes on and your mind is blank.

You would think after so many years at so many microphones, I'd stop having that dream. But there it was again, on the eve of my return to the air, after traveling around for many weeks on a book tour, talking about *Talk*. There's something reassuring to me in the fact that I still have that Radio Dream. It means I love the medium enough to be anxious about doing it properly. I hope it means there's still room for growth, doing it better. And I *know* it means I was glad to be done talking about myself (the job description of a book tour), and more than ready to resume a more natural state: talking with others.

Still, on the road I learned some things about this book that might be useful to share.

First, although it is organized chronologically, you can certainly read *Talk* at random and out of order, flipping from a 1991 conversation to something said back in 1977. But those who began at the beginning and went straight through said, read that way, *Talk* becomes an unfolding story of our times, accumulating the weight of an oral time capsule. A passage through time. Younger readers liked encountering the seventies and eighties through conversations and reports rather than "boring history lessons." Older readers said they relived their own lives on these pages—bumping up against things they'd forgotten (who remembers that in 1971 shag haircuts were in, or that 1985's big song was "We Are the World"?). They found little shocks of recognition, laughs and sadnesses in these remembrances of things past.

One earnest and inspired summer at a camp in Connecticut years ago, I fashioned a motto by which I thought I might try to live: consider the past; savor the present; anticipate the future. *Talk* attempts to honor that motto. What's past, on these pages, carries lessons for today, about the abuse of power (Watergate), the intransigence of racial tensions (James Baldwin, in 1985, anticipating the Los Angeles riots, saying that color is always more important than class), the transcendance of art (Nadine Gordimer, in 1979, crafting powerful novels in a nation where her writing was banned). The present, here, is savored in visits with some of today's most effective communicators: Garrison Keillor, Philip Roth, Annie Leibovitz. And the future is foreshadowed in 1984 by Geraldine Ferraro's Vice Presidential candidacy, which anticipated the brace of women today who wield political power.

Talk revisits twenty years' worth of such encounters. Plus there's quite a bit of writing here, to give history and context to the conversations, and to be personal in a way a journalist cannot be on the job. There are more "I"s on these pages than you ever hear on the air. Not as written self-indulgence, but to explain how the personal and professional have interconnected in this radio work you're about to read. For in addition to being about the past twenty years, *Talk* is about radio, and about interviewing and reporting, and also about being a woman performing this work—the first woman to host a nightly network news program—and how that (plus the fact of being a wife and mother) affects and shapes what listeners hear.

For me, an experience is not complete unless I've told it to someone. I read a poem, or go to Prague, or meet a Vice President, and don't know how it was, really, until I've put it into words, communicated it aloud, turned it into talk. I think most of us are like this. We tell something to a best friend, or a relative, make what's happened into a story, and then we can fit the story into the personal narratives of our lives. Broadcasters are simply women and men with the need to cast the news more broadly—to tell stories to a wider range of people.

Talk aloud. At microphones.

That's the core of our work, and of this book, I think. Every encounter on these pages contains a lesson—in how to conduct a life, how to think about our world, how to present oneself, in joyous and difficult situations. Having had the privilege of helping to shape the experiences of so many many people into tales that got told on the air, I offer their stories to you in print now, as a kind of bouquet of communication, with the wish you find nourishing fragrances here, of memory and understanding.

Introduction

The moment I finish writing this sentence, I'll want to read it to you. It's the broadcaster's reflex. We work to be heard. There's more to it, of course. We read and think, evaluate, reassess. But the goal, always, is talk.

Since 1971, I've done my talking at the microphones of National Public Radio. Telling the events of the day. Asking questions.

"Why are you fasting?"

"Are you free to talk about Watergate?"

"Conducting, do your arms ever get tired?"

"How's your *hide*, Mrs. Bush?"

The answers—in public conversations conducted on the electronic hearth of radio—become a sound track of our times. On radio, without the distractions of shadows, bad haircuts, and sweeps weeks, we talk about what we do, and think, and dream.

And then it evaporates in thin air.

Our audio engineers tell me "evaporation" is not precisely correct. That once sent, radio waves—with no walls or barriers to stop them—keep on going for eternity; if there were a sensitive enough *receiver* out in the cosmos, it could pick up everything that has ever been broadcast. (A bit like stars that keep glowing through light years, though they burned out millennia ago.)

But it still seems evanescent. Gone, once the broadcast is over.

So . . . *Talk*. An attempt to catch back some of what's been said. Twenty years' worth of words from politicians, artists, a Great White

Hunter, a convicted felon, an obituary writer, assorted revolutionaries, others who individually and together trace some of the public themes of these final decades of the twentieth century. Today, at a time of more broadcast talk and less real insight than ever before, the mixed voices on these pages shed light—fixing a moment, vaulting us back to a memory, or forward to an anticipation that brings meaning, understanding. Also there are laughs, jabs, sighs, some sad good-byes. It's not a history book, but history's first draft is here, etched in the voices that gave these decades their vitality.

———

"Good evening. From National Public Radio in Washington, I'm Susan Stamberg."

For fourteen years, at five o'clock each weeknight, I greeted *All Things Considered* listeners that way. Then the stories began—a ninety-minute blend of reports from NPR correspondents around the world, reporters at member stations and the BBC, from free-lancers and stringers. And reports and interviews by the cohosts.

When I left *All Things Considered* in 1986, the staff's going-away present was a computer printout of my work—a list of all the interviews and reports, all the considerations. (I'd hoped for a yacht and bonbons, but this, after all, is public radio.) The single-spaced, three-inch-thick bundle contains some fifteen thousand entries. Now, after hosting *Weekend Edition*/Sunday for nearly three years, then reporting for *Morning Edition* and all the other programs since 1989, the number hovers around twenty thousand.

———

"Gonzales is at the State Department briefing. Cokie will have something on the Senate vote."

At the *ATC* morning editorial meeting, the producer reads out the day's story list.

"And the budget message is coming up."

My heart sinks. Economics. My second favorite subject after Law of the Sea. I duck out of sight to inspect a hole I feel sure will develop in the sole of my right shoe. Maybe they'll give this interview to my partner Noah Adams.

"We'll have a report from Ted Clark at the White House. Then, Susan, you can do some analysis with an economist."

The bulk of my cohosting work consisted of such assignments (most, except for economics, accepted with pleasure)—stories that had to be done that day because they were news. News is the bread and butter of our NPR broadcasts, the service we perform. My job on *All Things Considered* was to bring the news—tell what had happened that day. Very little of that daily work appears on these pages. Today's news analysis is tomorrow's dull reading. It dates quickly, like good reporting.

This book consists mostly of talk by choice, not assignment. If the news is bread and butter, what's here is dessert, conversations designed to keep listeners (and me) going in the middle of drab news days. *Talk* is my corner of National Public Radio. The talk I like best.

———

"People think that I'm this great ballerina," Dame Margot Fonteyn told me. "And so you start trying to be the ballerina offstage. You can't do that."

Artists are my favorites. People who are very good at a very demanding creative endeavor. (Remember what Thomas Mann said? "An author is someone for whom writing is more difficult than it is for the rest of us.") Always less interested in what people are running for than what they're dancing to, I speak with artists whenever I can. In explaining what they do, they help us understand ourselves.

"All of us write plays all the time in our heads, right?" dramatist David Mamet said. "Before we're going to go visit our girlfriend, before we're going to talk to a boss—we rehearse."

Always, whether it's an artist (conductor Jorge Mester saying his arms get tired only when it's not going well) or a newsmaker (former President Jimmy Carter, scanning page 1 of the paper for news), I'm catching stories with my microphone—a magic wand, waved against silence.

I've lately come to understand that I would have collected people's stories even without the broadcast equipment. It's what I do with or without a microphone. Story-gathering was my joyful habit before it became a career. Working as a broadcaster lets me turn an impulse into a profession.

———

"Have you had a single day, since your husband was taken hostage, when your waking thought has *not* been, 'My God, he's still being held over there!'?"

"Why do you think *you* were the one who chose not to move, that day on the bus in Montgomery?"

"Take my picture?"

Talk always begins with a question. Then comes the most important part. Listening. Listening for what's said and *not* said, listening for the silences, the cracks between the words, the hesitations, the contradictions, the glorious expositions.

Ever notice that the ear is shaped like a question mark? That's a cue for interviewers. The more carefully you listen, the more interesting the talk can be.

Even more than words, the *way* the words are said colors the telling. The voice is any story's most important instrument. It's the voice that puts you in the presence of a person and a life. A scratchy cassette of a friend singing reminds me he's gone, as no snapshot can. A home movie of my wedding is only bearable because it's silent. On film, my father, Robert Levitt, who died in 1970, walks around a table, waves at the camera, but does not speak. If he did, I might be overwhelmed by loss. The voice gives life, as photographs and films cannot. It wraps you in the aura of a person, starts pictures in the mind, makes connections to the heart.

These pages are filled with voices that, collectively, become the decades' voiceprint, a rearview mirror on the seventies and eighties. The talk here comes from rage, frustration, pain, pride, exhilaration. It's public talk, absorbed in private, that "private experience" Marshall McLuhan said was radio. It's also talk between strangers, although it can sometimes sound like friends. The "unearned intimacy" (photographer Richard Avedon's phrase) of a radio interview can make deep connections: two people who have never met, trying together, in a brief period of time, for clarity, understanding.

"I just want to ask you something for radio."

And then the talk begins.

War on the Home Front

June 1971

We mark time off in decades to create the illusion that our lives have some shape to them. It's handy to think in ten-year blocks—that in this country the fifties were about comfort and apathy, the sixties about revolution, the seventies decline, the eighties excess, the nineties realignment. In fact, events are anything but tidy and tend to spill beyond the decade lines we vainly draw to impose a sense of order.

The sixties, for example, didn't really end until 1973, when American troops withdrew from Vietnam. The war that had dominated the American psyche in the sixties had begun winding down by the time *All Things Considered* was launched on Monday, May 3, 1971, but our broadcast that first day documented the ongoing and wrenching national conflict about Vietnam. That day, antiwar demonstrators tried to close down the federal government. Thousands were arrested. We put it all on the air.

The first broadcast. I remember sitting on the floor over at our old offices on I Street the day *All Things Considered* made its debut. There were 65 of us on the original staff (today there are 437), and the network was so new there weren't enough desks or chairs yet. So we sat where we could at five o'clock that first Monday evening in May, riveted by what we were broadcasting across the country to 63 NPR member stations (more than 450 today). We heard shouts, screams, confrontations—an agony of protest against the Vietnam War.

"Excuse me, Sergeant," Jeff Kamen said to a police officer, in an approach that told the nation this was a new kind of radio. (Kamen was one of NPR's 5 original staff reporters. Today there are 50.) "Excuse me, Sergeant. Is that a technique? Where the men actually try to drive the motorcycles right into the demonstrators?"

"Naw, it's no technique," the officer replied. "We're trying to go down the road and the people get in front of you. What are you gonna do? You don't stop on a dime."

Washington police had been busy that spring. For more than three weeks there had been a series of sweep arrests of antiwar demonstrators—seminarians, veterans, Quakers, and others—at the Nixon White House, on the steps of the Supreme Court, at the Justice Department. Then, on May 3, more than seven thousand people—mostly young, impassioned, and long-haired—were arrested. An unprecedented number.

We scrambled, our first weeks on the air, to cover everything that was going on. (In fact, the scrambling went on for years. Still does.) There were so few reporters in those loose, wildly inventive, extremely uneven early days that everyone had a chance to get on the air. I was a part-time associate producer then, responsible for cutting tapes that came in from free-lancers and reporters at member stations. But early on, I got my own pieces on the air.

Seventeen days after the May 3 arrests, I interviewed an activist civil rights lawyer (in the William Kunstler tradition) who represented the People's Coalition for Peace and Justice—one of the organizers of the demonstrations. Philip Hirschkop's clients included some well-known radical activists—Rennie Davis and John Froines of the Chicago Seven—as well as thousands whose names Hirschkop did not know. The total number of arrests that entire demonstration week in Washington had topped 13,000.

STAMBERG: How many of those 13,400 young people were your clients?

HIRSCHKOP: Probably all of them. But most of them were arrested illegally. See, by the time you get to May third, you've had almost two thousand illegal arrests by the government, which is the whole pattern which sets the stage for the police to feel that they can just go out and pick up any kid who's got a knapsack, long hair, blue jeans; any girl who's wearing hot pants.

STAMBERG: But Mr. Hirschkop, they didn't just pick up kids on those

---

One thing is to ask yourself how things are going to look a century later, when we're not so preoccupied with the minutiae of this or that administration, and not so much in the thrall of a particular personality. For example, I think that maybe the single thing that is likely to be said about John F. Kennedy a century from now is that he was the first Roman Catholic president. And one of the things he did was to make it possible for other religious groups to hold the presidential office.

**—FDR biographer
William Leuchtenburg
on NPR, October 1986**

grounds. They picked up kids who were slowing down traffic, who were lifting small cars to block the roads, cluttering the streets with debris, and slashing tires, and ripping flags and benches at the Washington Monument, and dumping chicken excrement at the Pentagon.

HIRSCHKOP: Well, the chicken excrement was thrown at a handful of guards. It was hardened. It wouldn't . . . didn't bother anybody. There were about twenty kids involved. Certainly nothing of notable effect. The garbage dumped in the streets was of minimal impact on traffic. As a matter of fact, traffic was never slowed by more than fifteen minutes in any place in the city. If anything, the tactic was a bust.

The protest could have been stopped just as effectively by arresting people in the street, as opposed to going to Dupont Circle and arresting every secretary going to work for blocks around, which is what happened. And hundreds and hundreds of people—students, professors—in the George Washington University area. Just *being* in that area was a criterion for arrest.

STAMBERG: But this gets us to the very real dilemma of the Washington resident, the guy on the street, who's *not* demonstrating, wants to get to work, and whose private rights as a citizen are being interfered with.

HIRSCHKOP: He's got to suffer the punishments of people being able to exercise their rights. Now, I am not saying people sitting in the street are validly expressing their rights within the law. But if they sit in the streets, you arrest them. You don't go out and arrest a lot of innocent people so that a couple of dudes are not five minutes late to work!

Nothing that happened—whether it be some trash in the streets, whether it be traffic slowed five or ten minutes—justifies seven thousand arrests, the largest number of arrests in history. We've had *riots* in this country. We've had property destruction in the millions of dollars in cities, and not seen seven thousand arrests or anything resembling it.

STAMBERG: Attorney General John Mitchell has said that all police departments across the country are to employ mass arrests to counter mob force. Do you think that's a sign of the future?

HIRSCHKOP: I think it's the future of the Nixon régime. Their whole approach is to keep order for an upper-middle-class white power structure rather than to get equal justice for minorities or the masses of people. They will arrest every poor person, every black person, every dissenter, who threatens the order they're here to maintain.

STAMBERG: Final question. Do you think May Day changed anybody's position on Vietnam?

HIRSCHKOP: I don't think big demonstrations ever change anyone's viewpoint. But it's a healthy thing, because I really believe the American people have a certain amount of conscience. Now, maybe it's naïve of me, but I think they do. The problem is, it's buried beneath their Pontiacs and their television sets and a lot of luxuries they feel they have to have in order to endure. You have to somehow reach that conscience.

When the Civil Rights Act of 1964 was passed, it passed with very popular support. But it hadn't had popular support the year before. The trigger was four young girls being blown up in Alabama. That was the difference! When the 1965 Voting Rights Act passed, the trigger was three young men being buried in a dam in Philadelphia. These things shocked the public—and maybe it's only violence that reaches the American people. May Day was a form of violence. It was a nonviolent demonstration, but it was violence to the system. It jolted the public. And even though we speak of backlash and all these problems, I think it's good any time you make the American public think about an issue, regardless of which way they are going to come down. They'll generally come down pretty good, if they'll only think and deal with the issue.

——

I have a tendency to act out people's fantasies in a certain way. When the society demands that you fulfill a certain role, I've shown a reluctance to go the straight, conforming way. I have stood up. I went south to Mississippi in the early early sixties. Way before the media ever heard of Abbie Hoffman. I was involved for six years. The antiwar movement was a very unpopular movement. I think people who are connected with unpopular movements that are then seen by the general population as correct are considered, you know, sort of heroes, and things like that.

—Abbie Hoffman, November 1980

Welcome to the seventies. The passions of the time scream off the page, as they did off the radio. There was an involvement, an engagement in issues and public life that spread across the country—in protest groups, consumer groups, affinity groups of all kinds. Reading back on it makes the eighties and pre-Clinton nineties seem far tamer, more segmented. Special-interest groups expressed the emotions of public life in the Reagan-Bush years. They organized around abortion, obscenity. The general level of caring declined. Our public voices got less shrill. Where this book begins, it was hotter.

Hemingway and Friend

July 1971

Clipped to the top of a battered lampshade that has traveled with me through at least five different NPR offices, and bearing the splashes of something that looks like coffee but may well have been extremely strong tea, is a faded piece of paper torn from a spiral notebook. On that lined sheet, in the middle of the 1972 Munich Olympics murders, or maybe the 1973 energy crisis, or the 1974 kidnapping of newspaper heiress Patricia Hearst, my visiting poet-cousin Peter Levitt typed out a fragment of verse from William Carlos Williams's "Asphodel, That Greeny Flower."

> It is difficult
> to get the news from poems
>   yet men die miserably every day
>   for lack
> of what is found there.

That verse has gotten me through innumerable world crises since I first attached it to the lampshade. It has also helped me articulate, to editors, producers, and news directors, the need to include the arts when telling the day's events; to make the case that a new novel by Amy Tan, a new dance by Twyla Tharp, or a new film by Spike Lee vitalizes the culture in ways the latest piece of legislation can't.

This commitment to the arts began early. Creative people have attracted me since I was a kid sitting at the kitchen table listening to *Let's Pretend* on the ivory Bakelite Emerson radio, a paint box and pad at hand for making splotchy watercolors. When I got to do radio myself, I took my love of drama, poetry, painting, music, and literature to the microphone and spoke, whenever I could, either with or about the artists I so admired.

On NPR, Ernest Hemingway was my first encounter. Not, alas, the man himself—he died before I became a broadcaster. But I did meet two people who'd known him intimately and had stories to tell. One was a close friend of his. The other was that, too—as well as being his fourth wife. Between them, they helped reclaim a literary lion whose reputation had grown tattered.

By the seventies, the Nobel laureate who had reinvented the novel was considered a sexist fraud, a man who had put more energy into his macho life-style than into his art. I parted company with the Papa bashers. I loved Hemingway's writing, and wanted to know what this giant—who occupies so much space on my bookshelves, who taught me that in good sex the earth moves, who showed me Paris before I ever got there—was really like.

In 1971, in Washington, D.C., on the tenth anniversary of Ernest Hemingway's suicide, I talked to a man who had known Hemingway since World War II.

STAMBERG: He wrote more words for Buck Lanham than he wrote for his longest book. Major General Charles "Buck" Lanham, whom he met on the battlefield just after D-Day and to whom he wrote pages and pages of letters. Hemingway and Lanham didn't see much of one another over the years, but their friendship lived through the letters.

LANHAM: I met him in August 1944, right after the Normandy invasion. We had fought three days and three nights, and I got with my regiment to this little, tiny French town. We were absolutely exhausted, and I'd set up a command post in a little peasant cottage and was trying to get myself cleaned up and see what happened next when one of my staff officers came in and said, "Colonel, there's a correspondent here to see you, and a colonel. And the colonel's name is Colliers." So I said, "Show them in."

And the next thing I knew, here was this huge man standing in this rather small doorway, who looked very much like an eighteenth-century pirate, except he lacked the dagger in his teeth. He hadn't shaved for about four days; he was totally disheveled. And I said,

"Colonel Colliers?" And he said, "No, I'm a correspondent for *Collier's*. My name is Hemingway."

And at this point, mindful of the Livingstone incident in Africa, I made the most stupid wisecrack I'd ever made in my life and said to him, "Ernest, no doubt?"

And in this very quiet, low voice that he had he said, "Yes, my name is Ernest." And I said, "Well, for God's sake!" (*Laughs.*) This was the beginning of a friendship that lasted right up until his death.

STAMBERG: You said he had a very soft voice?

LANHAM: Very soft voice. Very soft, very low-key. People in general have the wrong impression of Hemingway. Of course, he was a great mass of internal contradictions. He . . . he . . . I wouldn't use the word "schizophrenic," but he was many different people.

In war, he was very modest, very simple, very unassuming—almost withdrawn—and a man of infinite compassion, infinite gentleness. Also a man of enormous courage, *enormous* courage, constantly proving to himself that he was not afraid. He didn't do foolhardy things. He was battle wise, but he was constantly proving something to himself. And this is where you really get to know a man, in war. You see everything that is fine in a human being and everything that is the worst.

In peace, on the other hand, all of the other side of him seemed to come out. He was belligerent. He was tough. Sooner or later he seemed to fall out with almost every friend he had. I suppose I was a friend that lasted longer than anybody else.

We had a standing agreement that when we were sixty years old—he was about two and a half years older than I—no matter where one of us was, the other would come and we would really turn one on, on our sixtieth birthday.

Well, he was just outside of Málaga, Spain. He had wanted me to come over early and chase the bulls up at Pamplona. Well, I was not in the business of bull chasing, but I went. (*Laughs.*) We had a hell of a time!

But I was shocked when I saw him there. He was terribly beat-up, you know. He had a liver and a spleen that went out of whack in Africa. He had a kidney that didn't work. He had high blood pressure. He had just about everything wrong with him that could be wrong. He tried to go back to recapture his lost youth, chasing the

SCOTT DONALDSON: A lot of Hemingway is so spare that you miss a great deal unless you do it out loud, because you don't hear the subtext, you don't hear the silences.

STAMBERG: People say that the first sentence of a book tells it all. That is, if the first sentence grabs you, you'll keep reading it. And here's the first sentence of *The Sun Also Rises:* "Robert Cohn was once middle weight boxing champion of Princeton." Is that a compelling sentence to you?

DONALDSON: I don't really think so.

STAMBERG: But the second sentence tells you you're in the hands of an interesting writer: "Do not think that I am very much impressed by that as a boxing title, but it meant a lot to Cohn."

DONALDSON: By that second sentence we know a great deal about two people already.

—December 1984

9

bulls. To me, it was an exercise in pathos to watch it. He was simply not the Hemingway I knew. And that was the last time I saw him. When I left, tears were rolling down his face. I think he knew we just weren't going to see each other again.

STAMBERG: How did you get the news of his death?

LANHAM: I was sitting out in the garden, sweating like a Baptist preacher in the Deep South, and just turned on the radio to get the news flashes. I heard that he was dead, and the circumstances of his death. And, you know, it was just as if the sun went out.

The last letter that I had from him was, curiously enough, the only pedestrian letter he ever sent me. He'd been in the hospital, and it was obviously dictated—quite short, and typed. And on the last page, the last words he ever wrote to me—in longhand at the bottom—were these: "Buck: Stop sweating me out. Sweat out only flying weather and the common cold." That's the last I heard. It ended on a typical Hemingway note.

STAMBERG: Were you surprised at the way he died?

LANHAM: No, I was not surprised either at the way or at the time. I was quite certain this would happen, given the condition he was in. He had lost all confidence in himself. Life had lost all of its savor; all of the salt had gone out of it. Physically, he was just falling apart: His weight had gone down to nothing, he could do none of the things that he liked to do—he was just physically unable to do them.

I think he did absolutely the right thing. Our argument was always, you know, *how* do you do it. Because I always said I'd use a forty-five, and he always said a shotgun was better, and we used to argue that—purely as a matter of principle. (*Laughs.*) That was the way it was. But we had some wonderful times together.

STAMBERG: General Lanham, what do you think led to the misery of his last years, the physical and psychological deterioration?

LANHAM: Well, I would say that there were fundamentally two things. First, he had been an enormously heavy drinker all of his adult life. When he got "in training" for a book, as he called it, he wouldn't take a drink until noon. Several times, he asked me to come down to Cuba and help him get in training, and if I was able to fly down for a week or so, I would.

He had an Olympic-size swimming pool, and part of his training routine was to go out there and swim eighty laps. He always did the breaststroke. He kept his wristwatch on the side of the pool. And about every lap he would go and look at that wristwatch to see what time it was, because he wouldn't take a drink until noon. That was the theory.

Well, at eleven o'clock sharp, you would see his majordomo in the white coat coming down the hill with a tray and the biggest damn pitcher of martinis you ever saw. And Hemingway would look at his watch and say, "Well, Buck, it's noon in Miami. The hell with it, let's have a drink!" (*Laughs.*)

The other problem was the great number of accidents that he'd had. He was accident-prone. And they always seemed to get his head. I think he'd had something like seven or eight major concussions. His doctor said later that almost any one of them would have killed a normal man. He had a skull that was twice as thick as normal.

STAMBERG: General Lanham, what do you think Hemingway saw in you that started a friendship that lasted twenty years?

LANHAM: Hemingway had a thing about military people. He often wished that he had been a soldier—a professional soldier—himself. And he would have made a damn good one!

STAMBERG: I think you've given me a very modest answer. You're sixty-eight years old, and you're trim, you're handsome, you're intelligent. In some ways you must have represented for Hemingway the perfect military man. Beyond that, you probably represented to him a figure whom he might envy, almost an ideal Hemingway character.

LANHAM: No, I don't . . . I . . . I can't accept that. That . . . I don't think that was so. I think Hemingway was totally and completely satisfied with his life and with himself as a man, and I think he had every . . . every reason to be. So, you're not going to seduce me into . . . (*laughing*) . . . into making such a statement! Various people have said that, but I do not subscribe to it.

You'd have to crawl into the heart and soul and mind of a man in order to make such a statement. You don't know what he thinks.

——

Hemingway scholars called Major General Charles "Buck" Lanham the prototype for the hero in *Across the River and into the Trees.* Lanham denied it.

Hemingway's official biographer, Carlos Baker, was given access to the Lanham correspondence, and his 1969 book, *Ernest Hemingway: A Life Story,* owed much to that privilege. The biography was dedicated to Buck Lanham. General Lanham was quick to point out that the biography was *also* dedicated to Carlos Baker's wife. Her name appears second on the dedication page.

Five years after this talk with Buck Lanham, Ernest Hemingway's widow came to NPR on her book tour. As you'll see some pages ahead, Mary Welsh Hemingway was very protective, describing life with Papa. But we had a remarkable visit.

Dick Gregory Protests

June 1971

Smoke from angry fires lofted over the streets of Washington, D.C., when our plane returned us home in April 1968. Martin Luther King, Jr., had just been killed, and there was rioting in the capital's black neighborhoods. National Guardsmen were our grimly armed welcoming committee; a curfew kept us in at night. We were back from two and a half years in India, where the State Department's Agency for International Development (the foreign-aid agency) had posted my husband, Lou. In New Delhi, sixties America reached us a week late, splayed across the pages of *Time* and *Newsweek*. We read with disbelief the stories of psychedelia and drugs and national hysteria that challenged everything we'd been taught as proper children of the fifties.

So to land in the fires of Washington was to arrive at the heart of sixties upheaval, to experience a culture shock stronger than anything we'd felt in the remotest Indian village, watching women carry massive brass water jugs on their heads or pat mounds of fresh cow dung into pancakes, to be dried and used for fuel.

India stays with me, as it does everyone who has experienced its rich harmonies and profound deprivations. In those early years back home, the pull was especially strong. In 1971, in one of my very first pieces for *All Things Considered*, India kept cropping up in the way I framed a conversation with a comedian who had run for president of the United States.

This interview was broadcast a month after *All Things Considered* first went on the air, in the week that Attorney General John Mitchell demanded that *The New York Times* suspend publication of the Pentagon Papers—secret government documents on the conduct of the Vietnam war. The interview ran on June 17, 1971, a year—to the day—before the break-in at the Watergate complex in Washington, the event that triggered the biggest story of the decade. But when I spoke with Dick Gregory, the big story was the war in Vietnam. It was his response to the war that had prompted this interview.

STAMBERG: Talking to Dick Gregory, you feel you're in the presence of a kind of missionary. He's been on a fast for nearly two months. He says he feels fine—runs five miles a day. He's very concerned with food and proper diet and is raising his children as vegetarians. He takes only fruit juices—no vegetables, no meat. It shows in his eyes. I've seen eyes like his in India: clouded, opaque with malnutrition. And the intensity with which he speaks reminds me of Indian ascetics and holy men.

Dick Gregory is both part of this world—concerned about it—and removed from it. I asked why he was fasting.

GREGORY: Against the war. I started on the twenty-fourth of April. In California, at the peace rally, I looked out over half a million young people, and I was very embarrassed. Because I realized that if my generation had been working for peace at that age—instead of trying to be cool and up on the latest bebop and Miles's latest record and all of that—that we would have a world of peace today. So, being embarrassed by my generation's attitude, I announced then that I wouldn't eat any more solid food until the war was over.

I was 150 pounds on April twenty-fourth, and I'm down to about 118 now. But every time you go to bed and that hunger runs through your body, you think about Vietnam—which I never did before. My daughter walked up to me a couple of weeks ago with an apple in her hand, and I was hungry. I looked at that apple and I thought about Vietnam. So now I constantly think about Vietnam—the people that's being killed, the things that's going on. In denying yourself, you get a certain strength. A certain amount of misery, too, but it will make you a better person.

I feel that the young people in this country could deny themselves and end that war in thirty days. And if they don't, they can't blame us older folks. If the young kids organized and decided to call for a nationwide boycott of celebrating Christmas until the war is over,

It is pretty much a serene park, a park within a park, where you are brought down to a level where the sounds of the city recede. You are there with the names of those that have died. If you had gone to war and came back, you will remember the names. You will remember the times. It's pretty much a living gift, and I felt that was an honorable way to pay tribute. As you turn to walk out, the Lincoln Memorial and Washington Monument are soaring there in front of you, and you are a part of the nation's scheme.

—Maya Lin, designer of Vietnam Veterans' Memorial, July 1982

Sears and Roebuck would have to get into the peace movement. The whole Japanese government, who sells this country more toys for Christmas than bombs and planes for war, would have to become very concerned about the Vietnamese War.

If young people organize and decide that we're not going to buy no more General Motors cars until the war is over—and we pick General Motors because it's the number one corporation in the world—the chairman of the board of General Motors would have to call the president of the United States and say, "Look, boy, don't mess up my stock!"

STAMBERG: You've written a book called *No More Lies*. Why that title?

GREGORY: It's what the young people need. Look at the situation we're in today, with The Man being more concerned about a kid getting a heroin habit in Vietnam than getting his brains blown out! I don't say we shouldn't be concerned about drug addicts, but how do you justify that? See, as long as you kill American boys, that's okay. But we more concerned about cats we going to bring back with a monkey on their back—junkies—than we are about these guys that have no legs and no arms. When you look at that madness, you say, *No more lies!*

STAMBERG: (*Narrating*) We finished the recording and Dick Gregory asked my birth date and month. He spent the next ten minutes working with my numbers, telling me things that would happen, things that had already happened, things about my family's health and money—all based on the numbers. Some of them were true, some not. I tried joking about it, but he wouldn't joke. I said I should be leaving, but he kept working the numbers, listening to what his head was telling him. Then his messages stopped, and I was dismissed.

In another country—like India—Dick Gregory would have masses of followers, people who were convinced he was a saint and who shaped their lives to serve his ideals. Here, he has students on college campuses. He gives three hundred lectures a year, and does nightclub acts just to pay his rent. Whether, in fact, masses of young people *will* boycott Christmas and General Motors is questionable in 1971 America. It's a question that may haunt Dick Gregory like the hunger he lives with. In Washington, I'm Susan Stamberg.

In Asia, because of the Vietnam War, there are hundreds of thousands of children without a country—half-American children who are anti-American. They feel that their fathers should have recognized them. They are father-oriented, because they are in Asian societies. I'm more than a little concerned about this, because I don't want to see the day come when we have to send American men to fight the children of Americans. These are very strong people. The Asian blood and the American blood make a new person, and there has never been such a mixture as this before in such large numbers.

—*Pearl S. Buck,
August 1971*

In the spring of 1992, more than twenty years after that conversation, Dick Gregory was fined ten dollars for blocking entryways to federal buildings in East St. Louis, Illinois. He was protesting the forced repatriation of Haitian refugees. He's still fighting against drug abuse, and demonstrates and marches against drug dealers in the St. Louis area. He says that God, his church, meditation, and action give him strength.

My Child, Your Child

March 1972

When Margaret Mead died in 1978, Cokie Roberts's obituary for *All Things Considered* noted that the anthropologist's life and work had run in parallel lines. As a young woman, Mead observed adolescents in Samoa; as a wife and mother, she studied marriage and family; and toward the end of her many years, she turned her attention to the process of aging. Death, Cokie said, became the only milestone that Margaret Mead would not be able to help us understand more fully.

Looking back on two decades in broadcasting, I see that I've done much as Margaret Mead did, converting the personal into the professional as I've passed through various phases. New motherhood, schooling, family stresses, premature(!) middle age, illness: I've explored them on the air with experts. I figure there are plenty of listeners in similar situations, and we can all learn together.

Parenthood was my biggest personal mystery during my first NPR years, so on the air I went after some on-the-job training. This, on a network news program, was innovative. On commercial television news, what got reported was events at the White House, on Capitol Hill, on Wall Street—the major American power institutions. No one saw the family as a major institution needing to be covered. But at NPR, then, we did. Family got on our news agenda for several reasons: The women's movement was forcing attention to child-care issues; the early managers of NPR were committed to breaking some news molds; we had ninety minutes of programming to fill each evening—time in which to go beyond traditional stories. Also, I lobbied for it.

I was sitting at this desk not knowing what in the world to do, because I was brand-new at the job. And the mail boy came in and dumped five sacks of mail on my desk. The first letter I opened up was from a woman who said, "Dear Ann Landers: I'm a Methodist girl and I'm in love with a Catholic boy. We want to be married. Do you know of anybody who will marry us? My mother and dad are pretty strict about religion, and his folks are absolutely unbendable. What do you say?" Well, I'm a nice Jewish girl from Sioux City, Iowa. What do I know about these matters? So I thought I better call someone. Father Theodore Hesberg is president of Notre Dame University. I called up Ted, and I said, "I've got a problem." And, of course, he gave me the answer. From that day on, I always went straight to the top—the best available person—for help.

—Ann Landers,
November 1979

Our son was fifteen months old when I joined NPR. I'd been home from the time he was born. Restless for some intellectual stimulation, ready to be in a place where "Goo-goo, gaa-gaa" was not the lingua franca, I began at NPR as a part-timer and increased my hours as Josh got older. Throughout my radio days, Josh's age—and mine—have affected what got on the air.

In the early seventies, psychologist Haim Ginott was much admired for his advice to parents. In his books *Between Parent and Child* and *Between Parent and Teenager,* Ginott did for children's psyches what Benjamin Spock had done for their diaper rash. In those times before child abuse (physical and emotional) was a national issue, Ginott offered parents language with which to handle their own feelings.

In the spring of 1972, I went to Dr. Ginott for some parent-to-parent conversation. I liked his old-world air and the Israeli tilt to his speech.

STAMBERG: Haim Ginott, I want to give you my impression of your theories. When a child (usually mine, who's two years old) has a tantrum in the middle of a large department store and lies down on the floor turning beet-red and screaming, I am not to say to him, "*Get up,* darn it, I can't *stand* these scenes. You're making a fool of yourself and of me. *Get up!!!*" Which is how I would normally, spontaneously react. Instead, you suggest that I say, very sweetly and matter-of-factly, "Oh. You are angry. You are lying on your back on the floor. You are thrashing your feet in the air. You are flailing your arms. You are turning beet-red."

GINOTT: Don't be ridiculous! That's making me sick! If I were the child and you talked to me like that, I would say, "My mother is putting on a show. My mother is not authentic."

STAMBERG: But that's exactly *my* reaction to many of the things you tell parents to say in situations like that.

GINOTT: No, no. I distinguish between two situations: when I'm angry and when I'm not angry. Suppose I go in and see two children fighting. I get angry. Now, what should I do at this moment? Should I talk the way you just did? Or should I look at what's going on and say, "*I am angry! I am mad! There'll be no bloodshed in this house! People are not for hurting! People are for cherishing!*"

Here's my point. As a culture we have not learned how to deal with anger. Neither teachers nor parents have gotten lessons in how to express anger. When we are happy, what do we say? "I'm happy." When we are sad, what do we say? "I'm sad." But the minute we get to anger, instead of saying "I," we say "You." "You are such an *idiot*! You are such a *pest*! You are such a *nuisance*!" I'm telling parents to express anger with the word "I" and not with the word "You." That way, you protect your child against your fury.

Not only that, it's a wonderful opportunity to teach English vocabulary. Can you imagine looking at a child and saying, "I'm annoyed. I'm displeased. I'm uncomfortable"? Or, in a more difficult situation, "I am chagrined. I'm indignant. I'm aghast. I'm irked. I'm aggravated"?

STAMBERG: But, Dr. Ginott, an angry mother doesn't take the time to become *Roget's Thesaurus*. She gets ANGRY!

GINOTT: That's the whole point. A pianist does not start by playing symphonies. He has to learn scales first. The same thing with adults and how they express emotions to children. We need to learn an emotional vocabulary so that at a moment of crisis, instead of being spontaneously destructive, we can learn to be spontaneously helpful to children.

STAMBERG: Some of your suggestions require such calm, such self-control. It's unnatural.

GINOTT: That is not true! That is so completely untrue that I'm getting annoyed! I feel uncomfortable when you say these things. It makes me mad inside. I am chagrined.

STAMBERG: You forgot "irked."

GINOTT: I am *irked*!! (*Laughs*.) Another point. Do not deny your child's feelings. If the child says, "The milk is too hot," don't look at the child and say, "What do you mean it's too hot? Your brother drank it." Acknowledge his experience by saying, "Oh, it's too hot for you." (*Long pause*.) The reason I shut up is because I wanted to show you that after I make a brief statement of acknowledgment, I do not go on talking.

STAMBERG: You don't go on to say, "Wait a few moments and it'll cool off"?

GINOTT: That's *exactly* the point I wanted to make! I deliberately do *not* say, "Wait a few moments, it'll cool off." I wouldn't even say, "Blow on it a little and it'll cool off." Why? Because I would like the

child to take the initiative, so he develops initiative. If I make a
suggestion, then I'm the one who develops initiative. And I've already
got plenty.

———

I don't know. I went on to suggest to Dr. Ginott that *I* had plenty of
initiative, and I had been raised by a mother who said, "Blow on your
soup and it'll get cool." He didn't seem impressed, but at least he didn't
get irked.

I took Dr. Ginott's principles home and practiced them, as I would
many other child-rearing lessons collected over the years. By 1974, I was
planning ahead: Josh was four, and I interviewed about saving money
for college. By the fall of 1988 (Josh was born in 1970, so by now he was
eighteen), I was talking about empty nests and asking how to help make
the transition from home to freshman-year college. Soon I'll get up the
nerve to ask a director how a young actor becomes a movie star so that
he can buy his parents a lavish home somewhere warm.

Minding the Moon

December 1972

"We leave as we came," Apollo 17 astronaut Eugene Cernan said as he left the moon after the sixth manned lunar landing. "And God willing, we shall return—with peace and hope for all mankind." These would be the last words spoken on the lunar surface. It was the last moon landing.

The Apollo 17 crew—Cernan, Ronald Evans, and Harrison Schmitt—arrived on the moon December 11, 1972. There was other news that day. It was announced that George Bush would succeed Robert Dole as chairman of the Republican National Committee. In Paris, peace talks resumed between the United States and North Vietnam. (Trying to follow those talks, said Robert Conley, the first host of *All Things Considered,* was like watching a kitten playing underneath a scatter rug. The minute you thought you knew where the cat was, it scurried somewhere else.)

But the moon landing was most on my mind that day, and inspired this on-air telephone call.

STAMBERG: In the midst of all our news today, I must confess to you that I keep pulling away to think about those men who are at this very moment on the moon. It's probably less staggering now than it was the first or second time it happened. And there *are* all the criticisms about expense and priorities. But still, there's the fact of it. Men on the moon!

This afternoon, just before Apollo 17 landed there, I telephoned

Lucy Meeker to talk about the spacemen. Mrs. Meeker and her husband, Floyd, run a small farm in Bowling Green, Ohio. I discovered that Lucy Meeker, too, has a sense of wonder about men on the moon.

MEEKER: Well, I . . . I just don't even think . . . I don't know . . . everybody thinks they went to the moon. I *don't* think they went to the moon. Because it would be like Columbus discovering America! It would amount to that! We never would hear the end of it. They wouldn't be holding back so . . . because, right now, you ask them anything and you don't get no answers!

STAMBERG: Do you know other people who feel the way you do about this, Mrs. Meeker?

MEEKER: Yes, I do! And I don't bring it up. I have people come here to the stand—we sell our fruits and vegetables, y'know—and several women come out here. It was storming one day and this woman said, "If they'd just quit monkeying around up there with the heaven above," she said, "we wouldn't have the weather we got." And I've had several people talk about this. See, if you run a vegetable stand, you hear a lot of things, y'know—a lot of comments about different things.

STAMBERG: I've met other farmers who've said exactly the same thing. They feel some of the problems we're having with weather—the hurricanes and the flooding—have to do with the fact that men are up on the moon. They say men shouldn't be on the moon, that if God wanted that, He would have put men there Himself. Is that how you feel?

MEEKER: That's the way I feel! I'm sixty-some years old, and all my life I lived in this vicinity—it isn't like I lived in different vicinities and I wouldn't know the weather, see. And I have never known, from a child up, that we have had the weather that we are having. It was rain every day, or rain every other day. And now we're getting snow and sleet. We've never had this.

STAMBERG: Have you ever spoken to any weather expert about it?

MEEKER: No, I didn't, but I listened on the radio the other day—this guy was talking on the local news, y'know? And he said that he talked to a weatherman, but he didn't give him no answer, either.

STAMBERG: Well, you know, Mrs. Meeker, this is the last in the series of Apollo shots. How do you feel about that?

MEEKER: Well, I feel this way. They haven't gained anything. I think they spent a lot of money for it, but as far as us getting anything or finding out anything, I don't think we've accomplished anything for our money, to be honest with you!

————

Seems to me the weather *has* gotten worse and worse since that final moon landing. But I've not checked back with Lucy Meeker to ask her views on global warming.

The Apollo 17 crew stayed longer, traveled farther (driving around the moon's surface in the lunar rover for as long as an hour), and collected more lunar samples than any earlier crew. They made significant discoveries about lunar soil. And they left behind a plaque that says:

HERE MAN COMPLETED HIS FIRST EXPLORATIONS OF THE MOON
DECEMBER 1972, A.D.
MAY THE SPIRIT OF PEACE IN WHICH WE CAME
BE REFLECTED IN THE LIVES OF ALL MANKIND

All the younger people like my science-fiction books. By young I mean under thirty, or even thirty-five. And I maintain there's a different sensibility in people who were born with the era of moon shots and space shots. All the young people were brought up with it. They see the planet as a little planet amid a parcel of other planets, and subject to cosmic influences we now know as fact, and not some kind of crazy mystic thought. They think like this naturally. Whereas older people are very earthbound.

—Doris Lessing, April 1984

Let Them Eat Legumes

April 1973

Grass roots consumer movements sprouted up all over in the seventies, motivated, perhaps, by Ralph Nader—the conscience of the decade—who first battled Detroit for safer cars. In the spring of 1973, several consumer groups called for a nationwide boycott of meat. With inflation at 7.6 percent, meat prices were soaring. A pound of supermarket T-bone steak cost $1.79 in Chicago then—pricey by 1973 standards.

That April, three months after the Supreme Court's *Roe* v. *Wade* decision, just days after U.S. troops had withdrawn from Vietnam, and a month before a Senate committee began its hearings on the Watergate scandal (in this book, my big Watergate take lies ahead, in 1976, for reasons that will become perfectly clear), we made time to talk about cheap, healthy alternatives to meat. A listener suggested we contact Frances Moore Lappé, whose 1971 book, *Diet for a Small Planet,* dealt with protein in a revolutionary way. Lappé urged a nation of meat eaters to change its habits. The message was as startling then as it would have been to ask secretaries to give up their typewriters. In those days, pasta was still called spaghetti, and there were still more Thai restaurants in Bangkok than in New York City. Lappé's thesis was that meat cost too much—and not just in dollars and cents.

LAPPÉ: It's the land cost, really. You see, because we concentrate on meat and think it's the only source of protein, we devote eighty percent of our grain—half of all our harvested acreage—to feeding animals. So a steer, which is our favorite source of meat, is fed twenty-one pounds of protein to get back only one pound as a steak on our table.

STAMBERG: And you claim that it's edible protein we're feeding the livestock?

LAPPÉ: Yes, much of it is edible. We feed them high-quality soybeans, for example, which are an excellent source of protein. We feed them fish meal, grains—wheat and oats and barley—all of which are very nutritious for humans.

So the livestock depletes this vast amount of protein that could be available to humans. We could reduce our livestock population by, say, one quarter, and still provide every single American with half a pound of meat a day.

STAMBERG: You're specifically talking about Americans, aren't you, and the "peculiar"—as you call it—hang-up we have about meat eating?

LAPPÉ: Yes. We are just so culturally focused on meat. In the diet of many cultures, meat is basically a supplement to plants. We don't need the amount of protein Americans believe we need.

STAMBERG: You write about "usable" proteins. I wonder if you could define that for us?

LAPPÉ: Virtually no protein is perfect. Egg is the closest. With all the other proteins, only part of them are used by the body. But you can take less useful protein and make it more useful by eating two foods together in the same meal. The most common combination throughout the world is a grain product—whether it be rice or wheat—eaten with a legume—peas, beans, or lentils.

For example, in Latin America, beans are often eaten with rice—say, black beans and rice, the famous Brazilian dish; or pinto beans and corn in Mexico; or lentils and rice in India. And with these combinations, if you ate the two separately, you wouldn't have as much usable protein as you do when you eat them together.

STAMBERG: What happens with calories?

LAPPÉ: Even if you trimmed off all the fat, ten ounces of steak would have almost seven hundred calories. Whereas a whole cup of brown rice is less than two hundred calories.

The U.S. Department of Agriculture . . . estimates that the average American eats from 10 to 12 percent *more* protein than his body can use as protein. Since excess protein cannot be stored, it is converted to carbohydrate for use as an energy source. A very costly fuel!

—from *Diet for a Small Planet*

Isn't it interesting to see what a culinary Cassandra Frances Moore Lappé was in 1973? Most of her message, which we initially pondered as if it were a menu in a foreign language, has become second nature by now. And meat eating in America went from eighty pounds per capita in 1973 to sixty-seven pounds by 1990.

Will Marriage Ruin *Rhoda*?

October 1974

On one of my first days as host of *All Things Considered*, sometime in early 1972, the producer *du jour*, one Mr. Dave Cooper, looked at the proposed rundown of the program's first half-hour and frowned. The lead story was mine: Indira Gandhi, then prime minister of India, was in Washington for talks. The second story, something Michigan Representative Martha Griffiths was doing on Capitol Hill, Barbara Newman reporting. After that, a report by Kati Wetzel on Germaine Greer's appearance at the National Press Club. Finally, in that half hour, Connie Goldman's interview with an actress in Minneapolis. Mr. Producer Cooper was displeased. "That's too many women in the first part of the program." I drew myself up to my full and not inconsiderable height, sucked in my breath, and replied, "Do you say the same thing when Walter Cronkite introduces Dan Rather to report on what Richard Nixon did today, followed by Daniel Schorr on Capitol Hill with Senator Hubert Humphrey?" Dave Cooper blinked, as I remember, nodded, and left the half-hour as it was.

Not exactly a shot heard round the world. But there *was* a revolution going on. The feminist revolution. And I was one of its Minutepersons. As the first woman to anchor a national nightly news program, I kept gender watch, and felt the responsibility of all "first" people—to be vigilant and persistent. I urged our producers to put women on the air and to find female experts whenever possible so that all our analysis wouldn't be done by men. (It was more difficult then. Women hadn't cracked academia and the think tanks in big numbers, and we sometimes had to scrounge. Today our programs are regularly filled with expert women reporters and analysts.) In doing that kind of lobbying, I was replying to Sigmund Freud's question (seen as either mildly humorous, wildly patronizing, or both): "What does a woman want?" My answer: "To hear and see herself on the air."

In the early seventies, women were making news. The revolutionary winds of the sixties had blown in changes that were now felt by everyone. These social alterations, engineered by women, may have been the most important thing about the decade. Feminists were on the march. Helen Reddy had a big hit singing, "I am strong. I am invincible. I am woman." The Boston Women's Health Collective said that the vaginal orgasm was not all there was to sex. The word "sexism" entered conversations with stunning regularity.

When *Ms.* magazine made its debut—a consciousness-raising exercise in print—Linda Wertheimer and I spent twelve minutes—*twelve minutes!*—reviewing it on the air. We began by spelling out the title: "Em. Ess. . . . *Miz.* . . . Capital *M,* small *s* . . . period." The construction was so strange, it needed to be explained.

In 1972, the Senate passed the Equal Rights Amendment, and scores of women ran for public office. The National Women's Political Caucus pushed the Democratic party to enforce guidelines on selecting delegates for their national convention, and women's representation jumped from 13 to 40 percent. *Roe* v. *Wade,* the Supreme Court ruling allowing abortion during the first six months of pregnancy, was in 1973, the same year Ms. Billie Jean King beat Mr. Bobby Riggs in a $100,000 tennis match. The Equal Opportunity Act, barring discrimination on the basis of sex or marital status, was enacted in 1974, the same year girls got into the Little League and Erica Jong published *Fear of Flying.* But in 1974, women earned only fifty-eight cents for every dollar earned by men. (Two decades later, it's still uneven: seventy-one cents to the dollar now.)

Through most of the seventies, *The Mary Tyler Moore Show* was a television favorite. In 1974, there was a spin-off. Rhoda Morgenstern, Mary's best friend, got a show of her own. And on that new program, *Rhoda,* an event occurred that raised some feminist issues.

I look to popular culture for clues as to what is going on in society in general. Television programs, films, books, and songs take off because their messages are what the public wants to hear. Murphy Brown's early-nineties unwed and most welcome pregnancy would not

The physical source of our orgasm is based in the clitoris, not in the vagina. Our sexual response to having a penis inside us depends very much on how much stimulation our clitoris receives either before or during actual intercourse.

—from Our Bodies, Ourselves

have been tolerated on the small screen of the seventies. On the other hand, in 1972, a middle-aged TV heroine named Maude could choose to have an abortion. For Murphy, abortion would have been legal but impolitic.

Rhoda's big event, in 1974, was utterly traditional. That, in fact, was the issue. I explored it with Pat Dowell, an insightful woman who taught courses on film at the Smithsonian Institution. Before the broadcast, Pat and I discussed how she would be introduced. The decision we made tickles me today.

STAMBERG: Tonight at nine o'clock, Eastern time, on CBS-TV, Rhoda Morgenstern becomes Rhoda Morgenstern-Gerard, as the heroine of the new season's most popular comedy series changes from Ms. to Mrs. Will marriage ruin *Rhoda*? That's what we want to talk about with Pat Dowell. Pat is a radical feminist film critic. Pat, who is Rhoda?

DOWELL: Well, Rhoda is an unmarried young woman who is making her own way in the world—supporting herself. But primarily, Rhoda is a woman who lives very much with the fears of inadequacy and personal adjustment that we find in today's women. In other words, Rhoda is a walking casebook on the contradictions of growing up female in America.

STAMBERG: Does she satisfy female liberationists—feminists—like you?

DOWELL: No. She isn't a constructive character women can look to as some kind of role model.

STAMBERG: Why not? She's attractive. She's got a good job. She's fun. She's popular.

DOWELL: Primarily, the thing that bothers me about Rhoda is this incredible gulf of personal insecurity that she constantly voices. In a way, this is one of the strengths of the program. Rhoda voices for women everywhere those fears that we have been discouraged from making public. In other words, our inability to live up to the kind of feminine standards that our society sets for us. We've been given so many impossible images of womanhood—primarily by television and the movies—that we cannot hope to meet.

Rhoda—and this, I think, is her greatest strength as a character—provides an outlet, a kind of relief, for us. She says the things women would like to say about wanting to be pretty, wanting to be

What's the legacy? Well, Mary was the first TV comedy heroine to be single, working, and obviously not a virgin, *and* she never got struck by lightning. Ted was the first to show the world that behind the TV anchorman's façade of pearly teeth and empty pomp lurked a core of pearly teeth and empty pomp. Rhoda proved you could leave one neighborhood, join another, and still get viewers—all it took was a radical change in your basic nature. And all of them together showed that Minneapolis just might be a town to take seriously.

—from an S.S. essay on last Mary Tyler Moore Show, March 1977 slim, wanting to be loved and liked, wanting to be a woman as society defines it.

On the other hand, she's a character who is totally confined by those values and by her sense of inadequacy. I think it would be very constructive for a program to start out with a figure like her and let us see her learn self-esteem from within—from her own strengths.

STAMBERG: So the answer to the question, "Will marriage ruin *Rhoda*?" is . . . no. It's going to bring her the fulfillment she's been looking for, because she's a pseudo-independent working lady.

DOWELL: And that is where, in a sense, American women are betrayed by a program like *Rhoda*. The feeling you get when she marries is that finally, she is *somebody*. And the reason she's somebody is because she snared a man. She has a man to approve of her.

STAMBERG: Do you see *Rhoda* as part of a pattern of TV comedy series starring women?

DOWELL: She represents, I think, a new turn for women. In the fifties, we were treated to a whole line of women as morons and idiots with harebrained schemes and irrational behavior, who were funny and affectionate. We liked them, but at the same time we were really degraded by that picture of women: Lucille Ball, Gracie Allen.

Now we find comedy series that reflect women who are a little more human and sympathetic and intelligent—Mary Tyler Moore, for instance.

And Rhoda, I think, is somewhere in between those two. She is a woman who trades on her own self-deprecation to gain her comic points and be likable. And yet she is obviously more intelligent and more human than the women of the fifties.

And even though I feel she represents no great gain for feminists on television, there are elements in her life that certainly reflect the changing roles of women. For instance, tonight, instead of the traditional ceremony, she and Joe make up their own. And though she is getting her approval and self-affirmation from a man, the vow that they choose to exchange, I think, expresses how women's roles have changed.

Their vow is this: "To stay together, to grow together, to trust each other, as long as ye both shall love."

———

I came up in the sixties, so I had topics to talk about. I had a point of view. I had a mother who was desperate to get me married—I had been a bridesmaid nine times. I had a fiancé who bought me a fur coat during hunting season in New Jersey. I mean, everything was wrong in my life, and that's what I talked about.

**—Joan Rivers,
July 1972**

Rhoda stayed on the air until 1978. But she had to get divorced to do it.

The issues of self-image, feminism, and women's power remained on *our* air much longer. A few years after Rhoda got married, there was an outpouring of writing by women dealing with, among other things, lesbian affairs (Kate Millett's *Sita*) and the pressures of color (Ntozake Shange's *For Colored Girls Who Have Considered Suicide/When the Rainbow Is Enuf*). The most powerful and disturbing book on the feminist shelf was written in 1977 by Marilyn French. When we discussed *The Women's Room,* I asked French whether she hated men. My husband hated her answer. You may, too. It's several pages forward.

Pat Loud and Family

September 1974

Mention the Louds—Pat, Bill, and their five children—to anyone who watched public television in 1973 and their eyebrows lift in quizzical pleasure, as if the memory was summoning up some family friends who disappeared years ago but had been lively enough at a few Thanksgiving dinners to be talked about well into Christmas. We took the Louds into our homes just as they took us into theirs—through television. And did we talk about them!

From January through March 1973, PBS broadcast a series that became a cultural landmark. It was the early-seventies equivalent of *The Jewel in the Crown* or *The Civil War,* full of drama and conflict and colorful characters. But this series was neither a Raj dramatization nor an historical reappraisal. It was a cinema verité documentary, called *An American Family,* about the comings, goings, couplings, and uncouplings of a wealthy and attractive-looking family in Santa Barbara, California.

Over the course of twelve weeks we got to see what the Louds ate for breakfast, what they fought about, how they acted with friends and pets. The children—Lance, Kevin, Grant, Delilah, and Michele—became as familiar as our own neighbors' kids. We saw the vapidity of the Louds' lives, their noncommunication. And the series about them is, in retrospect, a document of an era.

The times were full of mixed news about the American family as an institution. In 1973, some social scientists were predicting the family's death; others said that "death" was an exaggeration but that the family was certainly changing. Here's how it was: The marriage rate was the highest it had been since 1950; the divorce rate was twice what it had been in 1960 (one in every three marriages was ending in divorce); the remarriage rate was rising; sex and money were the big divorce issues (sexual satisfaction was becoming more important in a marriage than procreation); and it cost forty thousand dollars to have a baby, raise it, and put it through college.

On commercial television, the number one show was *All in the Family,* a pioneering social comedy that examined some pretty tough contemporary themes: racial prejudice, abortion, breast cancer, the Vietnam War. The number two show was also a family series, but unlike the Bunkers, *The Waltons* took us back to the comfort zone of loving mom, dad, brothers and sisters, and apple pie at most meals.

And then there was *An American Family*. Again, family was the subject. But something very different was going on. Real life.

For seven months, a production crew moved in with that family and photographed them day and night. In those months, on camera, the Louds' twenty-year marriage broke up, Pat told Bill to move out, and twenty-year-old Lance Loud informed his family that he was homosexual (in 1973, to most people, the word "gay" just meant happy and full of fun).

It was outrageous. And so public. Back then, before *Oprah* and *People* magazine, we were still capable of being shocked by personal revelation and the invasion of privacy. That period was ending, however, and *An American Family* helped end it.

A year after the series ran, I went to New York to meet Pat Loud.

(Footsteps on echoey marble floor.)

STAMBERG: Good morning. I wonder what apartment Pat Loud is in, please?

DOORMAN: Seven-D.

STAMBERG: Seven-D. Thank you!

(Elevator door opens and closes.)

STAMBERG: Gorgeous day!

ELEVATOR OPERATOR: Yes, it is.

STAMBERG: *(Narrating)* Pat Loud moved to New York a year ago, into one of those undistinguished dark brick apartment buildings on the fancy East Side. She's spent the year writing a book. *Pat Loud: A*

We held an oxymoron contest and invited listeners to send in samples of contradictions in terms. The examples we gave: jumbo shrimp, airline food, military intelligence, instant coffee. Listeners' response: funeral party, British passion, remarkably dull, dreadfully plain, pretty ugly, perfect mess, good grief, bad luck, civil war, still life, good morning, drip-dry, typewritten, self-service, postal service. Married life.

—from an S.S. essay, September 1981

Woman's Story is about her family and the TV series. Now, at forty-six, she's decided to move back to California.

LOUD: I am truly a daughter of the Golden West. I feel so much more comfortable there. I like my life to be a little bit more relaxed than it can be here.

STAMBERG: You've been doing some thinking about the difference between easterners and westerners. You call people on the West Coast "lotus-eaters, the optimists, the innocents, the naïve"—people who can accept simple reasons as causes for problems. Have you found that easterners are the reverse? Always looking for some sort of mammoth meaning behind each tiny event?

LOUD: There *is* a tendency to overexamine here. I was talking to a French friend about it, and he said, "People on the East Coast always ask why, why, why. In Europe and on the West Coast, there is an understanding that sometimes there is no 'whyness'—that it is all right to do something and then decide why you did it later."

STAMBERG: You write that you came here to get really divorced—emotionally divorced. Are you?

LOUD: I am. As of this sitting, yes. I was in Chicago recently, promoting my book on a morning TV show, and as a surprise they brought in my ex-husband. There was no palpitation, no shiver. There was pleasure. I was glad to see him. And when we parted company, it was like saying good-bye to an old friend.

STAMBERG: It's funny, I want to talk to you about the TV series, and yet it must seem like ancient history to you. You're a very different lady now. You're on your own. Your kids aren't wandering in and out the way they did in California. I don't hear any of that perpetual rock music in the background.

LOUD: It *is* a different life for me. That part is gone. It's just like it happened to somebody else, almost.

However, doing the series was a fascinating experience. It really was a great thing to have happened to us. But I would never want to do it again.

STAMBERG: That gets us to the central question I want to ask you. *Why* did you do it? You've said you thought anybody would have let those cameras into the house.

LOUD: I think anybody would. People here in the East say we didn't get paid for it, so why did we do it? But I don't think it was a matter of

money. One man said to me, "God, if I had a fight with my butcher,
I wouldn't want my laundress to know about it. How could you do
that with your whole family?"

It isn't that easy to explain. In exposing ourselves the way we
did, all we were saying was "Look, humanity and our institutions are
not working well together. Maybe we have to stop and think about
ourselves and our needs and revise some of these things that we have
clung to for so many years."

STAMBERG: Wow! You're creating a lot of very cerebral East Coast
answers to . . . (laughing) . . . to what's basically a simple question.
You give a much simpler and maybe more truthful answer in your
book. You say, "Anyone would have done it, because we all want to
be TV stars." There was clearly something very flattering about the
whole opportunity.

LOUD: Certainly there was. A New York producer comes to your house
and says, "I find your family fascinating. I'd like to do a series on
them." Oh, really? How flattering! We'll do it! (Laughs.)

We thought we had the marriage fairly well stabilized, that
they wouldn't be around very long, that it would be nothing more
than a chance to show ourselves as a lovely family commercial—
zing!

STAMBERG: The original commitment was for a one-hour program.

LOUD: One hour. And seven people in one hour are certainly not going
to be able to get into very many family and personality problems. We
just leaped into it in a great spirit of adventure.

STAMBERG: What about the presence of those cameras? Could you
ever be unaware of them?

LOUD: At the beginning—oh, maybe for like two or three months—we
were really very nervous. Alan and Susan Raymond would sit around
and talk and chat, and then Alan would pick up his camera and
immediately the atmosphere would change.

Alan says that in cinema verité you get your best footage at the
very first, because that tension is there. The way you react, knowing
you're being filmed, is far more revealing than what happens later on,
when you get more accustomed to the camera and perhaps—as he
says—you play to it.

We did try to be as open and as natural as we could be. But
that little piece of information lodges itself in the back of your

mind—that whatever you are doing at that moment is going onto a piece of film that is going to be there eternally. And it's very hard to forget.

And the presence of the camera has another effect. There are times in everybody's day when you sort of withdraw down into some place inside yourself. You're not even thinking, you just sort of *are*.

STAMBERG: You "let it all hang out"?

LOUD: Yes. You just sit there and stare out the window or scratch your arm. Something is going on inside of you, but you don't know what it is.

Well, in those moments you're really restoring yourself, you're thinking out your problems but on a comfortable, almost dreamlike, level. We *have* to have these times. People who don't are very nervous. It's as necessary to the human restorative process as rapid eye movement is to sleep.

When you are being filmed, these moments go out of your life and you don't realize it. I never thought about it until I started writing about our experience . . . just how vital that kind of time is to your life . . . that you use it to plan and think and find out why you do things. Well, with the camera there, those moments are gone.

STAMBERG: How much do you think the absence of that kind of downtime influenced the decision to divorce?

LOUD: Oh, I would have been divorced anyway! I think everybody who has been married and divorced knows when the moment comes. You know that you really have done everything you could to save that marriage, and about nine tenths of what you've done has been wrong and is debasing—incredibly psychologically damaging. Well, that moment just happened to me at the same time that the filming was going on.

STAMBERG: The divorce came after years of acrimony. He was having affairs. But there are lots of marriages that aren't much more meaningful than yours, and the husband isn't having an affair. Those marriages often don't end in divorce, and maybe they should.

LOUD: That's true. In California, two out of every three marriages end in divorce now. Incredible? Of the remaining third, at least half of those are unhappy. At least *half*! But if marriage is unhappy, divorce is supposed to be unhappier. I think we have to change our way of thinking about that. I think we have to think of divorce as possibly a creative step rather than a diminishing one.

Perhaps there is more than one marriage in all of us—which is a rather difficult idea for us to come to. But people live longer now than they did in the days when divorce was considered a total no-no, a very tragic thing.

Okay, well—(*doorbell rings*)—in those days, people died, often they were women who died in childbirth . . .

(*She stops to get up and go to the door, then she returns to the living room with a young man.*)

LANCE: Hi, how are you?

STAMBERG: Hi. I'm Susan Stamberg.

LANCE: Hi. I'm Lance.

STAMBERG: Nice to meet you. I've seen you on TV!

LOUD: Right!

STAMBERG: We're nearly done.

LOUD: How are you, honey? Did you get your mail?

LANCE: What should I do about my tax thing?

LOUD: Well, we'll save it.

LANCE: Michele was on TV last night. She looked so good! For the opening of *Frankenstein*.

LOUD: Oh, really?

LANCE: She and I were on, and she looked *soooo* good. She was so funny on it! Because she didn't say anything. She . . . she didn't say *anything*. But she reacted to everything I said. And she was so much more funny! She had these great *face* looks.

LOUD: But, you know, whenever someone turns a camera on you two, you just start poking at her and prodding her and you . . . you get her so she doesn't want to talk to anybody.

LANCE: Listen, I get her to give a performance, and that's good enough!
    (*Laughter. Lance leaves.*)

STAMBERG: I'm glad he passed through! Mrs. Loud, we're about to finish up. You were saying, in the days when people didn't live as long—

LOUD: Yeah, women died in childbirth and the husband remarried. So there were several chances to marry, without having to divorce. Now we're living longer and we're vital through a longer period of our middle years and may need to make changes without having a sense of shame about divorce.

All our mothers, all our aunts, we always imagined them to be much older. Women in those years were older. They were tired, they were centered on everyone but themselves, they were doers, martyrs, caretakers, and they were gypped by life in a way that made them older. My character in Broadway Bound, Kate Jerome, is only forty-nine years old. But I know that she was an old person inside.

—Linda Lavin, December 1986

STAMBERG: Who are the ones who are able to make it?

LOUD: Do you know what I think? I probably will make a lot of people angry—but I think the people who make it are dull people! There are exceptions, of course, but generally, they're people who have a very low level of competition, of desire to achieve, who do not expect much from life, people who just like to be comfortable.

STAMBERG: You write, "I think the one thing you have to get over is the idea that you're supposed to be happy."

LOUD: You bet. *You bet!* Happiness to me is simply a by-product of getting to know yourself and actually growing up and accepting yourself as you are, as an adult.

We talk about love. Love is wonderful, but it doesn't crawl inside your body. Your loved one never knows you as you know yourself. So you have to get to accept yourself and like yourself. And I think once you do that—that you are reasonably happy.

———

Revisiting Pat Loud in print some twenty years later, I am surprised by an innocence of values I hadn't remembered as part of the early seventies. Vietnam, Nixon, and Watergate made the period so dark. But I see in Pat Loud's conversation a tender tentativeness that makes today's emotions and reactions seem quite hardened. Divorce was a shock, then. The idea of living long enough to have serial marriages was new, something to be contemplated. Homosexuality in the family—another shock. To have a child so different, in sunny upper-middle-class California (or anywhere, then, really), took adjustment. Some big gulps.

Pat Loud and her family have made those adjustments, and others, in these intervening years. Past sixty now, Pat lives in Los Angeles and works in a talent-booking firm. She never remarried. Bill Loud, now in his seventies, did remarry, and divorced again. And Lance Loud, past forty, writes about show business for magazines and appears on various cable television programs. He lives with his mother.

So the Louds are alive and well and living in various parts of the country. The family, so mesmerizing and different to us two decades ago, seems part of the crowd, somehow, today. Reviewing Pat Loud's book for *Ms.* magazine in 1974, Susan Lester, an associate producer of *An American Family,* wrote: "Pat Loud is not the great American heroine nor the ultimate victim. She is just like the rest of us. The tragedy is that as a people we do not like ourselves well enough to learn from someone who is no more and no less than ourselves."

That may be the reason, more than anything else, that we watched the Loud saga on television and remember it even now, when we have all grown up and beyond it.

Starting Kindergarten

September 1975

Pat Loud, Parent, interested me most. As the mother of a young child, in the early seventies I kept working the family beat in and out of the rest of the news—Nixon's visit to China, the Yom Kippur War, the fall of Saigon. I did interviews about the effect on children of working mothers (on the theory that a minimal amount of guilt-tripping is probably good for the complexion) and produced short essays on the high cost of new tennis shoes and on getting the notebook ready for school each year. These were personal essays, also new from a news anchor (to my knowledge, Walter Cronkite was not ruminating on CBS about the utility of lunch boxes versus paper bags)—brief observations on routine events at home.

One early essay got aired after an editorial meeting at which I described the big news in our house on a particular day in the fall of 1975. Jim Russell, the *All Things Considered* producer at the time, said, "Why don't you write about it? It's one of those universal experiences." So I did.

STAMBERG: School started today in our household. Kindergarten for our five-and-a-half-year-old. It's been a busy, magic time these past few days. The air has had a brisk, anticipatory zing to it. There's been much discussion about new sneakers and *Shazaam* T-shirts—the 1970s equipment that makes this rite of passage only superficially different from mine or yours.

We went over to the school the other day and noticed that

without the children, the brightly decorated rooms and cheery pieces of equipment—jungle gyms painted yellow and shaped like turrets and castle tops, swings, seesaws, a sandbox—looked incomplete, as if they were on standby, waiting for the laughter and touching and bumping that would bring them life.

The teachers were there, reminding us of just how long ago it was that we were spoken to so gently, with that degree of kind encouragement.

Revisiting kindergarten makes you examine the spaces in your own life, and how you've filled in the years between that first touch of formal education and the kinds of over-the-years learning that brought you to today. Wistfully, perhaps, you see how far you've come or strayed from those early exposures.

Our son was excited last night. He had a hard time getting to sleep. We sat and talked for a while, and he said he was a little scared about today. His stomach sort of hurt. He wondered whether his old nursery-school friends would be back and whether the teacher would be nice.

I tried to reassure him, and told one of those important secrets mothers share with their children from time to time: that probably all the other kids were feeling exactly the same way about starting school, and that grown-ups feel funny, too, when new things are about to happen.

That seemed to be some comfort, and he settled into his sheets, his eyes shut and his face peaceful. Then he sat up and asked one of his stumpers—one of those why-is-the-sky-blue? questions, one of those puzzlers that particularly unsettles a parent whose professional life is spent asking other people hard questions and waiting for answers that can illuminate.

"What are the rules?" he said.

I groped for an answer, made a few false starts. But he couldn't wait. He answered himself.

"Don't fight," he said. "Share things. And if you're climbing, don't push anybody else off the castle."

I figured those were pretty good rules, and I said good night.

———

Longtime *All Things Considered* listeners often ask about Josh. They feel as if he'd grown up right in front of their ears.

> The notion that to learn anything important you have to go to a place called school and be taught it by a teacher who doesn't do anything except teach is a very recent idea in human history. Nobody ever used to think that. I think it's a bad notion.
>
> Anything you can learn in school you can learn outside, except where very complicated pieces of equipment may be involved. And most of what we learn we not only *don't* learn in school, we don't learn it by being *taught*. We learn it by looking around, by talking to people, hearing them talk, reading.
>
> —educator John Holt, April 1978

Aiming at President Ford

September 1975

BARBARA WATTERS: Mr. Ford is not going to finish his term.

STAMBERG: According to your astrology, what's going to happen?

WATTERS: This I can't say. You know, we have a precedent, now that presidents and vice presidents have resigned, and this might be happening again.

STAMBERG: Does the possibility emerge from political pressure?

WATTERS: I think it's more likely to be something more personal. It might be an accident to his health or something in his personal life that would make him decide he didn't want to finish.

—*January 1975*

On September 5, 1975, in Sacramento, California, Lynette "Squeaky" Fromme, a member of the Charles Manson "family," pointed a gun at President Gerald Ford. It didn't go off. On September 22, in San Francisco, Sara Jane Moore did fire a shot at the president. Someone grabbed her arm as the revolver went off, and her bullet missed.

A day after the second attempted shooting, I phoned Robert Altman, whose brilliant film *Nashville*—which touches, in part, on leadership and assassination—had recently opened. This conversation is a reminder of the tenor of public attitudes in that post-Watergate period. In it I can see the country preparing itself for a man like Jimmy Carter to become president—a leader who promises never to lie to us.

ALTMAN: The political base of *Nashville* was the idea that our culture has come around in its values, and in its advertising and public relations and attitudes, in such a way that we condone political assassination. And we try to point out that it is a totally senseless act in most cases—I mean, it's my belief that it isn't plots or undercover, covert operations. Assassins are just people trying to elevate themselves. It's a basic psychological phenomenon. People feel if they can eliminate or destroy someone who's important, *they* gain importance.

With these Ford assassination attempts, I don't think there's a surprise at all. There's no reason why anyone should assassinate Gerald Ford, other than the fact that he is a president. But I think that the guilt of the matter lies in ourselves. When *Time* and *Newsweek* magazines publish pictures of that Fromme girl on their covers, they're literally inviting God knows *how* many people to say, "Hey, I'll show my mother and dad! I'll get my picture on the cover of a magazine and also kill a president!"

STAMBERG: I saw some interesting parallels, though, between your country singer—the woman who gets assassinated at the end of *Nashville*—and this attempt on Mr. Ford. Both of them embody American values: mom, apple pie, being straightforward, having integrity.

ALTMAN: Yeah, I agree with that. And you used to have the same feelings about our presidents. But I think we've been lied to so much that it doesn't make any difference what presidents say.

STAMBERG: But talk a little more about the possible relationship between Ford as a conveyor of values and your heroine in *Nashville*.

ALTMAN: Well, I don't want to bring any attention to my picture because of this shooting. I mean, my film was my statement, it was an opinion I had—my view of the state our culture is in right now. I don't want to make the same mistake *Time* and *Newsweek* did.

All I was trying to say was that we have come to the point that we will condone a political assassination. We would not condone the assassination of Barbra Streisand, for instance, because nobody will support that. But in politics it's different. And I don't think the attempt was on the person—Gerald Ford. It was on the *president*. It's the title that those people are after. And that, I think, is *anarchy*.

———

Robert Altman was proven horrifyingly correct five and a half years after this conversation when John Hinckley, Jr., shot President Ronald Reagan in order to impress actress Jodie Foster. Despite Altman's conviction that a tolerance for assassination would be confined to political circles, in 1980 one of the most important entertainers of the century was indeed killed. No one condoned John Lennon's murder. But it happened.

I have seen throughout the day the reaction of other members of the family. Mine is fury and rage and anger that in this country this kind of garbage still goes on. And it is *not* going to happen to this president! My God—it is *not* going to happen to this president! I think the American people have got to become angry about the crime in the country, about the ability of people to do this to other human beings. And we have got to stop it. We have got to stop it right now!

—Maureen Reagan,
March 30, 1981

John Ehrlichman on Watergate

June 1976

RECIPE FOR A THIRD-RATE
BURGLARY:
1 flight bag
39 rolls film
2 spotlight bulbs and clamps
1 extension cord
1 small battery
1 screwdriver
1 piece white plastic
4 sponges
1 pair needle-nose pliers
Surgical gloves
1 roll masking tape

A bungled break-in at Democratic National Committee headquarters at the Watergate—a complex of office and apartment buildings that edges the Potomac River—gave the early seventies a name and a language of its own. Phrases like "a cancer on the presidency" and "twisting slowly, slowly in the wind" and "I am not a crook" and "What did the president know, and when did he know it?" popped up in hearings conducted by Senator Sam Ervin and his committee as they interrogated members of the Nixon White House, the president's campaign committee, and others in his shady circle. The phrases then became catchwords at animated breakfast, lunch, coffee-break, and supper-table discussions of the burgeoning scandal.

The break-in, it turned out, was the least of it. It merely labeled the time, and was shorthand for a much broader text of power plays and paranoia that pitted the presidency against some of the other major institutions of our government, and that found the president or his men turning still other governmental institutions against American citizens themselves.

The Vietnam War, a catalyst for protest, was also the catalyst for Watergate. Protesters became "enemies," as did Nixon critics of all stripes. In Richard Milhous Nixon's White House, enemies needed to be watched, their phones tapped, their files inspected. The FBI and the CIA could be instructed to conduct surveillance against dissenters. Anything could be done in the name of national security. And anything could be covered up.

It was a dreadful time. For many Americans, Watergate was a watershed, a sharpening of the old saw about power corrupting, a painful lesson that government could not be trusted. When it was over, when Richard Nixon resigned on August 8, 1974, there was the feeling of shell shock across the country. Recovery took a very long time, and when it came, we had become a different people.

We kept talking about Watergate for years, analyzing its events, assessing its legacy, observing its anniversaries, and trying to explain to ourselves and others how it could have happened. We moved into the Ford years, then the Carter years, and Watergate was still there in the background. Whenever the name of any of its principals cropped up— John Dean, H. R. Haldeman, John Mitchell—attention was paid; their imprisonments, moves, deaths, were all reported.

In 1976, smack in the middle of America's bicentennial, John Ehrlichman, one of the president's most prominent men—his counsel, then his assistant for domestic affairs—published a book. The year before, Ehrlichman had been convicted of conspiracy, obstruction of justice, and two counts of perjury; not surprisingly, he was disbarred. He moved to Santa Fe, started writing his novel, did voluntary community work, and petitioned federal judge John Sirica for permission to work with New Mexico's Pueblo Indians as an alternative to imprisonment. The judge turned down that request, and Ehrlichman eventually served eighteen months of a thirty-month sentence. Four months before he went to a federal prison camp in Safford, Arizona, Ehrlichman came to National Public Radio to be interviewed.

I was more nervous about this encounter than about any other interview I have done. Ever. Seventeen years after the fact, I remember the nervousness more than the actual conversation. And now, seeing the exchange in print, I am surprised at how aggressive I was. In memory, nerves made me a kinder, gentler interviewer than I actually was when we sat down in Studio Two. But it's the nerves I remember, and the nerves that prompt the answer "John Ehrlichman" whenever the question is "Who was your most difficult interview?"

The Company, Ehrlichman's novel, was an uninspired spy tale set in CIA country. But it was not the anticipation of an encounter with a marginally talented fifty-one-year-old novelist that made my palms sweat. It was that John Ehrlichman had been, in my view, the most frightening member of the Nixon White House. Although his impassive and stony-eyed cohort H. R. Haldeman was a big vote getter in many of the Who's More Malevolent? debates, there was a cockiness about Ehrlichman, a sneering self-satisfaction that oozed out of radio and television sets whenever he appeared in news clips or during the Watergate hearings.

To be in the presence of such a person—one with or without White House connections—unnerves me. And the thought of having to discuss Watergate with him (which is the only reason any broadcaster wanted to interview him, as he and his publisher were well aware; no one cared about yet another indifferent spy story) . . . well, the idea of a Watergate wallow with Ehrlichman was both tempting and most unpleasant.

I knew I had to be very aggressive, but I did not want the conversation to sound like two dogs worrying a towel: I make a statement about Watergate, he contradicts it; I challenge, he rebuts. My mind doesn't work quickly enough for me to be very good at that kind of prosecutorial apache dancing. I can't store up facts in a mental quiver, ready to retrieve and release before the target moves. Even if I could, it's not my style. And if he wasn't much of a fiction maker, John Ehrlichman was certainly a sharp attorney. He would be able to win any dispute over facts or intent.

So I thought of what I might do in the course of the interview that would get Ehrlichman to address Watergate obliquely, in ways that might be revealing. I decided to ask some personal questions about what his life was like in those early post-Watergate days, to see how he might react, whether there was any guilt or remorse, any inner legacy from what was surely one of the country's worst political and moral upheavals.

Bob Edwards and I were cohosting *All Things Considered* then, and we decided to interview Mr. Ehrlichman together, an unusual arrangement, then or now. Hosts rarely double up. It's hard to keep a conversation focused when two people are asking the questions. More important, there is usually so much work to be done that it's an inefficient luxury for *both* hosts to read the same book and do the same interview. Still, Bob and I had both come of age professionally during Watergate. It was the first big story I had handled as an anchor, the biggest one he had done as the *All Things Considered* newscaster before joining me as cohost in 1974. John Ehrlichman was the first Watergate principal to be available for interviews, and Bob and I each wanted to "do" him. We agreed to share, and I'm glad we did. Bob's questions are the interview's turning points. They are surgical and direct, and they freed me to conduct the kind of interrogation that makes me comfortable. We did some brief, preliminary planning about how to divide up subject matter. Bob remembers it this way:

"Bob, I'll do the first seven questions, then you come in."

I don't remember that! Nor do I remember *any* detailed discussion between us, no "You be the good cop, I'll be the bad cop" stuff. But some of that sort of routine does occur in this conversation, which we broadcast on June 17, 1976—the fourth anniversary of the Watergate break-in. I began by asking Ehrlichman to read aloud. I can see evidence of jitters in my very first response to him. I flatter him for absolutely no reason. That's nerves.

EHRLICHMAN: (*Reading*) "John Ehrlichman was graduated from UCLA and Stanford and served as lead navigator in the air force in Europe.

"He was White House counsel and became assistant to the president for domestic affairs in late 1969. For many years, he has lived and practiced law in Seattle, Washington.

"*The Company* was written in an old adobe house in Santa Fe, New Mexico."

STAMBERG: You're a good reader! John Ehrlichman reading the description of John Ehrlichman that appears on the dust jacket of his new novel, *The Company*. Is that, Mr. Ehrlichman, a complete description of you? Are there not certain omissions in that description?

EHRLICHMAN: Oh, a page wasn't big enough for a complete description!

STAMBERG: There's no mention of Watergate there.

EHRLICHMAN: No mention of Watergate. No mention of my vegetable garden. No mention of my kids. There are all kinds of things that are left out that are important to me. But that was what was important to the publisher, I guess.

STAMBERG: You didn't have any say over it?

EHRLICHMAN: No.

STAMBERG: But it occurs to me that if somebody had been in outer space, say, for the last four years and picked up the book and read that description of John Ehrlichman, they would really miss what to most of the people in this country is the kernel of your life—the thing

I think the only people who tell the truth are novelists.

The real book about Watergate is going to be a novel. And it's going to be a novel with an entirely imagined president and his court, and entirely imagined senators and their court. There's not going to be a single identifiable person in it.

But that book is going to get to the heart of Watergate exactly as *The Great Gatsby* got to the heart of the twenties and beyond. The green light at the end of Daisy's dock is going to exist as an American symbol as long as people read and write. Exactly the same thing is going to be done about this period. It's going to be a very great book.

—Ward Just, September 1975

that has become the central, defining force of your life—and that is your association with the Nixon White House. The name Nixon doesn't even appear on the dust-jacket description.

EHRLICHMAN: I guess they figure not too many people from outer space are going to wander into bookstores this week. And I guess everybody else knows that.

EDWARDS: What is your legal status right now?

EHRLICHMAN: I have a couple of cases on appeal. And I have about a half a dozen civil cases in various stages of getting ready, down from a total of about sixteen at one time—the others all having been thrown out at one time or another.

STAMBERG: Are you free to talk about Watergate?

EHRLICHMAN: I'm admonished by attorneys and by the realities of this situation not to talk about the issues of those cases, because one of the grounds of our appeal is that it was impossible to get a fair trial in view of all of the pretrial publicity. Now obviously, I can't be complaining about pretrial publicity on the one hand and contributing to it in the event of a new trial on the other. So, I just don't talk about those things.

STAMBERG: You *are* talking about your novel, a book for which your publisher gave you . . . was it a fifty-thousand-dollar advance?

EHRLICHMAN: Well, yes. I ordinarily don't talk about my financial affairs, either, since I'm no longer in public life.

STAMBERG: You have spoken to some people about it, because I read that you're—

EHRLICHMAN: Well, I think they got that from the publisher, as a matter of fact.

STAMBERG: But I also read that you're something like four hundred thousand dollars in debt with legal fees and all that.

EHRLICHMAN: They didn't get that from anybody, because—

STAMBERG: That's not true?

EHRLICHMAN: No, I'm sure that's not accurate. I never try and estimate a number. I'm sure the lawyers don't, and it would be one or the other of us. But as you know, that doesn't stop people from writing things! (*Laughs.*)

STAMBERG: But I wondered why you decided to write a novel? Is it for economic reasons?

EHRLICHMAN: No, matter of fact, I had written the rough outlines of the book before I had incurred those obligations, and had a thriving private practice at the time, so it was very much a sideline.

STAMBERG: But now you've been . . . you're disbarred, so you really—

EHRLICHMAN: Well, that's all transpired since. But you ask what my motives were, and back in that time I started out to write a mystery story. And the central thread of it was going to be that the director of the CIA was going to try and rig a presidential election. That thread still exists in the story, but obviously the story has become much more in its final development.

EDWARDS: Why a novel and not memoirs?

EHRLICHMAN: Well, for a couple of reasons. I'm not in any shape to write memoirs, even assuming that I decide to do so, which I haven't decided. I'm not in any shape to do it because of the lawsuits. And also because the federal government has all my files and diaries and the notes of all my conversations with the president locked up, and I can't get at them. Anything that I did of a nonfiction nature, I would want to have as accurate as possible. I haven't really decided whether to do that or not. I don't know just how much I'm going to be able to contribute.

EDWARDS: Well, you have chosen fiction, and you've written about the CIA and foreign affairs as opposed to your old specialty of domestic affairs. Why?

EHRLICHMAN: Oh, it lends itself to a thriller, to an adventure story or a mystery, I think, better. I probably could have written a real shocker about a struggle between bureaucracies over the question of adding three more GS-14's—

STAMBERG: That *is* a shocker! It gives me shivers just thinking about *that* plot! (*Nervous laughter.*)

EHRLICHMAN: But I decided not to.

STAMBERG: Well, but you *have* written a shocker. You've written about a president of the United States who gives direct orders for the murder of a foreign leader.

EHRLICHMAN: Three presidents, actually. I very deliberately laid the plot over three different administrations because I didn't want to lend myself to the suggestion that these problems in government somehow crop up in one administration and are exclusive to that one administration.

STAMBERG: Why was it important for you to do that?

EHRLICHMAN: Well, I think it's very misleading.

STAMBERG: Is that what happened with Watergate? Is that what happened with the public perception of the Nixon administration?

EHRLICHMAN: Oh, I think there are a lot of stereotypes that carry with it, but I wouldn't oversimplify it by agreeing with your question.

STAMBERG: Why should we read this book, Mr. Ehrlichman?

EHRLICHMAN: Oh, I hope you read it for entertainment.

EDWARDS: About your characters—you seem to give them a cynicism, a super-cynicism, that has just about everyone in your book running around protecting a career, advancing his own ambitions. If these are not thinly disguised characters, but rather people who bear the same characteristics as people you might have known, they are portrayed as anything from fools and martinets to crooks. I'm wondering if you feel any contempt or bitterness toward people you worked with?

EHRLICHMAN: In real life? No, I really don't. I really don't. My . . . I have . . . none of that is to my . . . people that I formerly worked with. Haldeman, I still consider a friend. I don't have any occasion to see any of these folks anymore. They're all scattered around in different towns.

STAMBERG: Do you talk to them on the phone? Do you keep in touch?

EHRLICHMAN: I have talked to them on occasion when there's been something to talk about. I haven't talked to Mr. Nixon for many years. But I don't have any sense of animosity or resentment.

STAMBERG: Why not?

EDWARDS: Any regrets for having taken part in this thing?

EHRLICHMAN: Oh, of course, you can't help but have regrets.

EDWARDS: You ever wish you hadn't come to Washington?

EHRLICHMAN: Well, it's . . . you get a sort of a feeling, like after you've been in the army, as I was, and been to combat and seen a lot of things that were hard . . . hard to take, and you come back and you think, "Well, that's an experience I would rather not have had." But at the same time, there are a lot of valuable things. And I have a feeling that I was able to make some real affirmative contributions, particularly in the area of domestic policy and domestic problem solving. And I don't really regret that aspect of it at all.

But—at the same time—you can't be associated with a flawed enterprise without looking back on it and wondering if there weren't times, occasions, where if you had been smarter or more alert or better in some way, you might have prevented the disaster from occurring.

STAMBERG: You feel that President Nixon misused you, though. You've said that in the past.

EHRLICHMAN: Well, that gets into the area of these lawsuits, that I just really don't want to get into here.

STAMBERG: Why don't you bear any animosity? It seems to me it's totally human to be damn mad.

EHRLICHMAN: I had a lot of problems when I first came out of these trials. But it seems to me that there is no more corrosive and self-defeating emotion than resentment and hatred. And I finally realized that I simply could not pack that around with me. That it would eat me up. And so I have done a lot of thinking, I've done a lot of praying, I've done a lot of living, in an effort to drop that out of my being. I think it's very important for me to do. And I'm very grateful for the extent to which I have been able to do it.

EDWARDS: You don't have that feeling of having twisted slowly, slowly in the wind?

EHRLICHMAN: No, I really don't.

STAMBERG: (*Long pause*) Mr. Ehrlichman, if Watergate hadn't happened—and I suppose by that I mean if the burglars hadn't been caught—what would you be doing today?

EHRLICHMAN: I have no idea. I probably would be trying to figure out how to get away for the Fourth of July weekend and get all my work done.

I would not have had the chance to read or think or fish or sketch or do the other things that I've done. I'd not know my children as I know them, nor would they know me. And I think I'd be a net loser.

STAMBERG: What an extraordinary statement! Strikes me that if Watergate hadn't happened, you'd also be a part of an administration which would be preparing to make its graceful exit from Washington.

EHRLICHMAN: No, I'd be long gone.

STAMBERG: How come?

EHRLICHMAN: Well, I was ready to leave. And I had agreed to stay a short time after the election. But I'd be long gone from Washington. Probably be practicing law or in business or, you know, there's no telling where I'd be in those terms, but I doubt seriously that I would have had the courage to reconstruct my life along the lines that I

The main course at D.C. Jail, where the Watergate figures are being held while awaiting trial, was baked haddock. Of course, it was frozen. There are very few places except excellent restaurants that serve anything but frozen fish. I thought it was good. Tartar sauce was served with it, and I was amazed to learn that it was made from scratch. There was coleslaw, which was finely chopped and passably dressed. The portions were good. A prisoner can have four ounces of meat or fish, and one dessert. In this case canned peaches of good quality. Dinner cost eighty cents.

—Donald Dresden, restaurant critic, The Washington Post, June 1973 really, in my heart, would like to think that I have reconstructed it. And being blown out of it has given me the opportunity that I would probably not have taken on my own.

STAMBERG: (*Very softly*) Mr. Ehrlichman, I wonder, when you drive into a gas station or go into the Laundromat in Santa Fe—whatever ordinary housekeeping tasks you do—and a stranger suddenly comes to realize who you are, what kind of reaction do you get?

EHRLICHMAN: Friendly.

STAMBERG: Yeah?

EHRLICHMAN: Umm-hmm. Sometimes they ask questions.

STAMBERG: What kinds of things?

EHRLICHMAN: I had a couple of young guys come up to me in a restaurant and say, "Hey, who's Deep Throat?"

STAMBERG: Did you answer? Do you know?

EHRLICHMAN: Oh, no. Don't know and don't care. (*Laughs.*)

STAMBERG: You ought to care!

EHRLICHMAN: Why? But, no, people are . . . people are really nice, really friendly. And I've met some terrific people that way.

STAMBERG: Sympathetic towards you? Sympathetic to your situation?

EHRLICHMAN: Generally speaking. Generally speaking.

STAMBERG: Not resentful, not feeling somewhere—

EHRLICHMAN: No.

EDWARDS: No hostilities?

STAMBERG: Not feeling somewhere this guy was involved in taking our democracy away?

EHRLICHMAN: No. I think the only hostility would be in a totally safe situation, where they didn't have to face me. If they could make an anonymous phone call, maybe there'd be some of that.

There was some guy in California who wrote me hate mail for a while. It was kind of funny, because he had written me an earlier letter and put his name and return address on it. And when the hate mail started to come, it was anonymous. But it was obvious that it was the same guy. And so I just wrote him a letter and said, "Please don't write me this kind of stuff. It's not worthy of you"—he was a doctor—"it's just not worthy of you, and it's certainly disturbing to me."

STAMBERG: Why do you think he did it?

EHRLICHMAN: Well, I don't know. He was getting some sort of psychic release. The same reason you boo the umpire at baseball games,

I suppose. I don't know why people engage in that kind of thing. It's kind of sick.

STAMBERG: Do you sense, though, that there really might be a tremendous public resentment towards you, towards all of you White House people who were so deeply involved?

EHRLICHMAN: No, I think that this is much sharper in the minds of people in Washington than it is in the real country.

STAMBERG: Is that so?

EHRLICHMAN: Folks in the country think that the people in Washington are out of touch. And they're right.

EDWARDS: About Watergate?

EHRLICHMAN: About everything.

EDWARDS: You're not saying that the people beyond Washington, D.C., don't consider Watergate a big deal! I mean, you're not implying that it was a small matter to the rest of the country, surely?

EHRLICHMAN: No, but at this point it's pretty much a dead letter around the country. At least in the context that I have. And people can't understand why you all here are still beating a dead horse.

STAMBERG: What do you pick up in the course of talking with folks? How do they define what Watergate was?

EHRLICHMAN: Well, I think a lot of them recognize it as being a part of a whole rather than an isolated incident. And that it's not too much different from what has gone on before and continues to go on in the abuse of power, in misleading people, and so on. They know they're misled.

STAMBERG: And if it was part of a continuum, why then did it get so much public attention? Why, then, did it lead to the resignation of *one* president, when *many* might have been in similar situations?

EHRLICHMAN: I don't know the whole answer to that. Part of it is, I think, that the Congress was of one party and the White House of another. But the things that went on in the Johnson administration that were not made huge, celebrated causes are at least partly explained by that, and possibly the Kennedy situation the same. And possibly the Truman situation the same.

Secondly, this was the first one in the media age, and I think the Senate hearings, almost to the exclusion of every other factor, set the climate and prepared the skids, so to speak, for the president's resignation.

Without that prolonged, intensive media attention, without that

FRANK WILLS: Well, I'll tell you the truth, that particular night I thought it was just somebody just breaking in to steal a typewriter or something. I finished my rounds, from twelve midnight till eight that morning, and it wasn't until about four or five days later I really found out. Someone from the FBI or someplace came knocking on the door.

STAMBERG: How much longer did you stay working as a guard at the Watergate after that?

WILLS: Not long.

STAMBERG: How come?

WILLS: I was a corporal at that time. I got promoted to sergeant. And I got a fifteen-cent raise. And, you know, I said, "My God." Not necessarily that I was looking to be promoted to major or lieutenant or anything like that. But when I seen exactly how important it was, really, I said, "My God." I got really fed up, I just couldn't deal with it anymore.

—June 1977

preparation and without the obvious mistakes that the White House made in response to it—for an organization that supposedly understood the media, I think the people in the White House, myself included, underestimated that whole process terrifically in its impact and importance—without that, I think it would have been a very reticent Congress and very reticent people, unprepared to turn a president out.

And then there are undoubtedly all the other things, the climate in the city created by the two newspapers, particularly the *Post,* and so on. All of these things undoubtedly contributed in their way. So, it's . . . it's a mixed and complex answer that I would have to give to your question, and a very incomplete one, because I haven't really thought it through.

STAMBERG: I must say that I myself, just trying to think what Watergate was, have an awfully hard time.

EHRLICHMAN: Well, it was a media event, among other things.

STAMBERG: Well, yes, and it was a kind of—

EHRLICHMAN: Certainly not exclusively.

STAMBERG: It was a kind of a carefully charted tampering, essentially, with the ballot cast by every American. I mean, I don't know which to pick of what seems to me an octopus of—

EHRLICHMAN: You know, having sat there on sort of the other side of the screen . . . when people make political speeches and say, "These fellows were trying to steal the Constitution" or "They were trying to steal the country" or so on, it's very hard for me to equate what actually took place, and what I heard going on, with those kinds of rhetorical charges. There was just nothing like that in anybody's mind.

STAMBERG: You mean, in a premeditated way?

EHRLICHMAN: Well, either premeditated or—

STAMBERG: Nobody ever said, "Hey, guys, let's all get together today and steal everybody's constitutional rights?"

EHRLICHMAN: Or even, "The people be damned!" There wasn't even any of that . . . which would have been . . . I don't mean to denigrate that. That would have been pretty bad, too.

It was very much a day-to-day dealing with pragmatic problems that seemed to be part of a continuing battle between the White House and the media. And there were probably a thousand failed attacks on the White House that had been successfully blunted in one way or another by quick admission of wrongdoing, or by firing somebody, or by changing tactics, or by media response, or whatever. And this one took. The Committee to Re-elect could have been reorganized quickly, and people responsible could have been fired and punished, and the White House could have survived it very nicely. But it was by clutching the mistake to its bosom and by trying to deal with it as just another partisan attack that the problem became so severely aggravated.

EDWARDS: Was the mistake one of wrongdoing or in letting it get out?

EHRLICHMAN: Well, the mistake, obviously, was in how the wrongdoing was responded to, as I see it. That's what brought the president down.

If one had gone out quickly and said, "This was terribly wrong and these people ought to be punished and the campaign managers responsible ought to be fired and we're going to clean house over there and set up a new campaign organization," I think that would have been the end of it.

EDWARDS: Why didn't that happen?

EHRLICHMAN: Here, again, I'm getting right into the guts of this lawsuit that I really can't go into.

EDWARDS: How much of this came from paranoia—"We" versus "Them"?

EHRLICHMAN: Oh, I'm sure a measure of it did. And it was a continuing attitude. I don't know if paranoia is the right diagnosis. Because there isn't any question there was a "We" and a "They" attitude, as there always is in Washington. In Washington, there's always somebody who's the king of the mountain, and there are always eight hundred guys trying to pull him off.

There's nothing benign about the relationship of the president to other elements in the city of Washington, and there never has been. I think he's entitled to a healthy paranoia, if there is any such thing.

STAMBERG: Today I read in the paper that Jimmy Carter says he hopes, when he becomes president, that he can establish a benign relationship, rework the ties between the White House and the Congress and get them moving in concert.

EHRLICHMAN: Well, it isn't just the Congress, but I wish him *rots a ruck*!

STAMBERG: You doubt that he's going to have success?

EHRLICHMAN: Well, I just think anybody who's king of the moun-

tain, whether it's a little mountain or the biggest mountain, is immediately in a contest with the people who are trying to pull him down.

EDWARDS: If a friend of yours said, "John, I've just been offered this
great job as a White House aide and I've been invited to go to
Washington to serve on the president's staff," what would you say to
him?

EHRLICHMAN: Well, I would be very happy for him. I'd start to lobby
him for some money for an Indian school I know.

STAMBERG: Thank you very much, Mr. Ehrlichman.

EHRLICHMAN: You're very welcome.

EDWARDS: John Ehrlichman, former assistant to President Nixon for
domestic affairs, convicted felon, and author of the novel *The Company*.

⸻

By the end of that twenty-three-minute encounter, I think we got to meet
the real John Ehrlichman. Or at least the Ehrlichman who had paced the
corridors of the White House, strategizing.

Noah Adams, who is now a host of *All Things Considered,* was a
production assistant on the program when that interview was broadcast. (A noble beginning, by the way. Linda Wertheimer, another *ATC*
host; Liane Hansen, who hosts *Weekend Edition*/Sunday; and I also
started our NPR careers as production assistants, cutting other people's
tapes.) Noah told me, after listening carefully to the Ehrlichman conversation, that he thought it had been a seduction. By me, not Edwards! On
paper, I see nothing seductive in my approach. It's straightaway—a
series of direct questions, follow-ups, theories floated, the usual stuff of
interviews.

But here's the curious thing about radio and the power of the voice.
Listening to the tape now, I *hear* what Noah means. Toward the end of
our time together, I begin speaking very, very gently to Mr. Ehrlichman.
My voice is as soft as the belly of a kitten. But I am asking killer
questions: trying to define the meaning of Watergate, suggesting that the
White House tampered with our votes and interfered with our constitutional rights. Nearly every one of my questions has claws. But I place
them gently.

Bob Edwards's questions are more consistent and even-toned, in
print as well as on tape. It's Bob who raises the crucial matter of White
House paranoia, which leads to the pivotal moment in this interview:

I remember when our investigators found the White House tapes—when we learned for the very first time that a president of the United States was putting microphones in his offices and recording, twenty-four hours a day, all conversations in the Oval Office and the other offices. I called Senator Ervin and I told him what we learned. "My God," he said, and quoted from the King James Version of the Bible, something to the effect that you can't really do anything and conceal it from the Lord. And having quoted it, he said, "Didn't the president know that?"

—Sam Dash, chief counsel, Watergate committee, on Ervin's death, April 1985

Ehrlichman's statement about how Washington works—his "king of the mountain" theory—a stunning nutshell revelation of the Watergate mentality. That revelation may not have come out without the softer questions—about strangers' reactions in Santa Fe gas stations and what Ehrlichman would have been doing if Watergate hadn't happened. But with that revelation, John Ehrlichman takes us inside the Nixon White House. Even now, almost twenty years later, it's a chilling place to be.

Margot Fonteyn on "Margot Fonteyn"

May 1976

Describing Margot Fonteyn in *The New York Times* some years ago, critic Clive Barnes wrote that the ballet superstar "has always danced like a shy diamond." Both qualities—the shyness and the brilliance— came through in our 1976 conversation.

The Royal Ballet's one-time prima ballerina was fifty-seven when she came to NPR. Tiny (five feet four inches) and fragile-looking, with dark eyes and pale skin, she was easy to imagine as the teenage Juliet, a role she had danced not so many years earlier to the Romeo of Rudolf Nureyev, who gave her a second career in the 1960s.

We spoke of fame, of what life at the top meant to her.

FONTEYN: When I was younger, people would look at me and ask, "What ever must it feel like to be a famous ballerina?" Well, most of the time I wasn't feeling like a famous ballerina. Only when I stood on stage at the end of the performance and all the flowers were thrown down and the applause . . . then you feel like a famous ballerina. But a lot of the time you don't.

And for a long time, I didn't find the person that I could love. And I'm one of these people who needs to love more than I need to be loved by somebody else. And during all that time, I was essentially rather lost and, in a way, lonely. I had many friends, but I was lacking . . . missing something.

I did have this marvelous escape of putting myself into Giselle and Coppélia and all these characters in the ballet. So that became real. When I was Giselle, I knew exactly who I was and what I was supposed to be feeling and doing. But when I came out and went to supper afterwards, I wasn't really sure . . . (*Pauses*.)

STAMBERG: . . . who you were? Were you bewildered?

FONTEYN: A bit lost in a way. Then one falls into the trap of, well, "I . . . I am 'Margot Fonteyn.'" People think that I'm this great ballerina. And so you start trying to be the ballerina offstage. And then I realized that that isn't right. You can't do that. You have to be yourself not only *off* the stage, but even *on* the stage. You have to find the way to be yourself when you're being Giselle.

STAMBERG: Is this how temperamental artists get created? You are told so often how good you are that you not only begin believing it but demand that everyone else treat you that way?

FONTEYN: No, I think very often the temperamental artist is something else. People expect "Margot Fonteyn" to come out on the stage and to give them some special excitement in her performance. They say, "We are going to see you dance tomorrow! We're *so* looking forward to it. It's going to be marvelous!" And then you think, "Well, what ever am I going to do? How am I going to be marvelous?" That is, I think, usually the basis of what is called artistic temperament. It's really nerves. It's a feeling of this responsibility that maybe you won't live up to what is expected of you.

Of course, one does the very best one can, always, on the stage, but it's not always as good as one would like.

STAMBERG: How do you know?

FONTEYN: That's another point. I've talked to many, many artists, actors, even the Japanese Noh dancers, about that. Very often I have thought, "Oh, it was really terrible tonight. I danced so badly!" But people who are very close to me and have watched me many times say, "That was a really good performance." "But it wasn't," I say. "I was terrible." "No, no," they tell me. "You don't know how good it was." Another time, exactly the reverse.

STAMBERG: Have you had times on stage when the technical specifics simply left your mind and you became totally transported?

FONTEYN: Oh, yes. That's fleeting, but certainly there are moments when you completely give yourself over to some step. But that step leads into other steps and those steps also have their complications of time and space and balance and . . . it's very hard to explain because there are so many things going on in your mind at once.

STAMBERG: **As a conductor, how do you feel after a performance you are not really happy with, but the audience stands for five minutes clapping and the reviews are magnificent the next day?**

JORGE MESTER: **I feel almost as bad as when I've done a magnificent performance and get a lousy review. Almost as bad. Because at the moment, when an audience goes nuts over a bad performance, you feel certain doubts as to the value of what you're doing. You say, "Well, my God, if they really don't know when it's bad, how are they really going to know when it's good?"**

—February 1977

When Pablo Casals was in his seventies, a friend came to visit him. Casals's routine was to get up in the early morning and take a walk along the beach. They did that. Then he went back home, took out his cello, tuned it, and began to play a C-major scale. Casals played the open string C. No problem there. Then he played the D, first finger holding down the D. That was all right. Then he played the E, then the C again, and then he'd shift back to the D string. This went on and on and on. Casals couldn't seem to get past that third note. And his friend was sitting there thinking, "What in the world is going on here? Here's the world's greatest cellist, he's just trying to play a simple C-major scale, and he can't get past the third note!"

Casals knew exactly what the friend was thinking. "For fifty years," he said, "every day, I have to find the E."

—John Holt,
May 1979

STAMBERG: Do you remember what Isadora Duncan said years ago? "If I could tell you what I mean, I wouldn't have to dance it." Here I am pressing you to put into words something that is—

FONTEYN: Yes. Yes. Well, you're really asking me things that I don't know and I'm only a bit guessing at the answer. But it may be that one shouldn't inquire too closely into one's self. I think of something Isak Dinesen wrote about there being some things in the nature of people "that demand darkness and that need to go unobserved in order to grow soundly."

It's spontaneous; it's something alive and living. And if you lay it all out and look at it, it's lost a little bit of its life.

———

Off-mike, on one of those strolls to the exit door when you curse yourself for not getting the "walk talk" on tape, Margot Fonteyn said two things that stayed with me almost longer than what she said on the air. I had deliberately *not* asked about her fifteen-year partnership with Rudolf Nureyev. Everyone was asking that. But on her way out, his name came up and she told what it had been like performing with him. "I would just stand in the wings, watching him as Romeo," she said, "and it was so thrilling that I simply couldn't wait to get out on that stage to dance with him."

Dame Margot also spoke about stage fright, the terror she had experienced before most performances. Although it never went away, she said she finally learned to *use* the fear, to control it until it propelled her like an arrow, and actually brought out her best onstage. I've lost track of the number of times I've passed that observation along to new broadcasters or reporters or actors or athletes. Nor can I count the number of times I've told it to myself before a new undertaking.

Margot Fonteyn died of cancer in February 1991.

Mrs. Ernest Hemingway

October 1976

Mary Welsh Hemingway was the writer's fourth wife, and a fourth wife is a special breed. Undaunted by risk, she has chosen a man who has had three prior marriages. Even if this one lasts, the man is no longer young and will need much tending. A fourth wife is a caretaker.

The fourth Mrs. Hemingway was a small woman with fine cheekbones and a heart-shaped face crowned with short white hair. Her gestures were contained and precise, her skin was weathered, and her voice had been sanded by many years of whiskey and cigarettes. She was unassuming and direct. I liked her at once.

The interview, much anticipated, was also worrisome. *How It Was,* her book about her life with Hemingway, had made me wonder how it was that she'd been able to put up with him for seventeen years. There was also the matter of his death. At the age of sixty-two, Ernest Hemingway put a twelve-gauge double-barreled shotgun into his mouth and blew his head off. Mrs. Hemingway had written about it, but asking her to talk about it was a different matter. I feared it might be difficult for her, and in my early years of interviewing it was hard for me to raise troubling personal matters with guests. I was reluctant to invade their privacy. I suppose I've learned to move into delicate areas with a bit more facility over the years, but it's never easy. Maybe now, older myself and having heard and sought out so many sad stories, I've simply come to know how resilient people can be, and have grown to understand that if I ask difficult questions with respect and compassion, the answers will come less painfully.

STAMBERG: There's Marilyn Monroe.

INGE MORATH: This was on the set of _The Misfits._

STAMBERG: The film your husband, Arthur Miller—who was then _her_ husband—wrote for Monroe?

MORATH: Yeah, I was there to photograph for magazines. I didn't know Arthur. She was rehearsing a scene, and I thought that she looked much more sensually interesting doing that than in other poses she was doing just for my camera.

STAMBERG: Have you ever, in subsequent years, wished you had paid more attention to her then? There you'd been, in the presence of an earlier wife.

MORATH: Well, no. I think you have to be yourself. Even if you are the first, the second, or the third wife. If you try to take on or imitate anything, I think it would be a disaster.

—February 1987

This half-hour conversation with Mrs. Hemingway is filled with difficult questions and painful memories. There is great joy in it, too.

HEMINGWAY: And there was this thing that held us very closely together. The Gulf Stream. Fishing on the Gulf Stream.

And I loved being on _Pilar_. We didn't have any ship-to-shore radio. We were on our own. No matter what the weather, no matter what the circumstances, whatever things might be happening to the boat, or what kind of fish we'd run into, we were alone and independent. It was our own particular world, and I loved that.

STAMBERG: And that probably was your salvation. Whenever there got to be too many guests at lunch, or too many changes or improvements you had to make in the house, or in the life—

HEMINGWAY: We'd beat it off on _Pilar_.

STAMBERG: (_Narrating_) Mary Welsh Hemingway speaks the way Ernest Hemingway writes. Simply. Without adornment. About _Pilar_, their fishing boat, about the Finca Vigía—the home in Cuba which she ran as his fourth, longest, and last wife.

She's almost seventy now. And he's been dead for fifteen years—as many years as they were married.

She was thirty-five and someone else's wife when they met in London in 1944. Mary Welsh was a highly successful reporter, covering World War Two for _Time_ magazine. Ernest Hemingway was forty-four, also married—to the correspondent Martha Gellhorn—and very famous. He had written the major books by then, _The Sun Also Rises_ and _For Whom the Bell Tolls_. He came to London to cover the war for _Collier's_ magazine.

Here's how they met: Mary was having lunch with her friend Irwin Shaw, another writer. It was a warm day, and she took her jacket off in the restaurant. She was wearing a white sweater. Underneath the sweater she wore nothing, which was her habit since the age of thirteen, when her mother for the first and last time tried to harness her into a brassiere.

When Mary Welsh took off her jacket, Irwin Shaw said two things: "God bless the machine that knit that sweater" and "Wait till you see how many people will drop by our table during this lunch." Ernest Hemingway dropped by. His words: "Introduce me to your friend, Shaw." That was the beginning. But Mary Welsh didn't think much of him at first.

HEMINGWAY: Well, the thing I disapproved of particularly was that he had just arrived. He was one of the new batch of stars, big important names who were then coming over to London to handle the big story, which was going to be D-Day, the invasion of France. And us old-timers, who'd been there through thick and thin, and through the Blitz, and through . . . (*hesitates.*)

STAMBERG: You felt you'd paid your dues, and in comes this fancy whippersnapper?

HEMINGWAY: *We* knew! They didn't know anything. And I disapproved entirely of their ignorance. And also of the need sometimes to sort of coach them and enlighten them. I thought, "If they're such hotshots, let them find out for themselves."

STAMBERG: So you didn't like him terribly much. You saw him only a handful of times, and then he said a most extraordinary thing to you. He said, "I don't know you, Mary, but I want to marry you. You are very alive. You're beautiful like a May fly." What does that mean? What is a May fly?

HEMINGWAY: You have to ask a trout! I don't know what it is that makes a trout snap at a May fly. But I suppose he meant something attractive.

STAMBERG: What attracted Hemingway? What was it about you? It had to be more than the white sweater.

HEMINGWAY: It was all my glorious charms, of course! (*Laughs.*) Oh, I don't know. I don't have any idea.

STAMBERG: Is that an embarrassing question? Surely, people have asked you this before and you've had to think about it—had to wonder, "Why me?"

HEMINGWAY: Really, I . . . (*laughs self-consciously*) . . . I guess I'm not really enough of a self-analytical creature. Because it . . . it was good enough if he . . . if he felt . . . thought that well of me . . . I was pleased. But I still was not sold on the idea of getting hooked up with him.

STAMBERG: Why *did* you marry him?

HEMINGWAY: Why did I marry Ernest? Well, it was a complete break, as you can imagine, from the busy life of being a reporter around London. I knew everybody in the government, all sorts of interesting writers and actors and musicians.

STAMBERG: You were going to Lady Astor's country house for weekends.

HEMINGWAY: Yes.

STAMBERG: You were having dinner at Julian Huxley's.

HEMINGWAY: Yes.

STAMBERG: You were very well connected. What an exciting life!

HEMINGWAY: I was having fun. *Whammo!* Sharp break! Housewife in Cuba.

STAMBERG: But before we get to the change in life-style, I'd like to know what it was about *him* that attracted you. Why did you think about giving up all of that?

HEMINGWAY: Just because he was more interesting than any other man I knew.

STAMBERG: Is that it?

HEMINGWAY: Yes. Continuously more interesting, more thoughtful, with a wider perception of people and things and events. Our heads were totally . . . *enmeshed,* I suppose you might say. And then, he was a great big loving hunk of a fella.

STAMBERG: A big, sexy guy?

HEMINGWAY: I thought so.

STAMBERG: And so famous. Weren't you fascinated and curious about that? Wasn't there the idea, too, of living with a living legend?

HEMINGWAY: Absolutely not!

STAMBERG: Anhhh, I don't believe you.

HEMINGWAY: Look, I was married to a *man*. He was my husband. Period. There was none of this "I'm the big writer" kind of thing. He was a guy. And if he was a good husband, fine. If he was a bad husband, I told him so.

STAMBERG: There was a point when you made up your mind that you were going to leave him.

HEMINGWAY: I got all steamed up about something.

STAMBERG: It was 1950. You'd been married for six years at that point, right?

HEMINGWAY: Yes. I don't remember what caused it now, but—

STAMBERG: You sent him a letter. You wrote, "What I expected to contribute to the marriage were loyalty to you and devotion to your projects, your family and house and possessions, care of whatever things or jobs you entrusted to me, and in daily living a certain good balance, alertness and tenderness towards you. I think we must now both admit that this marriage is a failure. Therefore, let us end it." But you didn't leave.

. . . M. Picasso . . . welcomed Ernest with open arms, and while Picasso's girl, Françoise Gilot, a slim, dark, quiet girl with serpentine movements, and I kept ourselves behind them, Picasso showed Ernest the big, chilly studio and much of the work he had done in the past four years. "*Les boches* left me alone," P.P. said. "They disliked my work, but they did not punish me for it."

—from **How It Was**

HEMINGWAY: Obviously not.

STAMBERG: What happened?

HEMINGWAY: I don't know . . . whatever it was . . . oh, I think we got into a fishing tournament, I think that was it! I was going to fish in my own boat, which was called the *Tin Kid*. And everybody was betting I couldn't make it, couldn't stand it, because the Gulf Stream was seldom tranquil. Anyway, we did make it, and in three days of fishing, *we got the biggest fish!*

STAMBERG: (*As an aside to listeners*) Mrs. Hemingway just raised her head and jutted out her chin as she said that, and when she finished, she closed her eyes and nodded very emphatically. (*To her*) You're proud of it, huh?

HEMINGWAY: Oh, of course! Triumph. Absolutely!

STAMBERG: Look what you did, though. You met him on *his* level. You met him competitively, and you met him in terms of sports. You said, "You're not going to show me. *I'll* show *you*." And it worked out.

HEMINGWAY: I didn't feel I was going to show him, but I *was* determined. Natch, I was terribly pleased that our little boat, which was the smallest among something like fifty boats—lots of them, you know, with outriggers and refrigerators—was the winner. We didn't have anything. There's a certain panache, you know, to beating all those great big fancy boats.

STAMBERG: (*Laughs.*) Are you a fearless woman?

HEMINGWAY: Oh, I must have been afraid at various times of various things. I . . . offhand, I can't think what particularly—

STAMBERG: You weren't afraid of huge fish?

HEMINGWAY: No. A huge fish is more competitive and more stimulating than a little fish. Although little fish are fun, too.

STAMBERG: Would you say the same thing about people? It sounds as if Ernest Hemingway was some huge fish that was—

HEMINGWAY: I didn't fish for him.

STAMBERG: No, no, that's right! It was the other way around, wasn't it? You were the May fly.

Well, you weren't afraid of raw lion meat on a safari, when you had done some hunting and he slit it open and you ate it.

HEMINGWAY: Sometimes in Africa there were some walks, especially in very high grass, where we knew there were rhinos and other sorts of beasts that might be kind of hungry. And sometimes, going

Ernest was tired from his long effort to finish his book . . . and it seemed to me his weariness blurred his personality. . . . I had heard him say "truly" in solemn voice too often, and "daughter" . . . and "how do you like it now, gentlemen?" I was also bored with his war. But these were all new to Jigee, and she listened with devoted attention, rather like our Black Dog . . . while Ernest, wrapped in his voluminous plaid bathrobe I'd had made for him in Cortina . . . expounded. I found them thus in our sitting room every afternoon, recognized the risk I was taking and dismissed it.

—from How It Was

through the high grass, I thought, "Hmm . . . any minute now," you know. But it does stimulate the circulation.

STAMBERG: You weren't afraid of seventeen-year-old gorgeous Italian women and all the others who were always lionizing him and to whom he was very much attracted . . . one woman in particular?

HEMINGWAY: Yes. Yes. "Afraid" is not the word. I thought about it and decided that no matter how much he might be attracted, any of these people—but particularly one of them—would not be a good thing for him *at all*. He would have to readjust downwards. He would have to do so much educating. And it . . . the . . . the other thing of . . . would diminish in its power or its strength.

STAMBERG: The sexual attraction?

HEMINGWAY: Yes. I felt quite sure I could look after him much better than any of these other people could. (*Small, slightly devilish giggle.*) I . . . that's, I suppose, terribly egotistical, but I had by that time learned a lot about how to care for him, how to look after him. I did feel that I would be better for him. And also I wanted him for *me*!

STAMBERG: This was a flirty Italian girl who came to Cuba and moved in with you for a while.

HEMINGWAY: Yes.

STAMBERG: And you were taking her places, showing her things?

HEMINGWAY: Oh, certainly. Oh, certainly.

STAMBERG: How could you do that?

HEMINGWAY: We got along very well.

STAMBERG: How could you not march up to her room, pack her suitcases, and hand her a ticket to the next boat out?

HEMINGWAY: No, no. Oh, no. I knew Ernest was enjoying her. Why shouldn't he enjoy her? She was very carefully chaperoned by her mother. And I, of course, looked after her mother as well, and tried to see that she had a glorious time. Why not?

STAMBERG: There is a largess in that that I, as a married lady, find very difficult to understand.

HEMINGWAY: I suppose people have to take risks. I didn't think of it particularly as a risk because I felt, basically, that our association was so firmly footed that this temporary—I hoped it was temporary, and, of course, it proved to be temporary—thing would sort of wear itself away.

STAMBERG: You know, as you tell this story, I'm absolutely struck by how you changed from your early years as a journalist, when you were such an independent, tough lady. You *were* a tough lady, and a hardworking one, too—

HEMINGWAY: I was hardworking. I wasn't tough.

STAMBERG: (*Laughs.*)

HEMINGWAY: I wasn't tough.

STAMBERG: All right, thank you for the correction. Anyway, the change, then, to a life in which you essentially catered to every one of his wishes. You sustained him.

HEMINGWAY: That was my job. Quite different from any other I'd ever had.

STAMBERG: It's clear that you came to a realization of that, in the course of living with him. And I sense that you grew and—

HEMINGWAY: I learned a lot!

STAMBERG: But in some ways, *he* didn't. I mean, there he was, in his fifties, having these flirtations, these drinking parties, and there you were, *sustaining* him through all of it. It felt to me as if you were far more mature than he was—that the change, the education, happened for you in ways that it didn't for him. Do you think that's true?

HEMINGWAY: I hadn't thought of that. I really have no idea of whether it would be . . . whether he was learning. He certainly was forever reading, and learning whatever it might be from books.

STAMBERG: That's not really what I mean, though.

HEMINGWAY: You want to know whether or not he was learning to live.

STAMBERG: I think I am. I remember a few years ago interviewing Buck Lanham, who was a dear friend of your husband's—maybe yours, too?

HEMINGWAY: We're friends, yes.

STAMBERG: Buck Lanham told me that he thought Ernest was "frozen in adolescence." That was the phrase he used to describe your husband. And I think it's *that* that I'm getting to. The changes in your life were made by you, not him.

HEMINGWAY: I wouldn't agree with Buck that he was frozen in adolescence, because that indicates that a man doesn't know very much. And Ernest knew a great deal, about people . . . humanity and individuals. And he had great general knowledge. He was a very well informed man. He was, for example, awfully good at foreign languages.

STAMBERG: So is a high-school senior! A young person also has that mental agility. That's what you're really talking about, the ability to learn and absorb. That's a wonderful talent to have.

But . . . but I'm saying something else. I'm talking about a man in his fifties who is unable, somehow, to recognize or live with his changing self, the fact that he's aging, that he needs to settle down a bit, or take it slower, or not have all the parties, and all the champagne, and all the daiquiris, and all the caviar.

HEMINGWAY: Well, actually, you know, the champagne and caviar was not a daily occurrence by any means.

STAMBERG: It reads as if it were. (*Gentle laugh*.)

HEMINGWAY: No.

STAMBERG: There was a lot of it, though.

HEMINGWAY: Yes, thank goodness! Good gray, true, big-grain caviar.

STAMBERG: You're still not really answering me. Was I just getting too close, or is it something—

HEMINGWAY: No, it's just that I am . . . I don't consider myself . . . I haven't thought about it, for one thing, and I don't know whether I'm capable of judging.

STAMBERG: (*Long pause*) Well, Mrs. Hemingway, I'm just sitting here thinking what a great gift for living he must have had. You can look at it that way, too. You can say he was frozen in adolescence, or you can say he lusted for life all the time, and in lots of ways.

HEMINGWAY: Yes. He retained the exuberance of an adolescent—the ebullience, the warmth, the excitement about anything. I would make him a new bouquet at the Finca. I used to ask him to come look at my new bouquet. And he'd say, "It's the most glorious one you've ever done! It's the most *exuberant* bouquet you've ever done. It's lovely, my kitten." Well, you had to appreciate that, you know. That has a certain youthfulness.

STAMBERG: The last years were . . . were very difficult ones. His progressive madness—

HEMINGWAY: The last year. It really was . . . lasted about a year.

STAMBERG: What year did he shoot himself, what was the year?

HEMINGWAY: What was the what?

STAMBERG: What was the year when he committed suicide?

HEMINGWAY: (*Looking puzzled*) I don't get it.

STAMBERG: What was the year, what was the year when he died?

HEMINGWAY: It was '61.

STAMBERG: In 1961?

HEMINGWAY: Yes. July.

STAMBERG: And it came after a series of paranoid events and a change in his personality.

HEMINGWAY: Quite entirely different. Almost a reverse of the man he had been before.

STAMBERG: He was hospitalized.

HEMINGWAY: Yes.

STAMBERG: He had shock treatments. And then on July second, 1961, he committed suicide.

HEMINGWAY: Yes.

STAMBERG: And you first said it was an accident with the gun. Why did you do that?

HEMINGWAY: This was a pure attempt to save myself. I couldn't face it. I couldn't . . . I . . . it was a fact. But I couldn't admit it. It . . . I'm sure it sounds . . . it was a matter of self-protection, somehow or other.

Even though I had known, and should have known much better, that this was in the works, it . . . I don't know . . . it . . . you know, one attempts to protect oneself against any sort of . . . of quick destruction of oneself, and in a sense part of me was destroyed at the same time.

And I didn't mean to lie. I really . . . I had to say it, because I couldn't, myself, believe that . . . that it was intentional.

STAMBERG: And you saw signs? There were signs?

HEMINGWAY: Oh, yes. Oh, yes, plenty.

STAMBERG: He was worried that the FBI was watching him, that he was under surveillance.

HEMINGWAY: Yes. He was worried about money.

STAMBERG: And no need to worry about money?

HEMINGWAY: No, no. No! We called his banker. We were reassured that, you know, he was . . . we had no . . . no problems, no financial . . . after all, we were not buying *yachts,* anyhow!

STAMBERG: And you got the bank figures, you presented them to him, and nothing could get through?

HEMINGWAY: He didn't believe the banker. He had turned from being a man who had great faith in things going properly—he was a hopeful man—and suddenly he became a suspicious man. Not of me, amazingly. Thank goodness.

STAMBERG: Weren't there things that could have been done sooner?

Stopping the parties, or insisting that he get help when you first saw the signs? Something that could have been done sooner, that might have prevented it?

HEMINGWAY: I kept asking myself that, you know, for years.

STAMBERG: I'm sure you did.

HEMINGWAY: For a year, at least. And I couldn't find any answers. And of course, I did consult psychiatrists, quietly.

STAMBERG: And would you say, "He's acting this way, what do you suggest? What should I do?"

HEMINGWAY: Yes. But they didn't have any answers. They didn't have any answers that were satisfactory.

STAMBERG: Yes.

HEMINGWAY: I know that . . . that . . . I guess, generally, when anyone dies, a loving husband or a wife gets this terrible sense of guilt, and feels that there must have been something . . . something . . . something. I didn't suffer very much of that because I really had tried so hard to do everything possible that anyone suggested. And so I didn't live with that . . . that shadow darkening my life.

STAMBERG: (*Pause. Breath, and smile.*) So now, you have the book, you have your life. You're in Ketchum . . . are you still . . . Ketchum, Idaho?

HEMINGWAY: Oh, yes, of course. Of course.

STAMBERG: At the house you bought in the last years of—

HEMINGWAY: Ernest bought it in 1959.

STAMBERG: And you are surrounded by friends, and you're cooking, and taking care of people and things—including his manuscripts. Tell us about that. What are you sorting through? Is there the definitive novel that's never been published, that's going to come out in four months?

HEMINGWAY: No. No, there isn't.

STAMBERG: Five months?

HEMINGWAY: (*Laughs.*) No. There is a long novel, but it's certainly not definitive, and may not be good enough to publish. We have still quite a lot of manuscript, and it's just a matter of going back to work and finding what may be publishable. I have one principle—two, actually. One is that I won't publish anything, or will not permit the publication of anything which in consultation with Scribner's editors we decide is of inferior quality to that which was published during Ernest's life.

TOM JENKS: When I first heard this manuscript existed—*The Garden of Eden,* **an unpublished Hemingway novel, fifteen hundred pages—my response to editing it was NO. What I really wanted to do was new writers.**

STAMBERG: What turned you around?

JENKS: Well, they convinced me to read it, and I was hooked. I saw that there was a book here that should be published—not for historians, not for scholars or critics or reviewers, but for readers.

—December 1985

And the other one is that while we may cut where he has been redundant or repetitive without an artistic reason, we will not fuss around with his words. There will be no changes. We will not rewrite him or add anything except the obviously important comma or something like that. So if it comes out under Ernest's name, it'll be his book and nobody else's.

STAMBERG: Can you tell us what it's about?

HEMINGWAY: Well, I have got to go through this massive manuscript. I have to go now—pretty soon—and take up this thing again. I think there is maybe a collection of short stories and semi-reportage, non-fiction things, which might be made into a good book of the quality that is really Ernest. But this takes careful, careful reading and research and judgment, you know. And as far as I'm concerned, there isn't any terrible rush about that.

STAMBERG: Sure.

HEMINGWAY: I can go fishing a little bit, I hope. Some things like that.

STAMBERG: You like going out walking, and you do some shooting. Don't you go hunting?

HEMINGWAY: I do bird season, as a rule, in Idaho, but mostly we shoot clay targets. And when I do get a dove in my sights and I know that I could kill him, I say, "Go on, baby. I'm not going to shoot you. You're too beautiful alive." I'm really no menace to the doves at all!

STAMBERG: Are you still doing these annual get-togethers on his birthday, of people who were important—

HEMINGWAY: Oh, yes. We give Papa's birthday party every year. All the old friends, you know. The guests are limited to those who were his personal friends, and there are still seventy or eighty or ninety around, you know. Just an evening of music and dancing and, I trust, good food and decent wine—things like that. And usually, in the middle of it, some friend stands up and says, "Here's to Ernest," and we drink a toast, and that's it. I mean, there's no formality. It's supposed to be a cheerful evening, and it is.

STAMBERG: He wrote about you, once: "Miss Mary is durable."

HEMINGWAY: Ah! (*Laughs.*) You'd have to be durable to live . . . to, you know, to mesh in . . . with a man like that.

▬▬▬

When the taping was finished, I walked Mary Welsh Hemingway to the door, and we shook hands. "Well," she said, smiling, "that was just

71

dandy." After our conversation was broadcast, a friend of hers called. "That was absolutely the Mary I know," the woman said. "You got close to the bone."

Mary Hemingway died in 1986, after a long illness. She was seventy-eight years old. Before her death, she published three of Ernest Hemingway's manuscripts: *A Moveable Feast, Islands in the Stream,* and *The Dangerous Summer*. In the years they were married, Hemingway wrote *Across the River and into the Trees* and *The Old Man and the Sea*. His greatest works were written before her time. *Her* greatest work, she would say, was her care for and about him.

Warming Up to Garrison Keillor

January 1977

Here's Garrison Keillor before he became GARRISON KEILLOR. Garrison in 1977, when he was doing a local morning radio show in St. Paul and helping his listeners get up, get out, and tackle the brutal Minnesota winter. This conversation on *All Things Considered* was prompted by what the National Weather Service called the coldest winter "since the founding of the Republic." It is Garrison's network-radio debut, and when it's done, I'll tell you how it came to pass that shortly afterward, he wound up performing his wildly successful monologues, skits, and musical mixes on *another* network. But (as we say in the radio business) first . . .

STAMBERG: One very early morning last week it was forty-four degrees below zero when Garrison Keillor got up to go to work. Actually, Garrison Keillor always gets up in the middle of the cold, still Minnesota nights, because his radio program, *The Prairie Home Morning Show,* begins at six A.M. The program originates from KSJN in St. Paul, and it's heard also on the five other stations of Minnesota Public Radio.

Garrison Keillor has created for his show a mythical but well-patronized sponsor, Jack's Auto Repair, offering—on very cold mornings—the Jack's Auto Repair Warm Car Service, featuring Raoul, the award-winning Warm Car Driver.

KEILLOR: It is simply a warm car which comes by your house on cold mornings and picks you up—sometimes right out of bed, you know—

wraps you in a quilt, and carries you out. The catch is, the warm car only seats six.

STAMBERG: Six.

KEILLOR: But our surveys, you see, show that we have three times that many residents. So, that leaves twelve who are not going to get a ride to work. And those twelve people can just sit there and wait for the warm car, fully expecting it to come, and stay at home all day.

STAMBERG: What's the phone number for that place?

KEILLOR: (*Laughs.*) Well, it's one of those telephone exchanges that hasn't gone to seven digits.

STAMBERG: (*Laughs.*) I see. They also bring something warming for your stomach, don't they?

KEILLOR: Well, we do have some other products at Jack's. There's the Jack's Hot Oatmeal, which when eaten hot (as our mothers taught us to eat it, you remember) teaches children where food goes in the stomach, and gives you a lower center of gravity for better traction on the snow and ice.

STAMBERG: And Raoul himself brings that with him, does he, when he comes to pick you up?

KEILLOR: He does, indeed! It's the very first thing he does—slips a little bit between your lips. So, we put out the Jack's Hot Oatmeal, and we have other survival gear, such as the Warm Coat.

STAMBERG: You can get that from Jack's too?

KEILLOR: Yes, you can. The Warm Coat is kind of a unique invention—weighs over one hundred pounds and keeps you warm just by the exertion of carrying it around with you. Lets you get there and take it off. I've got one like it here in my closet.

(*Laughter.*)

But winter was so much worse when I was a kid. I used to have to wait for the school bus out at the end of the long driveway on those cold mornings. And that just seems to be so much worse, you know, to have to go stand and wait for something to come and take you someplace where you don't want to go. And you don't get paid for going there.

That's really how I got into radio in the first place. I was working in a parking lot to put myself through college, and I really just couldn't bear the thought of spending another winter standing out there in the cold and making change for five hundred or so cars with my bare hands. I just took the first inside job I could get, which turned

When it came time for me to record "Moonlight in Vermont," I told Johnny Mercer I didn't know what the lyrics meant. I was a California girl. It was about a place I'd never seen. All I knew was maple syrup and skiing. When we got to the middle, I said, "I don't know what ski tows are." And he said, "Well, if you don't know, then we're going to change it." And he called the composers and said, "Can it be ski trails?"

—Margaret Whiting,
October 1983

out to be radio. Which really, in comparison to what other people have to do, I mean—it's just a waltz, I think.

STAMBERG: What's the line, "It's inside work and no heavy lifting"?

KEILLOR: That's right. (*Laughs.*) That's the truth!

STAMBERG: Garrison Keillor, host of *The Prairie Home Morning Show* on Minnesota Public Radio.

———

Two years later, Garrison Keillor was doing some very heavy lifting—hosting a live national Saturday-evening vaudeville show on which he called attention to a hard-to-find lake somewhere in the middle of the American imagination. *A Prairie Home Companion* was distributed by the Other Network—American Public Radio—and thereby hangs a tale, since it turned out to be the most successful series they've ever had.

At one point, National Public Radio could have had the Keillor phenomenon, but our then president, Frank Mankiewicz, put the kibosh on the deal. The Minnesota people sent Frank an air check of Garrison's show and asked whether NPR would be interested in distributing it to member stations. Mankiewicz, one of the wittier men you'll meet, listened to the tape and decided it wouldn't work—too middle American, too "provincial." So Minnesota took its business elsewhere. And NPR ended up woebegone.

This story, which has become part of the National Public Radio Body of Knowledge, was much on my mind in 1987 when we were putting *Weekend Edition*/Sunday on the air. As host, I was involved in conceptualizing the program and helping make decisions as to commentators, regular features, etc. WBUR, one of our Boston stations, sent over tape of a weekly program that had been on their air for ten years, with the suggestion that we use a bit of it on Sunday morning. Here's what happened. (This is my version. Everyone involved in this story has a different version. I like mine best. No names have been changed to protect the innocent.)

The News Director (Robert Siegel, then) listened with regrets. The Executive Producer (Jay Kernis) agreed with the News Director. The Producer (Katharine Ferguson) agreed with the Executive Producer. The Husband (Louis Stamberg) agreed with all of them. Not me. "These guys are *great*!!" I insisted. "They have those accents, their timing is perfect, and everybody cares about cars."

And so it was that Tom and Ray Magliozzi, proprietors of the

Good News Garage in Cambridge, Massachusetts, and dispensers of invaluable and hilarious information about cams, struts, axles, hoses, and the American Way of Life (it's really Zen and the Art of Automotive Repair), came to National Public Radio and stayed there, moving from five minutes on *Weekend Edition* to a full hour of their own, distributed nationally each week. *Car Talk* is a jewel in NPR's crankshaft, a Wobegon on wheels, and we all have Frank Mankiewicz's mistake to thank for it.

Marilyn French on Men

November 1977

Women—and men—who read Marilyn French's first novel, *The Women's Room,* when it came out in 1977 can still remember the *rage* of it, and the rage it inspired. It was as if a sexual hand grenade had been tossed onto bookshelves.

In 471 pages, French set out the story of a generation of middle-class women raised in the 1940s, married in the 1950s, divorced in the 1960s. The 1970s brought them self-discovery, sisterhood, and an often lonely, isolated, angry freedom. Her bleak conclusion: Mutually nourishing relationships between men and women are impossible.

The Women's Room was on the best-seller list for almost a year and has been published in twenty-seven languages. I wonder whether this interview helped sell the book or made listeners decide to stay away from it.

STAMBERG: Something in the conversation you are about to hear will outrage you. Something in the conversation you are about to hear will strike you as cutting about as close to the truth as you can get. Which is what is so infuriating about Marilyn French's brilliant new novel, *The Women's Room.* It angers you to the point of wanting to heave it out the window, but it contains so much truth that you can't get up from the chair.

The Women's Room is didactic, narrow, simplistic, bitter, angry, tender, powerful, insightful, clear, and often truer than true. A very dangerous book. Marilyn French.

I think that women like Bess Myerson and Jean Harris, women of that generation (which is my generation) who were successful—we were solo women in a man's world—were made anxious by it. Men are made anxious by failure. Women are made anxious by success. You felt vaguely unfeminine if you were doing something in the world as well as trying to run a household or a marriage or a family life.

Women of accomplishment scare off a lot of men. So when a man like Herman Tarnower or Andy Capasso comes along, someone who is not afraid of you, that's a very nice feeling. You meet a friend and sometimes a lover, and it means a great deal.

—Shana Alexander, September 1988

FRENCH: My heroine, Mira, is intended as a more or less typical character. She's a sensitive, intelligent child. As she grows up, things happen to her. She can't handle them. She's been given no tools for handling them by her culture. This is what it's like.

STAMBERG: But look how she ends up! She's completely alone and fearing for her sanity, certain that she's mad. Her closest friends have seen their daughters raped, or been dumped on by their husbands, by lovers, found comfort through lesbian relationships, or moved into women's communes and written men off entirely. That . . . I can't . . . no! I won't do that, Marilyn French! I won't believe that that's the inevitable ending for today's woman.

FRENCH: You don't have to. The fact is that your experience is your experience. But I didn't draw this book out of a vacuum. Most of the women I know are alone, even those women who are married. They are essentially alone.

Betty Friedan, at a party the other night, said to me, "The ending made me unhappy." And I said, "Oh? What's *your* life like?" And she said, "Well, it's true!" And I said, "I'd like to introduce you to a few of my friends." There were about seven of them standing around, and I said, "We're all alone, every one of us." It is what happens to a great many women. Once they become fully themselves, there are no men out there for us.

STAMBERG: How is that possible? Is it because men's interests are so diametrically opposed—

FRENCH: Because they still expect women to do their bandaging. And if you're not willing to do the bandaging, you're out.

Anyway, you don't really want their company, because they're really essentially empty and mechanical. They're emotional children. They're dull.

STAMBERG: I can, you know, I can cite you names, addresses, and telephone numbers from my little black book . . . well, one address, anyway . . . where my husband happens to live, which is my house—

FRENCH: I see, okay.

(*Laughter.*)

STAMBERG: You're really wrong, you know. This movement for liberation can't just be called a women's movement anymore. It's touched men. Men who—

FRENCH: Some men.

STAMBERG: —have welcomed this liberation, opened their arms to it, saying, "Thank God, *I* can be a feeling human being too, *I* can show some emotion!"

FRENCH: Obviously, I know some feeling men. Of course, I know a few. But I'm not talking in this book about the few.

STAMBERG: Please read page 197.

FRENCH: Okay. (*Reads*.) "What is a man, anyway? Everything I see around me in popular culture tells me a man is he who screws and kills. But everything I see around me in life tells me a man is he who makes money. . . . If the men I've known haven't much indulged in killing and are no great shakes at screwing and have made money (for the most part) in only moderate amounts, they haven't been anything else either. They're just dull. Maybe that's the price of being on the winning side. Because the women I know have gotten fucked literally and figuratively, and they're great. . . .

"What I don't understand is where women suddenly get power. Because they do. The kids who almost always turn out to be a pile of shit are, we all know, Mommy's fault. Well, how did she manage that, this powerless creature? Where was all her power during the years she was doing five loads of laundry a week and worrying about mixing the whites with the colors? How was she able to offset Daddy's positive influence? How come she never knows she has this power until afterward, when it gets called responsibility?"

STAMBERG: A later paragraph begins, "You must think I hate men."

FRENCH: Yes.

STAMBERG: I think you hate men.

FRENCH: I do, part of me . . . a part of the time . . . yes. I hate qualities of male prerogative and male emptiness. It's funny, my son read this book and was very upset. He's not a child, he's twenty-three. He called me and said he thought it was great. But he was upset by it, and he said it made him feel guilty.

And I said, "Now, look, Rob, I wasn't attacking you. Remember, it's you who's helped keep me sane, and it's the way I feel about you that keeps me from going off the deep end with hatred."

And he said, "Yes, but the thing is, *I* hate men!"

And he meant the same thing that I mean when I say that there are qualities of behavior, qualities of consciousness, in men that are utterly hateful.

——

We are now offering a group for fathers and toddlers, where on Sunday morning, men bring their kids between the ages of about one and two and, with other men, run a play group and get a chance to talk in ways that many of them said they never have before—about the conflicts between being a father and having a job, and the mother's territory in the house, and the father's territory. I think it's somewhat parallel to what we saw with the women's movement, in the way women confirmed to other women that they have the same issues, same concerns.

—James Levine,
Fatherhood Project,
June 1982

Susan Sontag once said the artist is the memory curator, "the curator of consciousness." And I do believe that is the function of the fiction writer, and it is different from just creating a record. I've never heard of somebody reading a history book and bursting into tears every few chapters, or starting to laugh riotously. But that is a very common reaction to a fictional creation. And that's what I want to do. I want to move people to remember.

**—Alix Kates Shulman,
June 1978**

A decade and a half after *The Women's Room,* Marilyn French broadened her argument, made it global. Her 1992 book, *The War Against Women,* crammed with sobering statistics, reports that the subjugation of women is a worldwide phenomenon, that all institutions of a society wage war against women, that being under the influence of women is man's greatest shame.

In her gentle, sugared voice, French spelled out her findings recently at a sold-out Washington appearance. The audience—well-dressed women of all ages plus a man in every other row—grew increasingly quiet as she spoke. Leaving, people avoided one another's eyes. The outside air felt good. There'd been too much untempered accusation in that auditorium. Too much hatred, still.

David Mamet on Wrighting Plays

June 1977

Meet Mamet. The great American playwright David Mamet. Mamet, the 1984 Pulitzer Prize winner for *Glengarry Glen Ross*. Mamet, the writer who made Broadway buzz when Madonna appeared in his 1988 play, *Speed-the-Plow*. Mamet, the hot film writer and director—*House of Games, Hoffa, Charlie Chan*.

David Mamet was none of the above when we met in 1977. But you could see it coming. He'd won Off Broadway's Obie Award in 1976 for Best New American playwright and was just beginning to get big attention. "The new darling of the American stage" was how we introduced him on *All Things Considered*.

In those early years, in addition to writing plays for children and for consenting adults, Mamet was doing a good bit of teaching (it shows in our conversation), at the University of Chicago, Marlboro College, Goddard College. Speaking about his writing, he'd paraphrase Voltaire: "Words," he'd say, "were invented to hide one's feelings." The words David Mamet was putting down on paper were like prizefighter's jabs. They still are. Lightning fast. Lethal. In conversation, though, he sounded nothing like his characters.

STAMBERG: David Mamet has been called the American Pinter. Twenty-nine years old, author of twenty plays, his work is outrageous, brilliant, funny, obscene. His shows—*Duck Variations, Sexual Perversity in Chicago, A Life in the Theatre*—are playing in different theatres across the country. *American Buffalo* opened on Broadway this year, stayed there long enough for *The New Yorker* magazine to hate it, and then closed.

I asked David Mamet whether he ever writes straight narratives.

MAMET: I'm a contributing editor at *Oui* magazine in Chicago, and for a couple of years I have been writing what we refer to as *girlie copy,* things like "Bernice as a Way of Looking at the Universe": "She wrapped her silken thighs around my Maserati"—you know, things like that.

STAMBERG: Serious stuff.

MAMET: Very serious stuff. And I've been writing a lot of humor for them. Funny things. You want to hear some humor?

STAMBERG: Yeah, you could tell me some humor.

MAMET: This is a whole new category of humor I've invented. It's ethnic humor. It's called American Jokes. Here we go.

How many Americans does it take to change a light bulb?

STAMBERG: (*Laughs.*) It depends if they're Hungarian or not! Okay, I give up.

MAMET: One.

(*Pause.*)

STAMBERG: I'm afraid to hear more.

MAMET: How do you tell the planes of the American air force?

STAMBERG: The planes of the American air force? How do you *tell* them?

MAMET: Yes.

STAMBERG: You look for the stars and the stripes?

MAMET: Exactly so. That's one for you. And the last one is, How many Americans does it take to make popcorn?

STAMBERG: One.

MAMET: No, you're wrong there. Actually, it takes many, many thousands, starting from those who plant and cultivate the corn, those who create the farm implements which enable us to harvest it, and the home appliances which enable us to pop it. . . . I can go on forever.

STAMBERG: (*Hums "America the Beautiful."*)

MAMET: I'll do you . . . I'll do you . . . I'll do you some imitations. Are you ready?

STAMBERG: No, I want to talk about other things—okay?

MAMET: Can I do Roy Rogers and Trigger?

STAMBERG: *Quickly!!*

MAMET: Okay. It's Roy Rogers and Trigger, right? When I'm *speak-*

ing, I'm going to be Roy Rogers. When I'm *thumping,* that's going to indicate Trigger. Okay.

How old are you, Trigger?

(*Three thumps.*)

That's right, boy. And now, Trigger, what's the capital of Yugoslavia?

(*Three thumps.*)

That's right, boy, Belgrade!

STAMBERG: (*Laughing*) Can you stop telling jokes now for a couple of minutes, because I want to ask you seriously about this—

MAMET: I'm a little bit giddy today—I'm in the nation's capital, Susan, after all!

STAMBERG: Listen, but here . . . now, come *on,* stop a minute and let me . . . (*laughs*) . . . let me ask you this business about the transition from writing straight stuff—if it *is* straight—

MAMET: (*Settling down*) I wrote plays first, and then I started writing straight stuff later on. That's all I wrote for about ten years, was plays. Plays are written in dialogue, you know, and anybody who thinks they aren't is wrong. All that you have in a play is what the characters say to each other, and what they say to each other has to carry what they *do* to each other—you can't support it in stage directions.

STAMBERG: You mean you can't say, "He looked over there and what he was feeling was this and this"?

MAMET: Exactly. A lot of playwrights make that mistake—student playwrights, young playwrights, do that.

STAMBERG: You have to plunge us inside the characters' heads, inside their lives, with very little setup. Could you give us an example now—say, from *American Buffalo*? Three characters in a junk shop are planning a robbery—a robbery which ends up not coming off. What are the first words we hear?

MAMET: The play starts with the older character, who runs the junk shop, speaking to the younger character, who's his gofer. He says to the younger character, "So, so what, Bob?" The kid says, "I'm sorry." The other guy says, "Yeah." The kid says, "I'm sorry, Donny." "It's all right." And the kid says, "Maybe he's still in there." And the guy says, "If you thought that, Bob, what are you doing here?" The kid says, "I came here." The guy says, "You don't come in, Bob, you don't come in until you *do* a thing." The kid says, "I'm sorry." The guy says, "Don't tell me that you're sorry, I'm not mad at you." And that's the end of that first beat.

STAMBERG: So, what we know now is that some kind of mistake has been made, and there's a definite master-servant relationship between those two people.

MAMET: Exactly. You get that from the action, which is something that we've discovered from Pinter—that narration is useless in the theatre. You really don't have to narrate anything.

If the facts are important, they have to be in the action—that is to say, in what the characters are doing to each other, and the way the characters act toward each other. Through action they will recognize how they feel about each other, and what they are to each other. And if the facts aren't important, you better not put them in the play.

STAMBERG: Did you have other openings for *American Buffalo* before you settled on this one, or did it *have* to open that way?

MAMET: No, that evolved. The beginning and the end of *Buffalo* were very difficult for me and I rewrote them many many times over a period of about two years. See, I'm a playwright—spelled *w-r-i-g-h-t*. It comes from the verb "to work"—"wrought" being the past tense of "work," like "wrought iron" means "worked iron." And a playwright is someone who works a play, rather than someone who *w-r-i-t-e-s* a play. He *works* a play. She works a play. And what it means is that you have to write down as much as you can, see what it contains—divine the essence of it—and write it again, according to that essence. Divine the essence and write it again.

STAMBERG: And all of that is done in dialogue?

MAMET: Sure, sure, because every moment in a play affects every other moment in a play, just like every line in a painting affects every other line in the painting. Also, each moment has to exist on its own; no moment can serve a purpose other than putting forth the purpose of the play. A moment has to be logical and has to be essential. If it doesn't tell you something you must know, then the moment is wrong in a play. And if it tells you something that you know already, the moment is also wrong.

Arthur Miller's a great educator, a great education for a playwright. A play like, for example, *A View from the Bridge*—if you take away any moment, the play doesn't work, because every moment is critical. That's what a play is, it's a dramatic progression. And what Miller does so beautifully . . . if there's one moment in the play that's not essential, he takes it out. Which is why, even in his bad plays, we're rapt, we're spellbound by what's happening on the stage.

STAMBERG: Will you, as you write, say the words in your head?

MAMET: Sure.

STAMBERG: *Must* you do that?

MAMET: Sure. Just like we all do, when we have fantasies. All of us write plays all the time in our heads, right? Before we're going to go visit our girlfriend, before we're going to go talk to a boss, before we talk to our mother on the phone—we rehearse. It's a human faculty, it's part of the rational faculty. Subconsciously, to a large extent, we project future instances in an attempt to be able to choose between possible courses of action. We also do it consciously, sometimes. "Well, he's going to say blah, blah, blah, and then I'll say blah, blah, blah." And then we rehearse them unconsciously. It's the same thing.

STAMBERG: Do you do a lot of tinkering once a play of yours is on the stage?

MAMET: Oh, I would tinker forever. I would tinker forever!

STAMBERG: Do actors have trouble memorizing your lines?

MAMET: Most times when an actor can't remember a line, it's because the line is wrong. And it's my job to make the change before they know that it's wrong. *I* should know that it's wrong.

———

David Mamet has developed a cadre of actors, including W. H. Macy and Joe Mantegna, who speak Mamet as if his words were part of their breathing apparatus. Not an easy task. Despite Mamet's observation that if an actor has trouble with a line, the fault is in the line, most of his dialogue is daunting. Try reading Mamet aloud with someone. Here's a fragment from *Speed-the-Plow:*

GOULD: As I told you, the chances were, were astronomically slim that it would . . .

KAREN: Of course, but you said, you, you wanted to *investigate* . . .

GOULD: . . . yes . . .

KAREN: . . . "because once in a while" . . .

GOULD: . . . yes.

KAREN: And once in a while one finds a pearl . . .

GOULD: Yes . . .

STAMBERG: Do you think people will turn out to see *House of Games* just out of curiosity, to see Mamet's work as a director, even though it's not a great movie?

JULES FEIFFER: Well, Susan, I gotta make a sad response to that. David Mamet is one of our foremost playwrights, perhaps *the* foremost playwright. Which means that in today's culture, most people have never heard of him.

—*November 1987*

It's difficult, isn't it? His rhythms are so quick, the phrases so broken and repetitive, the dialogue so bereft of narrative, it's a miracle actors can memorize their parts. But Mamet's actors do. And once it's up, once it's on stage, everything becomes clear. On stage, Mamet's perfect ear turns out to have written all you need to know.

Interviewing Salinger

March 1977

On the day the Senate Watergate hearings revealed Richard Nixon's secret White House tapings, an *All Things Considered* producer whose name I shall graciously not disclose looked Linda Wertheimer in the eye (Linda was covering the hearings) and said, "I want you to get us those tapes for broadcast." With admirable restraint, Linda did not laugh in the fellow's face.

But we *have* had our scoops. Through grinding determination and intrepid investigative reporting, legal affairs correspondent Nina Totenberg got most of them—Supreme Court nominee Douglas Ginsburg's marijuana use, the Clarence Thomas–Anita Hill connection.

With me, it's been more coup than scoop. In 1979, I sat in the Oval Office with President Jimmy Carter for two hours, anchoring a national call-in program on which the leader of the free world fielded unscreened questions from ordinary citizens. (A later encounter with Mr. Carter and his wife appears ahead, in 1987.) Such proximity to the presidency might top any reporter's list of career highlights, and it certainly was a fascinating experience/wonderful opportunity for me. But a much bigger coup was putting William Shawn on the air. Almost as big as if I'd interviewed Amelia Earhart. Or Judge Crater.

William Shawn was the reclusive editor of *The New Yorker* magazine for thirty-five years. He never gave interviews, never spoke to the press. But in 1985, when E. B. White died, Mr. Shawn agreed to read *The New Yorker*'s obituary of one of its greatest writers over the phone

E. B. White was a great essayist, a supreme stylist. His literary style was as pure as any in our language. It was singular, colloquial, clear, unforced, thoroughly American, and utterly beautiful. . . . He never wrote a mean or careless sentence. He was impervious to literary, intellectual, and political fashion.

—William Shawn reading E. B. White's obituary

for broadcast. "Must we do this?" Mr. Shawn asked. "Yes, please," I replied. And we made a tape.

William Shawn agreed, I think, because he was too gentlemanly to turn down a direct request, also because he and I had spoken by phone, off tape, several times in the past when I'd called to ask for background information on some story or other. One such conversation had occurred in February 1977, and it concerned Mr. Shawn's best- and, at the same time, least-known author, J. D. Salinger.

Esquire magazine had just published, for the first time in its history, an anonymous short story. In an editor's note, *Esquire* said that the story was being run without signature, not because the magazine had decided to withhold the author's name, nor because the author wished to remain anonymous. "On the contrary," the note ran, "we are not entirely sure who the author is." But *Esquire* had concluded that lack of a byline didn't matter. The story was the thing.

The anonymous story, "For Rupert—With No Promises," smacked of J. D. Salinger, author of *The Catcher in the Rye* and numerous short stories, who has not published a word since the 1960s, nor spoken one, either—to the press, anyway. (Compared to Salinger, William Shawn was Chatty Cathy.)

"Rupert" was larded with clues—references to earlier Salinger characters (a dear, dead brother named Seymour, another brother, nicknamed Buddy—two members of the Glass family that the author had written of on a number of occasions), mysticism, Viennese logic, all sorts of Salingeriana.

Salinger's fans (they are legion, and "addict" might be a more accurate description) swamped *Esquire* with letters—ten-page single-spaced typewritten exegeses proving that "Rupert" *was* the work of their hero, J.D. (most correspondents felt the story was genuine). Other letter writers swore the piece was a hoax, a parody by John Updike or Philip Roth or Thomas Pynchon.

I arranged to interview *Esquire*'s fiction editor, Gordon Lish, and, before I did so, phoned over to *The New Yorker* to get William Shawn's view on "Rupert." As the magazine's chief editor, Mr. Shawn was intimately familiar with all of Salinger's writing, and also in touch with the man himself. When I said, "The only way 'Rupert' could be Salinger's is if he's had a hideous breakdown and hasn't written for years," Mr. Shawn laughed in his gentle, discreet way and assured me that this was not the case and that the story was most certainly not Salinger's. Back at *Esquire,* Gordon Lish, in the most level tones, said—on the air—that he did not know the identity of the writer but felt the work had merit.

A month later, *The Wall Street Journal* solved the mystery. The anonymous author was identified. It was Gordon Lish himself. Furious at having been lied to, I called him again.

STAMBERG: Mr. Lish, why did you do it?

LISH: Well, I'd like to say I did it because it was fun. It was fun to write the piece. I think I did it mainly because it interested me to respond to Salinger's silence; that is to say, Salinger's silence belongs to me.

STAMBERG: You mean the fact that he is silent is an open invitation to the Gordon Lishes of this world to come out and *be* Salinger—*pretend* to be Salinger?

LISH: No, I didn't pretend to be Salinger! I simply tried to imagine Salinger's psychological circumstances as they would pertain now. I think what belongs to me is the kind of feeling I have about Salinger, that he generated as a function of his work. You know, he *persuaded* me of things. He made me love him, and he made me love the people he wrote about. And then he stopped writing about those people.

STAMBERG: And you were mad?

LISH: I wasn't mad. I simply wanted more of it. And if *he* wasn't going to give it to me, I wanted to give it to myself.

STAMBERG: But you've pulled a hoax on innocent readers, especially Salinger lovers. Salinger readers are a cult unto themselves. I'm one of them. We can practically quote full pages by heart. We take him *very* seriously.

LISH: I think that every literary enterprise is fundamentally a hoax. All expression, in fact, is a hoax. So, I have no problem with that, either. I think that "For Rupert—With No Promises" is a true statement. It's a statement by me. I understand that Salinger regards this story as despicable, an absurdity, and I . . . I have a problem with that. I don't know how one can read that story and come away with the opinion that it is despicable or absurd. It's fundamentally a serious story.

STAMBERG: If it were a story that had been submitted to you through the mail, by someone else, would you have published it?

LISH: That's an excellent question that no one's put to me before. In

I'm interested that there is not more public outcry on behalf of Random House and Ian Hamilton, who wants to publish some private letters in his biography of J. D. Salinger. Hamilton has no permission to use the letters.

The oddity with Salinger is that he's become a public figure, apart from the excellence of his writing, *because of his privacy.* In a way, he created a life that is celebrated for that idiosyncrasy. I'd say the reason the public, by its silence, is probably going along with Salinger is that in some strange, circuitous way they cherish the oddity involved here and are siding with Salinger's right to have his way.

—Roger Rosenblatt, February 1987

fact, I would! Honest to goodness, I think I can be distanced enough from it in this case to say that. Yeah, I . . . my inclination is to say, "Yes, ma'am."

I want to stress this point: There was really no effort to *imitate* Salinger's style and there was no effort really to suggest this *was* Salinger. I mean, it's a complicated matter. There were certainly citations out of Salinger. But the story is *my* story. I mainly wanted to write a story that took readers firmly by the neck. And there was, in doing this, an effort to borrow the circumstances of Salinger's life and the circumstances of Salinger's fiction as I would imagine them to be. But not borrow Salinger's voice as such—not to imitate Salinger nor to parody him.

STAMBERG: Do you feel, Mr. Lish, that you owe anybody an apology—your readers, or Salinger lovers, or Salinger himself?

LISH: On the contrary. I think I'm . . . (*laughs*) . . . *I'm* owed something, because I think I . . . I composed the . . . a story that matters, that . . . that matters to grown-ups, that is worth adding to the word clutter. And I don't think anybody . . . you know . . . let me put it this way: a story . . . to take Salinger's position, as reported, that the story is despicable and absurd . . . I think that readers are safe from stories which are despicable and absurd. I think where we're endangered is where stories are lovable and real. That's where we are imperiled. Because then what's suggested is that we change our lives!

———

After all that gobbledygook, off mike I asked Gordon Lish why he hadn't published the story under his own name. "As fiction editor, I felt it would be inappropriate to publish my own story," he said, adding that he didn't think authorship mattered—"It's the story that counts"—and that "it was fun" to publish "Rupert" without an author's credit.

Earlier on these pages, I spoke about decades not really staying within the lines but, rather, spilling over into one another sloppily. This 1977 Me Decade conversation with Gordon Lish may be an illustration of that point. In it, I perceive the opening themes of the eighties, a period in which opportunism and doublethink ruled the day, and even some trusted guardians of the culture dipped their pens into sheer ego.

"I quit smoking. . . . If Mom would tell you *any-thing*, she'd tell you *that*— and you promised me you were going to start *listen-ing* to Mom, remember?"

"Smithy? Hey, buddy, you there?"

"Don't buddy me right now, Buddy. Please."

—from "For Rupert—With No Promises"—Esquire, February 1977

Joan Didion on Writing

April 1977

Favorite interview? The best out of twenty thousand? A very tough call. There was the brilliant, incisive (not to mention trenchant) exchange with dancer Edward Villella, sometime in the early seventies, which I—far too old by then to be a rookie but, nonetheless, rookielike—totally erased. By mistake, I recorded an interview with Pete Seeger over it. Seeger was terrific, but he was no Villella. With absolutely no way to prove it, and probably *because* there's no way to prove it, the Villella was my Best Interview. Unless . . . Mary Hemingway. Unless . . . the five-year old in Baltimore beginning her first day at school. Unless . . . whatever happens day after tomorrow. In commercial broadcasting, they say you're as good as your last interview. I like to think I'm as good as my *next* interview. A very public-broadcasting point of view!

In fact, I think the best interview I've ever done is this conversation with Joan Didion. But our encounter started off poorly.

Didion's journalism has had much influence on my own work, and I took special care in getting ready to interview her. I read, or re-read, all her fiction, essays, and reportage, as well as the thickest clip file I could put together—reviews, profiles, critiques. When she arrived, in a black Chanel-looking suit with a flower tucked behind her ear and circles under her dark, worrying eyes, I couldn't wait to begin.

But after we settled into our chairs and started recording, it was a near disaster. I began a question, stopped, paused to look at my notes, launched into another question, decided it wasn't coming out properly, said so, apologized, started again.

> A book has to start a dream in my mind. I read the first three pages and I fall through the print on the page and I'm in Russia watching a train go across a field. I never wake up in *Gulliver's Travels*, either. I just start and I'm in the dream all the way. The same thing with Shakespeare and Chaucer.
>
> **—John Gardner**

"Miss Didion, how come . . . uh, remember in that speech you gave at . . . no. I'm sorry. I'm so sorry! Let me try again. Miss Didion . . ."

I was overprepared, overawed. A mess. This went on for the kind of fifteen minutes that feels like years and makes you bless the creator of audiotape, which lets you throw away the jumble you're making.

"Miss Didion, when you . . . no. Sorry."

Didion's big eyes got more worrying. So did my small ones, and my stomach was in loops. Then, mercifully, probably because I'd finally run out of unease, something clicked and we began talking together so effortlessly that there were times when the broadcast miracle occurred: I actually forgot we were making a tape.

That rarely happens—forgetting there's tape. A broadcast interview, when it's really good, should *sound* as if the tape's been forgotten, should sound absolutely *natural,* like a real-life conversation. But it never really is. There's nothing natural about it.

You sit across the table from a complete stranger in a room lined with gray foam egg-carton-shaped acoustic padding; you wear a headset that lets you monitor the quality of the sound; you glance at a digital clock that counts off elapsed time; you nod to a wall of glass behind which sits an audio engineer, possibly an editor and producer, all of whom are taking notes so that they can cut the tape you are making; and then you talk into pieces of electronic wizardry that will eventually carry your voice, and the voice of your interviewee, outside this equipment-laden room and into people's cars and kitchens. Nothing natural at all.

A conversation designed to be overheard, a broadcast interview forces the interviewer to listen with a kind of third ear, to make constant mental notes about follow-up, about when to change the subject, about how to get a more concise response, about where the tape might be cut. And when it's done very well, a broadcast interview gives twelve million listeners the illusion that they're eavesdropping. This 1977 exchange with Joan Didion is the closest I've come to creating that illusion.

A Book of Common Prayer was Didion's novel that year. Like the rest of her fiction, it was crafted with elegance and style, but the prose here was dark, cheerless. The paper world Didion had created was parched, her characters' lives empty. I hated entering that world. Her point of view seemed to be that aridity is most of life, a reality to be dealt with. My point of view was that aridity is a nightmare, something to avoid. This difference would be the subject of our conversation. But I wasn't sure how to bring it up.

STAMBERG: You've said there are no terrific stories, there are only terrific ways of writing them down. Is that really true? Aren't there some terrific stories that are terribly written but still fascinate the reader?

DIDION: Well, yes, there are. But most stories are banal stories. *Anna Karenina* is a banal story. It could be called a soap opera. *Madame Bovary* is a banal story. It is the way they are written down.

STAMBERG: But what about mystery stories, where the twists of the plot become much more important than the language the author uses?

DIDION: Oh, I don't know. Do you ever read Ross MacDonald? The film *Harper* was based on one of his mystery novels. For years, he's been writing the same book. The detective, Lew Archer, goes out on a case and always finds that the solution lies several generations back. But Ross MacDonald has been writing closer and closer and closer until his books are all plot, almost like geometric exercises. They're very exciting. If he wrote that story down any other way, I'm not sure it would have such tension. His books are very, very peculiar and frightening.

STAMBERG: I find *your* books very frightening, especially *Play It as It Lays* and *A Book of Common Prayer*. The tension is distasteful.

DIDION: *A Book of Common Prayer* is not as ugly as *Play It as It Lays,* though. It's not a great deal more *cheerful,* but I think it's not as ugly!

Writing *A Book of Common Prayer* aged me a great deal. I don't mean physically. I mean that in adopting Grace, the narrator's, point of view, I felt much sharper, harsher. I adopted a lot of the mannerisms and attitudes of an impatient sixty-year-old dying woman. I would cut people off in the middle of conversations. I fell into Grace because I was having to maintain her tone.

It's a very odd thing with novels. You don't know where they come from. They don't exactly come from you, and while you're writing them they seem to influence your mood more than your mood influences them. You begin by trying quite consciously to maintain the mood, simply because you don't want to break the tone of the novel.

STAMBERG: John Gardner says that when he reads, he gets inside the dream of the book and doesn't wake up until the book ends. Is that what happens to you in the course of the actual *writing*? Does the world you are writing about become more real than reality?

DIDION: Yes. More real. And I really resent any intrusion. I didn't

> "My name is Grace Strasser-Mendana, *née* Tabor, and I have been for fifty of my sixty years a student of delusion, a prudent traveler from Denver, Colorado. My mother died of influenza one morning when I was eight. My father died of gunshot wounds, not self-inflicted, one afternoon when I was ten. From that afternoon until my sixteenth birthday I lived alone in our suite at the Brown Palace Hotel. I have lived in equatorial America since 1935 and only twice had fever."
>
> —*from A Book of Common Prayer*

answer mail for a long time while I was writing this book, and I didn't talk on the telephone very much, and if I had a certain amount of business that *had* to be conducted during the morning before I started work, I resented it because it was easiest to move from being asleep directly into this dream without waking up entirely.

STAMBERG: But in your fiction, you are in the middle of a dream that is consistently a nightmare. It's on the edge of horror all of the time. You write about people who are not connecting, who have no real relationships and very little happiness or fulfillment in their lives.

DIDION: I've always thought of my novels as stories I tell to myself. They are cautionary tales. Stories I don't want to happen to me. *A Book of Common Prayer,* to some extent, has to do with my own daughter's growing up. My child is not anywhere near the age of Marin, the girl in the novel, but she's no longer a baby. I think that part of this book came out of the apprehension that we are going to both be adults pretty soon.

STAMBERG: Cautionary tales you don't want to happen to yourself, you said. Do you really mean it that personally? Or do you mean it as cautionary to all of us, to every one of your readers—

DIDION: No, no, no. They are just cautionary tales for me.

STAMBERG: Why do you jump to say that?

DIDION: What I work out in a book isn't what the book is about. I mean, this book isn't about mothers and daughters. That's part of what it was for me, but I don't think that's what it is for a reader.

STAMBERG: Alfred Kazin called you "a professional moralist." I thought maybe that's what you were getting at. Cautioning us to pay attention to certain grim possibilities.

DIDION: I *am* a moralist, but I grew up in such a strong West Coast ethic that I tend not to impose my own sense of what is wrong and what is right on other people. If I do impose it, I feel very guilty about it, because it is entirely against the ethic in which I was brought up, which was strictly laissez-faire. But I myself tend to perceive things as right or wrong in a very rigid way. And I don't necessarily perceive the same things as wrong that large numbers of people perceive as wrong.

STAMBERG: I think I want you to be telling me, through all of these books, that these women and their life-styles are wrong. I want you to tell me that because I find them so distasteful. I find them to be people I must read about (because you're *that* good a writer) but people I would never want to know or be near. It's okay to enter their nightmare for a while as a reader, but I want to be very sure that *you* know—sitting there with your pen or your typewriter—that it's wrong.

DIDION: You see, there I can't make a judgment, because they are *other* people. They are not me. I just want to tell you the story. I can't make a judgment on it.

STAMBERG: What about the judgments in your essays about Haight-Ashbury in *Slouching Towards Bethlehem*? When did you do those?

DIDION: Spring of '67, just before the Summer of Love.

STAMBERG: You went to that section of San Francisco, tooled around, made connections with people who were living there, and gave us bare snapshots—quick glimpses—of some of their lives.

DIDION: That was an extremely frustrating piece to do research on, simply because you couldn't make appointments. To begin with, nobody was up before noon or one o'clock, so you lost the morning. Then, too, it was a very suspect thing to make appointments.

STAMBERG: You might have been a Fed, or you were too old—over thirty—and they didn't want to talk to you?

DIDION: Right. You just had to hang around.

STAMBERG: Your tone is as cool in these sketches as it is in the pieces of fiction, until you get to the end. It's been sheer description, a catalog of what you saw, who said what—until the end. There, it seemed to me, the moralist came out, the right-and-wrong lady. At the end, you told about the three-year-old child.

DIDION: Yes. I had spent a lot of time hanging around a place called the Warehouse, a place where a lot of people lived. It wasn't actually a warehouse—it was the basement of an abandoned hotel—and there were a great many people living there on a fluid basis. One of the long-term people living there had a child who was three. It was very dark in this place. There were no windows, or the windows were walled up. It was a very theatrical place, with colored spotlights all over. The child was rocking, always, on a rocking horse in a blue spotlight. That was where its rocking horse was. But one day I was over there and the child had somehow started a fire and burned his arm. I was terribly worried, because my child was almost that age. His mother was yelling at him in a kind of a desultory way. There had been a floorboard damaged in the fire and some hash had dropped down through it, and everybody else was trying to fish around and get

The center was not holding. It was a country of bankruptcy notices and public-auction announcements and commonplace reports of casual killings and misplaced children and abandoned homes and vandals who misspelled even the four-letter words they scrawled. It was a country in which families routinely disappeared, trailing bad checks and repossession papers. Adolescents drifted from city to torn city, sloughing off both the past and the future as snakes shed their skins, children who were never taught and would never now learn the games that had held the society together. People were missing. Children were missing. Parents were missing. Those left behind filed desultory missing-persons reports, then moved on themselves.

—*from Slouching Towards Bethlehem*

this hash back. I wanted to take the child out, but I had no business doing that.

STAMBERG: And that's where you lost your coolness. The child was badly burned. Nobody had grabbed him in time or knew that he had to be rushed to the hospital. That's where it all broke down for you. You could be a reporter just that far, and then you really had to make a judgment. And in making a moral judgment, you gave a context to the whole experience.

The essay, "Slouching Towards Bethlehem," became the definitive portrait of Haight-Ashbury in the 1960s and also the title piece of that collection of your journalism. In the introduction you write:

"My only advantage as a reporter is that I am so physically small, so temperamentally unobtrusive and so neurotically inarticulate, that people tend to forget that my presence runs counter to their best interests. And it always does. That is one last thing to remember: *Writers are always selling somebody out.*"

This past November, I went to a journalism convention in New York, and at three separate sessions that same passage was quoted. Incidentally, none of the people who read it aloud was in any way unobtrusive or inarticulate!

DIDION: It's very odd to have written things that people quote. (*Laughs.*) Especially that introduction. I had written it late one night and hadn't thought much about it. Usually I spend a great deal of time finding a tone that is not my own and then adopting the tone and getting it right. But with this, I just typed it out very fast, and rather in my own voice. Normally, I have difficulty "expressing myself" in any natural way. I'm not that open. Anyway, I had just written it out as a rough draft. John read it in the morning—

STAMBERG: This is your husband, John Gregory Dunne.

DIDION: Yes. And he said, "This is fine, don't change it."

But to get back to that passage, the statement "Writers are always selling somebody out" means that it is impossible to describe anybody—a friend or somebody you know very well—and *please* them, because your image of them, no matter how flattering, never corresponds with their self-image.

STAMBERG: But I hear it in a very different way for *my* work. I hear it right now, sitting here wanting to talk to you about the things that most concern you in your life, and feeling that I could never do that because there is no reason why I should rip off your emotions and your privacy to make my living. That's how *I* hear that line now.

DIDION: Really?

STAMBERG: Yes. I'm thinking, "Give me my great story, give me my great radio tape." And knowing I could never dare, never dare to ask, because it simply would invade a kind of privacy that's nobody's damn business.

DIDION: Yes. It's not what I meant in that passage, but I know what you mean. I can never ask people even simple questions that all reporters know how to ask, like, "How much money do you make?" I don't like sitting in all those Best Western motel rooms trying to make the first telephone call to the district attorney. Many reporters have mentioned to me that they feel the same way. David Halberstam, who seems to me a very aggressive reporter, very confident, said that he hates to make that first phone call, and just sits on the edge of the bed for a while first.

Maybe that's why we chose this work of writing, so we could disappear, in a way. I'm not sure that people who write had much sense of themselves as the center of the room when they were children. I think the way people work often comes out of their weaknesses, out of their failings. In my case, I wasn't a very good reporter. If I got into a town where a story was and found a *Life* team there, I'd go home. So I had somehow to come out of every story having *interpreted* it, because I wasn't going to get it from anybody else.

STAMBERG: You found a way around something that other people can do straight on?

DIDION: Right. If you can't go to the mayor, then maybe if you sit around the gas station long enough, you can figure out what it's all about. In a lot of situations—particularly when you're dealing with people who are interviewed frequently, like politicians or anybody who is in the middle of a breaking story—they tend pretty much to have an answer to every question you're going to ask them. I mostly use interviews, when I do them in that kind of a situation, as just a way of insinuating myself into the person's day. The actual answers aren't ever very significant.

I'm never happier than if I go on a story and I find myself with the person and they are doing whatever they do—say it's a movie set—and it turns out that they are too busy to give me twenty min-

DORIS LESSING: I'm sixty-four. When I was young, I was quite pretty. I'm sorry all that's gone. But I don't care all that much, you know. I personally don't mind getting older. I think there's a great deal to be said for it.

STAMBERG: What are the advantages?

LESSING: Well, you become invisible. I mean, no young woman is ever off show—she's always presenting herself, or people are looking. Also young men now, because they're also peacocks—which I quite enjoy. I love watching all that! But the thing is, when you become middle-aged and onwards, you literally become sort of unnoticed. And that's very good. You can sit and watch and listen.

—Doris Lessing, April 1984

utes. Then I am there without having to go through the interview! (*Laughs.*)

STAMBERG: What about all this business of fragility? "Joan Didion is so fragile, so delicate." I notice, talking with you, that you have a thin, almost whispery, voice. You speak very softly, but with great firmness.

DIDION: I think my physical size is deceptive.

STAMBERG: You are very small.

DIDION: I am not only small, I am too thin, I am pale, I do not look like a California person. It generally makes people think that I must be frail. I'm not actually very frail. I'm very healthy. I eat a lot. I don't cry a lot.

STAMBERG: But do they say that about you because of your physical size or—getting back to the people and things that you write about—is it because the fragility of your characters and the kind of perceptions you have make people think you must be emotionally fragile? When I read the essays in *Slouching Towards Bethlehem,* I thought of you as someone who was just trembling with antennae that were constantly vibrating, picking up on things that other people simply weren't sensitive to.

That desolate landscape that you create and those characters who move through it in their parched ways—it seems to me that you'd never get a Nobel Prize for Literature. Not because of any lack of *skill,* mind you, but because that prize is usually given for optimistic and positive views of life.

DIDION: I think that's probably true. I am more attracted to the underside of the tapestry. I tend to always look for the wrong side, the bleak side. I have since I was a child. I have no idea why. Talk about unexamined lives. . . .

I'm rather a slow study, and I came late to the apprehension that there was a void at the center of experience. A lot of people realize this when they're fifteen or sixteen, but I didn't realize until I was much older that it was possible that the dark night of the soul was . . . it had not occurred to me that it was dryness . . . that it was aridity. I had thought that it was something much riper and more sinful.

One of the books that made the strongest impression on me when I was in college was *The Portrait of a Lady*. Henry James's heroine, Isabel Archer, was the prototypic romantic idealist. It trapped her, and she ended up a prisoner of her own ideal. I think a lot of us do. My adult life has been a succession of expectations, misperceptions. I dealt only with an *idea* I had of the world, not with the world as it was. The reality does intervene eventually! I think my early novels were ways of dealing with the revelation that experience is largely meaningless.

(*Long pause.*)

STAMBERG: You've spoken in the past about the picture that's in your mind before you do a book, and said the act of writing is to find out what's going on in the picture. For *Play It as It Lays,* you imagined a blond girl in a white halter dress being paged at one o'clock in the morning at a Las Vegas casino. For *A Book of Common Prayer,* the picture was of the Panama City airport at six A.M., heat steaming up from the tarmac. Do you have a picture in your mind now of something that you're going to have to be working on?

DIDION: Yes. My next novel is to take place in Hawaii. I can't describe the picture except that it is very pink and it smells like flowers, and I'm afraid to describe it out loud, because if I describe it out loud I won't write it down.

———

That novel turned out to be *Democracy,* published in 1984. The "I" who narrates it is Didion herself. Edgily, she tells the Vietnam-era story of a man, a woman, a U.S. senator, a CIA operative, scandal, murder, adultery, another scandal, death. "Deeply mysterious, cryptic, enigmatic, like a tarot pack or most of Joan Didion's work," wrote Mary McCarthy in a review. Again, Didion, inspecting the underside of the tapestry.

Sex and Shere Hite

February 1978

Before sex was dangerous, it was ubiquitous. The sexual revolution of the seventies meant singles bars, multiple beds, and a top drawer filled with the sort of underwear that only porno stars used to wear. A study of commercial television found that from 1975 to 1977, depictions of flirtatious behavior quadrupled and instances of seductive behavior tripled—up from one sexy bit per hour in 1975 to more than three an hour in '77.

Recently, I came across an instructive piece of paper from that period. It's the introduction I read on the air in October 1976 for an interview with Shere Hite about a book she'd just written. *The Hite Report* gave results of a study conducted in cooperation with the National Organization for Women. Three thousand women between the ages of fourteen and seventy-eight told Shere Hite about their sexuality. "The study's not scientific," I dutifully informed listeners. "She changed her questionnaire in the course of collecting the answers." But Hite's work gave new insights into women's sexual perceptions.

Now, along the bottom of the yellow copy paper on which that introduction was typed—and surely this is the reason I saved it—there are batches of hatches, sets of four vertical lines crossed diagonally by a single line—the way you count in fives, quickly. Bunches of these are strewn across the script, clusters and clusters of them. And next to each bunch, a scrawl in my handwriting: *intercrse . . . vag . . . orgsm . . . clit . . . thrust . . . mastb*.

Apparently, this conversation with Shere Hite was so riddled with language that was *never* heard on the radio that I started keeping count of the number of times she used various words. This is as close as public radio has ever come to talking dirty. (The tallies from that six-minute conversation, in case you're interested: *intercourse* 13, *vagina* 1, *orgasm* 14, *clitoris* 7, *thrust* 3, *masturbation* 6. Did you see that? Fourteen orgasms in six minutes. A new record!)

Two years later, Shere was back. In the interim, I had learned to speak Hite.

STAMBERG: In the fall of 1976, sex researcher and feminist Shere Hite published a report on female sexuality in the United States. *The Hite Report* is an admittedly unscientific survey. But its findings—that eighty-two percent of the women surveyed masturbate, and of those, ninety-six percent always reach orgasm through masturbation, whereas only thirty percent reach orgasm through intercourse— struck home with American readers. The book was a runaway best-seller here. Now *The Hite Report* has been translated into a number of foreign languages. This past year, Shere Hite went around the world promoting her book. She discovered she had written an international best-seller.

HITE: Sex really is defined in a cultural way, and that hurts women. Sex as we define it is macho. I found this to be true everywhere.

STAMBERG: All the women who answered your questionnaire felt that men's sexual fulfillment was a lot more important than their own. They would go to all sorts of lengths to make sure their men were sexually fulfilled. They went so far as to fake orgasms.

HITE: That's right. That's right! And my publisher and I thought women in Europe wouldn't be like American women about sex. But it seems that everywhere in the world it's the same. The overwhelming majority of women everywhere say they have been faking orgasms. And they are really tired of it and don't want to do it anymore.

STAMBERG: What about Japan? Was *The Hite Report* a best-seller there, too?

HITE: Yes, which is very unusual. In Japan, translations don't usually make the best-seller list. But it was on for months and months, and it's still selling.

Japanese women said, "We never thought that American women

> I think a woman would make a much better sex researcher than a man. First of all, you have to understand my basic prejudice. I think women are generally smarter than men. And when it comes to anything involving emotions, women are better at understanding them and dealing with them than are men. So if you're going to be a sex researcher, obviously emotion is going to play a considerable part. I think that's a field in which women would be superior to men.
>
> —Roy Cohn, November 1982

would fake orgasms. Of course, *we* do. But we thought American women were so liberated, they would just hit their husbands over the head with a broomstick!" (*Laughs.*)

In Japanese, there is no written character for a female orgasm. There is only ejaculation, which means, of course, male orgasm. Similarly, there is no term for masturbation. There is only a character which means "a thousand strokes," which also refers to men. So, a lot of Japanese women didn't really identify that what they were doing was masturbation.

One of the things I heard in Japan was that aside from having the same bad pattern of sex that we've had here—you know, foreplay, penetration, his orgasm, and it's over—women were also complaining that they just very rarely *had* sex. The husband comes home very late at night and has to get up very early, because it's usually a long commute. So their life is not very pleasant.

————

In 1981, Shere Hite produced a report on male sexuality, which was thoroughly slammed by reviewers—mostly male. In 1987, her *Women and Love* was greeted with similar venom.

Hite's been married (for the first time) since 1985 to pianist Friedrich Horicke, who is twenty-one years her junior. When the attacks on her—her research methods, the conclusions she drew—got too sharp, Horicke went on television to defend her.

"I'm a feminist too," he'd say. "What's all this nonsense about?"

Ethel Merman Delivers

July 1978

In the days when fame was more the result of accomplishment than exposure, on a few square blocks northwest of Broadway and Forty-second Street a woman with a brass band for a voice ruled American musical theatre.

Ethel Merman starred on Broadway in the thirties, forties, fifties, sixties, and forever. She spiked energy and pep into musical comedy. Merman was a belter, solid and indomitable. Without a microphone, she could spit lyrics to the top of the balcony and be thoroughly understood.

"What is it about Ethel Merman?" Martin Gottfried asks in his big 1979 coffee-table book, *Broadway Musicals.* "The lady was never a great beauty, never a comic, never an actress. She acted the way she sang, squaring off with the audience and yelling at it." But, says Gottfried, she had "that voice, a physical thing," and with it, she shoved songs into the audience's face.

Merman began as Ethel Agnes Zimmermann in Astoria, Queens. She could carry a tune at age two (as much of an achievement in 1911 as it is today), fell in love with vaudeville a bit later, and wanted to sing professionally but gave in to her mother's urging and took a four-year business course at William Cullen Bryant High School in Long Island City. Her first job was as a twenty-three-dollar-a-week stenographer. When a better offer came in (twenty-eight dollars a week), she took her shorthand pad over to the B-K Vacuum Booster Brake Company.

Eventually she met a producer, changed her name to something that would fit more handily on a marquee, and ended up having George Gershwin, Cole Porter, and Irving Berlin write some of their best Broadway scores for her.

Growing up as I had to the recording of her *Annie Get Your Gun,* I was delighted to meet Ethel Merman in 1978. Not only was I sitting across the mike from a musical-comedy czarina, I was sitting across the mike from a woman *who had known George Gershwin.*

But as she spoke about her work—the work of "doing" a Broadway show—I felt there was something robotic about her. I fastened on it, and despite her good manners, you can see that my line of questioning began to annoy her.

My radio piece opened with a primal sound: Ethel Merman singing. We played two versions of the same song, segueing from a thirties recording to something she had taped more recently. Except for an improvement in audio quality, there was no difference whatsoever in the two versions. The segue telegraphed, in sound, the theme of our conversation.

(*Merman singing "You're the Top."*)

STAMBERG: Ethel Merman has been the top since 1930, when she opened on Broadway in George and Ira Gershwin's musical *Girl Crazy.* In 1934, she introduced "You're the Top" in Cole Porter's *Anything Goes.* And she's singing it today, almost fifty years later, exactly as she sang it then—the same beat, same key, same style.

In some ways, Ethel Merman is a singing machine. The perfect enunciation, the absolute pitch. She never changes a note or a word, even when she gets the chance! For instance, when she met George Gershwin for the first time.

MERMAN: I was singing at the Brooklyn Paramount, a young gal singer with the stage show. And I thought that was pretty good. They were casting for *Girl Crazy,* and the talk got around about this gal singing over at the Paramount. So the producer, Vinton Freedley, came over one day, unbeknownst to me, and he . . . well, as they say in my profession, he "caught my act." I guess he thought I was pretty good, because next thing I knew he had contacted my agent, and my agent and I and Mr. Freedley went up to see the great George Gershwin.

I was petrified. And not only in awe of meeting Gershwin, I was in awe of the building! I . . . you know, it was up on Seventy-second Street and Riverside Drive, overlooking the Hudson River. I had never seen anything like that. I was still living with my parents in Astoria.

And so up we go into this *beautiful* penthouse. After a few minutes of conversation, Gershwin sat down at the piano and he played three songs, one of which was "I Got Rhythm."

STAMBERG: That was the song that made you!

MERMAN: Yes. And he said something to me that I'll never forget—I mean, here's this great genius, and me, a complete unknown. Gershwin says, "Is there anything about these songs that you don't like? I'll be most happy to change them."

STAMBERG: What did you say?

MERMAN: Oh, I went bananas! I didn't know what to say. "Well, mmmmm, ummmmm, uhmmmm." (*Laughs*.) I couldn't believe what I was hearing! Finally, I managed to get out something like "No, Mr. Gershwin, they'll do very nicely."

And he used to come to the Alvin Theatre and sit in the pit on a Wednesday matinée day. He loved to play "I Got Rhythm" for me, and sit with the pit orchestra.

STAMBERG: During performance? He just joined the band?

MERMAN: He joined the band! The boys in the band! And I never had to look down, because he had a certain touch—that Gershwin touch—I didn't even have to look, I knew he was down there. And then I'd get through with "I Got Rhythm" and he'd leave, and that was it.

I have a wonderful picture in my living room of George seated at the piano. In pen and ink, he wrote in a few bars of "I Got Rhythm," with lyrics underneath the notes. And then next to that, he said, "Dear Ethel, a lucky composer is he who has you singing his songs. All the best, George Gershwin."

STAMBERG: (*Narrating*) George Gershwin wrote Merman's first Broadway show, and our very best composers followed his lead. Merman introduced songs by Cole Porter, Jule Styne, Stephen Sondheim, and, of course, Irving Berlin.

(*Merman medley: "Alexander's Ragtime Band," "It's De-Lovely," "They Say It's Wonderful," "Small World."*)

STAMBERG: Do you like to listen to your own records?

MERMAN: No, never play them!

STAMBERG: Is there one way to play the "Moonlight Sonata"?

MISHA DICHTER: I *hope* **not!**

STAMBERG: There is no one Misha Dichter way, and you'll play it that way over and over again, no matter where you are?

DICHTER: No! That is the scary thing about records. People tend to think of records as definitive. All they symbolize is the way a person played *on that* **day. That's all.**

STAMBERG: So if I've heard your record a hundred times and memorized it all, and then go to hear you in a concert hall, I think you're not doing it right?

DICHTER: Right! It may not be better, but it will be different three days later.

—January 1978

STAMBERG: You don't?

MERMAN: *Nooo.*

STAMBERG: Do you own them?

MERMAN: Do I *have* them?

STAMBERG: Yeah.

MERMAN: Sure I have them.

STAMBERG: But you don't play them?

MERMAN: No. I've heard them! I don't want to listen to them. No. And I hate it when I go to someone's house and they put on one of my records. I don't like it. It . . . (*deep breath*) . . . I'd rather listen to someone else.

STAMBERG: Do you get uncomfortable listening? Does it make you feel uneasy?

MERMAN: It bores me.

STAMBERG: You're *bored*??

MERMAN: Yeah, I've *heard* it. *Gypsy* has been done in various places—even in New York—and people ask, did I go to see it. I say, "No!" And they say, "Why?" "Because," I say, "I've *seen* it." (*Laughs.*)

STAMBERG: But really, you wouldn't be curious to see how somebody else would do a role that you created, that was written for you?

MERMAN: I don't care! I don't really care. Really. No.

STAMBERG: If you did hear a recording of yourself and listened to it carefully, would you think, "Gee, I should have phrased that line differently"?

MERMAN: Oh, no! No, no, no! The recordings are perfect. The recordings of albums are done a week after the show has opened.

STAMBERG: You know, I talked to Mary Martin about that, and she really objected. She didn't like that at all.

MERMAN: Why?

STAMBERG: She said that's much too soon to do the recordings. You need to record later, when you've really grown and settled into the role. And also, she said that in those first weeks of performance, you're so frazzled, there's so much going on, that you don't have the energy or full attention—

MERMAN: I beg to differ with her, though. No, I mean, I think the performance should be down on the record the same as you gave it to the audience on opening night.

STAMBERG: Where's the room for growth in that, though? Some performers say a part is never set until their last performance of it.

MERMAN: Oh, *no*, no, that's not true.

STAMBERG: No, huh?

MERMAN: *Nooo!*

STAMBERG: Then how do you know how to change? How do you know how to make it better?

MERMAN: You don't change.

STAMBERG: How do you know how to—

MERMAN: You don't change. *You don't change!* You come into New York completely prepared. I've never been nervous on an opening night—*never!*—because you go on the road for three, four weeks, and that's what you go on the road *for*—to perfect a show.

Whenever I've gone out with shows, before the opening in New York I always request that the producer freeze the show for the last week out of town. That way, you get eight performances under your belt just as you are going to play it on opening night. And if you play that show eight times, you pretty much know what you're going to do on opening night. That's always been my theory.

STAMBERG: But if it's the same, night after night—how do you keep doing it?

MERMAN: It's your job!

STAMBERG: But how do you do that song over and over again and keep it fresh?

MERMAN: Because I *enjoy* doing what I am doing. I never got tired of going out there and repeating things over and over again, night after night.

STAMBERG: Was it Buddy De Sylva who said about you, "Watching Merman is—"

MERMAN: "—like watching a motion picture; she never varies."

STAMBERG: And you said that was the greatest compliment you ever got.

MERMAN: One of them. One of them. Yeah.

STAMBERG: He meant that night after night—

MERMAN: Consistently.

STAMBERG: —it was always the same.

MERMAN: Never varied, never let down. Right. And I . . . that used to *bug* me so in a show, when people would let down in a performance.

The way I work, my worst performance is the first one, and my best is the last, and in between it gets progressively better. When I finished *Streetcar*, I felt I'd just begun, and I was dying to have a lot more time to complete the work. I felt I didn't finish it. To be really good at it, it takes a very long time!

**—Shirley Knight,
June 1978**

TYNE DALY: I think Rose is about a woman with frustrated ambitions, and no talent to back it up. Nothing but want. She wants something so much and it's so unspecified and she'll take it in even its remotest imaginary form.

STAMBERG: You're playing Rose in this thirtieth-anniversary production of *Gypsy.* Did you ever see Ethel Merman as Rose?

DALY: Umm-hmm. I was twelve years old and it was fascinating. She was formidable, and I remember that I'd not seen a show where the hero went crackers at the end. That was pretty amazing.

There are critics who think they saw Merman as Rose and they couldn't have, they're only forty-three, like I am. They do comparisons and don't know what the hell they're talking about. Sometimes I think all the people who thought they saw Ethel Merman should all get together in a room and play the album to one another.

—August 1989

It . . . it used to drive me *crazy.* If they don't want to do it, then they shouldn't sign a contract to do it. I mean, it's like anybody going to do their day's work. You do the best that you can, it's your job!

STAMBERG: Yes, but what I don't understand is how . . . then why not go to a movie of you? I mean, if you're going to do it the same, night after night, then—

MERMAN: *Because people enjoy live theatre!!* I know people who have come to see *Gypsy* dozens of times. They just love live *theatre*!!

STAMBERG: I loved learning—we're almost finished—I loved learning that all you wanted to do was sing. You didn't have a special thing to be a Broadway star.

MERMAN: Well, it was wonderful when it came along, but I think I would have survived if I had not become a star on Broadway. Sure.

STAMBERG: You didn't really care where you sang. If it was radio, that's fine; if it was on the screen—

MERMAN: No. Well, I've covered most all the mediums. I don't know what else there is to do.

STAMBERG: What *is* there? I know! You could go on a rocket ship. The *moon,* you have never played!

MERMAN: (*Laughs.*) To the *moooon,* one of these days. To the *moon*!
   (*Merman singing "Some People": "Good-bye to blueberry pie. Good riddance to all the socials I had to go to, all the lodges I had to play . . ."*)

——

We ended with a song and a smile, but it had gotten a bit tense there. Ms. Merman did not like the direction of my questions toward the end, and surely thought I was some dumb broad! I noticed her glancing at the clock. (That's why I said, "We're almost finished," and then left it in for broadcast. My aside could easily have been edited out. But I wanted to signal to listeners that Merman was getting fidgety.)

Thinking about this great lady of the American musical theatre, who died in 1984, I realize that a clue to her lies in that early work as a secretary, taking dictation. By her own accounts, she was an excellent stenographer and typist. In those pre–word processor, pre-Dictaphone days, the boss dictated a letter, she took it down in shorthand—Isaac Pitman method—and then typed out her notes. A great secretary is methodical and steady, does not permit mistakes to get out, and doggedly pursues the perfect product. Isn't that exactly what she did on stage night after night? The personal qualities that made her good at office jobs also shaped her talents in the theatre.

Great secretaries have all but disappeared from the offices of America. So, too, the Broadway stage—bereft of new Gershwins, Porters, and Berlins—has yet to match the brilliance of Ethel Merman.

You will never forget her singing, never get it out of your mind or your heart. She's like the Statue of Liberty to me. When something happened to her, it was like the Statue of Liberty had fallen down. She was that strong.

—Mary Martin, on Ethel Merman's death, February 1984

Tom Wolfe Is Listening

January 1978

A handful of fiction writers write *about* radio—Garrison Keillor has invented broadcasters at a mythical radio station in Minnesota; other authors put radios on in the background of their characters' lives, to be overheard, like traffic. Tom Wolfe is the only author to actually write radio itself. In the New Journalism he helped invent in the 1960s, Wolfe put printed approximations of the sounds of real life right in the middle of his reportage. His very first magazine article, written for *Esquire* in 1963, was called "There Goes (Varoom! Varoom!) That Kandy-Kolored (Thphhhhhh!) Tangerine-Flake Streamline Baby (Rahghhh!) Around the Bend (Brummmmmmmmmmmmmmmmmm) . . ." Writing about the women's jail then located in Greenwich Village, he caught some inmates yelling out their windows at a passing twenty-one-year-old named Harry: "Hai-ai-ai-ai-ai-ai-ai-ai-ai-ai-ai-ai-ai-ai-ai-ai-ai-ai-ai-ai-ai - ai - ai - ai - ai - ai - ai - ai - ai - ai - ai - ai - ai - ai - ai - ai - ai - ai - ai - ai - ai - ai - ai - ai - ai - aireeeeeeeeeeeeeeeeeeee!"

On paper, Tom Wolfe did the same thing we radio people do—with fewer spelling errors—on the air. Always, on a story, we look for natural ambient sound that we can record to give listeners a sense of place. On radio, sounds are our colors. On location, instead of taking snapshots we collect a palette of sounds, then bring them back to mix into the stories we tell.

Sounds ought to be distinctive to a place, but that's getting harder to find. Just as most airports in this country look alike, so that landing in Boston isn't much different from landing in Los Angeles, our sounds have become homogenized, too. Traffic in Dallas snarls like traffic in Chicago. (Asia is wonderful for traffic sounds. In India you get cars and bicycles and cycle rickshaws and bullock carts and carriage horses with bells tied to their bridles and meandering, mooing sacred cows.) Muzak's the same in shopping malls in Rehoboth Beach, Delaware, and Santa Rosa, California. Now that the typewriter is dead, offices from St. Paul to Tallahassee emit identical muted taps, as if legions of baby Nicholas Brothers got trapped inside millions of computer keyboards and are sending out continual encoded messages for help. Even the natural world has aural limitations. The Atlantic Ocean breaks, in sound, just like the Pacific. Geese, whether north or south in season, honk alike. The rain, on any plain, sounds the same.

The trick, then, is to find the *dis*similar sound, a noise that is unexpected in a particular landscape. In Haverhill, Massachusetts, for a profile of Andre Dubus, a writer who lost the use of his legs in a terrible automobile accident, I surely didn't expect the grinding sound of a motorized chain being lowered from the top of Dubus's car. A hook on the end of the chain grabbed his wheelchair, pulled it up, and stored it on the car roof so that Dubus could drive. I put that sound at the very start of my profile. It gave listeners an image, from the beginning, of a man grappling with disability and not letting it prevent him from getting out into life. (The Dubus portrait is toward the end of this book, in 1991.)

When Sir Georg Solti left the Chicago Symphony after twenty-two seasons as its music director, I spent a rehearsal afternoon at Orchestra Hall with symphony members, asking about the Solti era. In addition to recording the interviews, Flawn Williams, our Chicago engineer, prowled backstage with his tape recorder and microphone, collecting the unrehearsed sounds musicians make before they perform. Flawn taped violinists sawing, oboes and clarinets climbing scales, the French horn making hunting calls. Putting the piece together, I decided to begin with the broad and cacophonous sound of the full orchestra tuning up. But Gwen Macsai, who was mixing audio for the report, disagreed. "It's so predictable," she said. "Every orchestra piece starts that way. Do you have anything else?" We spun through the reel with Flawn's sound effects and found something utterly unmusical that would capture listeners' attention against their expectations of symphonic sounds. In the wings, Flawn had taped the sound of a heavy cart, loaded with more than a hundred scores that would be placed on individual music stands, rolling clunkingly toward the stage. That lumbering, mysterious noise opened our Chicago Symphony piece. It gave me a chance to describe events backstage before a performance: how scores are marked with half squares or vees so that the string players know when to bow up or down; how a violinist rubs a bit of furniture polish into his instrument; how the management keeps a glass ginger jar stocked with throat lozenges on a shelf in the wings in case one of the musicians feels a cough coming on. And the clatter of the cart was annoying enough, and lasted long enough, that when we finally *did* present the orchestra tuning up—about a minute into the piece—it was a fine release from the aural annoyance. Listeners could settle in comfortably with the real story— the relationship between a Hungarian conductor and 106 musicians who, in 1969, after working together for only three years, began to be called the best orchestra in the world.

The sounds of real life—carts on rollers, chains and pulleys— intrigue Tom Wolfe, as well. And when the author came to NPR in 1978, sound was very much on his mind. This was nine years before *The Bonfire of the Vanities,* his first novel that became such a blockbuster. But he'd produced, by then, a group of brilliant books of reportage, including *The Kandy-Kolored Tangerine-Flake Streamline Baby* and *The Electric Kool-Aid Acid Test.* And in our studio, Tom Wolfe was busy considering how to make his work sound as contemporary as possible.

WOLFE: I find myself—and I see other writers doing this, too—using a lot of really old-fashioned imagery. Expressions like "barking up the wrong tree" and "a hard row to hoe" are still used, and these are from the days before agricultural technology. You still see people write about someone who has blinders on. Well, I bet there are very few people alive under the age of forty-five who have ever *seen* blinders. Blinders were on horses, and you don't see that many horses anymore! And they write about people with craggy brows. Well, who has seen a crag in the last ten years? You have to go to western Oregon to see one!

So, I keep trying to keep my eyes and my ears open for the sounds of right now. One of them is the desk calculator—that little sound it makes as you punch in your figures? And another—I was thinking about it this morning—is the sound of the motor on a Nikon or Leica camera. It makes a kind of whine which I don't think I can even

Mmmmmmmmmmmm-mmmmm These are nice. Little Roquefort cheese morsels rolled in crushed nuts. Very tasty. Very subtle. It's the way the dry sackiness of the nuts tiptoes up against the dour savor of the cheese that is so nice, so subtle. Wonder what the Black Panthers eat here on the hors d'oeuvre trail?

—from "Radical Chic"

duplicate with my voice, but . . . (*tries various screeches but sounds more like a cat meowing*) . . . every time the film advances, you hear it. And if you ever listen on the radio to a press conference with Henry Kissinger or any great big public figure, this is the sound in the background. You're never told *what* this sound is. But it's like this chorus. First it sounds like a lot of cicadas with a voice change. In fact, it's the still cameras whirring.

When I was working here on *The Washington Post*, we'd be sent out to cover parades—that's the kind of story I usually was assigned to, parades or communion breakfasts. I would notice that at parades, there were no more American flags being waved. Now, this was way back in the late fifties and early sixties, long before there was this national sag in morale because of Vietnam and Watergate. And the reason was that everyone had cameras. They didn't have any hands left to wave flags *with*! They were all sitting there with cameras. In fact, at that time it seemed to me that if the United States had made the camera the national symbol, instead of the flag, then we would have been way ahead of the game and become an extremely patriotic country. If every time you pick up a camera you're picking up the symbol of America, everything would have worked out!

(*Laughter.*)

STAMBERG: You're obviously going to write something about this. How are you going to translate that camera sound? What letters would you use?

WOLFE: Well, it's hard. A lot of writing depends on the reader's memory, anyway. For example, it's very hard to even describe a face in print. You really have to pick out one feature and hope someone has seen a face like that and can conjure up the image.

So, I think you have to *describe* the sound, and then . . . I think I would probably just use the word "whine"—I might say *whi-i-i-i-ne,* that kind of spelling. Perhaps. I'd have to think about that. But I probably will try to use that sound, because it's the sound of right now.

——

Tom Wolfe in 1978, with his whirring cameras at press conferences, reminded me of something I'd first noticed two years earlier in the 1976 presidential campaign. That year, NPR reporters and others were coming back from early primaries talking about this Georgia peanut farmer who struck them as a really impressive candidate—smart, well prepared, moral. When Jimmy Carter's campaign came to Virginia, I crossed the Potomac on a sunny Saturday afternoon for an in-person look at him. And failed entirely. Jimmy Carter was there. I was there. But between us, in addition to a fair crowd of supporters and curiosity seekers, were TV vans and sound trucks and, massed together on tripods up at the platform where Carter was speaking, dozens of cameras rolling and snapping and *whi-i-i-i-ning* away in such a dense configuration that they completely obliterated the candidate.

That day I witnessed, face-to-nonface, what Joe McGinniss wrote about in *The Selling of the President,* his book about how Richard Nixon used the media in the '68 campaign. There on the quaint and cobblestoned streets of Alexandria, Virginia, just down a parkway from the plantation home of our first president, I realized that the days of candidate-meets-voter encounters were over. The electronic image had become so dominant in our political life, and the candidate's need to capture and control that image so crucial, that local folks wanting a glimpse of some hopeful who was in the neighborhood didn't stand a chance. The candidate may have traveled all the way from Chicago to Lanark on his campaign trip. But what was important about Lanark was the cameras and microphones that would carry the campaign beyond the crowd in a small northern Illinois town and into the living rooms of the rest of the country. In the 1992 presidential campaign, the Clinton-Gore bus convoy deliberately drove candidates back to the people. But just as deliberately, the encounters were choreographed for television. Still, by '92, the crowds had begun to shout, *"Cameras don't vote!"* And some of the camera-wielders had the grace to try to crouch out of the way.

The Difference Between Men and Women

March 1978

Best-seller lists of the nineties prove that the women's revolution of the seventies remains a war unwon. In nonfiction, in the early nineties, the debris of the revolution was being swept up in print. Robert Bly's *Iron John* gave men permission to cry and flex their muscles at the same time. Sociolinguist Deborah Tannen, in *You Just Don't Understand,* told men and women that their communication problems stemmed from their speaking different languages. (I always thought the difference between men and women was pockets.) "Ohhhh!" we said, with perfect mutual understanding, snatching up copies of the book for friends of the opposite sex.

Who was it who said, *"Plus ça change, plus c'est la même chose"?* Probably some guy who didn't speak the language. Because here we are in the nineties, still wrestling with all the gender issues we started half-nelsoning back in the seventies.

"Power" was the big word then. It's how I began a 1978 conversation with Lois Gould, whose 1970 novel, *Such Good Friends,* fired an early shot in the feminist revolution. Eight years later, Gould was still loading her musket.

STAMBERG: "Power is the ability not to have to please." Want me to run that by you again? "Power is the ability not to have to please." It's novelist Elizabeth Janeway's definition, and it crops up in Lois Gould's new essay collection, *Not Responsible for Personal Articles.*

Gould says that is the *female* definition of power. Then there's the *male* definition.

GOULD: Power for men means the ability to make things happen, which is a more assertive use of autonomy. Not only do *you* not have to do something, but you are able to make *others* do something—which gives you a sense of authority, a sense of being a mover and a shaker.

STAMBERG: But those two definitions are not necessarily mutually exclusive. The female one—power as the ability not to please—is a first step that can get you to the other definition—power as the ability to make things happen.

GOULD: One hopes!

STAMBERG: You give a very interesting example of the difference between men and women—that men can put up with, and use, people whom they cannot stand, while women feel that's hypocritical.

GOULD: Yes! I have found that's a very powerful thing to think about. Men are constantly doing business with each other to get things done. That is how the world has been changed. People of totally opposite and presumably hostile opinions and backgrounds and convictions get together to make deals. We see Begin and Sadat—sworn enemies for generations—talking together about matters of mutual importance.

According to the old female tradition of snubbing enemies, a woman in that situation would not be able to sit with someone who had slighted her. She would say, "What, *me* sit at that table with so-and-so?? Do you realize she took my boyfriend?!"

STAMBERG: So, withdrawal and avoidance is woman's way?

GOULD: It has been, and it's unfortunate, because you never get off that dime. If you have to change things, if you have to transcend where you are, it becomes necessary to have something to do with people that ordinarily you would not call friends.

STAMBERG: You make a terrific point that men do this kind of thing—putting up with people they can't stand—almost from birth.

GOULD: Yes, because in childhood, boys are trained to play on teams. Obviously, if your team requires eleven kids to play football, they are not going to be eleven best friends, all of whom love each other. But boys know they have a choice to make. Either they can play only with their best friend, or they can play football. And women—little girls—are never given that choice, that incentive. They play either by them-

---

Real women are afraid of the dark and Alexander Haig. In Los Angeles, they're afraid of George Hamilton. They're also afraid of losing their reputation. They look for the union labels, and they tip well. Real women are concerned about nuclear war, world hunger, life after death, and finding the perfect dress, though not necessarily in that order.

—writer Barbara Cady, June 1982

selves or with one other best friend. And they play small, solitary games.

STAMBERG: Women will play tennis, or they'll swim.

GOULD: As children, they are gymnasts, they are solitary skaters, rope jumpers, hopscotch players, and tea-party givers. None of those things require getting along with a lot of other people to do a big thing.

I'm not sure that this was true a hundred years ago when women had communities, and had to work together in order to survive. A quilt was a community project; so were a number of other things. But we've lost that. We lost the community of women somewhere along the way, with the creation of the so-called nuclear family, where women went off with a mate, and 2.3 children, and a dog named Spot, and lived totally alone with very little contact with other women, and thought of themselves as rivals rather than as friends and teammates. We need to get that sense of community back.

Paying Attention with Marcel Ophuls

October 1978

STAMBERG: Every day, in preparing this radio program, we choose the stories we want to cover and then budget lengths of time for each item. For the most part, the lengths are determined by the quality or the nature of the story, but—and it's a big "but"—our stories usually run from three and a half to five minutes.

Which brings us to our next tape, an interview I did with film-maker Marcel Ophuls. Edited, it runs about ten minutes. The original was maybe twenty minutes, or twenty-five. And ten is probably four minutes longer than we would ordinarily give to an interview like this, if Marcel Ophuls had not directly addressed the issue of attention span—this drive communicators have these days to make their productions concise, efficient, self-contained.

Marcel Ophuls asked audiences to spend four and a half *hours* viewing his 1970 film, *The Sorrow and the Pity,* a documentary about French reaction to Nazi occupation during World War Two. His 1976 film, *The Memory of Justice,* an examination of the consequences of the Nuremberg trials, ran nearly five hours.

Ophuls has just become a producer for ABC television, where his unwillingness to compromise content for style will likely be tested.

OPHULS: There was the fellow who wrote the letter—a very long letter—to his friend. At the end, he apologized for writing such a long letter. He said that he didn't have the time to write a short one.

We're living in a period of managerial myths, and one of them is that the more concise, the shorter something is, the more structured and profound. I think that's bull. It makes it easier for people who only want to read synopses, but I don't think we ought to mythologize it.

STAMBERG: It also makes it easier for people who only have three minutes' worth of anything to say.

OPHULS: (*Laughs.*) That's right! That's right!

STAMBERG: It has to do with span of attention, too. But in your documentaries, you insist that people go *through* it. I mean, you will not spoon-feed little thirty-second clips and give fast fixes on a subject. You make your viewers sit and watch and watch and watch and become, in a way, drenched by your topic.

OPHULS: Well, you know, there's a great danger in my doing that, because life is short. There are still a few things left that may be pleasant, like making love or lying under trees or looking at the grass grow. And anyone who goes around asking for that much attention to his work is under very great danger of not only seeming pretentious, but *being* pretentious. But I suppose that the excuse I give myself, which is not always a good excuse, is that I think there's a relationship between attention span and morality. I think that if you shorten people's attention span a great deal, you are left with only the attraction of power, and the power of power.

This pollutes the spiritual atmosphere by making things more and more superficial instead of more reflective. And finally, by shortening attention span, since attention has to go somewhere, finally it goes on your own navel and you finish up with narcissism.

STAMBERG: Okay, but still, recognizing that in the modern world those collapsed tastes are the tastes that are being catered to—that this is the current way to get the message out—how do *you*, having made the kinds of documentary films you've made, now go to work in television and not compromise the need to take the time to really understand the fact that you're now in a medium which is much faster, much pizzazzier, sharper, and more truncated?

OPHULS: Well, I don't know if I can.

STAMBERG: But here's the problem. If you have messages you want to get across and nobody's listening—

OPHULS: I know—

STAMBERG: —how will you get them out?

OPHULS: It's not messages, I'm not a conveyor of *messages*. I'm very reluctant to use the word. The idea I'm more comfortable with is that my four-and-a-half-hour talking-head marathons are a form of show business, and also a form of game playing, and that it is no more noble or serious or profound than, uhh . . . (*sighs*)

STAMBERG: *Charlie's Angels?*

OPHULS: . . . than a medium-sized, medium-qualified nineteenth-century novel. I have no political sense of mission at all, I don't think. It's just a side of show business that I got stuck in.

STAMBERG: How can you say that? Everything you do is deeply political, carries political messages!

OPHULS: Doesn't everything? Mine is perhaps more *overtly* political, which I sometimes regret. I mean, I don't think that being overtly political gives you a badge of depth or profundity or nobility.

My greatest hero in show business—which, as I say, I think I'm in—is Fred Astaire. There, structure and balance is so dignified and so rarefied and so marvelously controlled that content is almost entirely removed.

STAMBERG: Yes. But you deal in content—right and wrong, values, morality.

OPHULS: Yes. Morality is fine. I'm very comfortable with that word. It's not fashionable, but I love it!

One of the reasons that my films worked for a while (they may not work anymore, because there are things happening in the shortening of attention span that I can't control), the reason relatively few people walked out of the theatre once they were there, is because, in fact, I was trying to *broaden* attention span by using very modern and sophisticated public sensibilities.

McLuhan's perception of the television generation being able to absorb certain things faster . . . I certainly tried to use that in the structure of my work. I didn't use traditional narrative to say, "This is where you are, and this is the connection between the last person you heard and the next person you hear." I left that up to the public. That absence of narrative gave the film speed and fastness. But I use that speed and fastness and still make long movies, because our world is so complicated and because these themes are so complex.

———

Ten years after that conversation, Marcel Ophuls made *Hotel Terminus: The Life and Times of Klaus Barbie*—another documentary (four and a half hours) about responsibility and complicity during the Second World War. In it, M. Ophuls found a way to include his show-business hero. As bitter commentary at one point, Fred Astaire appears—in a clip from the movie *Swing Time*—and sings, "Pick yourself up, dust yourself off, start all over again."

Our world has grown increasingly complicated since my 1978 meeting with Marcel Ophuls; our attention spans have undergone continual changes and are serviced now in new ways by new media that shrink—or stretch—our concentration. Not long ago, two studies showed that on TV evening news shows, sound bites of presidential candidates had shrunk from forty-three seconds in 1968 to nine seconds in 1988. On the other hand, we seem to have infinite time when there's a crisis. During the Gulf War, Radio Shack stores in downtown Washington sold out of portable radios. People were taking them to work so that they could follow the conflict at their desks. C-SPAN, television's gavel-to-gavel history witness, was born since the Ophuls chat. So were Court TV and other cable channels that operate in long form.

CNN, Ted Turner's twenty-four-hour news operation, popped up just in time for the decline of traditional commercial TV network news. The technology that lets CNN's cameras broadcast *to* anywhere *from* anywhere has indeed turned the world into a global village. American reporters in Beijing watched the Tiananmen Square demonstrations on CNN in the safety of their hotel rooms and reported back to their news organizations on the basis of what they saw on-screen. American tourists in foreign hotel rooms can see CNN news from home.

Similarly, satellite technology and portable cameras let local TV news shows expand their coverage beyond the boundaries of a particular city. Network anchors, threatened by obsolescence, make ten-year predictions that put themselves out of the news picture. Dan Rather's wife reportedly once tried to comfort her husband by saying, "Remember, Dan, more than a billion Chinese have no idea who you are." Well, they may never learn. Dan Rather, Peter Jennings, and Tom Brokaw may end up as nonprofits in their *own* country—the victims of mergers, takeovers, the high cost of network TV news, and technology that puts everyone out there where only the networks used to tread.

But thanks to this information explosion, what do we, as a society,

SAUL BELLOW: I think everyone has developed a taste for shorter communications, vital communications that are brief. Even in the nineteenth century, one of my favorite English essayists, a man named Sidney Smith, used to cry out, "Short views, for God's sake! Short views!" Don't bore us with tedious explanations, expositions, and fill our ears up with a kind of flowery mixture.

STAMBERG: Yes, but in publishing this new one-hundred-nine-page book, *A Theft*, don't you risk being accused of pandering to our shortened attention spans?

BELLOW: You always risk being accused of *something.* I really go by my own feelings, which are in a temporary revolt against *longueur*, to use the French expression.

STAMBERG: Length.

BELLOW: Length. Excessive length.

—March 1989

know that we didn't know before? The answer is mixed. We know what SCUD missiles look like at the very moment they arc down through the night skies over Riyadh. We know what tanks look like at the very moment they enter the most important square in the capital city of the People's Republic of China and begin bearing down on students and other protesters. We know what we see. But we know very little beyond that.

This may just be the freshest evidence of the truth of Marcel Ophuls's comment about the relationship between attention span and morality. He said that if we shorten our attention span too much, we are left with only *the attraction of power*. Isn't that what drives us to our screens? That we can see war in real time, see protest crushed in real time, eat dinner to the thrilling spectacle of power being exerted? And keep on watching, at least until it's time for our favorite sitcom to begin!

Saul Bellow, in a 1982 *Esquire* interview, spoke about the socially corrupting possibilities of this kind of reporting. "One week the president is shot," Bellow said, "another week the pope is shot." Some two centuries ago, either event, let alone both, would have caused a holy war. Today, assassination is only something to titillate the public's appetite for sensation. "We live," said Bellow, "in this alleged age of communication, which really comes in the form of distracting substitutes for reality."

I'm especially tough on television because *someone* has to be, because it's an easy mark, and because it has such overweening power. But radio's guilty, too. NPR takes pride in its reporting and analysis—the content and context of its news programs. Nonetheless, at this fountainhead of information, this safe haven for long form, we've done our share of concentration trimming.

I see it in my own recent work as Special Correspondent. *All Things Considered* and *Weekend Edition* accommodate longer pieces—a ten-minute interview, a fifteen- or seventeen- or twenty-two-minute report. But *Morning Edition* is more tightly formatted. The longest piece there can be only eight and a half minutes. My reports for *Morning Edition* generally go into a seven- or seven-and-a-half-minute slot. And sometimes that's just too short.

Marcel Ophuls's beloved Fred Astaire once said that his rule in films was "Get it as perfect as you can—and then cut two minutes." But

I lament the pileup of audio inches on the cutting-room floor when perfection-minus-two-minutes is an imposed goal.

For all my quibbling, seven minutes is the equivalent of *two* Ophuls documentaries at any other news operation. That's major time in TV news, where the end of the world will be a minute-and-a-half stand-up.

Still, I'd give the world to see all those two minutes that Fred Astaire cut, spliced together end to end.

Fourscore Fred Astaire

May 1979

(*Music: Astaire tapping to "Top Hat."*)

STAMBERG: He danced in ballrooms, on ships, in parks, on roller skates, on the ceiling. Fred Astaire, eighty today, dances even when he's standing still. There's always a restless quality, the sense that he's poised for flight, that at any moment one hand will come out of his pocket to stroke some passing breeze, and his body and feet will simply have to follow the breeze to find out where it's going. Repose, for Fred Astaire, happens on the balls of his feet. There's more sheer dancing when Fred Astaire *walks* than in most other people's five-minute musical extravaganzas.

One year, this consummate dancer got an award for singing. He has a well-intentioned voice, but it's awfully thin. That really doesn't matter, though—the judges were right. His singing dances! The phrasing is perfect. He jogs into the beat to make a counterpoint that's almost another song. And composers like George Gershwin and Irving Berlin stretched beyond their own talents in writing for him.

(*Astaire singing "Top Hat."*)

Fred Astaire turned a sailor suit into top hat and tails. Playing a cobbler in an apron, with his sleeves rolled up, you could still see the white tie. His costume is really grace and elegance; the top hat is simply the perfect metaphor.

Arlene Croce, in *The Fred Astaire and Ginger Rogers Book,* says their dances were Astaire and Rogers's way of expressing their love for each other—that until he dances with her, he hasn't possessed her.

The dances were their love scenes. There were other partners: his sister, Adele; Cyd Charisse; Joan Crawford; Leslie Caron; Lucille Bremer; Gene Kelly. But as wonderful as those companions were, nothing was as wonderful as watching Fred Astaire dancing all alone, with a prop as simple as a tall coatrack.

At eighty, Fred Astaire will dance no more in public. He says he doesn't want to be "the oldest performer in captivity." It doesn't matter. He dances still. And makes us realize that the only thing we ever really wanted to do was dance with him.

(*Astaire, singing and dancing "Top Hat" to end.*)

———

This birthday salute ran on *All Things Considered* on May 10, 1979. We repeated it five years later, on Astaire's eighty-fifth birthday, "because," as I observed on the air, "nothing has changed."

Stassen for President

November 1979

In February 1992, 176 voters in the New Hampshire Republican presidential primary cast their ballots for Harold Edward Stassen. I'm not sure which part of that sentence is the more amazing—that at the age of eighty-six Mr. Stassen was still running, or that 176 New Hampshire souls gave him their vote.

Harold Stassen is the losingest candidate in American presidential politics. He ran for president in 1948 (he was a leading contender that year, but Thomas E. Dewey got the Republican nomination), 1952, 1964, 1968, 1980, 1984, and 1988. The Perennial Candidate, people called him, with a smile, at first; later, a sneer.

His life story is written in Early American dazzle—the farm boy who graduated high school at fifteen, became Minnesota's governor at thirty-one—the youngest governor in the nation's history—and was known as the Boy Wonder, carving a brilliant Republican liberal-progressive record during his four years in office. The Roosevelt White House pulled him out of World War II, where he'd built a distinguished naval career, to serve on the U.S. delegation that drew up the United Nations charter. Stassen was president of the University of Pennsylvania, then had top jobs in the Eisenhower administration, including a cabinet-rank position as special assistant on disarmament. In 1956, he led a campaign to dump Vice President Richard Nixon from the Republican ticket, and when Nixon ran for president in 1960, Stassen opposed him again.

But most of all, and in between all the rest of it, Harold E. Stassen ran. And ran. And ran. And lost. In addition to the presidential bids, he tried to be vice president, governor of Pennsylvania, mayor of Philadelphia, U.S. senator from Minnesota, and congressman from Minnesota. Throughout, he was called (reverentially, by his fans) The Governor, in honor of the only big election he ever won—back in 1938.

Harold Stassen is a string of contradictions: brilliant/misguided, serious/laughable, eager/irrelevant. In his seventies when we met, with an ill-fitting toupee and smooth cheeks as rosy as waxen apples, Stassen hadn't been a contender in years, but he wouldn't stop trying.

Our 1979 encounter was both brutal and heartbreaking. Running for president yet again, his belief in himself was unshakable, if largely unshared by others. His idealism and love of country shine through this conversation (a friend remembers sitting near The Governor at the 1980 Republican convention in Detroit and spotting tears in his eyes as he sang the national anthem), as does a refreshing openness to actual colloquy.

Although it's clear he had an agenda to get across, unlike most politicians Mr. Stassen was willing to engage my questions. Most unusual. Political figures often act as if they have a limited and carefully predetermined number of Rolodex cards embedded in their brains, through which they will flip to produce a fixed set of answers. But Harold Edward Stassen is no ordinary politician. Which might be why this man, who once seemed so unstoppable, got stopped.

STAMBERG: Considering that he has been unsuccessful in all of his presidential bids, starting in 1948, the most optimistic current candidate we can think of is Harold Stassen. People remember Stassen as the losing candidate. But we forget that he was an early advocate of disarmament negotiations with the Soviet Union, and of recognition of two Chinas. I asked him what other early stands or accomplishments go unnoticed by today's voters.

STASSEN: Well, I took the first stand against the war in Vietnam, along with General Gavin, the retired Chairman of the Joint Chiefs. He and I, at the beginning, were the only ones that said, "Don't do this." Way, way back, I worked with Senator Arthur Vandenberg on the first establishment of federal deposit insurance with the banks.

STAMBERG: You helped draft the charter that created the U.N. and were one of the original signers. When you were governor of Minnesota, you helped shape legislation that gave blacks equal opportunity on the job market.

STASSEN: Very first. But I . . . you know, on the other hand, my thoughts are of the future . . . of the eighties . . . what we're going to do in the eighties!

STAMBERG: Yes, but there are some things in the middle that I'd like to talk with you about first. Why did I have to discover all those accomplishments of yours on the pages of an out-of-print *Current Biography,* and why, now, when the name Harold Stassen comes up as a candidate, do people say, "What?! Again?!" What happened in there?

STASSEN: Well, I think for one thing, of course, my stand against Richard Nixon tended to move me to the outside of the Republican party—somewhat in eclipse, so to speak. And then my stand against the Vietnam War when almost everybody was saying that you just had to go in and win.

STAMBERG: But others have taken unpopular stands and been able to reach high office and hold on to that office.

STASSEN: Well, of course, I have been in high positions, too. You know, I did very extensive work with President Eisenhower, and also, you know, I worked with President Roosevelt, President Truman.

STAMBERG: Governor Stassen, what keeps you going?

STASSEN: When I was a student in college—that far back—I decided that in my lifetime I wanted to make a contribution toward world peace and toward progress for humanity. And then I realized that you had to get in the active political arena to have the best impact. You know, you can write, you can lecture, you can have books and so forth—this can be good. But to really move things, you've got to get right into the political arena—and I knew that meant a rough, tough go. So, I haven't been surprised by what's happened.

STAMBERG: Could you have imagined it would have been *this* tough? That the door to that arena would have been shut against you year after year after year?

STASSEN: No. See, the door has never been shut. You know, you can do a lot of things without ever being president. Just think of the fact that I started out with that kind of an aim as a farm boy in Minnesota, keeping the aim in college, having President Roosevelt call me back from the war, then taking part in starting the United Nations.

STAMBERG: That explains the early days. But you haven't been called in many, many years. And it's clear you've been on the right side of a number of issues—maybe *ahead* of a whole lot of other people—for many years. Yet it never got you elected.

STASSEN: I have a kind of a deep feeling that it may be that I can make my greatest contribution in the 1980s. I am in good health. And, of course, having started so young, I had the opportunity to work with Winston Churchill and General de Gaulle and Konrad Adenauer. And I saw those men in their seventies literally save their countries. So, that, perhaps, is what keeps me going.

STAMBERG: You must have a very good set of personal blinders, though, that can shut out some of the criticism and . . . *derision*.

STASSEN: You have to be aware that critical views develop. But you do not let that stop you. I ran for governor when I was so very, very young—I took more ridicule then than I have ever since, you know. They said I was trying to lead a "diaper brigade."

STAMBERG: Do you think taking that kind of flak so young was helpful? Did it give you a thicker skin?

STASSEN: I think so. You know, I'd put it another way. I think that the strain of the presidency tends to make inexperienced young men old before their time. The challenge of the presidency tends to keep experienced senior men young!

STAMBERG: You can understand, though, that it is astounding to think how you do it. What aren't you telling us? What is that inner thing that really drives you and keeps you going?

STASSEN: Well, it has to be a kind of a deep conviction that you can make a contribution, literally, to all humanity on this earth under God. It's as basic as that.

———

Harold Stassen left the studio that mid-November day in 1979 to continue running for president of the United States. The final national totals in the 1980 Republican primaries—the totals that affected him—were these: Harold Edward Stassen, 24,753 votes, or 0.2 percent; Ronald Wilson Reagan, 7,709,793 votes, or 60.8 percent.

And still . . . and again . . . Stassen ran.

Chester Bowles's life was committed to public service. Even when he was in the advertising business he wanted to go into public service, and swore he would retire at the age of forty a millionaire and then put that money someplace so he could free himself for public life. Which, in fact, he succeeded in doing. I once asked him when I was a young man whether it made sense to try to achieve financial security before going into public service, and he said, "No, no. Don't do it that way. You'll waste too much time, and you'll always regret it."

**—Douglas Bennet,
obituary for Bowles,
May 1986**

Nadine Gordimer of South Africa

October 1979

Through all the darkest years, when little was known about daily life in
South Africa, Nadine Gordimer was a conduit. Her novels were the
closest we could get to the heart of the particular darkness that was
apartheid. When newspaper and magazine accounts offered dry, fact-
laden stories of detentions and voting patterns, the fiction of Nadine
Gordimer gave the feel and taste and smell of the land and its people.
The winner of the 1991 Nobel Prize in Literature, she has taught readers
what it has meant to be South African.

Against all expectation, given her persistent, sharp, and uncompro-
mising criticism of the South African government in ten novels and nine
collections of stories, Nadine Gordimer has the voice of a little girl—
high and a bit soft. Her consonants are clear, her accent international,
with a British edge. She speaks rapidly, then pulls up sharply, searching
for the correct word or a more precise phrase, finds it, and plunges on
again. Small and unpretentious, she is elegant in her person and her
writing.

I first interviewed Nadine Gordimer in 1979, when apartheid was
in full throttle. She had come from her home in Johannesburg on the
occasion of the American publication of *Burger's Daughter*—the story
of Rosa Burger, the child of white South African radicals (underground
Communists) who devoted their lives to ending racial separation.
Burger's Daughter was denounced by the South African government,
state censors banned it, and then the ban was lifted. That was my
starting point with Ms. Gordimer. Wasn't the lifting of the ban a mixed

blessing? A public-relations gesture to make the world think the Republic of South Africa was becoming more liberal?

GORDIMER: Yes, but you know, you must take what chances come, so to speak. When there's a loophole and you slip through it, you're just glad about it. I am, of course, very very glad that it will now be read there. Because if you read that banning order, you certainly get the impression that this is a bad book from a literary point of view. And I really feel that the important thing is to read the book and forget about the banning. Because, to me, it's not . . . it's only narrowly about the . . . the situation in South Africa. I was fascinated with the whole question of commitment. What is it like to put some kind of commitment—whether it's religious commitment or, in this case, political commitment . . . to put this before your own ambitions, your loves, the whole business of your individual life. This is something that's fascinated me.

STAMBERG: As the child of revolutionaries, Rosa Burger is aware that outsiders were curious—"had a sense of wonder about"—passionate activists. So that's *your* curiosity, too, is it—about the stamina it takes to be able to lead a revolutionary life? Your need to spend time thinking about that, and writing about that?

GORDIMER: Yes. I've seen it happening around me. It's impinged upon my own life. I've looked at people like Rosa Burger. They have been a fascinating mystery to me. And this is an imaginary exploration of those areas of their lives that are hidden.

STAMBERG: You raise questions about the emotions that have to be shut down in order to lead a life of political commitment.

GORDIMER: Near the beginning of the book, when Rosa's only eighteen years old, she puts on an engagement ring and pretends to be the fiancée of a young man who's in prison. Only a near relative like that can get in to see him. This is all planned by her parents. She's used as a device to keep in touch with him, and to keep him in touch. But at the same time, she really is in love with this young man. And she's in the incredible position of writing the five-hundred-word monthly letter that such a prisoner is permitted to receive—writing it as a love letter, and at the same time disguising all sorts of messages in it, in a kind of private code. But it's a double deception for her, because she really *is* in love with him.

This kind of situation does arise for people like that, and I find

Rosemarie Burger, according to the headmistress's report one of the most promising seniors in the school in spite of the disadvantages—in a manner of speaking—of her family background, came to school the morning after her mother was detained just as on any other day. She asked to see the headmistress and requested to be allowed to go home early in order to take comforts to her mother. Her matter-of-fact and reserved manner made it unnecessary for anyone to have to say anything—anything sympathetic—indeed, positively forbade it, and so saved awkwardness.

—*from Burger's Daughter*

it fascinating. How do you feel inside? What sorts of resentments do
you build up when you have to live like this? Resentments against the
very ideology and people who ask you to do these things, even for the
best of reasons.

STAMBERG: I am curious about you as an author, living in that country. How do you sustain your artistic perceptions? How can you keep
on writing and living there?

GORDIMER: Well, I always think that wherever you are, the ideal way
to write is as if you were already dead. As if it didn't matter what
anybody said about what you write. You simply write what you want
to write—what you know. Your job is to explore things as deeply as
possible and forget about who's going to read it, what they're going
to think. This applies to the censors and everybody else.

STAMBERG: It's a question that can also be put to Soviet dissident
writers. How does the art flourish? How does it continue in an
environment which you yourself describe as being so painful, so
difficult?

GORDIMER: You don't think of what is surrounding you, oppressing
you. You don't think of the political surveillance looking over your
shoulder. You're absorbed in what you are writing.

Writing is such a lonely business and such an intimate business,
and it's such a struggle with the material itself, that truly it's sometimes almost to the point of being foolish. You may be writing
something that probably will never see the light of day in your own
country. It's likely to be banned. That doesn't stop you writing it. I
can't explain how this is. You simply go on, ignoring the outward
circumstances. And since writing is my way of dealing with life, it's
also my way of dealing with the pressures around me.

———

I spoke with Nadine Gordimer again, seven years later, this time about
one of her short stories. "A City of the Dead, a City of the Living"
presented daily life in Soweto in such detail—down to the greenish
brocade curtains subdividing a room in the heroine's small house—that
I wondered how Gordimer could have known it so well. She told me she
had been to such houses many times and knew how they were furnished.

But at the time we spoke, in 1986, tensions were such that it had
become dangerous for her to go to Soweto.

"What's the fear?" I asked. "Is it fear for you, or for them?"

"The fear is that you're just a white face in the street, and you might meet a mob that had been in conflict with the police. And instead of seeing red, they'd be seeing white."

Yes, but surely they'd not be seeing just *any* white. They'd be seeing Nadine Gordimer. In fact, I imagined her to be something of a heroine in Soweto—a white South African who fought on behalf of blacks.

"Oh, not at all," Ms. Gordimer said. "When I go to Soweto, no one has the slightest idea who I am."

I don't think you ever would come to the end of the stories anywhere you lived, because you're really writing about human beings. You have to find a place to lay the scene and cast of characters. But you're not writing from the outside. So it wouldn't matter where you write, except that you like to have what you know as the skeleton of it.

—Eudora Welty,
May 1983

Picturing Lord Snowdon

November 1979

Radio and television always get bunched together. I'd like to unbunch them. To me, the true media affinity is between radio and print—the newspaper, the magazine—where the means of communication is also language. Language lets you deal with ideas. Pictures—the moving images of television—prompt emotional reactions more than they do intellectual ones. It's the difference in how we process information.

But if there is a visual equivalent of radio, it's the still photograph. The news photo grabs a single moment of an event and makes it stand *for* that event, just as the radio report selects a few of the many things that were said at a particular scene. The photographic portrait tries to "get" the individual in the brief snap of a shutter, as the radio profile works to capture a life in a few minutes of tape.

This affinity is probably what has drawn me, over the years, to photographers. Like me, they are professional observers. Unlike me, they never get to tell what they've seen. And I've found that photographers have plenty to say. Even the shy ones.

STAMBERG: (*Sweetly*) I want you to take my picture.
(*Long silence, guest not responding. Stamberg plunges on.*)
You're a working photographer, and I know that you get a very pretty price for portraits. This doesn't have to be fancy. But I think we can learn about you and the way you work by asking you to do it as we're here together in this radio studio. Are you willing to do that?

SNOWDON: I haven't got a camera with me.

STAMBERG: I have two cameras. One is a Polaroid . . . (*Fade interview tape.*)

STAMBERG: (*Voice-over, narrating*) I'm talking with Lord Snowdon. He stopped in to promote his new book, *Snowdon: A Photographic Autobiography.* My gimmick is to ask him to take my picture, and he's going to refuse.

(*Fade interview back up.*)

STAMBERG: . . . and they both have flashes. Would you be willing to work as you talk, so we can pick up tips as to what your methods are and how you—

SNOWDON: It wouldn't work.

STAMBERG: —and how you manage to get these wonderful photographs?

SNOWDON: It absolutely wouldn't work.

STAMBERG: Why not?

SNOWDON: (*Pause.*) First of all, because I work with a camera that I know. And secondly, the whole thing will be phony and a gimmick. If I was going to do a photograph of you—which I'd love to do at another time—then I would need to come here to do my research about you, to do my homework. The most important thing about taking photographs, just as much as for a writer or an interviewer, is homework.

You see, the camera is unimportant. It's the kind of mood one's trying to create, which is typical of that person, that's important. I'd find out everything you've done, get all the clips, go right back to square one. We certainly might not be in this maze of microphones and equipment.

STAMBERG: Well now, that's an interesting point. Don't you like to take a picture in the milieu in which the person is most comfortable—or, anyway, spends the most time?

SNOWDON: It depends. It depends on luck more than anything else.

STAMBERG: Luck has little to do with research.

SNOWDON: Oh yes it does! It's research first, then having no preconceived ideas of what you're going to do. Then the terror of opening the camera box and your mind's a blank. Then trying to make luck work for you.

If you're at home here, surrounded by microphones and angle-poised lights, it may well be one would start here and do something,

> **What you're trying to do is capture an instant where the whole situation can be seen. See, that's the great beauty of still photography. With motion pictures, the images are flickering past you. But still photography—if it captures that great moment that says the whole thing—can often be taken deeper into the mind than all the flickering of motion pictures.**
>
> **—former White House photographer Yoichi Okamoto, August 1971**

reject it, go on to something else that is also typical of your life, in the mood of your life, but not necessarily show these machines—which are too powerful visually. I want a photograph to be as simple as possible, to impart or to evoke an emotion.

STAMBERG: You said something interesting about the terror of opening the camera.

SNOWDON: That gets worse.

STAMBERG: It should get easier and better, no? I mean, as you're more successful, as you do it and do it and do it?

SNOWDON: I don't think it has anything to do with success. I think it's the thing of getting older. People think that because you've been taking photographs for thirty years, it gets easier. It doesn't. You get more and more frightened. You actually get to a situation where, when you arrive on an assignment, you long for the people to have gone on vacation or something. Your adrenaline is running to such an extent that you're sort of half looking forward to it. You're in a desperate state.

You've done your research, you've done your homework. And then, suddenly, you're on your own. What are you going to be faced with? You might be going to be faced with a room that doesn't reflect their character. You've got nowhere to go to get that kind of mood. Have they put on a façade? Have they changed? Have they dressed up to be photographed?

One always never thinks anyone else is shy. I'm desperately shy. You're never shy, probably.

STAMBERG: Everyone is—at least a little.

SNOWDON: Shyness affects people in different ways. It puts up certain façades that can be either quiet or aggressive—different forms of masks. Those, I've got to break through.

And to make it even more difficult, I believe in terribly quiet sessions. Sometimes total silence for two hours, and there's . . . that . . . I mean, you looked strangely at me then, but the point is that out of silence and out of embarrassment, you can sometimes get nearer to the truth.

> **The whole shooting of Robert Penn Warren was remarkable to me because the whole time he was, like . . . *staring at me*. You know? Like straightaway, like that. It was just unnerving! It was as if he was so completely comfortable with himself that he was not afraid to give himself over, to look me straight in the eye with complete abandonment. He had nothing to fear.**
>
> **—Annie Leibovitz, September 1983**

———

Annie Leibovitz, the best-known portrait photographer of her generation, also confessed to shyness—her difficulty in making conversation—when we spoke in 1991. But Leibovitz found a way to make the shyness

work to her advantage. Early in her career as a portraitist, she decided
to give her subjects some business—things to do while she was taking
their picture. She wrapped Clint Eastwood in rope—a pale rider lassoed
for delivery. She planted Ella Fitzgerald, wearing a bright red suit, in the
middle of ferns and greenery—the ultimate songbird. The celebrities she
was photographing got so involved with what they were doing, Leibovitz said, that she didn't have to talk with them.

I began my interview with Annie Leibovitz exactly as I did this one
with Lord Snowdon—asking that my picture be taken. Leibovitz's response, as you will see, was quite different.

Inventing Velcro

August 1980

Quick as a camera blink, we're in the eighties. 1980, the year of Abscam and U.S. hostages in Iran, the year Mount St. Helens blew its top and Ronald Reagan won the presidency. A new decade, bringing new connections.

In my earliest weeks hosting *All Things Considered,* I kept chasing them. Connections. It was important to me to build bridges between stories, tie events together, find patterns. I used to write links from one story to the next—verbal segues from a chat with a Vietnam veteran, say, to a report on farming in Kansas. "Speaking of veterans," I'd announce, "two veteran farmers in Kansas . . ." Dreadful! Forced! But I felt impelled, as anchor, to put things together. Maybe it was the old Barnard English Lit. major's search for coherence.

Producers mucked it up by changing the order of stories at the last minute. While one story was on, I'd scramble to find a quick hook to the next one. I remember feeling like the Dutch kid with his finger in the dike, trying to stave off an avalanche of water. The flood of events, late-breaking stories, technical demands, drowned my efforts. Finally I gave up. Sadly but realistically I decided that whatever connections there were would have to be made *within* reports and interviews, not between them.

In August 1980, producer Jay Allison and I, for no earthly reason I can remember or even make up with a straight face, did a piece about connections—literal, physical connections—on *All Things Considered.* We saluted an invention that was popping up in new places: on waistbands, shoulder pads, backpacks, straps of all sorts. We spent ten minutes and forty-five seconds of America's time broadcasting a little item we called "Voilà Velcro!" The piece featured a range of unidentified voices and original music Jay wrote with his friend Bill Vanaver.

MALE: You know, it's two pieces of material, you put them together and it sticks automatically.

STAMBERG: Do you know what Velcro is?

FEMALE: Velcro? Like a brush, that you pull? I don't know how I'd explain it. It's kind of like what he said.

STAMBERG: Do you know what Velcro is?

ANOTHER MALE: No.

　　　(*Sound of Velcro, sticking and unsticking.*)

STAMBERG: It holds up our pants and paintings and keeps our pillowcases fastened. It took us to the moon, up and down the sides of mountains. It monitors our blood pressure, keeps haircuts tidy. Velcro has held us together through the sixties and seventies. Nylon hook-and-loop fasteners gave zippers a run for the money and introduced a new sound to the environment.

A THIRD MALE: Well, you know, it's sort of a tearing sound. It goes *chhhhhurrrrrrrhhhhhh.*

A FOURTH MALE: Well, sort of like *CKCKCKCKCKCHH HHHH KKK*—but softly.

ANOTHER FEMALE: It makes a wonderful noise—*brrrrr*. Like that. *Brrppppp*. Nope, I can't do it anymore. *Bbbrrrriiiippppppp*. How's that?

STAMBERG: George de Mestral gave us the sound and the hook. And loop. Or pile. George de Mestral of Switzerland. Monsieur Velcro. He speaks no English, but *Madame* de Mestral does.

MME. DE MESTRAL: My husband, George de Mestral, his favorite hobby is to go shooting—hunting. And one day he got very fed up with all the little burdock burrs that were sticking in his trousers, and in the dog's ears, and all over. You know what these things are?

STAMBERG: Sticky burrs?

MME. DE MESTRAL: Yes. You throw them at somebody and it sticks. He began to wonder *why* they stuck, you see.

STAMBERG: (*Narrating*) So, *annoyance* can be the mother of invention!

　　　Now, George de Mestral, hunter, is also George de Mestral,

engineer. Monsieur Velcro took the prickly intruders home to learn *how* they intruded. Why the burrs stick.

(*Dramatic guitar chord.*)

STAMBERG: Hooks. Thousands of pointed hooks, right there under the microscope.

(*Another dramatic guitar chord.*)

STAMBERG: The answer to George de Mestral's question raised another question. He had unfastened the secret of an annoyance. Wasn't there a way to put the secret to good use? Weren't there things you *wanted* to join together that might join better this way than the ways they were joining then? This was in the middle of the 1940s.

(*Yet* another *dramatic guitar chord!*)

STAMBERG: Voilà! Nature helps George de Mestral to reinvent the hook and eye. Or hook and loop. Or hook and pile. Or—

MME. DE MESTRAL: So, at about this time, which was, as I say, during the war, he was aware that there were certain problems with zippers. You know, when they get stuck, you really can't do anything about it. So, he wondered whether there was some way to make use of this invention of nature.

STAMBERG: (*Narrating*) By now you must realize that if George de Mestral is a man who would not stand by while burrs adhered to his hunting trousers, he was surely not a man to stand by his microscope while burrs revealed their sticky secrets. De Mestral went from the microscope to the bank. He got money to finance some experiments. The mission: to *re-create* the burr.

What materials could he use? Did a textile with such properties exist? The search took him to weaving school in Lyons. But nothing on the looms of Lyons could match the stick-to-itiveness he'd found in nature.

MME. DE MESTRAL: Suddenly, he heard about the invention by Du Pont de Nemours of new nylon thread. Nylon was coming in. In a way, it was a stroke of luck, you see. It's a coincidence that it came along at that time. He realized that nylon was the answer to his problem of how to make these hooks stay put.

STAMBERG: (*Narrating*) Nylon! The answer was nylon! The patent was easy enough, but then the problem was to create a fabric with the nylon, to find a factory where looms could be built to produce the material.

Sylvan Goldman was a grocer. After he invented the shopping cart in 1936, his problem was getting people to use them. Women said, "Well, it's just like a baby carriage, and I've pushed enough of them!" And the men said they were strong enough to carry their own groceries. After a week or so, Goldman got the idea of hiring people—men and women of various ages—and he had them use the carts and pretend they were shopping. They walked up and down the aisles, gathering food. And as people came in, he had an attractive lady at the door offering them carts and pointing out how people were using them and how wonderful they were. So customers began using them, and they caught on.

—Philip Lambert, Oklahoma Historical Association, November 1984

(Guitar again, playing "Come Back to Sorrento"—up, then under.)

STAMBERG: It was a lonely search. No one would gamble on him and his new idea, until a factory owner's wife perceived its value and convinced her husband to build the looms. The first factory opened in Italy, and soon the idea spread throughout Europe. It arrived in the United States in 1959 and gradually became a household word.

("Sorrento" ends.)

STAMBERG: Where did the name Velcro come from?

MME. DE MESTRAL: "Vel" is "velvet," or *velours* in French, and then the *croc* is the word in French for "hook." It is a cross shape.

STAMBERG: So this velvet hook, Velcro, entered our lives on blood-pressure tourniquets, barbers' capes, backpacks, parkas, shoes, gloves, sleeves, watches. Velcro marches on!

(Music: "The Caissons Go Rolling Along.")

It's even in the trenches. Boston's Natick Laboratories test material for the U.S. armed forces. Herman Madnick is their spokesman.

MADNICK: We use it for dog booties, which is a very good application. They would wear them in the extreme cold environment to keep the bottoms of their feet from scratching. And instead of lacing these little booties onto a dog's feet, you use this touch-and-go material.

(More marching music.)

STAMBERG: Touch and go, hook and loop, hook and pile, velvet hook. If it can keep booties on dogs' feet, Velcro can do anything!

A MALE: I don't know any silly ideas. Do you?

STAMBERG: Now that you mention it, yes, we have heard a few.

(Excited silent-movie music on piano, plus sound of Velcro pulling apart.)

ANOTHER MALE: Well, one thought that I had was that Velcro could probably be used very efficiently for harvesting burrs.

(More piano and Velcro sound.)

ANOTHER MALE: I guess you could sew it on the feet of paralyzed bats and then line the roof of their cave with it so they could sleep comfortably.

(Really excited music and Velcro sound.)

LITTLE BOY: Tonight for dinner, we had manicotti. It's not a solid food. It moves around a lot. So I think that if you made a little container with a cardboard bottom, you could put Velcro around it and just have a little part that was loose where you could undo the Velcro and pour the manicotti out little by little and then seal back the Velcro. When the food was finished, you could just wash out the Velcro, let the felt dry, and then use it over again the next time you have manicotti.

(*Guitar: "Lucky, Lucky, Lucky Me!"*)

LITTLE BOY: I don't have manicotti that often, but I think it would be a good idea.

(*Song by Allison and Vanaver—very country and western:*)
Hold on to me . . . like Velcro.
Hold me tight, dontcha let me go . . .

M. DE MESTRAL: *Allô?*

STAMBERG: Hello, *monsieur.*

M. DE MESTRAL: Here is George de Mestral. I will say that all that my wife have said upon Velcro is absolutely exact. And I will thank you very much for your interview.

STAMBERG: *Merci beaucoup, monsieur. Et merci pour le Velcro aussi!*

M. DE MESTRAL: *Merci.*

STAMBERG: *Au revoir!* Good-bye!

Them hooks and eyes,
They got me by surprise.
Got a hook-and-pile fastener round my heart . . .

The Secret of a Long Marriage

July 1980

Talk about sticking together (oh, Lord, the Linking Affliction is back!), in 1980, California State University psychologist Judy Todd described her study of couples who had been married for fifty years. Those marriages had survived the Depression, the world wars, and, for some, the struggles of assimilation as immigrants. Having survived all that, you'd think they would have had the secret to a happy marriage. But *no*.

TODD: They're pretty happy as individuals, but if you investigate their happiness with their marriage, you find a great deal of disappointment. That surprised us. It turned out that rather than the marriage lasting so long because of their own efforts, it was more due to cultural prohibitions against divorce. They had just stuck together in spite of a lot of disappointment with the marriage itself.

STAMBERG: And was the disappointment there from the beginning?

TODD: A lot of the things that were aggravating them in their spouses had bothered them when they got married. They entered into the marriage with expectations that ended up not being met, and they developed rules for surviving together that got *around* the disappointment but never solved it.

STAMBERG: But how important was happiness as one of their early expectations? Did they get married to be happy?

TODD: The men didn't, but the women did. I think the women had romantic illusions. The men went with more practical views. They knew that they had to make a living. Their life orientation was

At the end of the day, the couple gets together. She'll start telling him everything that happened during the day, who she met, what they said, what she thought, how what they said made her feel, what they told her about other people. She'll feel this is a good conversation because she's communicating the essence of her experience of the day. It makes you feel like you're not alone. You're sharing your life with someone. Then she'll turn to her husband or her boyfriend and say, "And how was your day?" And he'll say, "Fine."

—*sociolinguist Deborah Tannen, July 1990*

towards business. They expected their wives to help them. The men were more likely to get their expectations met than the women.

STAMBERG: So, if they weren't particularly happy, why did they stay together?

TODD: I think, for them, there just wasn't an option for divorce. We would ask them things like, "Was there ever a point when you reached a crisis and you thought of leaving the relationship?" They would look at us like we were crazy!

STAMBERG: How were they able to stay together, being unhappy?

TODD: I think they developed little behavior rules that let them keep going. You also have to remember that the men worked sixty-hour weeks, they never had vacations, and they were basically not home— so there wasn't much time for discussion.

STAMBERG: These people must be in their seventies now. The men are retired, and around the house more. What difference is that making?

TODD: There was a big change at retirement. There's a shift in power. The men are home, and often ill—they get heart attacks or other things around that age—and they're not able to do as much as they used to. Whereas the women *start* doing things they had never done before. They were forced to take over certain things. "I finally got my own checking account. I never had written a check," some said. "I learned to drive. I hadn't driven a car for fifty years."

STAMBERG: Did that make them happy?

TODD: The women *were* more happy after retirement. They had more say; they were more competent. For instance, we asked the couples, "What years would you like to relive of your marriage?" The men usually said, "Gee, I'd like to re-live the first ten years, when I was president of the company." And the women usually said, "The last five years."

STAMBERG: You know, Ms. Todd, I don't find much cause for optimism in anything you've discovered. Did you?

TODD: No, we got quite depressed doing the interviews, actually!

━━━

Well, here's something optimistic. Maybe. In 1980, the year of that conversation, the divorce rate was 5.2 percent. Ten years later, in 1990, the divorce rate was 4.7 percent. Cheer you up? Of course, the marriage rate was down, too. From 10.6 in 1980 to 9.8 in 1990.

Read a book called *Madame Bovary*! Read a book called *Anna Karenina*! Don't we know that half the marriages in America end in divorce? And I bet half of those end in *acrimonious* divorce. A successful marriage is one in which you more or less negotiate the conflict without killing each other. Otherwise, we're talking about advertising images of marriage, which are banal and silly, aren't they!

**—Philip Roth,
September 1988**

Nancy Reagan to the White House

October 1980

In late October 1980, I drove through some extremely cold and unwelcoming snowy weather out to Middleburg, Virginia, to interview Nancy Reagan. This was Nancy Reagan before the White House, before the extravagant china, before the assassination attempt on her husband, before "Just say no." It was not before the astrologer, but we didn't know that then. It was Nancy Reagan before Kitty Kelley. She was still a candidate's wife, and we spoke the day before the Reagan-Carter debate. Election Day was a shade more than a week away.

President Carter had just spoken sharply against Ronald Reagan, criticizing his "naïve" ideas about foreign policy and warning that the anti-Communist hard-liner might bring the country closer to the brink of nuclear disaster. A Gallup Poll showed the president just a single percentage point ahead of the former California governor. This interview was taped two days after that poll, and—most unusual at that point in her political life—Nancy Reagan had just gone on the offensive publicly, expressing her exasperation with Jimmy Carter on network television and in a sixty-second campaign commercial that she insisted the Reagan people run nationally.

So it was an embattled Nancy Reagan I had driven out to see, and I must say that from almost the moment we arrived at the estate the Reagans were renting in fine-living Virginia horse country, I began to wonder whether she was angry with *me*. What else could explain the way engineer Gary Henderson and I were treated after we'd parked NPR's beat-up station wagon at the foot of the hill just inside the gate?

We were right on time, in fact somewhat early for our 3:30 appointment. After a Secret Service agent emerged from a sentry shack and checked our credentials, we climbed into an open golf cart and were driven up the hill toward the house. And then Gary, carrying a thirty-three-pound tape recorder plus a supply kit containing fifteen pounds of mikes and mike stands and cables, and I, bearing only a weighty intolerance of the cold, were made to stand outside under mean late-afternoon skies in the unseasonable and freezing snow for half an hour. In less than five minutes, we felt as if a decade had passed. As the year 2000 began wrapping itself around our imaginations, just moments before frostbite nipped our audiotape, someone came out and ushered us inside the mansion to a motelish-looking back bedroom that might have come in third in a Kmart interior-design contest. There we sat for another thirty minutes, wondering why we'd raced to leave M Street so quickly.

The living room, when we finally encountered it, was a large, cheerfully furnished space with a warming fireplace and big mullioned windows that framed a Christmas-card view of the soft, snow-covered Virginia hills. Inside, with our fingers beginning to thaw, it was easier to appreciate aesthetics. Again we waited. Mrs. Reagan had had interviews stacked up all day, we were told, and was just wrapping up the last one.

Gary set up the Nagra recorder on a table, and we decided where we'd ask Mrs. Reagan to sit for the taping. Gary fussed with cable and mikes while we waited; I looked over my notes. Then Mrs. Reagan arrived. She entered through a door at the fireplace end of the living room. Gary and I were at the other end. Mrs. Reagan crossed the big room, but instead of coming over to the couch where we were seated, she walked around deliberately and quite methodically emptying a number of ashtrays that were perched on various end tables. Then, and only then, did she come up to us and extend her hand in greeting.

Finding this behavior utterly fascinating, I dined out on it for days. Haynes Johnson, the *Washington Post* columnist, said it was the most interesting thing he'd heard about Nancy Reagan. And it *was,* in those extremely careful, watch-yourself-because-everything-hinges-on-it, pre–White House days. I'm still not sure how to interpret it. Emptying the ashtrays is the act of a good housekeeper, surely. Also the act of a person who wants to dress the set before the next appearance. Also the act of someone more concerned with appearances than with making human connections.

She looked marvelous, tiny and trim in a beautiful red suit with mohair loops in it—very designer-made. But despite the meticulous grooming, Nancy Reagan was not a *presence*. You didn't forget about the weather when she entered the room. She was contained, closed off. It was difficult to believe she'd spent so many years in the back-slapping how-ya-doin' world of politics.

In conversation, her sound was like . . . air. She put long pauses after almost every word, and her voice and face were expressionless. Several times after posing a question, I found myself starting to suggest the beginning of an answer, trying to help her understand what I was after. Getting the question seemed to be a problem for Nancy Reagan.

STAMBERG: I have to say from the start that you surprise me. This is the end of what must be an extremely busy day for you; I'm probably—what?—maybe the tenth interviewer—

REAGAN: (*Laughs.*)

STAMBERG: —you've had to face, and yet I sense a great quiet in you. I would think you would either be exhausted or strung out with nerves, and you don't seem to be either.

REAGAN: (*Hesitates, looks at tape recorder.*) Are we . . . ?

STAMBERG: Yeah, we're going.

REAGAN: Oh! . . . Well, I think you reach the point, especially towards the end, where you feel that you've done all you can do. You've tried; you've worked hard. Now it's in somebody else's hands. This *is* the longest week ever. (*Laughs.*)

STAMBERG: I bet it is.

REAGAN: *Ever!*

STAMBERG: I was thinking that a week plus two days from now, you'll know, won't you?

REAGAN: Umm-hmm. Umm-hmm.

STAMBERG: I wonder what that feels like? Is this just so anti-climactic now? Are you just marking time?

REAGAN: Well, you just wish that the days would go by. When I think back to a year ago and the primaries and New Hampshire and all of that, it . . . it seems like another world.

STAMBERG: Is there anything you could say, Mrs. Reagan, into that microphone that would assure your husband a victory on the fourth?

REAGAN: Well, I don't know if . . . (*laughs*) . . . I can assure my husband a victory on the fourth. I can . . . I can say what kind of a

STAMBERG: **Kitty Kelley, what's the most scandalous or news-breaking piece of information in your unauthorized biography of Nancy Reagan?**

KELLEY: **I think the fact that Mrs. Reagan was as powerful as she was. When I started the book, I thought we were dealing with an influential first lady. I had no idea that we were truly dealing with someone who had a control of the presidency.**

STAMBERG: **You are not saying she was president of the United States for eight years?**

KELLEY: **I am saying that she was your president, Susan, indeed she was! Make no mistake about it. She was our petticoat president.**

—April 1991

man he is. If I had to pick one adjective over any other adjective to describe him, it would have to be "integrity." Very rare quality these days. He's strong, he's compassionate . . .

(*Pause.*)

KITTY KELLEY: She was a great president. I really mean it! I think we owe her a great deal. We would have never had dialogue with the Soviet Union had it not been for Nancy Reagan.

—*April 1991*

STAMBERG: Do you know what? I'm sitting across the table from Nancy Reagan, and it occurs to me that if I were with Rosalynn Carter and asked that question, she would have given me the same answer. She would!

REAGAN: I don't know . . . I don't know Rosalynn Carter.

STAMBERG: Because these are exactly the grounds on which Jimmy Carter ran in 1976. And those are the words that were used. Remember? "We need a government that is as compassionate as the American people. . . . I am a man of integrity." How interesting!

REAGAN: I don't know. I don't know Rosalynn Carter, I don't know Jimmy Carter. All I know is that I deeply resent the kind of campaign that he's been waging against my husband. Deeply!

STAMBERG: You resent it so much that you have just taped a series of ads in which you personally . . . (*fade*)

REAGAN: (*Tape of her campaign spot:*) I don't often speak out in campaigns, but I think that this campaign now has gotten to the point and the level where I have to say something. I am deeply, deeply offended by the attempts of Mr. Carter to paint my husband as a man he is not at all. I'm offended when he tries to portray Ronald Reagan as a warmonger, or someone who would cut off Social Security . . . (*campaign spot fades under*)

STAMBERG: Very uncharacteristic of you. How come?

REAGAN: Because I am so angry. I think . . . (*laughs*) . . . I think that this election is the most important election, certainly, in my lifetime. I think it's going to determine which way our country goes—indeed, which way the world goes.

STAMBERG: What *got* you, though? What got you so that you said, "I'm going to break character—"

REAGAN: It started with the speech that Mr. Carter gave in Chicago, which I deeply resented. That was the speech in which he said that my husband was going to divide the country—(*pounds on table*)—North from South, black from white, Jew from Gentile. It was a terrible speech—a terrible, personal attack on a man.

STAMBERG: But I'm curious about the timing in all of this. Do you perceive that this is something new on President Carter's part, or is it your concern that he's catching up in the polls, and maybe—

REAGAN: No, no, no.

STAMBERG: —you do what you have to do, and if it takes going on—

REAGAN: No, no, no.

STAMBERG: —and making these ads, you do them?

REAGAN: No, no, not at all. Not at all. I . . . just . . . *had* it!

STAMBERG: Part of leadership is the ability to give the people a sense of themselves. There are several ways to do that. One is to hold up myths in which the country can believe. "Vision" is another word to use—a candidate's perception of what the country should be, what the people can aspire to. What would your husband's vision be for America?

REAGAN: To get the government off their backs, and turn the people loose to do what the people can do better than anybody else can do for them. And *they'll* be just fine, and our *country* will be just fine.

STAMBERG: If Ronald Reagan becomes president, can you imagine what difference it will have made to us a year from today? What sort of shape will we be in? What will be different about the country?

REAGAN: Well, now, you know, I'm terribly superstitious . . . (*laughs*) . . . and really, that's a question you should ask me eight days from now. (*Laughs.*)

STAMBERG: But what about the *idea* of it? Would we be stronger as a nation? Would the hostages be released? Would inflation be reduced?

(*Long pause.*)

REAGAN: That we would have less government interference in our lives, that we would not have the growing bureaucracy that we have, that you would have somebody who would level with you. Campaigning is very character revealing. Very! How you choose to fight your battles. It's very revealing. Character revealing.

STAMBERG: What has it revealed to us about two people? First, Jimmy Carter, and then Ronald Reagan.

REAGAN: Well, about Ronald Reagan, that he—

STAMBERG: No, no, let's start with Jimmy Carter.

REAGAN: No, I'm not going to, because—

STAMBERG: You won't do that?

REAGAN: No, because then that . . . that . . . then I would be doing

KITTY KELLEY: Writing the Frank Sinatra book, I had to put up with physical threats. People thought they were going to lose their lives. This was tougher.

STAMBERG: Why?

KELLEY: With Mrs. Reagan, they were afraid of being discredited, kicked off corporate boards, having spouses fired.

STAMBERG: With *that* many people *that* scared, how come so many talked to you?

KELLEY: Well, there were some people who really wanted to set the record straight for history's sake, but they were still scared to use their own names. Secret Service agents, doctors, neighbors of the Reagans', White House aides. Some of these people are in George Bush's cabinet. They're in George Bush's White House!

—April 1991

exactly what I'm criticizing *him* for. And I feel very strongly about the way you campaign. Very!

STAMBERG: In other words, you avoid personal attack and explicit criticism?

REAGAN: Unless it's on an issue. I mean . . . (*long pause*) Now, where were we?

STAMBERG: What it reveals about Ronald Reagan.

REAGAN: (*Laughs.*) Ronald Reagan! It reveals that he's a very strong man who has the courage of his convictions and his ideas, which have not changed. And he campaigns on the issues and does not resort to personal attacks.

STAMBERG: Are you worried that you're taking it *too* personally, maybe? That it's getting too close now, and you may be making a mistake in that way?

REAGAN: No.

STAMBERG: You know, when things start to *get* to you—start to get under your skin—then you've lost control in some way.

REAGAN: No, no, no, I don't. I think it's something that has to be said.

STAMBERG: You were talking about the kinds of traveling you've done this year, and what you pick up from the people. I've done a tiny bit of traveling, too, and in the course of it pick up something quite different that I want to ask you about—and that is a sense of despair on the part of voters at the choices they're being asked to make this year.

REAGAN: I read that all the time, but I'm certainly not seeing it. I'm certainly not hearing it.

STAMBERG: Well, wouldn't you tend, though, to see Reagan supporters, so that they would be the most enthusiastic people?

REAGAN: Not necessarily. I would see demonstrators. I would see . . . you know . . . I mean, you see . . . (*laughs*) you don't just see Reagan supporters. And apathy? I don't see any apathy out there at all.

STAMBERG: Not apathy. I think there's a real rage, there's a real anger, the kind of thing you were talking about before. And then that huge swath of the undecideds. If people felt there really were a choice, would there be that big a clump of those who said that they—

REAGAN: Yes, there would. Because of the kind of television commercials that have been run, that have confused people, so that there is a large undecided vote.

The idea that she's involved in governmental decisions and so forth, and all of this, and being a kind of a Dragon Lady—there is nothing to that, and no one who knows her well would ever believe it.

—*Ronald Reagan, March 1987*

STAMBERG: But these undecideds were there before any of these ad campaigns began. In other words, people who were looking—

REAGAN: No, no.

STAMBERG: —at the candidates themselves seem to feel there wasn't—

REAGAN: No.

STAMBERG: —there wasn't anybody they could be enthusiastic about—

REAGAN: No, I don't agree with you.

STAMBERG: No?

REAGAN: I don't agree with you.

———

For all that she disagreed with various observations of mine, for all her anger with Jimmy Carter, for all the "No, no, no, no, no"s, there was a marked absence of passion in Nancy Reagan. Passionless, presence-less—surprising in a person who had spent so much time in the public and ego-driven worlds of politics and entertainment.

Driving back through the snow to Washington in that week before Nancy Reagan became first lady, I felt that there was no weight to her—neither physically nor emotionally nor intellectually. She was like a glass of champagne without the gaiety of bubbles. It wasn't that the champagne had gone flat. It seemed, instead, as if the bubbles had just never been there.

A first lady's foremost job is to be a support system for her husband. Nancy Reagan has done that, and she's done it with great zest and perhaps more colorfully than some other first ladies. I admire her for that. And I have great sympathy for anyone who's living in the White House. I know what a fishbowl it can be. People are going to find fault with you. You have to have confidence in what you and your husband are doing, and you've got to give him that confidence. And I think she's done that.

—Betty Ford, March 1987

Pump Who Up?

August 1980

STAMBERG: In his new book, *Aerophobics—The Scientific Way to Stop Exercising,* Don Lessem says exercise is an epidemic that has struck at least one hundred million Americans. Terminally active people. Lessem lists some of the symptoms.

LESSEM: You become gaunt. Your attention wanders. You begin to speak in disjointed phrases like, "Did you do your five?" Oftentimes, you get sweaty and breathless. It's a bit like the symptoms of sex, only there's no cigarette smoking.

STAMBERG: Now, you feel these are warning signals of a dangerous situation, but there is a solution to this problem. What is that solution?

LESSEM: The aerophobic program of fatness fitness.

STAMBERG: What is aerophobics?

LESSEM: It's really just a scientific catchall term for what we've been doing all our lives. It's the life of Riley. It's what the French call *joie de vivre*. Eddie Cantor called it whoopee.

STAMBERG: In other words, aerophobists do nothing?

LESSEM: Eating. Sleeping.

STAMBERG: That doesn't sound very hard!

LESSEM: No, but we try and do it twenty-four hours a day.

STAMBERG: What does the aerophobist eat?

LESSEM: Try and avoid greens. Take anything that's in a wrapper and has over twenty additives and no vitamin content.

STAMBERG: Mr. Lessem, our listeners can't see you, but I can. You're skinny and you look to me as if you're in pretty good shape. So you're making all this up, aren't you?

LESSEM: No. Since I've been on this fatness fitness program, I've gained 70 pounds. I'm over 160. By Christmastime, I should be a natural Santa, about 250.

STAMBERG: So, it really does work?

LESSEM: Yes, it does. In fact, you can eat the book!

When I was a little girl, women who were forty-six—the age I am now—were old. They thought of themselves as old, they looked older, they didn't live as long, and they were much more victimized by the stereotypes, and they didn't expect much out of their lives. But today we have higher expectations. More of us are working and have identities that are not uniquely bound up with being mothers and wives. More of us have taken health into our own hands and improved the quality of our lives. For all of these reasons, we see mid-life as the extremely vital and dynamic center third of our lives.

—Jane Fonda,
January 1985

The Art of Obituary Writing

June 1980

When Miles Davis died in September 1991, you could hear his probing, muted jazz trumpet curling in on itself on radio stations all weekend long. That's the way to mark the end of such a life. Surround us with the talent for forty-eight straight hours. Let us hear what we've lost.

In a *Washington Post* column some years back, Richard Cohen wrote that when he died, he wanted the entire world to call a time-out. He wanted his paper to stop publishing for two days, wanted all his women friends to wear black for six months, and hoped that years after his demise, people would spontaneously burst into tears at the very thought that he was no longer around. And truth to tell, who among us doesn't want attention to be paid for a *long* time?

In radio news, there's never a long time. A radio obituary usually lasts four minutes or so, and in that mere splinter of an hour you need to relate the life that's just ended and explain to listeners how it was important, and to whom. It's an immense responsibility. For *All Things Considered,* I fashioned fourteen years' worth of obituaries and never felt I'd done justice in a single one of them. You have to work too quickly. Usually, the news of death arrives in the morning; by the time you can even *begin* working on the obit, it's noon; and in the afternoon, there are four *other* stories to do before the five o'clock broadcast. The lives and deeds to be encapsulated demand much more reflective work time than is ever available. That's true of almost everything we report on each day, but in cases of death the lack of time is especially frustrating because you know that the obituary you're writing may be the program's last word on the subject.

We developed a routine after a while, and the very routine of it began to bother me—it became so formulaic—pull the file, read the file, make the notes, find a friend or expert, tape an interview, intercut the interview with music or a film or stage clip, or a few seconds of the deceased's voice on tape (lifted from our archives), write the copy, run the piece. Next.

There was no time to think, much less feel. Certainly no time to mourn. When I heard the news that Miles Davis died—this was long after I'd stopped hosting either *All Things Considered* or *Weekend Edition*—I caught myself sighing with relief that I didn't have to *do* anything about this death—didn't have to process it, report it, turn it around quickly. I could simply feel sad. And I did.

At the same time, in the morbid but necessary business of preparing obituaries, there are people you very much want to write about because you admire them and want the chance to "get" them right. I remember feeling that when Fred Astaire died on a day I was off the air. The same thing happened with Irving Berlin.

The master of the obituary, the man who created a new form for it in print, was Alden Whitman of *The New York Times*. At the paper, they called him The Mortician and were always asking him, "Who'd you pack away on ice today, Alden?"

Although enduring gallows humor was his occupational hazard, Alden Whitman elevated obituary writing to an art. From 1964 until his retirement in 1976, he did what no one had done before: He *interviewed* his prospective subjects—sought them out while they were quite healthy, in fact—and talked to their friends and associates, as well (he promised his sources confidentiality during their lifetimes). Whitman looked for personal details, anecdotes, information beyond the cold facts in *Who's Who* or on a résumé. After conducting the interviews, Whitman wrote the obituary. Often, ghoulish as it may sound, the obit would then be set in type, ready to run when death occurred. When I interviewed Mr. Whitman in 1980, I asked whether his was grisly work.

WHITMAN: No, of course not!
STAMBERG: Morbid?
WHITMAN: No! The people were alive when I wrote about them, after

Starting precisely at 5:30 A.M. Mountain War Time, July 16, 1945, J. (for nothing) Robert Oppenheimer lived the remainder of his life in the blinding light and the crepuscular shadow of the nuclear test bomb that was exploded at that moment, at Alamogordo, N.M.

—Alden Whitman obituary for J. Robert Oppenheimer, The New York Times, February 1967

John O'Hara, the pro-
lific American novelist
who took the public poses
and the private hells of
the small-town rich as his
theme, died of a heart attack yesterday morning in
his sleep at his country
home in Princeton, N.J. He
was 65 years old.

—Paul L. Montgomery
obituary for John
O'Hara, The New
York Times,
April 1970

all. You can't possibly be writing about somebody and visualize him
as lying in a coffin or on a morgue table and hope to survive. You'd
go up the wall. You'd go crazy.

STAMBERG: Who died on your day off?

WHITMAN: John O'Hara, alas. I interviewed him and I wanted to do
him, but I put him aside because he was sixty-five years old and
looked to me, when I saw him, in absolutely perfect health.

STAMBERG: And you never had a chance to write up your notes, so the
obit wasn't shelf-ready when he died?

WHITMAN: It wasn't shelf-ready, alas. I'd love to have done it because
I liked John O'Hara. I felt he was vastly underrated as an important
American writer.

STAMBERG: You retired four years ago. What's left of your writing on
the shelves, still unpublished at *The New York Times*? An obituary
for the shah of Iran?

WHITMAN: No. I did not do that. There *is* one of Erik Erikson hanging
around.

STAMBERG: Is there a Nixon obituary of yours?

WHITMAN: Well, there is, but I'm certain it will be revised, because it
was written at great speed at the time when there was word that he
was threatening to commit suicide after he left office. And of course,
there is a man who will *never* commit suicide.

STAMBERG: I wrote one then, too, when he had very bad phlebitis. It's
sitting on my shelf.

WHITMAN: That's when I wrote mine.

STAMBERG: Alden Whitman, have you written your *own* obituary?

WHITMAN: No, I have not. But I may. The one reason I would write
it is not out of any immodesty but simply because I would like to set
down the facts correctly as I know them—simple, short and sweet,
and that's it.

STAMBERG: Should we trust you?

WHITMAN: I think so. To be perfectly fair.

STAMBERG: Do you read the obituary pages first in the paper every
day?

WHITMAN: I read page one and then I turn to the obits.

STAMBERG: Did you do that before you became the *Times*'s number
one obituary writer?

WHITMAN: Yes, I think I've always been interested in obituaries. I am really interested in biography. And obituaries are a form of biography.

STAMBERG: The average obituary is about five hundred words or less. Is that what a life is worth? How do you decide between five hundred words and five hundred thousand words?

WHITMAN: Well, every life is worth something, obviously. My feeling is that there are neglected lives and lives that shouldn't be neglected. The class system operates on the obit page as well as everywhere else. People who are rich and famous tend to be treated more adequately than those who are unrich and unfamous, and yet those lives may be as interesting, and certainly as worthwhile, and contribute as much to society, as the rich ones.

Alden Whitman, a retired reporter for *The New York Times* who pioneered the use of interviews of notable people to personalize and energize their obituaries, died yesterday at the Hotel de Paris in Monte Carlo. He was 76 years old and lived in Southampton, L.I.

—collectively written obituary for Alden Whitman, The New York Times, September 1990

The Hostages Come Home

January 1981

The face above the fold on page 1 of the Sunday paper was so familiar that at first I thought it was a family member—a distant relative, to be sure, but someone related. That first reaction was right and wrong. It was Terry Anderson, the journalist who had been held hostage in Lebanon for six years, and finally released in December 1991.

Anderson was the last of eighteen American hostages to be released. But in a sense, he was the last in an even broader arc of terrorism that began in November 1979, when Iranian militants seized the U.S. embassy in Tehran and held fifty-two Americans captive. That 444-day ordeal gave this country a stern lesson in vulnerability. Tehran and the accident at the nuclear power plant on Pennsylvania's Three Mile Island tied for first place when we asked *All Things Considered* listeners to choose a single event that stood for the seventies—something that summed up everything that went before it and changed the direction of everything that followed. Listeners said that the hostage situation—and the Carter administration's inability to resolve it—ended the illusion that America could control everything. They also expressed an apprehension (eventually to be reversed by the glittering Reagan Revolution) that in the United States, more had become less. At the end of the seventies, American power had dwindled.

We got tremendously involved with those hostages in Tehran. We tied yellow ribbons around trees and committed the prisoners' names to memory—Laingen, Ode, Queen, Lopez, Swift, Rosen. A month after the hostage taking, I phoned Dorothea Morefield, whose husband, Richard, had been general consul at the embassy, and asked if she'd had a single day when her waking thought had not been, "My God, he's still being held over there!"

"No, no," she said. "It's always my first thought. I wake up very early, turn on the radio, or sometimes call Washington. And I always call in hopes that something positive will have happened overnight."

For 444 days, nothing at all positive happened. Mrs. Morefield and I kept talking by phone. But our relationship wasn't unique. In October 1980, on a trip west to meet her in person, I found the Morefields' San Diego home strewn with the wires and cables of television crews camping out there. As I was recording my interview with Mrs. Morefield, one of the network TV morning shows called. I poked my microphone at the family television set and taped the live broadcast of Mrs. Morefield as she spoke to the TV people on a phone in the next room. The scene would have taxed George Orwell's imagination. "I guess giving all these interviews is my way of coping," she told me.

Finally, the ordeal ended. On January 20, 1981, moments after Ronald Reagan was sworn in for his first term as president of the United States, the hostages were released.

On January 21, we groped for what to call them—hostages? . . . former hostages? . . . returnees? In an essay on *All Things Considered,* I observed that they'd become more to us than those terms could imply.

STAMBERG: They're husbands, friends, lovers, sisters, brothers, children, relatives. And strangers. Except that the fifty-two Americans became part of *our* family in the last fourteen months, and we feel a kind of closeness that passes for family feeling. Like family, we want to know everything, to ask everything. It's that eager and loving wish *to know* that troubles me today, even as I share the curiosity and make mental notes of questions I would ask. And then I stop, and am troubled. Because they're strangers and should be permitted to *remain* strangers.

They *look* like us, of course. Paler, maybe, hairier. But in their T-shirts and pants and parkas, they're people you'd see in the seat next to you on the bus, or at the car wash. And they're not. They've been through an experience we cannot begin to imagine. So we don't want to imagine it. We want them to tell us what it was like.

One of them, stepping onto non-Iranian soil for the first time in four hundred forty-four days, said, "It's great to get away from the masses." Well . . . he ain't seen nothin' yet! Wait until he encounters the masses of *us*—citizens, broadcasters, reporters, camera crews, shoving lights and lenses and microphones and notepads at him, probing and pressing. "Just one more question!" "One more statement, *please??*" We're entitled to ask for more. But it's troubling.

The dilemma in a democracy is to find the middle ground between the competing demands of the public's right to know and the individual's right to privacy. Maybe, to satisfy our curiosity, there should be a twenty-four-hour orgy of a news conference very soon, in which everyone asks everything and tells everything, until there's nothing more to say. And then let's leave them alone. Let's leave them alone! Let's give them their private time, space for readjustment and re-entry.

It seems extremely important today that we all be careful not to turn these newly freed men and women into hostages again. Hostages to our own curiosity, relief, and love.

Dave Brubeck's Musical Education

February 1981

What's it like when it's going right? What makes it happen? How do you make it happen again? Can you? Why? Why not?

If this were a sheet of music, that would be the refrain. Questions I've asked over and over again, trying to get to the heart of creativity. The answers are as varied as the artists themselves.

Jazz musicians are especially good on these questions, possibly because so much is on the line every time they perform. In jazz, it's not just getting the notes right and well shaped, it's also forming them into spontaneous little ongoing compositions—tunes within tunes—that will mesh with what others are playing and also stand up alone, with a beginning, middle, and end.

Hazen Schumacher, who hosts the longtime public radio program *Jazz Revisited,* once said that jazz players are special because they walk out on stage with absolutely no idea of what they're about to do, and then they sit down and do it. They invent the music note by note.

What's it like when it's going right? Joe Williams, the great jazz singer who spent years in front of the Basie band, had this answer:

"On some nights, you can hear it. You and the musicians are so together, there's such an empathy between you, and the support and the soloist are reaching inspiring heights. And you know you can't capture and hold these moments. Because they're spiritual moments that are only given to you to have for a little while. You're allowed to have them for just a little while. You're not allowed to keep them."

STAMBERG: As a child, did you feel you were happier playing the piano than just about anything else you could think of?

BARBARA CARROLL: Oh, yes. And you want to know something? I still am!

—June 1986

161

What's it like when it's going right at the piano? Dave Brubeck said that it involved courage:

"You can't be totally inspired night after night in public, with the spotlight on you, and so many things that will kill creativity: the lights, a different piano, a different PA system, the audience. But some nights, something happens right there in public—it's like a feeling almost of bravery or something. All of a sudden you're out of your shell, you're out of the things that hold you back. Sometimes it's because of the crowd, how they reacted to the last number; their encouragement feeds your inspiration. Or you feel something which you can never say, because if you knew what it was, you'd set it up every night.

"When you write music, what you have going for you is, if it's bad, you can tear it up and start again. When you're improvising, you can't. You play it if it's bad *or* good, and you keep going. If it's great improvisation, it's better than anything you can write. If it's bad improvisation, you're sorry it left you. It could be on a record forever. So you've got to give a little and take a little in the two. But I prefer to play badly some nights for the chance of playing great some nights."

Picasso said, "You can't be a sorcerer every day." But you can try. And to my ear, Dave Brubeck approaches sorcery just about every time he sits down at a piano. Once, in 1981, he sat at *my* piano. The piano in my house. Please understand what this meant to me. An Elvis fan, seeing The King risen from the dead, couldn't approach what I felt. "Ecstatic" is an understatement. It was one of those times when the impulse to go to the NPR personnel office and expunge the word "job" from my job description was almost overwhelming.

Since the 1950s, I have gone through four copies of the Brubeck Quartet's *Jazz Goes to College* LP, and I can sing, by heart, every note of Brubeck's nine-minute, twelve-chorus solo on "Balcony Rock." Brubeck at my piano!! It's tricky, now, playing through twelve-plus years of key dust. But I could no more clean the keys than I could improvise four choruses of "Out of Nowhere."

NPR didn't have a piano until 1987. It was a gift from the Baldwin people (the news director called it our "baby grant" piano) when we put *Weekend Edition*/Sunday on the air. In *Weekend*'s first almost-three years, when I was host, Stefan Scaggiari sat at that piano and provided musical interludes between the various interviews, reports, and features. On Irving Berlin's birthday, Stef would play Berlin. On Halloween, "Danse Macabre." He once played the "Minute Waltz" in fifty-three seconds, and "Rhapsody in Blue" in sixty. His former teachers at the Eastman School of Music in Rochester would have cringed, but Stef understood our time constraints and met them masterfully. We taped the program on Fridays, and my favorite part of the week was the short trip from our news-laden, pressure-cookered second floor down a short flight of stairs to Studio Three, where Stef sat warming up, the piano pealing swirls of notes that seeped through the soundproofing and brightened the hallway and corridor.

But in 1981, NPR had no piano for Dave Brubeck, so I did the only thing I could think of: invited him to my house to tape. And he agreed! I couldn't believe his generosity. We have a respectable Knight upright with decent sound. Surely not a piano fit for Dave Brubeck. But there he was, sitting at it and playing, at my request, my favorite Brubeck tune—his tribute to Duke Ellington.

(Brubeck playing "The Duke.")

BRUBECK: That's one of my favorite things that I've written. I remember writing it in my mind, when I took Chris to nursery school. He was about four years old (now he's playing for me!), and just coming back in the car, I started singing this song to myself. I got back home and went into the house and wrote it. I was going to call it "Duke Ellington Meets Darius Milhaud," but the title was just too long, so it was shortened to "The Duke."

In this tune, you go through every key, all twelve notes. I didn't realize this. I was playing it at a concert, and a college professor who knew a lot more about twelve-tone music and harmony heard it and said, "You know, that's a twelve-tone piece." And I said, "No, it isn't. I don't like twelve-tone music!" *(Laughs.)* And he said, "Well, it goes through all the keys in the first eight bars, all twelve chords of a scale." And then I realized it. You see, I had studied with Schönberg, and I didn't like it because of the twelve-tone row. I also studied with Darius Milhaud—he's the one I really studied with. And Ellington's my favorite jazz composer. So the piece should really be "Schönberg Meets Ellington and Milhaud." *(Laughs.)*

(Plays more of "The Duke.")

These are the kind of chords I played when I first met Paul Desmond in 1944, and he thought I was crazy. I was in the army in '44, going overseas as an infantryman. And I wanted to get into the band at the Presidio in San Francisco. They auditioned me, and I had

STAMBERG: May I see your hands, please?

JULIAN BREAM: Sure.

STAMBERG: The right hand has nails of different lengths.

BREAM: They have to be a millimeter above the tip of the finger. And the nails on the left hand have to be fairly short.

STAMBERG: And the pads of the fingers on your right hand?

BREAM: Very soft. And on the left hand, they're like . . . I don't know what you'd say they were like. . . .

STAMBERG: Rocks.

BREAM: Rocks! Yeah! Callused. Very hard.

—February 1987

STAMBERG: A violinist's hands would be like that, too, wouldn't they? Except for the nails?

BREAM: They'd have little calluses, perhaps, but the strings are much thicker on the guitar. And if you look at my two little fingers—

STAMBERG: (Gasps.)

BREAM: —you wouldn't think they belonged to the same person. The little finger on the left hand is twice the size of the right.

STAMBERG: And the colors are completely different, too. The tip of the pinkie on your right hand is a very nice pink. What you'd find on a baby.

BREAM: That's right.

STAMBERG: The left-hand pinkie is almost colorless because it's so callused.

BREAM: You'd find it on someone who had just died.

STAMBERG: Well, it's years of difference between the two. Years of work.

—February 1987

to play some jazz. One of the guys I was playing with was Paul Desmond. And he said, "Let's play the blues in B-flat." Well, the first chord I hit was this: (*Plays chord*). And he thought I was stark raving mad. Because, you see, it's a G chord in this hand (*chord*) and a B-flat chord in this hand (*chord*). That's the way I played when I was a kid.

STAMBERG: Before you even knew that's what you were doing?

BRUBECK: Yeah, before I knew the terms.

STAMBERG: How did you do that?

BRUBECK: Well, it's a crazy explanation, but it's the only one I can tell you. I was raised on a cattle ranch, and I rode horseback hours a day, alone. The ranch was forty-five thousand acres, which is one of the largest ranches in northern California. My father was the manager. And so, being raised on that ranch, I was alone a lot. I worked for a dollar a day for years as a cowboy, and sometimes I worked in the hay, and sometimes I worked pumping water—because you got to have water for the cattle. And the gasoline engines go *chug/chug/chug/chug/khBOME/khBOME/khBOME/khCHUG/khKAKAKAK-AKAKA/kaGOWG/kaGOWG*, and they go on like this for hours.

(*Recorded music sneaks in, same rhythms as engine sound. Brubeck Quartet and "Take Five."*)

And there's nothing to do. You're all alone under a water tank and it's maybe a hundred, hundred and five degrees. And you just lie and you wait for that tank to fill, and it's the only cool place and you're . . . you're out there. So you start singing against the engine, because you're there for a couple of hours. And then you move to the next tank.

(*"Take Five" up full for a while.*)

I had this strange background. My father . . . I can describe him as like the father figure on *Bonanza,* you know. That's the kind of guy he was. He was a champion rodeo roper, just a fantastic cattleman. And my mother was a classical pianist. And I had two brothers. Both are fine musicians. And my mother wanted three . . . well, to tell you what she wanted, she wanted three genius sons, and she drove all three of us.

Well, my dad said that one son had to take after him. And I was the last one. So you know who wasn't the musician, was me. I was going to be a veterinarian, went to college as a pre-med the first year in Stockton, California, College of the Pacific. Hated zoology. Chemistry. I was a C student working as hard as I could because I didn't want to be a failure. And I was, oh, depressed completely.

Across the lawn was the conservatory. And when I was supposed to be cutting up frogs and things like that, my mind would be on what they were playing over at the conservatory. And a professor, God bless him, came over and he said, "Brubeck, next year, just go over there!"

I couldn't read music, but I hid the fact for three years.

STAMBERG: How could you hide it for three years?

BRUBECK: Very simply. I never studied piano! And I had a good ear. I would get through harmony and ear training on my ear. (*Laughs.*) And the whole thing was, rather than learn to read, I had to learn how to operate so they wouldn't know. Can you imagine that?

STAMBERG: No! It sounds like an awful waste of time.

BRUBECK: Well, it was! Then, in my last semester, I took piano, and the teacher put something in front of me, and I couldn't read it. She went right to the dean and said, "He's a senior and about to graduate!" So the dean called me into his office, and he said, "I understand you can't read a note." And I said, "That's right." He said, "Well, doesn't that bother you?" And I said, "No, all I want to do is play jazz. It won't make any difference." And he said, "You know you're a disgrace to the conservatory." And I said, "Well, I guess so, but it doesn't make any difference." And he said, "It doesn't make any difference that I'm not going to graduate you?" And I said, "No, not really. I'm here because my mother insisted I go to college." So *he* said, "Well, I'll tell you what. If you'll promise that you'll never teach music, I'm going to give you your degree." I said, "I promise. I will never teach music!" (*Laughs.*) So, that's the way I graduated from the College of the Pacific!

STAMBERG: When *did* you learn to read?

BRUBECK: When *will* I learn to read?

(*Laughter.*)

(*Brubeck plays again, without reading a note.*)

It's always competitive. You don't think two piano players walk out on the stage thinking, "Well, I'm going to be nice and make him look as good as I can," do you? You're thinking, "Kill!" But in a nice way.

—Oscar Peterson, January 1985

Imperialism and Babar

December 1981

Before we leave 1981, a number of milestones should be noted. That year Sandra Day O'Connor became the first female Supreme Court justice. A U.S. test-tube baby made its debut. Prince Charles of England married Lady Diana Spencer. Walter Cronkite stepped down as CBS anchorman. And Babar turned fifty. I'm stopping right there.

Babar, the fictional elephant who would be king in the African colonies of the thirties, was created by Frenchman Jean de Brunhoff and beloved by children and their grown-ups. But in what might have been an early maneuver in the multicultural war against Eurocentrism (no more polysyllables like that for at least another forty pages, I promise), Chilean writer Ariel Dorfman suggested that Babar lovers were overlooking the book's subtext—a subtext that was patronizing and probably racist. Dorfman had published a collection of essays, *The Empire's Old Clothes,* which tackled a number of popular icons. He thought Babar's creator had certain cultural biases.

DORFMAN: Just as a child matures, a country must mature. Just as there are innocents in human nature—the children—so there are innocent countries which will acquire development. And how does this happen? Well, it happens basically by injecting Western values into these countries.

STAMBERG: Show us how your theory of imperialism civilizing the Third World is played out in *Babar*. He's a happy little elephant in the jungles of Africa.

DORFMAN: Babar's mother is killed, and he runs away from the forest to the big city—Paris. He is taken in by an old lady who takes care of him—teaches and civilizes him. She's like the Red Cross. She cares for the poor and the needy. She is on what the French call a *mission civilisatrice*—a civilizing mission. They go back to Africa. There, Babar becomes king.

It is this relationship that allows Babar and the children who identify with him to understand that there is only one way out of underdevelopment, and that is to imitate the Western world and Western values!

STAMBERG: But is it so terrible, what Babar is doing? He's a very benign ruler. He's extremely kind. He's thoughtful, even to his enemies. He keeps up strong family connections. What's so awful?

DORFMAN: Well, Babar is, in fact, a benign ruler, and he has created a sort of welfare state in the jungle. But this is not real. This is not what happened in history. It is telling a false story. It's giving a sugared, adulterated, beautiful version of something which was, in fact, bloody and exploitive. In fact, it was the worst barbarianism in the world—the destruction of all these cultures, the destruction of our natural resources, et cetera.

STAMBERG: But surely Jean de Brunhoff did not set out to tell the story of the impact of so-called civilization on the Third World. That's *your* interpretation.

DORFMAN: That was not his intention at all, I'm sure. He was probably a very kind man, and there's no doubt in my mind that he only wanted to tell the story of how a little elephant grows up. But in doing that, he used the colonizer's dreams of easy, trouble-free colonization.

STAMBERG: And your point is that for many children, this will be their earliest contact with a notion of Africa?

DORFMAN: Or a notion of what development is, what the poor countries are, and how they can get out of the situation they're in. The book teaches that the way for the dominated to *stop* being dominated is to be like Babar. It's basically *not* to rebel.

STAMBERG: What do you say to listeners who are thinking, "Boy, that's such a fancy theory! It's absurd! This is just a lovely story for children"?

DORFMAN: Well, they're defending their own innocence. They're defending their own childhood. They're defending their own children. They don't want to see that children can be politicized against their

Luckily, a very rich old lady who has always been fond of little elephants understands right away that he is longing for a fine suit. As she likes to make people happy, she gives him her purse. Babar says to her politely: "Thank you, Madam."

—from The Story of Babar

Cornelius, the oldest of all the elephants, spoke in his quavering voice: "My good friends, we are seeking a King, why not choose Babar? He has just returned from the big city, he has learned so much living among men, let us crown him King."

—from The Story of Babar

will. I would ask them to take another look at this book. Really, take another look at your whole world. Understand that there are hidden messages—not deliberate, not conspiratorial, but ingrained into what is happening. If there are hidden messages in advertisements, why can't there be hidden messages and political messages in children's literature?

Nyet Funny

July 1982

In Year Two of Ronald Reagan's America, there were certain clarities. Two superpowers: an Evil Empire; a Shining City on the Hill. The clarities would soon give way, but in 1982, no one could have predicted it.

It was Cold War time. The Soviets still had satellites, the Communist party still had muscle, the Old World Order prevailed. Three years would pass before Mikhail Gorbachev became head of the Soviet Union, bringing first the euphoria of change; later, the sobering recognitions.

Today's realities—the desperate economic situation and ethnic conflicts in so many of the former Soviet republics—have filmed over the old realities of political repression and tyranny that defined the U.S.S.R. in the Cold War period. The miseries of those years remain etched on the faces of citizens who endured the brutalities. And reminders crop up in all sorts of places—in plays and books, in conversations that now seem dated. The following, for instance. Dated, but daffy.

In 1982, comedian Yakov Smirnoff was making the rounds of the American comedy circuit. He'd emigrated from the Soviet Union five years earlier, and his act was an earthy mix of language faux pas, shrewd jabs at his homeland, and the wonder and confusion of a stranger in a new land.

(Comedy club, Smirnoff in performance:)
SMIRNOFF: It's nice to be here. It's nice to be in America, because you have all the freedoms, which is wonderful. You can go on the stage

Friends told us before we went to Moscow (and it was a good rule to follow): "Never introduce Russians who don't know each other to one another in your house." Because they'll be suspicious of each other, and wonder why you—a foreigner—invited them. One might think that the other was an agent. That's the type of atmosphere you're living in there.

—Jerrold Schecter, co-author, An American Family in Moscow, January 1976

and actually say anything you want to. You can go even to President Reagan and say, "I don't like Reagan."

We can do the same thing in Russia. We can go to Brezhnev and say, "I don't like Reagan."

(*Laughter.*)

Almost the same thing!

(*Comedy act fades to studio interview.*)

STAMBERG: Mr. Smirnoff, we don't tend to think of Soviets as very funny, because in all the pictures they're very grim-faced, never smiling. Is that wrong?

SMIRNOFF: No. The tension is there. That's what you see in the pictures. Tension, standing in line for bread or for milk or for butter—whatever the line is. Pressure is on in public transportation—everything. So people tend to tell jokes to each other just to release it. It's like in a funeral, people telling jokes sometimes.

STAMBERG: You had a pretty big career in Russia, performing all over the country. What made you decide to leave?

SMIRNOFF: I reached certain top of my career where I couldn't go any further, because they censor your material. You have to censor it twice for different agencies, and then you have to stay with the script. You can't go left or right, you have to stick to it. So, it got boring.

(*Again, Smirnoff in performance:*)

I like eat now the American food. It's a lot of food. You see, in Russia we don't have that much food. My mother used to put empty plate in front of me and say, "Starve, there are children eating in America."

(*Laughter.*)

In Russia, food stamps are stamps with pictures of food on it.

(*Laughter. Fade to studio interview.*)

STAMBERG: Can you remember a specific joke to which the censors said, "*Nyet*"?

SMIRNOFF: For example, there was some movies from East Germany, and I would just switch the name. Instead of *Red Horseman,* I would change it to *Red Comrade,* or something like that. And they would just go crazy.

STAMBERG: You're doing the same thing now when you talk about how American TV shows would play in the Soviet Union.

(*Again, Smirnoff in performance:*)

SMIRNOFF: Television is a little bit different, you know, because we

In Moscow, there seems to be a lot more trust than here. Like on the buses. It costs five cents to take the bus, and the metro, and all the public transportation. When you get on, you can either pay or not pay. There's a lot more trust that everybody *will* pay—you get in big trouble if you don't. Also, if you ask someone for a nickel, lots of times they'll give it to you. One time, I didn't have enough money, and I asked a lady if she could lend me some. She didn't know who I was, but she said, "Oh, well, to a Young Pioneer I lend it!"

**—Kate Schecter,
age 17,
January 1976**

have only two channels. First channel is propaganda, and the second channel there is a KGB officer who tells you turn back to Channel One.

(*Laughter.*)

Not much variety there. In Russia, I used to watch soap operas like *One Day to Live*, or *Last Days of Our Lives*. And game shows like *Bowling for Food*.

(*Laughter.*)

Shows like *Marx and Mindy*. *Love Barge*. Show about a guy who has an opportunity to leave Russia, but stays, called *That's Incredible!*

(*Fade out of act, back to studio.*)

STAMBERG: Are you limited here in any way by the fact that you are a Soviet, and you have an accent? Is that going to limit you to *Love Barge* jokes?

SMIRNOFF: I don't think so, no. I feel that it works for me, and I still can talk about anything I want. I just have my different point of view.

STAMBERG: You couldn't tell Henny Youngman jokes—"Take my wife . . . please."

SMIRNOFF: In Russia, I used to tell the joke, "Take my wife . . . please. And they did."

Craig Claiborne's Talk Soufflé

January 1982

Cranberries for remembrance. That's what I'll get. In my broadcast life I have labored to understand the difference between Sunni and Shiite Muslims, crammed to learn Senator X's voting record on abortion, and peered over maps to find Nagorno-Karabakh, all in an effort to enlighten (or at least inform) listeners. But that enormous effort will be as naught when the day of reckoning comes. On that day, only the single word "cranberries" will be heard. "Cranberries" is how I'll be remembered.

It's partly my fault, partly the fault of my late mother-in-law, and partly the fault of Craig Claiborne.

At the first Thanksgiving of my married life, in Allentown, Pennsylvania, my mother-in-law, Marjorie Stamberg, served a fabulous and fascinating cranberry relish. So fascinating that I asked for the recipe, which she kindly provided:

2 cups raw cranberries
1 small onion (that's the fascinating part)
½ cup sugar
¾ cup sour cream
2 tablespoons horseradish (that's the other fascinating part)
Procedure: Grind the cranberries and onion together. Add all the other ingredients and mix. Put in a plastic container and freeze. A few hours before serving, move the container from the freezer to

the refrigerator to thaw. The relish will be thick, creamy, chunky, and shocking pink. Makes 1½ pints.

I put the recipe for Mama Stamberg's Cranberry Relish on the air every year a few weeks before Thanksgiving, first at WAMU-FM, the local public radio station where I did my earliest air work, later at NPR for the immediate nation to enjoy. In the course of these one hundred and eight consecutive years in which I have offered this recipe for Mama Stamberg's Cranberry Relish, I have learned a number of things:

1. It wasn't her recipe. Her sister-in-law Marie Salinger gave it to her.
2. It wasn't Marie's recipe, either. Marie got it from Craig Claiborne.
3. Craig Claiborne didn't mind a bit. He said he'd gotten more mileage out of the recipe through NPR than he had since he first published it in *The New York Times* in 1959.
4. Listeners had distinct opinions on it. "Ychhh" was the concerted view of Emily, Robert, Herb, and Althea Glick. "Delicious," wrote Robin Atwood Fidler. Holly Gail Baumann called to say that she'd made it such a tradition that when she got divorced, her ex-husband asked for the recipe. On Thanksgiving Day, 1980, one listener passed a note card around the holiday table and collected these reactions from guests: "What a combination!" "Blah!" "It just wasn't very good." "You must be kidding!" "Disgusting."
5. I have extremely thick skin, and just kept on reciting the recipe every year.
6. A farmer's wife in Wisconsin puts up big batches of it, stuffs it into old honey jars, and sells it for two dollars a jar at the farmer's market in Madison on Saturday mornings. She calls it "Cranberry Horserad-ish Relish from the Land of Oo's." I know because I saw it there in 1991, when we were visiting Josh, his junior year. When I asked where she'd gotten the recipe, she said, "Oh, Susan Stanbur gives it on the radio every year." To which I replied, *"I'm Susan Stanbur!!!"* She was as thrilled as I was. I even bought a jar. Mine's better.

So the cranberries have become memorable. As has, for me, this 1982 encounter with their initiator, Craig Claiborne. In addition to mixing onions and horseradish with cranberries, in his thirty-one years as restaurant critic, food writer, and editor for *The New York Times,* this soft-spoken southern gentleman introduced America to other oddi-ties that we have also come to adore: quiche Lorraine, guacamole, bouillabaisse, pesto. He educated our palates, then whetted them.

I'll tell you precisely when it appeared be-cause I've got the original recipe in my files right here in my kitchen. It ap-peared on December first, 1959. The headline said, "Cranberries Are Availa-ble; Many Ways to Relish Them." In those days the federal government had contended that some of the cranberry crop had been contaminated by some sort of weed-killing agent. It was a false scare, not serious at all. What I was doing back on December first, when your mother-in-law's sis-ter-in-law got that recipe, was trying to tell the pub-lic cranberries were to-tally safe. Apparently she thought it was a great rec-ipe!

—Craig Claiborne, November 1983

In 1982, Mr. Claiborne had just written an autobiography containing a number of delights and one controversial, perhaps courageous, revelation. *A Feast Made for Laughter—A Memoir with Recipes* was filled with food and early memories of good southern cooking.

CLAIBORNE: My father lost everything by the year I was born. He'd been fairly wealthy, a well-off plantation owner. When he fell on hard times, my mother opened a rooming house, because that was the only thing that a highborn young southern belle could do and keep her chin up. I grew up in the kitchen there. She was a marvelous cook, and also I lived in that era when there were lots of black servants. They were my friends, and they were magnificent cooks. So at home I had a combination of southern cooking and soul food, Creole cooking, Cajun cooking. And my mother cooked out of *The Boston Cooking School Cook Book,* which was extremely sophisticated, that first edition. Fannie Farmer taught a lot of great French dishes—desserts, especially. They were fantastic. And my mother was a master of all these things.

STAMBERG: There's a feeling, still today, that there's something snobbish about fine food.

CLAIBORNE: I can only be reminded of a time I went down to Palm Beach, where the very rich, very fancy, very social types play. I turned to some woman and asked, "What do you really enjoy eating?" And she said, "We never discuss food in this community." I think it's some strange reverse form of snobbism when people say there's snobbery involved in good cooking today. I don't think it's at all true. We are the most educated people in the world where international cooking is concerned.

STAMBERG: And that's new?

CLAIBORNE: Of course it is! When I first joined *The New York Times* it was, oh, make another pot roast and open up a can of cream of mushroom soup or, you know, make a casserole out of tuna fish and potato chips. It was just—

STAMBERG: (*Laughs.*) You're turning your nose up! What is it that you simply won't eat? What else will make you turn up your nose?

CLAIBORNE: I don't like maraschino cherries.

(*Laughter.*)

And I don't like peanut-butter-and-grape-jelly sandwiches. I can't stand—

STAMBERG: What do you think is the secret of an English muffin?

CALVIN TRILLIN: Good crater man. You have to have the guy make the craters so that the stuff—like the butter and everything—soaks in there.

STAMBERG: Yes. See, now it's interesting you call them craters. For years I've heard them described as nooks and crannies.

TRILLIN: Crannies. That's the old name for them.

—November 1982

STAMBERG: Wait a minute! What about peanut butter on its own?

CLAIBORNE: The only way I like to eat peanut butter is when you turn it into a sauce like in an Indonesian *satay*.

STAMBERG: You have never snuck down into your kitchen—

CLAIBORNE: I have never . . . I hate—

STAMBERG: —at two in the morning and eaten a spoonful of peanut butter out of the jar?

CLAIBORNE: I hate peanut butter out of the jar! I hate marshmallows! I hate marzipan!

STAMBERG: (*Laughs. Then, quietly:*) In addition to your great and wonderful memories about food, your book is filled with a number of personal details which must have been extremely difficult for you to write about.

CLAIBORNE: (*Sighs.*) Right, they were.

STAMBERG: One is the acknowledgment of your homosexuality.

CLAIBORNE: Right.

STAMBERG: And another, an early encounter with your father—not child abuse, but a fascination with him, physically.

CLAIBORNE: Well, the reason I did that was not because of sensationalism, not to sell copies of my book, but I felt a really moral obligation. I think if you write an autobiography, you're obliged to tell the most motivating forces in your life, and that was by all odds the most monumental thing that happened to me in my childhood. I mean, sleeping with my father. Out of necessity. Economic necessity—because every bed in that house had to be filled. And I discovered him in the state of arousal and then it was like having this great gushing of adrenaline flowing all over my body. I was so *impassioned* with this feeling for him that I had never known before—because I had just reached the age of puberty—and I couldn't overcome it. And then he didn't . . . I don't . . . I think my poor, innocent father didn't know how to stop it. And I think he was aware of it. He pretended to be asleep. Anyway . . . but that . . . I had to bring that up because it was a thing that I think as much as anything made me who I am in one major way. But it was certainly not . . . did not *cause* me to be a homosexual.

STAMBERG: It's interesting that you choose to write it on the twentieth page of your book—that you explored his body, that the relationship was never consummated. It's also interesting that you can be so honest in talking about it. But I must tell you that a number of people

STAMBERG: The real reason I called was to get you to explain the difference between a nook and a cranny.

TRILLIN: You know, I've had a little trouble with nooks and crannies for a long time. Ever since a friend of mine who was working for *Time* magazine was sent to Alaska for stories, and he wired back that he couldn't find any, even though he had looked in every Nanook and cranny. Now, I know the difference *there*. Between Nanook and cranny. But between nook and cranny, that would be hard. That's one reason they're called craters now, 'cause of the confusion.

—*November 1982*

who admire your work enormously read this and got into long conversations—"Why does he have to tell us that?"

CLAIBORNE: Don't you think it's important? And also, there's a certain streak of altruism in me, and I mean that wholeheartedly. It's something I wish I had done ten years ago. Because if you are some sort of role model, perhaps you can help one kid who is gay to understand that he's not an evil person, or to feel excessive guilt.

I was born with these genes. And I know full well that there's nothing I could do to alter the situation in my life. So I lived with it all these years. I lived with excessive guilt too long. I've never tried to hide this fact. I've never come out and been blatant about it. On the other hand, I've never been ashamed of it. And I think I've been respected because of it.

STAMBERG: You just observed your sixty-second birthday. And you write something that I found very telling. You say you wish to be cremated.

CLAIBORNE: I do.

STAMBERG: And you're thinking about the possibility of your ashes being strewn over the oceans. Why?

CLAIBORNE: Because I have enjoyed eating so much fish in my life, and I thought I'd pay the fish back.

(*Laughter*.)

I'll tell you a funny story about that. I come from a long line of Methodists, and I went to a kinfolks' meeting which has been going on for a hundred and fifty years. When I went down, this book had just come out, and I was afraid I was going to shock a lot of people, a lot of my kinfolks. But after I got back I got a letter from the matriarch of the family. And she said, "Craig, I just read your book again, and I'm absolutely horrified at one thing." Well, I thought she was going to say something about what we've been talking about. But she said, "I'm horrified that you're going to be cremated. You have got to come down here and be buried right between your great-grandmother and great-grandfather!"

Barney Clark and Our Hearts

December 1982

This conversation began with science and, most unexpectedly, ended up being about the meaning of life, and about risk, and about bridges built between strangers.

On March 23, 1983, Barney B. Clark died at the age of sixty-two. A retired dentist from the Seattle area, Dr. Clark became known throughout the world in the last sixteen weeks of his life as the recipient of the first permanent artificial heart— a device that kept him alive for 112 days. Barney Clark had been on the verge of death before the seven-and-a-half-hour implant procedure, performed in early December 1982 at the University of Utah Medical Center by a team headed by Dr. William C. DeVries. The polyurethane artificial heart, designed by Dr. Robert K. Jarvik, beat 116 times a minute for most of the remaining minutes of Barney Clark's life.

There was one problem after another in those 112 days: convulsions, pneumonia, air leaks that needed to be closed, the entire left side of the device needing to be replaced. Dr. Clark suffered repeated spells of confusion. But in the month before he died, he was able to pedal a stationary bicycle for minutes at a time. Eventually, though, despite the mechanical heart's continued functioning, the rest of Barney Clark's body failed to keep up. The official cause of death was "circulatory collapse due to multi-organ system failure." After having beaten almost thirteen million times, the heart was turned off. Barney Clark died quietly.

No one expected Dr. Clark to walk out of the hospital a new man.

Physicians knew he was destined to spend the remainder of his life—however long it might last—hitched to hoses and the air compressor that powered the Jarvik-7 heart. This was frontier medicine, and Barney Clark was called its Columbus.

The experimental operation that placed the artificial heart in Barney Clark's body raised moral and ethical issues as well as medical ones. Two weeks after the procedure, Dr. Chase Peterson, the University of Utah's vice president for health sciences, explored some of those issues on *All Things Considered*. Barney Clark had undergone three additional surgeries by the time we spoke.

PETERSON: Minutes before the third operation, Clark's wife showed him bundles of letters pouring in from well-wishers around the world. It's a very isolating thing to go in to be a dependent patient in a surgical intensive-care unit. And it was nice for him to be aware of people who wished him well, even though they are strangers.

STAMBERG: And yet a very peculiar and subtle thing is happening. I find it happening in myself. As each day I come to know more about his medical condition and a bit about his personal life, I feel some sort of connection. Yet I know that if the day comes when he dies, I will say to myself, "Of course, it was inevitable. It was lucky that he lived this long." That's a peculiar set of feelings to have towards a perfect stranger!

PETERSON: That's right. But, you see, maybe that's why it's a story. I mean, it's Christmastime, we're looking for things in this world that are somewhat upbeat, and I guess we're looking for connections. You're describing the creation of some kind of connection, and I think that does have spiritual overtones as well as proper medical, professional, overtones. I think that's all right!

STAMBERG: But, you know, Dr. Peterson, I'm saying something a little different and I don't quite understand it myself—which is why I'm having a hard time explaining it to you. (*Pause.*) I think that the connection is as artificial as the new heart he has.

PETERSON: (*Laughs.*)

STAMBERG: And that if he dies—

PETERSON: It will sort of dismiss the whole thing?

STAMBERG: Possibly.

PETERSON: Yeah.

STAMBERG: In a way, that dehumanizes him.

STAMBERG: Kurt Vonnegut, fifteen years ago you foretold the emergence of artificial-human-organ implants in your play *Fortitude*. You said the play was a tragedy.

VONNEGUT: It is about a very wealthy woman being kept alive by her doctor. He's in love with her and continues to replace her organs as they fail. He not only holds a medical degree, but one in mechanical engineering and one in electrical engineering. She is simply, now, just a head on a sort of tripod. There's a big engine room down below which keeps her operating. A hairdresser comes in and combs the lady's hair twice a week. One time, she had a crying jag. It was simply a bad transistor in the control panel. (*Laughs.*)

STAMBERG: (*not laughing*) Good heavens!

—*January 1984*

PETERSON: Well, you and I won't know for sure what we're thinking for a long time. It'll take some sorting out. But I would propose that your attachment to him is more than artificial. Read Genesis again. Read the first chapters of Genesis. If you believe it metaphorically—or actually—it doesn't matter. A decision appeared to have been made by Adam and Eve to take on life, and to take it on with all its unpredictability. What they discarded was perennial comfort and ease in the Garden of Eden.

Now, Barney Clark had the immediate option to choose an honorable death without pain. His heart was going to stop—in fact, it did stop within minutes of surgery. But he—like Adam and Eve, I guess—actually chose the arduous and the unpredictable. And I think that's one reason that you're attached to him. That's the brave, mortal decision. And in some strange fashion, he made it not only fifteen days ago, but he made it again *two* days ago. I find that heartening.

STAMBERG: Are you aware, Dr. Peterson, of an editorial in *The New York Times* today? The headline is "Prolonging Death Is No Triumph."

PETERSON: I haven't seen that.

STAMBERG: Let me read you one passage from it. I'd love to hear your response to this: "Can all that pain and exertion be worthwhile? The purpose of medicine is to improve life's quality, not to make Methuselahs of us all. To prolong life beyond its natural span is no favor unless reasonable quality is also provided. Without it, the physician has succeeded only in prolonging death."

PETERSON: That's an entirely appropriate point of view, and that's the question that we're addressing. I would only differ if the editorial presumes to have an answer to the question, when *we* still say we're in the process of experiment. And if our studies on this man, and any others we do, would indicate that we are prolonging death—not preserving life—then I would agree with that conclusion. Of course you don't want to prolong agony.

If, on the other hand, our experiment—and that's exactly what it is, an experiment that Dr. Clark and Dr. DeVries and all of us are in *together*—if that experiment proves that we can prolong good life and let someone see a grandchild they haven't seen, and take care of their estate matters, and read some books they haven't read, and write a book they haven't written—all of which are well within Dr. Clark's

VONNEGUT: She gets the idea from the hairdresser that she doesn't want to live anymore.

STAMBERG: And what does she do about it?

VONNEGUT: Well, they have her fixed. She has no arms or legs anymore. So she's equipped with these very clever claws. She can, in fact, knit with them. But the arms are designed so that there is no way she can ever get poison to her mouth, or point a pistol or a knife at herself.

—*January 1984*

VONNEGUT: She tries to shoot herself and can't. So she shoots the doctor instead.

STAMBERG: (Gasps.)

VONNEGUT: (Laughs.)

STAMBERG: See, now you're laughing! I asked you if it was a comedy or a tragedy, and you told me it was a tragedy. It's awful, isn't it? And yet it's funny.

VONNEGUT: After the doctor is shot through several vital organs, his assistant takes his head and hitches him up to the same apparatus the woman is using. So he's on the tripod next to her, hooked up to the same circulatory system and kidney and pancreas and all that. And there they are. The closing piece of music when the curtain comes down is "Ah, Sweet Mystery of Life," sung by Nelson Eddy and Jeanette Mac-Donald.

STAMBERG: (Laughs at last.)

—January 1984

capacity, theoretically, if he recovers—then the answer to that editorial is, this process has prolonged goodness.

This is true of almost every experiment that has ever occurred. Artificial hips, when they were first put in, were all infected. People were worse for having the hip put in than if they hadn't. But then the techniques were developed, and hip replacement became successful. Other procedures have been developed and perfected. They used to freeze people's stomachs to cure intractable ulcers. That was a miserable thing to go through. But if it had succeeded, it might have saved cutting stomachs out. It didn't succeed. It turned out to be worthless, so it was abandoned.

This process of the artificial heart may be abandoned after a reasonable experimental trial, or it may succeed. But the development of an idea is the critical thing. We only have to be sure that no one is taken advantage of in the process—to be sure that the patient is fully aware of the hazards when he chooses to experiment with us.

———

After Dr. Barney Clark's implant, and his death, some 150 others received Jarvik-7 artificial hearts. In most cases the plastic heart was used as a temporary device, to keep patients alive while they waited for heart transplants. Attempts to use it as a permanent replacement failed. In 1991, the U.S. Food and Drug Administration banned the Jarvik-7 because of the many complications associated with it. But as a result of the Barney Clark experiment, it is now common practice to use other types of artificial hearts for patients awaiting heart transplants. Meantime, there is continuing debate on the cost of such technology, which benefits only a small number of people.

The eloquent Chase Peterson went on to become president of the University of Utah. He resigned in the summer of 1991 after championing, without question, university experiments with cold fusion—the attempt to derive nuclear energy from a test tube. When physicists in other laboratories dismissed cold fusion as fantasy, Dr. Peterson stepped down. He continues at the university, though, teaching medicine now.

All this is the aftermath of the Barney Clark experiment. But what also remains is the memory of a profound watch, kept around the globe for 112 days, for a man few of us knew except through his willingness to be first.

Radio Lady

June 1983

We women in broadcast news with some age on us don't have many role models. The media—radio and television—are young, and women's access to them even younger. There was Pauline Frederick at the United Nations, a pioneer reporter in the 1940s, who inspired NPR's Linda Wertheimer. Linda remembers being a kid in Carlsbad, New Mexico, in 1956, watching Pauline filing from the U.N. as Soviet troops crushed the revolt in Hungary, and thinking, "Look! A woman can do news!" (In the decade before she died, Pauline reported for NPR. Linda and I got to work with this legend.) In the 1960s there was Nancy Dickerson, the first female news correspondent at CBS (later, she went to NBC) and the first woman (in 1960) to report from the floor of a political convention. Beginning in the mid-sixties, albeit outside formal journalistic circles, Barbara Walters opened doors for all of us. And that was about it—on the national level, at least. The next phase was ours.

In the 1970s, as women entered the work force in record numbers, so, too, did we enter newsrooms. And I believe our presence makes a difference there. We influence the way stories are chosen and told. My lobbying, beginning in the early seventies, got and kept child, family, and other so-called women's issues on NPR's nightly news. In the early eighties, staff women pressed for reports on the gender gap, child care, and the sexual abuse of children. In 1984, when the third in a series of abortion-clinic bombings took place, a male editor spoke against coverage.

"We've already done it," Marc Rosenbaum said. "We covered the

Helen Chinoy, a professor of theatre at Smith College, is developing a whole theory about the fragmentation in women's work—ten minutes dropping off the kids, ten minutes making the beds, ten minutes picking up the groceries. Women's lives are chopped up into small slices, and that tends to get reflected in the work. We think that the scenes women write tend to be shorter. Women tend to write in a more circular fashion. We tend to share out the dialogue on stage much more generously, so that you can't always clearly see a protagonist and an antagonist according to Aristotelian terms. Rather than building to a *climax*—women playwrights tend to have smaller climaxes and many of them, and tend to come full circle at the end.

—Kathleen Betsko,
International Women
Playwrights
Conference,
October 1988

first two bombings," I answered. "Now there's a third. Why isn't the FBI stepping in to investigate? Isn't this domestic terrorism?" I posed those questions on the air that evening.

Twice, Nina Totenberg broke Supreme Court stories that I believe it took a woman to get. People who'd seen Douglas Ginsburg use marijuana socially and were upset by his indiscretion expressed their reactions in 1987 to Totenberg, a woman who asked the right questions and listened (in her careful, predatory way) to the answers. When the story came out, Ginsburg's chances for a seat on the Court went up in smoke. In 1991, Anita Hill went on the record for Totenberg with charges of sexual harassment by Clarence Thomas. The Oklahoma law professor gave a detail-laden interview to Nina, not to the male *Newsday* reporter who also had information about Hill's affidavit to the Senate Judiciary Committee.

Women have put issues of sexual harassment, rape, and abuse onto the agendas of news organizations. Men at NPR editorial meetings spoke against daily coverage of the Mike Tyson and William Kennedy Smith rape trials. "Circuses!" they scoffed. Women wanted coverage. "The men saw the trials as too tabloidy for us," Deborah George, an editor on the national desk, remembers. "To them it was just another crime story. But we said the trials raised serious legal questions affecting women."

Stories about women's health get on our air because women suggest them. On weekend *All Things Considered,* Lynn Neary's series on breast cancer was a primer on the sorry state of research. For *Weekend Edition*/Saturday, producer Laura Ziegler and I went to a Washington, D.C., jail to report on AIDS education for female inmates.

Women have certain attributes that are an advantage in telling the news. By gender, we have a greater capacity for listening, so our sources may talk to us more openly. We care more about relationships, so the atmosphere in the offices we run, or the offices where we work, can be more humane. We are nurturers. Katharine Ferguson, my producer on *Weekend Edition*/Sunday, regularly brought in flowers from her garden and put them on our conference table. It made our editorial meetings better, having something lovely to look at. (Women have no franchise on flowers, of course. Kitty's husband, Glenn, is actually the family gardener. And Noah Adams is the original NPR flower bringer. He'll leave small bouquets on desks where tense work is being done, or stick daffodils into a Styrofoam cup and carry it into the studio on days when news is breaking too quickly.)

Women have a greater ability to organize. (Again, not *always*. My husband, Lou, is enormously methodical.) Women are list makers and anticipators. And women teach the courses in organization.

We women have less confidence, and strangely, that works to our advantage in the newsroom. We check our facts more carefully and more frequently, to make sure we've got the story right.

We make fewer statements and ask more questions. Which means we get more answers. We make more use of the word "perhaps," and we're more gray than black-and-white. We see nuances where men see absolutes. So our reporting can be more subtle. More *frustrating*, surely—because absolutes are so much easier—but, perhaps(!), ultimately more accurate.

Before we haul out the halo polish, rest assured there's a fair share of inflexible women and nice guys, too—at NPR and elsewhere. But in these past few years, it's the women who have been breaking ground in broadcasting. Still not *enough* ground—never enough—but pioneer work is under way.

The real ground-breaker for us all—we microphone-wielding females—was an Englishwoman named Sheila Stewart. I interviewed her on *All Things Considered* in June 1983—the same month and year that another "first woman" was making news. Astronaut Sally Ride boarded the space shuttle *Challenger* that June and became American woman No. 1 in space. (Her first utterance to Mission Control from orbit: "Have you ever been to Disneyland? This is definitely an 'E' ticket." Flat! She should have said, "Come up and see me sometime.") Ride's ride was exciting, but for me the *real* "E" ticket was speaking with Sheila Stewart on the occasion of her first half-century in broadcasting.

(*Crackly old tape: Sound of Big Ben chiming.*)

STAMBERG: At the British Broadcasting Corporation, some traditions take a long time to die. Like the role of women on the air.

FEMALE ANNOUNCER: We are interrupting our program to bring you a news flash.

(*Bells ringing.*)

MALE ANNOUNCER: This is London calling. Here is a news flash:

The German radio has just announced that Hitler is dead. I repeat that: The German radio has just announced that Hitler is dead.

FEMALE ANNOUNCER: May I remind you that the next news broadcast in this General Overseas Service will be for listeners overseas at 22:45 Greenwich mean time.

(Music, as regular BBC programming continues. Fade.)

STAMBERG: Sheila Stewart was the woman who had that modest supporting role on the BBC news in 1945. And although it doesn't seem like very much today, it was a long way from 1933, the year Miss Stewart was hired as the BBC's very first female announcer/commentator.

STEWART: The BBC were taking no chances with me. I had a simple program of light music from a studio—fairly easy to do.

STAMBERG: When you spoke your first words, did your voice quaver a bit?

STEWART: I'm sure it did! I'm sure it did!

STAMBERG: You're very pleasant to listen to; your voice is rather low. Did you feel that was an advantage?

STEWART: I'm perfectly certain that's why I got the job, yes. Because all those years ago, the technique of broadcasting voices was much less sophisticated than it is now. The upper register of women's voices was very irritating and tinny-sounding on the air. So I'm sure this great foghorn of a voice had something to do with it, yes!

STAMBERG: How is it, though, that it took the BBC until 1933 to permit a woman to do such a job?

STEWART: Because nobody *else* in the world had! It wasn't just England, you see, it was the world!

STAMBERG: Was there any kind of opposition to you, as a woman, doing this work?

STEWART: Oh, yes, a lot! In particular from the women of England, who really didn't like the news given them by another woman.

STAMBERG: The women objected more than the men?

STEWART: Yes, much, *much* more, I hate to say.

STAMBERG: What were their grounds for objecting?

STEWART: They just said, "We don't want to hear the news from a woman." No one who wrote had anything to say about my voice; it was just that a woman should not give the news.

STAMBERG: Before the war, what was it like at the BBC? Is it true that announcers in those days had to dress up in evening clothes before they went in front of the microphone?

STEWART: Oh, yes. Dinner jackets for the men. I had to wear a long dress. And we changed clothes at six o'clock in the evening—while the six o'clock news was being broadcast. The six o'clock news broadcaster was allowed to change *after* the news. (*Laughs.*) This was whether we were going to be in the studio all evening, or out announcing at a concert.

STAMBERG: It didn't matter, you had to be properly attired?

STEWART: Nope. Certainly!

STAMBERG: Did that ever strike you as absurd?

STEWART: Oh, yes! It struck us as absurd even then. It took a war to stop that!

   (*Laughter.*)

STAMBERG: Did you have to pay for your own evening clothes?

STEWART: Oh, certainly, yes. And I was told very firmly that it must be very *discreet*. I don't know whether they pictured me coming in gold, naked to the navel, or what, but they said it must be very discreet!

——

Sheila Stewart spent twenty years at the BBC, and was part of the NPR family from 1970 until she died. Ms. Stewart had a music program on member station WUSF in Tampa, Florida. In January 1986, the day before her last scheduled radio program, she had a heart attack, and she died three months later.

Her story about negative audience reaction in 1933 reminds me of a story about myself, one I wasn't told until some twelve years after the fact. Bill Siemering, the first program director of NPR and the man who, along with producer Jack Mitchell, made the decision that I should host *All Things Considered,* told me that just after I went on the air as the first woman to anchor a nightly national news program, there was quite a bit of opposition, primarily from NPR station managers.

"A woman can't do news," they said. "People won't take her seriously." "Not authoritative enough." "Voice won't carry well."

Those were pre-satellite days, and the quality of our sound wasn't nearly as good as it is today, so voice carriage may have been a slight issue. Otherwise, the objections were simply grounded in history, prece-

> What I find appalling is that we women have to overcome a lot of fear and be just as courageous, if not more courageous, than the men covering Beirut. And we often find that instead of being received with praise and admiration, we are hit by resentment from male journalists and accused of enjoying violence or not getting enough of it. I have worked in a place where I've seen men correspondents break down and cry. When I felt like doing the same, I never dared do it in public. If *they* break down and cry, they're *sensitive.* I'm hysterical.
>
> —reporter Nora Boustany, Beirut, February 1987

dent, and, probably, prejudice. As far as I know, listeners weren't complaining. It was the station managers, *worried* about their listeners.

Bill Siemering dealt with the resistance and kept me on the air. And that he never told me about the objections until I'd been in the job for about twelve years was, to me, a mark of his leadership skills. He had confidence in me and felt that if I just kept on broadcasting, the "oddness" of a woman's voice (in those long-gone and much-lamented cigarette days, mine was a foghorn, just like Sheila Stewart's) would pass and the managers would relax. He also knew that if he told me any of this, it would upset me and affect my work. So Mr. Siemering—a tall, skinny, plainspoken visionary who's as close to Plato's Philosopher King as anyone I'll ever meet—just kept the criticisms to himself and gave me airspace in which to grow. Today, NPR is known for the number and strength of its female reporters and anchors, as well as for the off-air women who play vital roles as executive producers, producers, editors, and engineers. Just as we were pioneers in putting a woman behind the anchor mike, so we continue to be unusual in the number of high-ranking women in our newsroom. Studies of the three major television networks find only one in every six news items being reported by women. Blacks, Asians, and Latinos are far worse off. White males rule television news screens and offices. Even if they were all Bill Siemerings (and they decidedly *are not*!), that's too many of the same kinds of cooks stirring the broth.

Her Friend Picasso

May 1983

People who think a picture is worth a thousand words suffer from imagination deprivation. I'd trade a thousand pictures for the right grouping of words. Except, sometimes, when I'm reporting on the visual arts.

Seeing on radio. Getting listeners to see along with you when words are the only light. If the story involves a very familiar painting—the "Mona Lisa," say—the audience already has a mental image. But if it's something *un*familiar, you have to describe it, and not eat up all your airtime with ". . . and in the upper left-hand corner, about two inches from the top of the frame . . ." The description has to be like haiku—quick verbal jots that fill in just enough for visualization.

Biography is a major solution to the problem of covering the visual arts. If you think the work is hard to talk about, try talking about the artist. What was her life? What was his philosophy?

People like Rosamond Bernier help. In post–World War II Paris, she knew *everyone*—Picasso, Matisse, Miró, Braque. She worked for *Vogue* and, with her husband, founded the French art magazine *L'Oeil*. Her lectures at New York's Metropolitan Museum of Art, studded with slides and sharp perceptions, have been standing-room-only affairs for decades.

When we met in 1983, I wanted to hear about Picasso. Like Ernest Hemingway, Picasso was a giant I kept trying to know through the people who had known him—a kind of rolling-snowball approach to art: Keep asking, keep accumulating information. So over the years I

STAMBERG: Jack Fruin, the Museum of Modern Art has called you in to help with this massive Picasso exhibit—the biggest ever—that will open in May. You are a pedestrian-traffic engineer at New York Port Authority Bus Terminal, and they wanted your recommendations for an indoor traffic flow plan. What did you tell them?

FRUIN: We made some assumptions about average observation time. Ten seconds per painting.

STAMBERG: *Ten seconds?!!*

FRUIN: Yes. That's a fairly long time.

—*February 1980*

gathered details about Picasso from his daughter Paloma, her mother/ his mistress, Françoise Gilot, and—my earliest source—Rosamond Bernier.

STAMBERG: So, Mr. Fruin. The Picasso exhibit opened yesterday. Did you spend *more* than ten seconds in front of certain pictures?

JACK FRUIN: Oh, most assuredly! In some rooms, I actually sat down and looked at a painting for a minute. There *is* room for people to spend time with things they like.

STAMBERG: But if you spend more than ten seconds, wouldn't you be lousing up your own terrifically plotted traffic patterns?

FRUIN: No, it seems to work out. It's just that with the diversity of this artist, everyone seems to find something different to like.

STAMBERG: Isn't that wonderful! Picasso himself has solved the traffic problems!

FRUIN: I think so. If it were another artist, there might be a problem!

—May 1980

STAMBERG: One of my favorite images of Picasso comes from a David Douglas Duncan photograph. It's lunchtime, they're eating fish. Anyone else would scrape the fish off the bone, then toss the bone into the garbage. Not Picasso. He saves the bone and finds a flat slab of clay. Then he presses the skeleton into the clay, makes a fossil, creates art.

BERNIER: Well, that is typical! When we were in the flea market at Cannes, I saw him buy a pizza, which was served on a paper plate. When he'd finished the pizza, he took a flower that somebody had, rubbed the flower into the paper plate, and made a drawing with its juices. It was a sense of fun *and* an absolute compulsion to turn one thing into something else.

STAMBERG: That idea that art could be anywhere—that's so extraordinary with him, isn't it?

BERNIER: You felt it all the time, that anything he looked at . . . in fact, being with him, things became something else as *you* looked at them.

STAMBERG: He must have felt all the time the way we feel a few times in the very first moments of being in love—when all the world looks possible—

BERNIER: Yes, yes!

STAMBERG: —and everything is available.

BERNIER: High elation!

STAMBERG: It must have been like that for him most of the time.

BERNIER: Well, I would say *some* of the time. Being Spanish, he had a very black side, too—deep depression and fury. I think this stemmed from dissatisfaction with himself, when he felt the work wasn't going the way it should go. At those times, nobody could go and see him. It didn't matter if you had an appointment or if you had come especially from Zanzibar. The door was closed. So there was the reverse of the coin, you see. The tremendous life-flowing force, and then the negation of it.

He didn't want to hear about death, for instance. He died without leaving a will. And he never wanted to hear about illness. As he lived to be over ninety, most of his friends had died, and this was terrible for him. He told me once, toward the end of his life, that he used to say the names of his old surviving friends over and over to himself every day, and if he forgot one, he was afraid they would die.

STAMBERG: Was Matisse a complete contrast?

BERNIER: Complete, in that he was quintessentially French! That is to say, rational, reasonable, logical, persevering—

STAMBERG: You're describing a *banker*! Dull and plodding.

BERNIER: Well, he had that methodical aspect. And to me he seemed measured and controlled. Yet he told me that he had spent an entire life in the haste to bring order to his naturally chaotic nature. So inside was all the turmoil and all the tension, all the passion and tremendous self-centeredness which it seems to me any great artist has. He said to me jokingly—but it wasn't really a joke—"I'm a monster. My family—*nothing*—counts, compared to my work."

STAMBERG: As you look around today, in the eighties, in this country, do you have some sense of what our visual style is?

BERNIER: It's very eclectic. An enormous amount of people are working, and the atmosphere is electric with excitement. Artists who grew up in the television age are very aware of a rapid succession of images. They are aware of the speed with which our eye is now trained to take in images. And I think that affects them.

Don't forget, we are bombarded with images all the time. Fast-moving. It's not the quiet contemplation of the small jewel-like work anymore. Many of the works made today are enormous. They really come forward and grab you! I think that has to do with the television age. Many, many, many artists come right out and say, *Look at me!!*

───

In the slower days of the 1940s, Pablo Picasso's mistress watched him create a portrait of her. Matisse was involved, too. Françoise Gilot's description lies ahead, in 1991.

> "We must talk to each other as much as we can," Matisse told Pablo one day. "When one of us dies, there will be some things the other will never be able to talk of with anyone else."
>
> —Françoise Gilot, Life with Picasso

Learning to Write

July 1983

Why should we all use our creative power and write or paint or play music? Because there's nothing that makes people so generous, joyful, lively, bold and compassionate, so indifferent to fighting and the accumulation of objects and money. Because the best way to know the truth or beauty is to try to express it. And what is the purpose of existence here or yonder, but to discover truth and beauty and express it? That is to say, share it with others.

And so I really believe this book will hasten the millennium by two or three hundred years. And if it has given you the impulse to write one small story, then I am pleased.

—from **If You Want to Write**

This is one of the most popular interviews we ever ran. Brenda Ueland—ninety-two when we spoke in 1983—was vital and true, with a voice as sharp as dried pine needles and an endearing habit of tacking "Yeah!" in hearty self-agreement, onto the end of her sentences. She gave wonderful advice to writers.

In 1933, Carl Sandburg said that Brenda Ueland had produced the best book ever written about how to write. Sixty years later, that book—*If You Want to Write*—seems as clear and useful as ever. "Everybody is talented, original, and has something important to say," Ueland wrote, and then went on to prove that in her case, anyway, it was certainly true.

If You Want to Write (the subtitle is "Thoughts About Art, Independence, and Spirit") grew out of a class Ueland was teaching at the YWCA in Minnesota. In the thirties, she split her time between Minneapolis and Manhattan, where she said she was "the Queen of Greenwich Village." Her life, served up in a 1939 autobiography, *Me,* was like a zesty novel. A bohemian when the term was first applied to artsy Village types, she hung around with writers Willa Cather, Robert Penn Warren, and John Reed, the poet-adventurer who helped form the Communist party in the United States. She told her step-grandson Eric Utne (publisher of *Utne Reader*) that Warren Beatty had asked her to appear in *Reds,* his film about Reed, but that she had refused. She hadn't really liked John Reed, Ueland said. He'd tried to seduce her, but she wouldn't have an affair with "a man who ate with his fingers and dressed like he did." Still, she'd had three husbands and boasted of having had a hundred lovers. "But never a love affair with a married man, unless he brought a note from his wife saying it was okay."

"I know one thing for certain," Brenda Ueland declared in her ninety-second year. "I am not a bore."

UELAND: A diary, if it's kept in a headlong, unself-conscious way, often tells you what you're really thinking. You go to the point much quicker and more vividly. Most people write "writing," which is very tiresome. But if they keep a diary, they learn to write what they think. And it's very good for them.

STAMBERG: I like what you say about keeping a diary: "Write a true, careless, slovenly, impulsive, honest diary every day of your life."

UELAND: Yeah. Well, you sit down, you write what interests you. Maybe you're interested in your stomach ache. Well, write about it! But don't be pretentious or think you're a writer. Yeah!

STAMBERG: You keep telling people to write about what they know, what they can see, and what they feel. You also tell them not to be afraid to write something bad or too mawkish. What is your advice to writers if they write a bad story?

UELAND: At first, the streams that come when you're writing are very imitative and muddy. But you must have the courage to write terribly boring and dull things. And the streams get purer and livelier. Better things come later. Don't hurry, take it easy.

Write vituperative rage—maybe about your best friend. You read it again and you think, "Well, I don't really believe that." In other words, if you're not afraid of your own thoughts, there isn't this continual fakery and self-delusion. You get to know who you are, and you get to know what your honorable and talented self is, instead of your cliché self. Most people write simply a string of clichés that everybody in the world is saying all the time.

STAMBERG: Many people read over their writing too quickly, get discouraged, and want to tear it up. You say if you write a bad story, the way to make it better is to write three more.

UELAND: That's good! Very good advice. Yeah!

STAMBERG: I think so, too.

UELAND: That's absolutely good advice!! There are people, very talented people, who will write maybe one teeny little poem a year, or one in ten years. That's the end! Write a sonnet every day! If you're going to be grim about it and pretend you're Shakespeare, you won't do it.

STAMBERG: When you sat down to write a book, would you plan it ahead before you wrote it?

UELAND: No, I think planning is the end of all impulse, inspiration, vision, genius. Be impulsive!!

———

Brenda Ueland's hometown paper, *The Minneapolis Star and Tribune*, described her as a kind of "electrical storm of aphorisms and exclamation points." By the time she died, at the age of ninety-three, she had published some six million words, been knighted by the king of Norway, and set an international swimming record for over-eighty-year-olds.

Brenda Ueland was, indeed, not a bore.

If You Want to Write has been republished by Graywolf Press in St. Paul.

I don't think anything's ever wasted. Neither do I think it hurts you to read trash. I grew up reading things like *Bobby Brown and His Sister Sue* at *Camp Rest-a-While*. That didn't do me any harm! I also read good things. I read everything. But I think just to feel the word entering into your soul kindles something.

—*Eudora Welty,*
May 1983

Edward Kleban and
A Chorus Line

September 1983

Whatever I write here about Ed Kleban, it won't be good enough. Even if John Updike sat at this computer, it wouldn't be good enough. Or Neil Simon, or Lorenz Hart. Well, Hart might come close. Ed was a lyricist, too. Brilliant. Witty. Hart just might come close. But not-good-enough is how it always was with Ed. He made constant demands (on others, and even more on himself) that it be better, and better, and better.

Ed wrote a song called "Better." One section:

I've been good. I've been bad.
Bad is better.
Need's okay. Having just had is better.
I've been fire. I've been ice.
I've been naughty. I've been nice.
I've been naughty once or twice.
Twice is better.

After Kleban died, Marvin Hamlisch spoke about Ed's perpetual push toward betterment. Hamlisch wrote the music to Ed's lyrics for *A Chorus Line*. "What he taught me was that finally, you have to hold on to trying to do your best. If I'm sitting at the piano with another lyricist, that lyricist is going to let me get away with murder because I am who I am. Who but Ed Kleban would say, 'You can do better. Go back and write it again!'"

I sit down to write a lyric, and when I get up I'm usually about three pounds lighter.

**—Alan Jay Lerner,
March 1979**

193

Ed's intolerance for the ordinary defined his talent. It also showed, quirkily, idiosyncratically, in an interview I did with him in 1983.

In journalism, you're not supposed to interview friends. But it happens, sometimes, that friends make news. Old friends—people you grew up with—accomplish something worthy of reporting. So you report it, often with more care than usual—the bias alert working overtime to keep you in line.

In 1983, *A Chorus Line* became the longest-running musical in Broadway history. (Of course, the show had been making news from the very beginning, when it opened Off Broadway in 1975.) And Ed Kleban, *A Chorus Line*'s lyricist, who almost never gave interviews, was one of my oldest friends.

Essentially, we grew up together, or at least saw each other through some of the most important growing-up years. We met at New York's High School of Music and Art as kids, went to college—Barnard and Columbia—together, and had a long, intense relationship. At his funeral service (he died of cancer in 1987 at the infuriatingly early age of forty-eight), I said he was the most interesting man I'd ever met.

Edward Lawrence Kleban was the first person I knew who subscribed to *The New Yorker*. At the age of sixteen. *And* he actually *read* it! Red-headed and clever, he was also quite prickly. He had *lots* of long, intense relationships—friends he stopped speaking to, as well as friends he encouraged and helped.

In high school and college, he was a fine jazz musician. He would play the Steck baby grand in my family's living room for hours. His chord changes are scrawled all over my sheet music. Ed sang, too, sometimes, in his terrifically earnest piano player's voice, scratched low by two packs a day of unfiltered Camels.

In one of those years at the piano I heard the score to *A Chorus Line* before I ever saw the show. And I heard many stories of how the musical was created.

He told me how he'd fooled around with lyrics to various songs, was dissatisfied with everything, and then wrote the refrain for "At the Ballet": *Up a steep and very narrow stairway / To the voice like a metronome . . .*

"Once I wrote that," Ed Kleban said, "I knew it would be all right."

When *A Chorus Line* reached its long-run milestone, I put Ed on *All Things Considered,* which in itself was a milestone. He was aggres-

May 21, 1974
Michael wants me to call Ed Kleban. He's already picked him to do the lyrics for the show. Michael has heard some of his stuff and says he's the next Sondheim.

—Marvin Hamlisch,
The Way I Was

sively shy of publicity. "Marvin's the performer, not me," he said. "Hamlisch does the talk shows."

But after some urging, he agreed to speak with me, as usual, at the piano, where he thumped out some *Chorus Line* chords.

> *One singular sensation, ev'ry little step she takes.*
> *One thrilling combination, ev'ry move that she makes . . .*
> *(Fade and hold under briefly, then out.)*

STAMBERG: Edward Kleban, of all the words you wrote for *A Chorus Line,* are these lyrics—from the show's signature song—your favorite?

KLEBAN: Oh, no. Not at all, no. They were the hardest in a way, the lyrics to "One," because they had to say nothing and everything at the same time.

STAMBERG: "One" and "What I Did for Love" have become the two hit songs from *A Chorus Line.* Do you like "What I Did for Love"?

KLEBAN: No. I like that the least, actually!

> *Kiss today good-bye,*
> *The sweetness and the sorrow.*
> *Wish me luck, the same to you,*
> *But I can't regret*
> *What I did for love,*
> *What I did for love. . . .*

STAMBERG: (*Narrating*) Tonight in New York City, *A Chorus Line* breaks the record, becoming the longest-running show in Broadway history—longer than *Grease, Fiddler on the Roof,* even *Life with Father.* The Pulitzer Prize–winning musical opened on Broadway in July 1975. A year and a half before that, choreographer and director Michael Bennett held a midnight talk session with some gypsies—the dancers who travel from show to show. The conversations taped that night were shaped into a show in an extended workshop, then went Off Broadway, then *on,* and became a hit all over the world.

The story of *A Chorus Line* is simple. An audition. The director has to choose eight dancers from seventeen who are dying to get the job.

Edward Kleban says the initial workshop sessions helped him write his favorite lyric—for the song "At the Ballet."

KLEBAN: At those encounter sessions, the dancers talked about their

For the movie version, Marvin and I wrote two new songs. One had to be a production number. I lay there in my bath, thinking what this could be—it would have to be something incredibly universal for the entire company to be able to empathize and break into a huge number. So it could only be two things that I could think of: a scream of angst in the modern world, or the first time you had great sex. I opted for the latter.

**—Edward Kleban,
December 1985**

For the movie songs, I went back to the original process, did a number of interviews with chorus dancers. One of the questions I remember asking was "If you had to explain to someone who had never had great sex—a child or someone who just had no idea what you were talking about—and you had to use other than sexual imagery, how would you explain it?" And one male dancer said, "Well, it's like when you were six years old, you walked in thinking everybody had forgotten your birthday, and suddenly everybody in your life jumped out from behind the door and said 'SURPRISE!!!' " And that's what I called the new song.

—Edward Kleban, December 1985

lives at length—very honest, very compelling tales of unhappy home-life, and going into the artistic process as a salvation. I used their stories as a starting point for my lyrics.

STAMBERG: Is there one particular cluster of words in "At the Ballet" that give you pleasure every time you hear them?

KLEBAN: No, I love the whole song! I usually cry! It's the rare performance of "At the Ballet" that doesn't make me cry all over again. I don't know why. I cried when I wrote it. I can't tell you why.

> *Mother always said I'd be very attractive*
> *When I grew up, when I grew up.*
> *"Diff'rent," she said, "with a special something*
> *And a very, very personal flair."*
> *And though I was eight or nine, though I was eight or nine,*
> *Though I was eight or nine, I hated her. . . .*

STAMBERG: A major plot change was made in the workshop phase. One dancer at the audition, Cassie, had had an affair with the director. She's a better dancer than any of the others, went off to California to try to make it as a soloist, now she's back and trying to get onto that chorus line. Can you describe the shift in plot, and how it happened?

KLEBAN: In one of our original versions, Cassie did *not* get the job. After all, it certainly can be argued that in real life, someone's ex-lover who is being troublesome the entire evening is *not* someone you would cast in your forthcoming show that's going on the road in eight weeks!

We very carefully considered who would get the job at the end of the show. It's not arbitrary at all. Tall people get the job, good-looking people get the job, people who haven't been personality problems all evening get the job.

Except that when we sent Cassie home in those first two weeks of previews, Marsha Mason, Neil Simon's then wife, called Michael up and said, "You can't do that! You can't step on all the hopes and dreams of the entire audience and send Cassie home! You have to leave the door open a little—give them some hope. It's just too brutal."

STAMBERG: So you let Cassie get the job?

KLEBAN: We let Cassie get the job. Thank you, Marsha Mason!

STAMBERG: How many times have you seen *A Chorus Line,* do you think?

KLEBAN: Oh, goodness! Well, I've never seen a matinée, of course. I nap in the afternoon. The first year, many times, because, you know, all your good friends are coming and it's exciting and you're very tied to the epic that's unfolding. You see it not only in your hometown—which is New York—but you see it as you begin to mount it all over the world. But after the first few years, you go . . . oh, I don't know . . . every few months. And then, finally, when you get down to the seventh or eighth year, you tend to see it on New Year's Eve. You go New Year's Eve.

STAMBERG: And seeing it now, do you like every single minute of it? Are you satisfied with your work?

KLEBAN: Oh, certainly not! I mean, I only like maybe sixty-five percent of *A Chorus Line*!

    (*Music: "One."*)

STAMBERG: (*Narrating*) Tonight, lyricist Edward Kleban will see a very special performance of *A Chorus Line*—performance number three thousand three hundred eighty-nine. The current company will be joined by the original company and four touring companies, each performing sections of the show. The finale will bring three hundred fifty dancers on stage, all at once, sweating, smiling, and kicking out "One."

    (*Music up to end.*)

Sweet icicle hot, smooth as a lemon pie,
Sailing across the sky, into the ocean.
We liked it a lot. You can imagine why.
We had begun to fly. Feelings in motion.
And then we did it again.
I'm thinking, was it beginner's luck?
Or is it wonderful once in each three tries?
Surprise, surprise!

—*"Surprise, Surprise,"
from A Chorus Line, the
movie*

———

My favorite lyrics from *A Chorus Line* are almost simplistic, and it's their very simplicity that's so powerful. It amused Ed, a man who once rhymed *je t'aime* with *dilemma,* and who strung "palpably, tangibly, briefly alive" together in a lyric, that I chose his most pared-down words as favorites. Cassie, that excellent dancer, has a song—"The Music and the Mirror"—in which she expresses her need to be hired for the chorus line. "God, I'm a dancer. A dancer dances," Cassie sings. And in that cropped, conversational, highly charged shorthand, she shows how desperate she is for the job, and how her art anchors her very existence. In just seven words, Cassie brings the audience to the core of her feelings.

In addition to the *Chorus Line* lyrics, Ed left behind a body of unproduced work—a trunkful of words *and* music (he was an excellent composer)—dozens of theatre songs that gleam with humor and originality. Friends are trying to pull the songs together into a show—something Ed attempted to do himself, never (of course) to his satisfaction. He hoped others would do better.

America Meets Geraldine Ferraro

July 1984

It was one of those times when you remember where you were when you heard the news. I was whizzing in and out of Studio Five that summer afternoon of July 12, 1984, when word came that Democratic presidential candidate Walter Mondale had chosen a woman to be his running mate. I stood still for a moment and clasped my hands to my chest because it felt as if a balloon were going to burst out of me. Then I grabbed a phone to call Linda Wertheimer, our national political correspondent, who was in San Francisco covering the convention. It was like calling home to share good tidings—a rush of sisterhood over the wires.

"*Linda???!!!*"

"Isn't it wonderful!"

"I can't believe it! Never thought he'd do it!"

"Didn't think we'd see this in our lifetimes!!!"

Linda remembers the euphoria out in San Francisco among women reporters—tough, sassy, dedicated pol-watchers, hugging and crying in profound recognition that a massive door had swung open and that history—*our* history—was being made. And Nina Totenberg remembers the Mondale campaign's Ann Lewis, in San Francisco, walking past a group of male reporters, approaching Linda and Cokie Roberts, and, with her back to the men, mouthing these words: "*What now?*"

The woman was Geraldine Ferraro, forty-eight, a three-term member of the House of Representatives from the Ninth District of Queens, New York. She was tough, too. And sassy. An Italian American Roman Catholic, Ferraro was disciplined and politically astute. Speaker of the

STAMBERG: In 1984, we resolve never to do stories on Cabbage Patch dolls or Pia Zadora.

NOAH ADAMS: We never *did* stories about Pia Zadora.

STAMBERG: Yes, but you never know when her name might pop up.

ADAMS: In 1984, we resolve to avoid stories about pasta, and whether jogging is bad for your knees. And men getting in touch with their feelings. And new reports on the quality of education in the United States.

STAMBERG: In 1984, we shall not discuss coping over forty.

ADAMS: Or NPR's financial difficulties.

STAMBERG: Especially NPR's financial difficulties.

ADAMS: Especially coping over forty.

—*January 1984*

House Thomas "Tip" O'Neill was her mentor. As chair of the Democratic Platform Committee, she'd won respect from perpetually scrapping party regulars. She was pro-choice, pro-E.R.A., pro-Israel, anti-draft. A four-square liberal Democrat. Her widowed mother, Antonetta, had sewn beads on rich women's dresses and skimped on meat to help her daughter get ahead. Gerry Ferraro got ahead. Became the first woman to run for vice president on the ticket of a major party.

Plenty of women thought they would never see it happen. The autumn before the convention, at a forum of Democratic presidential hopefuls (including John Glenn, Alan Cranston, and Gary Hart, all of whom were on record as saying they would consider a female running mate), former Texas representative Barbara Jordan raised the question with Walter Mondale. In her slow, deep, meticulously articulate fashion, Jordan had mesmerized Democrats at their 1976 convention as the first black *and* first female keynote speaker. In 1984, she put Mondale on the spot about putting a woman on the ticket.

JORDAN: Mr. Vice President, much has been made of the possibility of a woman running as a vice presidential candidate. (*Applause.*) My question to you is not whether you would accept a woman as your running mate—because certainly you would! (*Laughter and applause.*) My question to you is, what are the *disadvantages* of having a woman as a vice presidential running mate?

MONDALE: None! (*Laughter and applause. Fade.*)

STAMBERG: Ms. Jordan, were you satisfied with Vice President Mondale's answer?

JORDAN: I was not satisfied with that answer, because everybody exercising common sense knows that if a woman had been a tremendous plus on a national presidential ticket, a woman would have been on a ticket long ago. There *is* some disadvantage, and I think the disadvantage is that a lot of people in this country are not willing to consider a woman for an office which ranks that high.

STAMBERG: What do you think is the reason for that reluctance? After all, Golda Meir has led Israel, Indira Gandhi has run India, Margaret Thatcher is prime minister of Great Britain at this very moment. Why are we lagging so?

JORDAN: We have been so brain-washed with the superiority of white male personalities that it is difficult to cut through and perceive a woman as a person of competence.

STAMBERG: Does it strike you as ironic that polls here show female voters are as reluctant as men are to put a woman on the ticket?

JORDAN: One problem we as women have is in perceiving ourselves as people of extraordinary competence. That is a function of history. It is a function of tradition.

STAMBERG: People do make the point that there's a lack of women qualified to be candidates.

JORDAN: That is a point which has been made, that there is not a woman with a broad executive governing base which would give her the hands-on experience of running a big company or a big government. But again, this is not an insurmountable problem. There is nothing which gives you the training to be a vice president. Certainly nothing which trains you to be president. If we think that serving as governor makes you a good president, we can look at some recent history and draw some conclusions about that! I certainly think we will have a woman as president of this country in the foreseeable future.

STAMBERG: You don't think, though, that we'll see a woman on any ticket in 1984?

JORDAN: I do not feel that we will see a woman on either ticket in 1984.

———

Nine months after that conversation, Walter Mondale proved Barbara Jordan wrong. But even a week before Mondale announced his choice, when the Ferraro possibility was being widely raised, there was skepticism expressed by people from whom you might not have expected it. By, for example, the first woman in the history of the country to have been asked to run as vice president.

In 1952, in a symbolic gesture, Democratic party leaders placed the name of India Edwards in nomination alongside that of their presidential candidate, Adlai Stevenson. After years of lively and important service to the party, India Edwards had become vice chairman of the Democratic National Committee. Although she was a crusader for women's rights, Edwards turned the Democrats down "flat and quick."

EDWARDS: First of all, I had no aspiration to be vice president of the United States. I also didn't think the Democratic party was ready for a woman vice president, and I'm quite sure that Adlai Stevenson

> We were naïve in many ways. We thought that if we went to state legislators and demonstrated to them convincingly that the majority of their constituents supported the Equal Rights Amendment, they would vote for it. But we forgot the majority of those constituents don't vote them in. It's special interests. And so, in many cases, they simply wouldn't listen.
>
> —Gloria Steinem, July 1982

wouldn't have had a woman as vice president. I'd known him for years, had great admiration for him, and was very anxious for him to be the Democratic nominee. But I knew Adlai well enough to know that he wouldn't want a woman.

STAMBERG: Well, now more than thirty years have passed, and we're talking again about the possibility of a woman on the Democratic ticket. What's your feeling about that?

EDWARDS: Well, I feel that this year we do not have a woman who would be an asset nationally. We have enough women who are *qualified* to be vice president, but you also have to look at that person as a potential president. And I just don't think this is the year to gamble.

We want to get Reagan out of the White House—that is the height of my ambition. I would do anything I could to defeat him. And if I thought a woman would be an asset to whoever gets our nomination, I would be not just one hundred percent for her, but two hundred percent.

STAMBERG: Why wouldn't Geraldine Ferraro, who seems to be everybody's favorite—

EDWARDS: She's not known nationally. If she had been a senator and had been going around the country making speeches for several years, and people knew her . . . but the only publicity that she's ever had nationally has been just in the last few months, since there's been talk of having a woman on the ticket.

STAMBERG: But you know, Ms. Edwards, communication is so much better these days. You can get publicity—a national message—out so much more quickly.

EDWARDS: I know, but you don't get a person . . . well . . . the vice president in this case must be an asset!

STAMBERG: Let me ask you this, Ms. Edwards: Was Harry Truman any better qualified at the time to be vice president than these women who are being mentioned today?

EDWARDS: Certainly! He had done a magnificent job as senator from Missouri. He had headed the committee that kept prices down during the war. He was very well known and admired by senators.

STAMBERG: I have a feeling a lot of feminists listening to you are going to be awfully mad at what you're saying.

EDWARDS: Well, I don't care! I care more about winning this time. I

I happened to be traveling with Gerry just as she went from being a rather obscure congresswoman being talked about as a potential vice presidential nominee right through the swirl of all her national publicity. But she never believed for a minute that she was famous until Barbara Walters came to interview her.

—*journalist Marie Brenner, July 1984*

do think there'll be a woman running for president in 1988. I hope I live long enough to vote for her!

———

India Edwards was eighty-nine when we spoke. She'd given up driving her own car a year before our conversation. She died in 1990. Her survivors include five granddaughters.

India Edwards's reservations notwithstanding, Geraldine Ferraro became a national figure almost instantly, and brought excitement to an otherwise lackluster campaign. Her opponent on the Republican ticket, Ronald Reagan's running mate, George Bush, was provoked enough by her, and worried enough by his own image as a wimp, that toward the end of the political season, after debating Ferraro on television, Bush said that he had "tried to kick a little ass." Wimp away! It was one of the campaign's loftier moments.

Ferraro lost, of course. Or Mondale did. Or Ronald Reagan won— overwhelmingly. The consensus was that no one could have beaten him. But Ferraro's was an ignominious loss. Ugly information came out during the campaign about her real-estate-developer husband, John Zaccaro, and his financial irregularities.

But for the handful of weeks before the Zaccaro story broke, there was a sparkle to the election season, the sheen of something brand-new.

That summer of '84 bustled with news about women, good news and bad news. First, the bad news. Toward the end of the month in which Geraldine Ferraro was nominated, Miss America's crown got tarnished. It was another female first. Vanessa Williams was the first black Miss America. And when nude photos of her appeared, in living black and white, on the pages of *Penthouse* magazine, she was also the first Miss America to give up her title. Feminists defended her, saying economic necessity, the same economic necessity that always keeps women powerless, had driven Williams to pose.

A week after that bombshell, while we were still catching our breaths at the magazine rack (actually, you couldn't find a copy of *Penthouse* for love—as it were—or money, that issue was such a sell-out), the Bureau of Labor Statistics informed us that for the first time since the founding of the Republic, white males no longer made up the majority of the nation's work force. They'd slid to 48.8 percent in 1983, down from 50 percent in 1982. And Professor Alfred Kahn of the

ROBIN MORGAN: If some years ago, for economic reasons, she posed for the photographs, it still is no excuse for the exploitation of them. It never ceases to enrage me, and feminists in general, how the woman who has been the powerless party is the one who gets blamed.

STAMBERG: Aren't you letting Vanessa Williams off awfully easily? These photographs — weren't there other ways she could have made money?

MORGAN: Scholarly studies have shown that the women who become involved in posing for such magazines or films do so from very basic economic necessity in a culture which still does not permit women equal access to education, to jobs, to job training, et cetera.

—Robin Morgan, Ms. magazine, July 1984

Columbia University School of Social Work told me it didn't take a Labor Department study to know that the work force was changing.

KAHN: A dramatic part of the change is the arrival of very large numbers of *women* in the labor force. We once had a situation in which only 20 or 30 percent of the mothers of children were working. Now, as of this month, of the mothers of children under age eighteen, 60.5 percent are in the labor force. And the arrival of these women creates an entirely new situation, because it raises all kinds of questions about child care, about double fringe benefits for husbands and wives, about the appropriateness of the benefits that exist, and about all sorts of related questions having to do with what goes on in the home and in the community if both parents work.

———

Those working women, however, as well as the nonworking ones, couldn't get Geraldine Ferraro and the Democrats elected. In fact, Ferraro may have hurt Mondale more than she helped him, even with women. Although there was much talk about 1984 being the Year of the Woman, and also much talk about gender gap, women chose Ronald Reagan over Walter Mondale by 55 percent to 45 percent. Because the main point about 1984 was that, above all else, it was the Year of Reagan. A troika ticket of Mother Teresa, Madonna, and Marie Curie couldn't have laid a glove on him.

In December 1985, Geraldine Ferraro was back in the news. Faced with the Justice Department's investigation of whether John Zaccaro had made illegal contributions to his wife's 1978 congressional campaign, and questions about whether Ferraro should have included information about her husband's income in her own financial disclosure statements, Geraldine Ferraro announced that she would not challenge New York Republican senator Alfonse D'Amato in 1986.

At the time, Ferraro told me that she very much wanted to be a senator, but that she'd already delayed her decision and felt that further delay was unfair to other candidates and the public.

FERRARO: I have no doubt that I'll be vindicated. But the problem about getting into a Senate race with an investigation pending is that it distracts from the issues of the campaign. I learned that in the campaign of 1984. For me to sit down and try to discuss what was

Ferraro said, "In this campaign, I don't want to appear frightened of Ronald Reagan. I don't want to come out and say I am scared of Ronald Reagan. As a woman, I would never want to appear vulnerable."

—journalist Marie Brenner, July 1984

wrong with Ronald Reagan's economic policies so that you end up
with the deficit that we have today—a debt that is over two trillion
dollars—I mean, we couldn't even talk about the issues because I
spent all my time talking about what was going on in the investigation! I don't want that to happen again.

STAMBERG: All the financial business that has shadowed you since you
emerged on the national scene—is that your Chappaquiddick?

FERRARO: Oh, God!

STAMBERG: Is that going to come up whenever—

FERRARO: No! I don't think you can compare the two at all. And I
. . . you know, I . . . I think that's . . . you know, what's happened
with our finances is . . . is over.

STAMBERG: So, you're not feeling that because of this whole financial
thing, which might haunt you for the rest of your public life, that—

FERRARO: Oh, it's not going to haunt me! I hate to interrupt you on
that, but it's not. That's past. What I'm worried about now is the fact
that with a pending Justice Department investigation, we would be
diverted from the issues.

STAMBERG: A last question to you, Ms. Ferraro. It's a difficult one for
me to ask . . . but I will.

    (*Laughter.*)

FERRARO: Ask me a positive one this time! (*Laughs.*)

STAMBERG: I wonder whether you have any three A.M. dark-night-of-
the-soul moments in which you just find yourself getting utterly furious, realizing that this business of your husband's finances—

FERRARO: Wait a minute!

STAMBERG: has in the past come between you and what could be a
brilliant political career, and might continue to do so, even though
you're saying what's past is past?

FERRARO: I have several concerns. One is for my family. My husband
and I are extremely close. He is . . . he is a person who has (and I use
this word advisedly) *allowed* me to be what I want to be. I say that
because in my marriage, my husband and my kids come first, and if
I had gotten opposition, I wouldn't have done any of the things I've
done. But I go to the second step, and say that I have a deep love for
this country and for my state. And if it's not right for me to do
something today—me, personally—I'll still work for the things I care
about, and the causes I care about, and for the people who do the

things I care about in Washington. So, you know, there is no . . . there is no need for me to have . . . wake up at three o'clock in the morning and have resentment.

———

In 1988, Geraldine Ferraro's son, John Zaccaro, Jr., was convicted of selling cocaine to an undercover agent.

In 1992, when Ferraro finally went after Alfonse D'Amato's Senate seat, she never made it past the primary. Her husband's finances and connections did indeed haunt her. The new wrinkle in '92 was that it was a female opponent who summoned up the ghosts. New York City comptroller Elizabeth Holtzman's campaign pounded Ferraro mercilessly on ethics. Holtzman lost, too.

But in other races, 1992 turned out to be the Year of the Woman people had hoped for back in 1984. Women tripled their numbers in the Senate (up to seven—it's a start), and doubled them in the House of Representatives, and there were significant jumps in state and local offices. Not to mention Hillary Rodham Clinton in the White House, the best-educated, most professional presidential spouse in history. The initial euphoria felt in 1984 because of Ferraro was brought home in 1992. Her breakthrough candidacy, albeit brief, helped pave the way.

Philip Roth and the Jewish Problem

January 1984

Alan Cheuse, a novelist and *All Things Considered*'s book reviewer, tells a Philip Roth story. Cheuse was in college, editor of the Rutgers literary magazine, when Roth's *Goodbye, Columbus* came out in 1959. The novella, published when Roth was twenty-six, is the story of Neil Klugman—lower-middle-class, Jewish, from Newark—and his summer romance with Brenda Patimkin, the original Jewish American Princess. The operative word here is "Jewish." Everyday, vernacular Jewish family life is Roth's supreme literary shtick.

"I should serve four different meals at once," Neil's Aunt Gladys complains. "You eat pot roast, Susan with the cottage cheese, Max has steak. Friday night is his steak night, I wouldn't deny him. And I'm having a little cold chicken. I should jump up and down twenty different times? What am I, a workhorse?"

And Brenda, the exquisite nouveau riche object of Neil's horny adoration, explains why she doesn't rush the net in tennis: "I'm afraid of my nose. I had it bobbed."

Alan Cheuse, young, Jewish, horny, a would-be writer from near Newark, remembers running across the Rutgers campus waving a copy of *Goodbye, Columbus,* and yelling to a friend, *"Someone's done it! Someone's done it!!!!"*

Philip Roth has by now written nineteen books. Hilarious, obsessive, brilliant books. (In 1983, reviewing *The Anatomy Lesson,* Cheuse said, "Roth has the mind of Henry James and the mouth of Lenny Bruce.") One of Roth's themes is being Jewish in America. And just as

Spike Lee has been criticized by blacks for exposing too much about their race in his films, Jews have blasted Roth for painting an unfair picture of his people.

In his eleventh book, *The Ghost Writer,* published in 1979, Roth introduces a hero named Nathan Zuckerman. It's the beginning of an author/character relationship as zesty and permanent as the bond between pastrami and rye. Zuckerman, middle-class, Jewish, a struggling writer from (guess where?) Newark, will preoccupy Roth's imagination for many many (many) books. In Zuckerman-1, *The Ghost Writer,* the twenty-three-year-old author gets an audience with the Great Writer—E. I. Lonoff. Zuckerman has written a story—a true story from his own family—about Jews who are fighting over money. Zuckerman's father says the story is bad for the Jews. At Lonoff's house, Zuckerman meets a mysterious girl about whom he has a remarkable fantasy.

"I met a marvelous young woman while I was up in New England," Zuckerman imagines telling his mother. "I love her and she loves me. We are going to be married." "Married? But so fast? Nathan, is she Jewish?" "Yes she is." "But who is she?" "Anne Frank."

When *The Ghost Writer* was dramatized for public television in 1984, I got my first chance to interview a literary hero. (I had run across the Barnard campus waving *Goodbye, Columbus.* I, too, was born Jewish in Newark—only because my mother happened to be there at the time. The state of my libido when I read that Roth is none of your business.)

Philip Roth and I talked about fiction that's bad for the Jews.

STAMBERG: How many terrific stories don't get written because of the family—because it's bad for somebody?

ROTH: I don't think any terrific stories don't get written for that kind of reason. The energy that goes into making a story terrific is not going to be obstructed by that kind of objection. Opposition often feeds the energy itself.

STAMBERG: I've heard some horror stories. One writer I know published a book very similar to the one Zuckerman wants to publish, and his mother sued him.

ROTH: That's a wonderful story! He should write that story!

STAMBERG: Yeah, maybe he will—if he can recover from the trauma of his mother having sued him!

ROTH: Yes, well, if he can't recover, then he oughtn't to be a writer.

Those scruples will only get in his way. It's a very unscrupulous profession, you know.

STAMBERG: What do you mean?

ROTH: One isn't really trustworthy, is one? That is, your material is raw life. Your material is the real thing. And you can't be any more squeamish than a doctor is, who opens a patient up and sees a big abscess. You have to go in there and take it out!

STAMBERG: You've certainly had to deal with enormous criticism in the course of your writing life, very specifically for *The Ghost Writer,* which many people feel is your best novel. But when it came out, there was *fury* from reviewers at the idea of your taking Anne Frank—the ultimate symbol of the Holocaust—and using her for a joke.

ROTH: From a few book reviewers there was some criticism—which amounted to nothing. I mean, it wasn't of the sort that one could begin to take seriously. And then I . . . I must take exception to your saying Anne Frank was used as a joke. There's no joke there at all! What Zuckerman is trying to do is bring her back into life, make her a living young woman, because sainthood is exaggeration. She was only a girl—charming, very bright, a very *engaging* girl, obviously. Not only does he take her seriously, Zuckerman's problem is he takes her *too* seriously. She's central to his imagination.

STAMBERG: Over the years there's been criticism of you for writing about Jewish themes, revealing certain things about middle-class Jewish life. How did you evaluate the criticism at the time, and what did you do about it?

ROTH: Well, we . . . we . . . best to be specific. The first opposition I got that meant anything to me, and that was sizable, was to a short story I published in 1957 called "Defender of the Faith." I was twenty-four when it came out, and it appeared in *The New Yorker,* much to my delight. I think it was my first story published in a commercial magazine. *The New Yorker* got a lot of letters from people who were very upset by that story.

STAMBERG: Can you remind us of the story, please?

ROTH: Yeah. If I can remember it! "Defender of the Faith" is a story about an American Jewish sergeant in the army during World War Two, named Marx. He is taken up by a Jewish recruit, a private, who comes to him and asks him for some favors. And the point he makes is "Look, we're Jews, why don't you help me out?" Marx feels himself put upon when this fellow proves himself not to be terribly

> **Is it worth bringing in the most famous symbol of the Holocaust just to add a clever touch? Am I a literary rabbi in saying this use of Anne Frank seems to me a failure of aesthetic judgment? . . . It raises our expectations . . . only to leave us with a self-conscious joke.**
>
> **—Jack Beatty, The New Republic, October 1979**

> **He does *not* have the right to use the life of an accidental celebrity for his Holocaust romance. That little pile of bones on Belsen heath is something more than raw material.**
>
> **—Rhoda Koenig, Saturday Review, December 1979**

I don't think I'm the only novelist who has as a companion a self-challenging voice. It's in the nature of the job. You're constantly attacking your own work daily, hourly, minute by minute. You write a sentence, and you look at it and say it's no good. Any novelist worth his salt is a hundred times more critical of himself than his worst critic. And the brutality with which writers attack themselves in private while they are working is . . . It's ugly. A critic would be imprisoned for being as brutal as a writer is with himself. I mean writers who are any good.

**—Philip Roth,
September 1988**

pleasant or terribly honest. And eventually when Grossbart, the private, says to him, "Look, can you arrange for me not to be shipped abroad? I don't want to get killed," Marx makes it his business to *have* him shipped abroad. It's a very strong story.

There was a kind of small furor—a *small* one, but there it was. And if you're a young writer—as young as I was—and you're just starting out, it sounds like a very *big* furor, because no one's paid any attention to you at all before that!

So—how did I respond? As a matter of fact, I got a phone call from an executive of the B'Nai B'Rith Anti-Defamation League who told me about the mail and phone calls *they* had received as a result of the story, and asked if we could get together and have lunch and talk about it. I said yes, and we did. It's a free country, we both knew that! There was nothing much for us to do except talk.

But for me it was a beginning of an education. That is, I realized there were readers out there! Forget Jews and Jewish writers—there were people to whom fiction *meant* something. They weren't students sitting in a class. They weren't people writing papers. They were people reading fiction. And saying, "No, this doesn't accord with my sense of life." Or, too, they would say, "Look, this is dangerous stuff. It can have dangerous consequences." Or they would say, "Look, there's something wrong with *you* to be writing stuff like this." And so on. So, it was the beginning of my sense of an audience.

STAMBERG: Umm-hmm. I'm curious. Why did you agree to meet with him?

ROTH: One, it was too serious an accusation to dismiss. Two, I was young, I wasn't terribly worldly; if summoned, I came. And three, I was interested! It was more interesting than sitting down and spending another three hours writing!

STAMBERG: But did you ever, as Zuckerman finds himself almost doing, ever say to himself, say to *your*self—I'm confusing you with your character, please forgive me!—"Gee, maybe I ought to drop this stuff; I'm making a lot of people mad out there"?

ROTH: Did I ever think that I ought to *drop* this stuff? No, how could I drop this stuff? This stuff was my *stuff*!

STAMBERG: Now, what about Zuckerman? We have this trilogy—*The Ghost Writer* from 1979, *Zuckerman Unbound* in 1981, *The Anatomy Lesson* in 1983—all about the life and times of Nathan Zuckerman. Have you finished with him now, do you think, with this last

book, *The Anatomy Lesson*? He's going to medical school to become
a doctor.

ROTH: (*Laughs.*)

STAMBERG: He's decided he needs people.

ROTH: Medical school is only the beginning! (*Laughs.*)

STAMBERG: Are you done with Zuckerman?

ROTH: I would . . . gee, I don't know. I . . . I don't know. I *thought*
so, a few months ago. But a friend of mine recently wrote me a letter
and said, "Why don't you *kill* him?" A very nice fellow said that. And
I . . . I've been thinking about it.

STAMBERG: Why would you want to do that?

ROTH: Well, these three books . . . that's it. I've come to the end
. . . or exhausted the themes that I wanted to deal with. And if there
were to be another Zuckerman, he'd be in some other predicament
entirely.

———

There was another Zuckerman. *The Counterlife,* in 1986. And another.
The Facts: A Novelist's Autobiography, in 1988. That last book led to
another visit with Philip Roth. And Nathan Zuckerman. Two for two.
Quite a privilege for a broadcaster. "You should know," Philip Roth
wrote in a thank-you letter for the tape I sent him of this 1984 interview,
"that that's the first radio interview I've given since 1959. I do this every
twenty-five years."

> I turn sentences around. That's my life. I write a sentence and then I turn it around. Then I look at it and I turn it around again. Then I have lunch. Then I come back in and write another sentence. Then I have tea and turn the new sentence around. Then I read the two sentences over and turn them both around.
>
> —from **The Ghost Writer**

211

Rosa Parks Tells Her Story

November 1984

There are certain stories that cannot be told too often. Rosa Parks's act of defiance on a segregated bus in Montgomery, Alabama, is one of them. But, as with most stories, there is more to it than we've heard. And more to it, even, than Mrs. Parks herself tells in conversation.

Rosa Parks has related the story so often that there are no pauses in her narrative, no "er"'s or "uh"'s. The telling is as smooth as a polished stone. And the story has the strength of stone, like the woman herself.

Initially, I felt reluctant to ask Mrs. Parks to describe what happened that day she refused to surrender her bus seat to a white man. Surely, in the thirty years that had passed since the event, she'd grown tired of going over and over it. Ultimately, though, I realized I couldn't *not* ask for the story. It's something we all have to hear.

On Thursday, December 1, 1955, with racism and segregation terrorizing people of color throughout the South, the deliberate inaction of a quietly determined forty-two-year-old seamstress led to a boycott, by blacks, of the buses in Montgomery. Initially planned as a one-day protest, the boycott lasted for a year. It was the nation's first mass public civil rights protest, and it propelled a new minister in town, the Reverend Martin Luther King, Jr., to national prominence. But Rosa Parks told me she hadn't been involved in any *plan* to start a boycott against segregation.

PARKS: I had no thoughts of it at all, not even up until the moment the driver said he would call the policeman and have me arrested. There was nothing that I had planned in any way.

STAMBERG: Did you think for a moment, "Why am I doing this? Why don't I just keep quiet and do what they're asking of me?"

PARKS: No, I didn't question myself or my intentions at all. I felt that it was the only way I could protest against the way I was being treated. By the time I got on the bus, there were a number of people standing in the aisle, and I took the last available seat, just back of what was considered the white section, at the beginning of what we considered *our* section.

The driver did not say anything or ask for us to move. When I say "us," I mean four people—a man who shared the seat with me (he sat at the window) and two women across the aisle. And when this one white man was standing up, that was when the driver wanted the four of us to get up. None of us moved immediately. But he said, "Y'all make it light on yourselves and let me have those seats." And at that point, the man next to me and the two women stood and moved out into the aisle. In fact, I permitted the man to move past me, and then I stayed where I was.

When the driver asked if I was going to stand up, I said, "No, I'm not." He said, "Well, if you don't, I'm going to call the policeman and have you arrested." And I said, "Well, you may do that." And he did get off the bus for a few minutes. In the meantime, everybody was rather quiet. A few people talked very quietly among themselves, but no one addressed me. When the two policemen came on the bus, the driver pointed me out, to let them know that *I* was the source of his trouble, that *I* didn't stand up and the other three *did*.

And then one approached me and asked if the driver had asked me to stand. I said, "Yes, he did." He said, "Well, why don't you stand up?" I said, "I don't think I should have to." And then I asked the policeman, I said, "Why do you push us around?" He said, "I don't know, but the law is the law and you are under arrest." The moment he said I was under arrest, I stood up, and one policeman picked up my purse, and the other my shopping bag, and we left the bus together.

STAMBERG: You were arrested. Where were you taken?

PARKS: I was taken to jail.

STAMBERG: How long did you stay in jail?

PARKS: Just a short while, a few hours.

STAMBERG: What was the charge, Mrs. Parks?

PARKS: They charged me with violation of their racial segregation law.

VIRGINIA DURR: Mr. Nixon, who was the president of the NAACP, came by, and Mr. Durr and I went with him to the jail and got her out. Mr. Nixon put up the bail. And we took her back home. And Clifford asked her what she wanted to do, and she said she wanted to carry the case on up to the Supreme Court if necessary.

—January 1986

STAMBERG: Did you realize how much worse it could have been for you, so much more than a few hours in jail?

PARKS: At the time of my arrest, I knew not only that it could have been worse than just being arrested, I knew I could have been physically injured or possibly killed or perhaps put in jail and not even have anyone to come to my rescue.

STAMBERG: Did you feel in some way that you were lucky to have gotten off so easily, Mrs. Parks?

PARKS: I didn't feel lucky at all! I felt that it was very ridiculous for any human being to have to be subjected to this type of humiliation in a supposedly free country.

STAMBERG: Your action that day was really the beginning of what grew into a concerted nonviolent civil rights movement that changed the course of American history.

You said you were one of four who was asked to move to the back of that bus. Did you ever hear from the other three?

PARKS: No, I did not hear from them. I didn't know them personally. I know that the two women lived very near me. Several years later, I was in Peoria, Illinois, and I met a young man who said the man occupying the seat with me was his uncle, but he had passed away.

STAMBERG: Why do you think it was that *you* were the one who chose not to move?

PARKS: I had had a number of confrontations of this manner, including one with the same bus driver. He evicted me from a bus in 1943. Because after I boarded through the front door and paid my fare, he wanted me to get off the bus, go around to the back door (as we did then), and get in from there, so as not to pass through the white section. I refused to do that, and he had me to leave the bus. But he did not call the policeman then, he just had me to leave the bus. Many times, I had had trouble with bus drivers.

But 1955 was the first time that people in Montgomery took enough notice to cooperate with each other and *remain* off the bus. That attracted the attention of the entire city, first of all, then other places around the country, and it just spread as our protest grew in strength.

STAMBERG: We often hear that you were weary that day, your feet were tired, and *that* had the most to do with your unwillingness to move. But it sounds from what you're saying as if there was a lot more than that involved.

PARKS: Well, at that time I was not having any trouble of any kind with my feet. Of course, anyone who works a full day at the type of job that I had would be weary. But that was not the utmost thing. The utmost thought in my mind was it was time. . . . It was far spent for all of us, as a people, to be treated as human beings.

———

Rosa Parks was fined fourteen dollars for her 1955 transgression on that bus in Montgomery, Alabama. Her gift to history has no price.

There is a back story to Rosa Parks's action, a story that rarely gets told. It's about her history of activism.

At the time of her protest, white supremacists were railing against the Supreme Court's 1954 decision against school segregation, the Ku Klux Klan was burning crosses on Negroes' lawns, and lynchings were occurring with some regularity. Efforts to organize against the brutality were brave, dangerous. But people tried. The National Association for the Advancement of Colored People, for instance, had chapters scattered throughout the South. And Rosa Parks was secretary of the NAACP chapter in Montgomery.

Mrs. Parks had other civil rights connections, as well. On the recommendation of Virginia Durr, a well-born white Southern liberal, Mrs. Parks had spent ten days at an interracial workshop at the Highlander Folk School in Tennessee. (Mrs. Durr and her husband, Clifford, a politically well-connected one-time New Dealer, had long fought segregation in Montgomery. It was the Durrs, along with E. D. Nixon, longtime president of the local NAACP chapter, who bailed Mrs. Parks out of jail.) And decades earlier, Rosa Parks had worked—"day and night," she told me—trying to save the "Scottsboro Boys," nine young blacks charged with raping two white women, from the Alabama electric chair. (Eventually, eight of the men were released. Their landmark case gave all defendants the right to adequate counsel.)

In her 1992 autobiography, *My Story,* Mrs. Parks says she learned of the Scottsboro case in 1931 from the man who would become her husband. Raymond Parks, a twenty-eight-year-old barber and longtime member of the NAACP, was "the first real activist" young Rosa McCauley met and the only black man she knew, apart from her grandfather, "who was never actually afraid of white people." Raymond Parks's late-night underground Scottsboro meetings were so dangerous, Mrs. Parks says, that the table around which they were held was kept

STAMBERG: What did the white women of Montgomery do to help in the bus boycott?

VIRGINIA DURR: Well, I never knew whether they did it wittingly or unwittingly, but the thing was that most of the people that rode the bus were the domestics who worked in the residential areas of Montgomery. And the custom was for the women to go and pick them up at the bus stop and bring them home. When the buses were boycotted, they took their maids all the way home, and they went and got them in the morning. The mayor came out with a proclamation. He said that if the white women of Montgomery would just stop doing that, they would kill the boycott in a week. But they wouldn't stop. What they said was, "If the mayor wants to do my laundry, or clean up, or look after the children, he can. But until he's willing to do that, I'm not ready to get rid of my maid!"

—*January 1986*

covered with guns. After the "Scottsboro Boys" were saved, Raymond Parks worked for voter registration. His wife's first incident with bus driver James P. Blake, in 1943, occurred, in fact, when she was on her way to register.

So Rosa Parks's work for racial justice began decades before that monumental day in December 1955 when she stood for her rights by remaining in her seat.

We think of heroic people as being larger than life. Rosa Parks is tiny, and so soft-spoken, with a rounded, liquid, southern lilt, that during the interview we had to move the microphone closer to make sure her story would be heard. It was heard. It will be heard again.

STAMBERG: Is it dangerous to think of it as ancient history?

JULIAN BOND: Oh, absolutely, because it's so much a part of us today. It's not always a straight line, but I start my discussions of the movement in 1953 with the bus boycott in Baton Rouge, Louisiana. I could easily have gone back to '47 to the CORE sit-ins in Chicago. I could easily have gone back even before that, to sit-in activity here in Washington, D.C. I mean, there's almost no real beginning point, and luckily there's almost no real stopping point.

—February 1989

Emmett Tyrrell and the Liberal Menace

November 1984

It's tough to pinpoint just when "liberalism" became "the L-word"—so out of fashion that you couldn't even spell it, much less say it, in front of the children. Eugene McCarthy may have killed liberalism, or maybe it was George McGovern, or Jimmy Carter. Whoever took the first swipes, the liberal dragon was ultimately slain by the Reagan Revolution. And by 1984, the year of this conversation with R. Emmett Tyrrell, Jr., editor of *The American Spectator*, syndicated columnist, author of *The Liberal Crack-Up*, and impassioned conservative, liberals were seen as Gloomy Guses—"Whole Earth catastrophists," in Tyrrell's words, "women of the fevered brow," who had fallen prey to that most disagreeable habit: exultation of the bleak.

TYRRELL: This is one of my gripes with what's happened to American liberalism. It's dissolved into a kind of running argument with the way normal people live. And I think if my liberal friends were to reappraise the value of being agreeable, overnight they'd find life on this earth a lot more comfortable.

STAMBERG: Give an example of the disagreeability into which liberalism has dissolved.

TYRRELL: Well, a constant absorption with rights, and contentions over rights, many of which are fanciful. And a kind of running horror of the present—a fear of your water, your air. The one way you can tell if the environment is indeed healthier is by measuring longevity.

By 1980, after years of ceaseless solemnizing and legislating, all [the liberals] had accomplished was an exchange of absurdities and injustices, those of the past having been heaved aside only to be replaced by new, more impregnable ones: quotas; consciousness-raising; legalized prejudice against men, mothers, and achievers of every variety. Moreover, the government was now empowered to force such abominations into the most intimate spheres of private life.

—from **The Liberal Crack-Up**

217

And by every standard, longevity has increased and increased over the last fifteen to twenty years.

STAMBERG: That's your evidence for not worrying about the environment and the quality of our drinking water??

TYRRELL: Well, you can worry about it and do something about it, but acknowledge your triumphs!

STAMBERG: Something else that bothers you are new regulations on behalf of the handicapped that led to those depressions in curbs so that wheelchairs can roll down more easily.

TYRRELL: I think they're dangerous!

STAMBERG: To whom?

TYRRELL: Well, I have a wonderful old friend, a wonderful old Washingtonian, Huntington Cairns. Huntington developed difficulty lifting his legs, and he has to walk, as a lot of old people do, shuffling his legs along the pavement. When he comes to one of those sudden indentations, he darn near falls over!

STAMBERG: On the other hand, there are handicapped Americans who are served and made more mobile because such depressions exist.

TYRRELL: Undoubtedly. The major point is, when did we get a chance to *vote* on what kind of indentations we were going to have? Or what kind of doorknobs are going to be placed on doors? Everybody should treat his fellow neighbor well. And everyone should show respect and added solicitude and attention for a handicapped person. But this matter didn't have to become politicized. The New Age is broken down into a lot of enthusiasts who practice masked politics!

STAMBERG: But do you see these people having any *power* at the moment? Aren't they gasping their last polluted gasps?

TYRRELL: Are you kidding?? I'll be lucky to get out of here alive!! (*Laughs.*) This whole building's dominated by you people!

STAMBERG: We don't have depressions in our walks here for the handicapped.

TYRRELL: At least I won't have to watch for that! But did you notice . . . I want you to notice that I came in here with a *woman* bodyguard. That shows how much I've accepted feminism! And believe me, anyone lays a hand on me, their arms will be broken. That woman is no one to fool around with!

STAMBERG: I'm glad you mentioned that, because I'd like to hear your exegesis on feminism. You're *very* troubled. What did you call them, "the anaphrodisiacs"?

TYRRELL: Anaphrodisiac women.

STAMBERG: Yes.

TYRRELL: I mean that they're the opposite of aphrodisiac.
(*Laughter.*)

STAMBERG: Which is the natural condition of women, is that it? Or what *should* be the natural condition?

TYRRELL: Well, it makes life wonderful! I can tell you.

STAMBERG: All right, please—

TYRRELL: No need to tell *you*, Susan!

STAMBERG: Thank you. (*Laughs.*) How come you're so handsome and you're so conservative? Now, let us get back on track here about your anti-feminist views. Anaphrodisiac? Surely there are other roles that women can and do serve in life.

TYRRELL: They can serve in the business world and the professional world, and they have. But to speak of "the women's movement" is a blatant misnomer. You mean *some* women's movement, and some women who are members of *that* women's movement are generally radical leftists whose greatest absorption is with advancing socialism and things of this sort upon our society.

STAMBERG: But that segment would probably thoroughly agree with you, and admit it. No?

TYRRELL: (*Laughs.*) Well, they haven't admitted it. They claim to speak for all women in this country. They don't speak for the women *I* associate with.

STAMBERG: One of whom is your mother, who really *did* own a parasol? What did you write in that essay?

TYRRELL: Oh, was she mad! She said, "Bob, I'm just reading what you say about me." My mother never had a parasol. But you got to have a little *fun* in this world, Susan.

American manners have grown very lax. . . . At universities idealists can hoot and howl at visiting speakers. Near-naked joggers sweat and wheeze up Fifth Avenue at high noon unmolested; they pass Saks and Bergdorf Goodman, but no lady shopper would dream of bashing one with her parasol. In fact, few ladies even carry parasols nowadays. My mother carries one, but she is an exception. Most carry whistles and small cans of mugger repellent.

—from The Liberal Crack-Up

The Cripple Liberation Front

February 1984

STAMBERG: Lorenzo Milam reads from his new book, *The Cripple Liberation Front Marching Band Blues*.

MILAM: "They taught her how to diagram sentences, and they taught her about Mozart and Beethoven. They showed her the difference between the Samba and the Rhumba, and between the Waltz and the Foxtrot; she remembers her teacher played "Besame Mucho" over and over again, so they could learn the Samba—but they never taught her about her lungs, the beautiful rich red alveoli, that lose the ability to aspirate themselves, so that one night, they think she is clogging up, suffocating, the doctor comes, with all the lights, and slices into the pink flesh, at the base of her neck, the blood jets up all over, and she can see the reflection of her neck as he cuts into her neck (no anesthetics permitted because they affect the dark gray nerves nestled in the aitch of the spinal column, and polio got there first). . . ."

STAMBERG: So, Lorenzo, your sister never learned those lessons about her body. She died. And a short time after that, you, too, contracted polio. How old were you?

MILAM: I was eighteen.

STAMBERG: What year was that?

MILAM: That would be 1952.

STAMBERG: (*Narrating*) Lorenzo Milam is a hallowed—some say revolutionary—figure in public radio broadcasting. In the 1960s and '70s, Milam organized more than a dozen community radio stations—in Seattle, Portland, San Francisco, Dallas, St. Louis—and then gave them away, back to the communities themselves. But that was a good decade after the day he woke up in a Florida charity hospital, paralyzed.

MILAM: No one really is prepared for something like this happening to the body. It's like some mystery that's inside of us all—the mystery of aging, or the mystery of disease, or the mystery of death. And when it hits you, no matter how much you read about it or hear about it, you're never prepared for what comes over you.

STAMBERG: It took years for you to come to terms with it, then years at a place in Florida where the treatment was brutal. Then you were moved to Warm Springs, Georgia, and you describe that as a kind of paradise. What was the paradise?

MILAM: First, the layout and design of Georgia Warm Springs Foundation—in that beautiful North Georgia country, with the soft nights and the stars and the sweet smell of magnolia. Then, hundreds of support personnel for the patients, and the freedom that came with not having to be subservient to some doctor. It was—and, indeed, still is—a paradise. It was Franklin Delano Roosevelt's keen sense of what people need—people in that sort of desperate part of their lives, when they wake up one day and find themselves helpless. He had the wisdom to set up something like this for that world.

STAMBERG: It was also a world of friends—people who were all in the same boat, or on the same gurneys, or the same kinds of crutches. A community.

MILAM: It's like being an eighteen-year-old person inside the body of a seventy-five-year-old. Our bodies were new to us. We were learning about that together. And we were learning freedom, too. Or sometimes, in some cases, we were learning what freedom we didn't have.

There's a passage where I describe a woman I was with at Warm Springs—in this book I call her Francine—on the day she was learning to walk: ". . . that summer day in August at the upper Georgia Hall walking court, during 'walking class.' When you try out your new braces and new crutches. For the first time by yourself. All the other times there have been pushboys and physical therapists to hold on to your belt. But the rest of us are getting up, me and John Longstaff and Margot, all of us in full triumph on our new feet, walking, friends out for a stroll together.

"We are full of the triumph of getting onto our own two feet, by ourselves, to try out our new stuff together. And you do too: you,

He was brave, that Roosevelt. O Lordy he was brave. He must have known that he would never be whole, but he was brave. A clear-cut nothing-from-the-waist-down case, and yet he forced himself to walk. With steel and fire, he forced his arms to take him across the room, across the lawn, down the steps. He knew, some part of him knew he would never be walking at the head of the Labor Day Parade again, but he kept on pouring his will into what was left of his muscles, trying to walk that walk again.

—from The Cripple Liberation Front Marching Band Blues

Francine in blue shorts and white blouse. You my Francine, my beautiful Francine: I never realize how tall you are. I never realize how tall you are until you are tall no more.

"A swing through, and you miss. Feet go forward, but the balance is wrong, the balance is all wrong Francine. And you begin to go backwards. Ah Francine.

"You fall backwards. There is nothing to stop you in your fall backwards. You don't have the muscles of the other 99 percent of humanity that would permit you to twist, to catch yourself. There is nothing you have to protect yourself from the ground.

"To this day, a quarter century later, I can hear the sound that your head makes when it smacks into brick pavement. I can hear it, and I see you now there, my helpless friend, my helpless love. We are all helpless. There is no one, no one of your friends there who can reach out to you as you fall; none of us can reach out to you after you fall. There is no way I can reach down to you, there is no way I can kneel down to reach you as you lie there on the ground my Francine.

"Your body is askew. You are so hurt by your fall that you cannot cry out. You don't see my gut soul frozen with the recognition of you all of us lying helpless there, the army of us cripples fallen over backwards to crack our heads and with the shock of it, just barely able to groan, barely."

(*Long silence.*)

STAMBERG: Francine had a concussion. She never walked again.

(*Another long pause. Even sitting in a distant studio, he's touched me deeply.*)

Lorenzo, why do you choose to call your book *The Cripple Liberation Front Marching Band Blues*? It's a wonderful title, but the fact that you . . . you can even use that word—"cripple." I know some people who don't even like to be called "handicapped," let alone "crippled." They prefer phrases like "differently able." But you come right out with it.

MILAM: I was looking it up today, and it's from the old English "crypel," which means "to creep." It's an ancient and historic and honorable word. The word "handicap" means you're at a disadvantage that's often self-imposed. It's from racing. Or the word "disabled." "Dis" is from the Latin. It means to turn away from. "Disable" means to turn away from mobility. I can't stand either of those words. With my friends who are crips, we would never use the words "handi-

capped" or "disabled." We call each other "crips"—even refer to each other as "basket cases." I want to defuse the rage that's implicit in that word—"cripple"—and indeed restore it to its place of honor.
STAMBERG: Lorenzo Milam. His book is called the *The Cripple Liberation Front Marching Band Blues*. It's published by Mho and Mho Works in California.

——

When I phoned for permission to publish the excerpts of his writing quoted above, Lorenzo had just one request, which I am pleased to fulfill: The address of Mho and Mho Works is Box 33135, San Diego, California 92163. He says that copies of the book are getting dusty under his bed, and he wouldn't mind selling some off. Lorenzo also said that at age fifty-eight, he was spending most of his time in a wheelchair, and working very hard to learn how to do absolutely nothing.

There are people who are good around cripples, and there are people who are dumb. I learn to avoid the latter. Like the ones who refer to my crutches as "Pogo Sticks." Or the people who spurt ahead of me as we are reaching the door and say, "Here, lemme help ya: looks like you gotta handful there!" Strangers with concern on their faces, always asking if they can help. "Can I help you?" "Can I help you son?" "Here, I'll get that for you." So many times I turn away, go back from where I came, leaving them holding the door. I won't let them do this to me.

—from The Cripple Liberation Front Marching Band Blues

A Nine-Letter Word for Puzzle

June 1984

When *The New York Times* Sunday crossword puzzle turned fifty in February 1992, it made the cover of the paper's magazine section. Those twenty-one-by-twenty-one-box brain ticklers had clearly become an institution. (Daily puzzles didn't appear until 1950.) The cover story quoted a wartime memo the *Times*'s first puzzle editor, Margaret Farrar, wrote to Sunday editor Lester Markel urging the paper to begin running puzzles. "I don't think I have to sell you on the increased demand for this kind of pastime in an increasingly worried world," Farrar wrote. "You can't think of your troubles while solving a crossword. . . ." Readers agreed. They said the puzzle helped their insomnia, their cognitive skills, their health.

When Margaret Farrar died in 1984 at the age of eighty-seven, Will Weng, her successor at the *Times,* did our obituary.

WENG: One day, the phone rang and a voice said, "This is the foreman in the composing room. Your puzzles for the next week have all vanished. Will you replace them?" And Margaret Farrar said, "You lost them. You find them!"

STAMBERG: And they did! Margaret Farrar, *The New York Times*'s very first crossword puzzle editor died this week. They were called "Word Cross" puzzles when she started editing them at the *New York World.* She went to the *Times* in 1942, stayed there as editor until 1969. Margaret Farrar trained Will Weng to take her place.

WENG: I think she was about as pure a puzzle person as I know. She really transformed the puzzle from child's play or just an ordinary time killer, to something that would be of interest to adult solvers.

STAMBERG: Did Ms. Farrar make up the actual puzzles herself?

WENG: No, no. Editors rarely do that. There's a whole stable of people, most of them amateurs, who love to make up puzzles. And they send them in. Then the editor picks out ones that are acceptable and puts them into shape—smoothes the definitions. A lot of the work is to check items for accuracy.

STAMBERG: Looking up all those obscure words like *gnu*—all those crossword-puzzle words. What was Ms. Farrar's greatest strength as crossword-puzzle editor?

WENG: When the puzzles were absolutely new, they were quite primitive. She single-handedly transformed the crossword puzzle into what you might say is a work of art, something that is respectable. You don't have to be ashamed to be working a puzzle, because of how she developed it into something that not only was fun to do but gave a certain amount of instruction as well.

——

Margaret Farrar was married to John Farrar, the Farrar in the publishing firm Farrar, Straus & Giroux. For another publisher, Simon & Schuster, she produced the first crossword puzzle book, in 1924. She was working on her 135th puzzle book when she died.

Will Weng upheld the traditions begun by Ms. Farrar, test-solving every puzzle, livening up the clues, checking them. But when he began the job, Mr. Weng suffered through a year of hate mail from readers. "Bring back Margaret Farrar!" they wrote, complaining that the puzzles had declined in quality. Weng said he even got those letters when he was still using puzzles Farrar had edited.

In later conversations with me over the years (as a crossword wrangler myself, I looked for ways to get the subject on the air), Mr. Weng spoke about his rules for the *Times* puzzles.

"There are no two-letter words. That's one rule. And I was careful about body parts and functions. I wouldn't let 'enema' in. I never ran a Watergate puzzle. Got a lot of them sent to me, because it was all over the paper, but I said, 'Why add another one?'

"You also have to keep in your mind that there are an awful lot of people in hospitals solving these puzzles. So I never defined 'cancer' as anything but a tropic or a sign of the zodiac."

Maybe your theme is flowers, and you have "chrysanthemum" and stuff like that. You take your large words and put them in, and then you put the black squares in and form your shorter words around them. Several people who do the daily puzzles will just take a pattern out of the *Times* and put their own puzzle into it. So the same diagram might appear over again.

—*Will Weng, March 1987*

We have about fifty to seventy-five people who regularly create puzzles for the paper. They range from sixteen-year-old boys to retired professors to housewives. Then there are others who just send in one or two. Some people have just one puzzle in them, just like some people have one book in them. Send in a very good puzzle, use it, and that's the end. You never hear from them again.

—Will Weng, March 1987

A few years ago, *New York Times* crossword puzzles were computerized. The Windows program lets you cheat. Choose a clue, click "Peek," and the answer gets filled in. "Undo" erases mistakes. Surely this modern breakthrough is causing Margaret Farrar some motion problems in the grave. It can't be successful, can it? As we all know, the truest pleasure of *Times* puzzles is working them in ink.

James Baldwin on Racism

December 1985

The Fire Next Time was James Baldwin's 1963 plea for reconciliation between blacks and whites. He predicted that the struggle for civil and human rights would end either in reconciliation or in chaos. Baldwin's title came from an old spiritual: "God gave Noah the rainbow sign./No more water, the fire next time!" After the 1992 riots in Los Angeles—the worst urban riots of the century—newspapers and magazines remembered the prophecy. "The Fire This Time" was the title of *Time* magazine's cover story on the war waged by blacks, Latinos, Asians (mostly Korean Americans), and whites on the streets of America's second-biggest city.

The acquittal of four white policemen who had bludgeoned black motorist Rodney King was a lesson in the grim truth of race in America in the nineties, a truth black Americans have known for generations: There is no equal justice for blacks.

In 1985, James Baldwin had illuminated this truth for *All Things Considered.*

BALDWIN: There are black people on every level of American life, including the middle class and the upper middle class. But to be a member of the black middle class is simply to be a member of the black class. It does not alter what one may call your stigma in this country if you're black.

STAMBERG: (*Narrating*) James Baldwin has been examining the relationship between blacks and whites in America for all of his writing

> I am very much concerned that American Negroes achieve their freedom here in the United States. But I am also concerned for their dignity, for the health of their souls, and must oppose any attempt that Negroes may make to do to others what has been done to them. I think I know—we see it around us every day—the spiritual wasteland to which that road leads.
>
> —*from* **The Fire Next Time***, 1963*

life. In books like *Notes of a Native Son, Nobody Knows My Name,* and his latest, *The Evidence of Things Not Seen,* Baldwin has explored—often in anger—the condition of American blacks. He finds few improvements for young blacks here—those between the ages of seventeen and twenty-five—although for blacks as a whole he says there have been some changes.

BALDWIN: Someone my age can say this is better than it was—this is improved here, or the enrollment of kids in various colleges has risen, or whatever—and that may to some extent be true. But it doesn't have any effect on the bulk of the black population, which still lives in the ghetto. Also, the black middle class is not really significantly divorced from the people on the bottom, because they're still black.

STAMBERG: But, Mr. Baldwin, I've heard so many complaints in recent years, as the black middle class has bulged, that as blacks move up the socioeconomic ladder they forget about the people in the ghetto. They don't pay the kind of attention they need to, in order to help their brothers and sisters.

BALDWIN: Well, that's inevitably true enough, but that doesn't really make any difference, since they are nevertheless, in the eyes of most white Americans, more black than they are middle class.

STAMBERG: Don't you reach a point where as a black person you say, "Who cares what I appear to be in the eyes of a white! If I am living as well as whites, if I have the advantages and opportunities that any white has, who cares what they think?"

BALDWIN: Well, even if you have those opportunities, you have paid more for them and *keep* paying more for them. And it doesn't protect your son or your daughter, who risk being raised in a kind of limbo between the whites and the blacks.

STAMBERG: I wonder how many conversations like this you find yourself having, when suddenly somebody says, "But what about Jesse Jackson?" There's Jackson breaking barriers with his Rainbow Coalition, running for president last year, winning almost four hundred delegates. Look what happened for the first time in the history of this country!

BALDWIN: Well, it's very, very important what happened to Jesse Jackson, you know, but it doesn't pay anybody's rent yet.

STAMBERG: Yet! You said "yet."

BALDWIN: Uh, I'm very . . . I'm very . . . I'm very glad . . . I'm very glad for the Jackson presence, because it has something to do with the morale of young people. It doesn't have any objective meaning yet, but the morale of the people is very, very important.

STAMBERG: You write a number of extraordinary things in this book, but one that puzzles me—just leaped off the page at me—was when you remember something an old black lady said to you. Standing on her porch in Alabama, she said, "White people don't hate black people. If they did, we'd all be black."

BALDWIN: Umm-hmm. Well, it's very true, isn't it?

STAMBERG: I don't understand it.

BALDWIN: Oh, it means—especially in the Deep South—it means everyone has been mixed for a very long time. Remember, years and years and years ago, at the beginning of the civil rights battle, black people were talking about desegregation, which was a social matter, you know—to desegregate the schools, desegregate the institutions, desegregate the living arrangements of Americans.

But white people talked about integration. No black person would have talked about integration, because we could tell by looking at the colors of our skins how long we had been integrated! It's this denial on the part of so-called white Americans—denial of his past, after all. And his present, too. You see what I mean?

My grandmother, for example, was a slave, and she had fourteen children. Some of them came out of her womb pale white, and some came out black. But they came out of the womb of the same woman. And some led lives of white men, and some led lives of black men, like my father. And that's true for the nation, really. That's part of our history.

STAMBERG: Before we began taping, you were saying you were sixty, and in the course of—

BALDWIN: Sixty-one, actually.

STAMBERG: Pardon?

BALDWIN: Sixty-one.

STAMBERG: Oh, be sixty!

(*Laughter.*)

You were saying that in your lifetime you've seen a number of changes, although not as many as you'd like to see. Do you think the new attention to the situation in South Africa will be good for American blacks? The kind of consciousness raising that Randall Robinson and his TransAfrica lobby are doing now—picketing the South African embassy, getting arrested, coming back to protest again, pushing

I never heard Malcolm X refer to a white person without referring to him as a devil. And he would often use it even when he was saying something quite complimentary. It was just "devil." I remember the first time I ever heard him alter that pattern. He was saying something like, "I met this dev—" and he stopped in mid-devil. And then he almost a bit embarrassedly said something like, "Well, he's this fellow that works for *The New York Times*." And I knew that whoever that fellow was had made some very considerable impression on Malcolm.

—*Alex Haley,*
December 1971

against apartheid, pushing the Reagan administration to toughen its policies?

Now, maybe one reason for the increased awareness is that we're more comfortable when it's someplace far away. But maybe the new consciousness of oppression *there* may come home to roost in valuable ways.

BALDWIN: It's *not* that far away! I think that may happen, because I am not a pessimist. And in some ways it is happening. Because it's very difficult to call for sanctions against South Africa and do nothing about Detroit.

STAMBERG: What do you find yourself saying to the incipient James Baldwins—the ones who will grow up to become the gifted writers, the ones who will speak out—about the need to hold on and keep the anger, and know how to temper it when necessary, and let it go at other times.

BALDWIN: That's right—how to *use* the anger instead of letting it use you. And to bear in mind that it is really not a racial problem, though it seems to be.

STAMBERG: Are you saying it's not race, it's economic, or—

BALDWIN: From my point of view, it has something to do with the American sense of reality. White people walk around with an image of black people in their minds, and react to this image. All the legends about black people in this country—you know, the *Gone with the Wind* nonsense, the happy darky, Mammy, Uncle Tom, the rapist— all of these images have nothing whatever to do with reality. Nothing whatever to do with black or white. It has to do with an image white Americans have created about black people in order to justify the way black people are treated in this country.

A black walking around on the streets of America does not carry around in his head some image of a white man. He doesn't *have* to. The white man is right there, you know—the cop or whoever—and it is a part of his reality to deal with that every day of his life. But in the minds of most Americans, as far as I can tell, *he*—the black—is a kind of fantasy.

Color is not a human or a personal reality; it is a political reality.

—from The Fire Next Time, 1963

━━━

James Baldwin did not live to see the Los Angeles riots that reflected so much of what he had said that day on *All Things Considered*. He died two years after we spoke, in December 1987.

Arthur Murray: A Life in Dance

April 1985

(*Music: "Arthur Murray Taught Me Dancing in a Hurry."*)

STAMBERG: Arthur Murray, happy ninetieth birthday!

MURRAY: Thank you very much.

STAMBERG: Are you going to dance today in order to celebrate?

MURRAY: Well, we're going out tonight. Some friends are giving me a party. And we'll probably dance.

STAMBERG: (*Narrating*) They'll definitely dance if his wife, Kathryn, has anything to say about it. Arthur Murray will dance on his ninetieth birthday as he danced on television for eleven years on *The Arthur Murray Party,* once described as the longest running commercial in the history of TV. Twenty years ago, Mr. Murray sold his nationwide chain of some five hundred dance studios. Since then, he has lived in Honolulu. Today, he explained how, at the age of eighteen, he got into the dance business.

MURRAY: Well, I worked for an architect, I went to architectural school at nighttime, and I expected to be an architect, because in high school a teacher said to me, "You're artistic, you should go into one of the arts." I couldn't think of anything to do except architecture that might be profitable, because I always heard that artists starved. So I took up architecture, but the most I ever made was five dollars a week. So at nighttime, I went to teach dancing in a dime-a-dance hall in New York. My boss the architect came in, and he was embarrassed that I should watch him learn to dance. So when I asked for a dollar raise, the architect said, "I'll give it to you if you quit dancing." I quit architecture instead.

STAMBERG: That was a very wise decision! Was yours the first chain of dance studios?

MURRAY: It was the *only* one. Then Fred Astaire's contract was not renewed, and some promoter talked him into going into the dance business—telling him, "Arthur Murray made a lot of money. Your name is much bigger, you can do better." But Fred Astaire never made any money out of the studios. In fact, when they did nothing, I would take them off his hands. So, actually, mine is the only one that has been successful.

STAMBERG: These days, there's a little boomlet in the world of ballroom dancing.

MURRAY: Well, ballroom dancing is a step towards getting acquainted with your partner. Today, all you have to do is say "Your place or mine?" You don't need dancing as an introduction.

STAMBERG: You don't need the amenities anymore, huh?

MURRAY: No.

STAMBERG: Could I ask you something long-distance, by telephone? Would you dance with me?

MURRAY: I'd love to!

STAMBERG: You count out the steps, please.

MURRAY: Count out the steps?

STAMBERG: Yes. You tell me what we're going to do.

MURRAY: Well, of course, the "magic step" is the basis of the fox-trot. You go (*music sneaks in*) forward, forward, side, together. Start with your left foot, going forward, one . . . two . . . and then side, together. Forward, forward, side, together.

STAMBERG: Forward, forward, side, together. I think I'm getting it!
  (*Music—very ballroom-sounding, lots of violins. Up full and hold for a while.*)

STAMBERG: Thank you for that dance, it was lovely. And happy birthday to you.

MURRAY: Thank you very much for calling me.
  (*Music full to end.*)

STAMBERG: Forward, forward, side, together. Arthur Murray at ninety, still teaching dancing in a hurry.

An AIDS Awakening

April 1985

Usually it's raining when I drive past her apartment building, and the rain feels too appropriate. On sunny days, I go to work a different route. Rock Creek Park, a wildway that snakes through the northwest section of Washington, provides what must be the loveliest urban commute in America, and is the quickest path from home to NPR when there's sun. But in the rain, the creek comes up in places, the park slickens with leaves and slowed cars, and Sixteenth Street is my long-way-round shortcut. I can get down that one-time "Avenue of the Presidents" (the White House sits on Pennsylvania Avenue at the bottom of Sixteenth) quickly in the rain. And en route, I pass the place where Sunny Sherman used to live. I went there only once, on an April day in 1985; we met and spoke for less than an hour. But there has not been a rainy-day driving time in the intervening years that I haven't seen that building and remembered our meeting.

Sonya "Sunny" Leisa Sherman was one of the first women in this country to have contracted AIDS and spoken out about it. She was also the first person I met who had the disease. Spring of 1985 may seem late for such a first encounter. But the history of the disease has shaped the way it has been reported.

On June 5, 1981, the U.S. Centers for Disease Control in Atlanta first reported the presence of a rare form of pneumonia in five members of the Los Angeles gay community. An apparent medical curiosity primarily affecting homosexuals, the disease was a science story before it became a societal one. Early cases were few, and reporting was spotty.

NPR did more than any other broadcast organization, and did it earlier, but the work was still sparse.

Less than a year after the initial CDC report, in April 1982, the NPR science unit produced a special "Gay Health" series, which ran on *All Things Considered* and *Morning Edition*. Five months later, in September 1982, the disease got a name: Acquired Immune Deficiency Syndrome. And the affected population expanded. In addition to homosexual men, intravenous drug (heroin) users were added to the high-risk list, also hemophiliacs and Haitians. "The four *H*'s" was our shorthand way of remembering the groups affected. Small groups, removed—it was thought—from the so-called general population. Stigmatized and reviled, gays gradually began organizing, forming activist coalitions, pressuring for AIDS research. In December 1982, NPR reported that the AIDS population had gotten larger, that some heterosexual men and women may have contracted the disease through blood transfusions.

AIDS stayed on the air at NPR, an ongoing science story of a disease affecting specific communities. Anne Gudenkauf, our science editor, says that her reporters' work was well accepted at first. Then came resistance from the news director and from *Morning Edition* and *All Things Considered* producers and staff who felt that listeners had heard enough about a disease that hit only marginal, isolated communities. One science reporter remembers NPR legal affairs correspondent Nina Totenberg flouncing down the hall one day, screaming at the top of her lungs, "If I hear one more of those goddamn AIDS stories, I'll puke!" Listeners, too, protested. "Why do you continue to cover a problem that perverts brought on themselves?" one letter writer objected.

As host of *All Things Considered,* I, too, cautioned against too much coverage. I felt that a disease with so many unanswered questions attached to it was becoming more and more difficult to handle as news. Profiles of AIDS patients were compelling and heartbreaking, but ultimately they began to sound alike. There was no way to advance the story. Nothing new was happening. On *All Things Considered* I introduced the various science reports but saw no reason or need to get personally involved—to move into the subject myself, doing stories or interviews as I usually did with important national and international issues. (In many cases, before reporters are available or assigned, it's a host interview that initially gets a story on the air.

ANN LANDERS: I'm still amazed in this day and age, Susan—you think that the kids are so smart about sex. You think that they're really street smart. But they're not information smart.

STAMBERG: Just look at the teenage pregnancy rate, and you know they're not so smart.

LANDERS: Right! Over a million teenage pregnancies last year. They need information. They need to know the symptoms of V.D., especially now that we have a new strain of V.D. called herpes simplex II, for which there is no cure.

—November 1979

And host interviews often keep a story on the air even without reporter involvement.)

Then, three months before the news broke that actor Rock Hudson
had AIDS—a revelation that brought dramatic and widespread national
attention to the disease for the first time—along came Sonya Sherman
and a way for me to get involved.

Producer Ellen Weiss spotted an article in *The Washington Post*
and handed me the clipping. "Look," she said. "Here's a local woman
with AIDS—there aren't very many of them—*and* she's going public
with it. Why don't we go talk to her? Her name is Sonya Sherman."

Ellen phoned and chatted a bit with Sherman to see how she
sounded, whether she was healthy enough to do an interview, whether
she was a good talker. A time and date was set for the taping. We would
go to Sonya Sherman's apartment on Sixteenth Street. "Ellen," I said,
"be sure to tell Gary about the health situation." I wanted Gary Henderson, the engineer assigned to us, to know we were going to see an AIDS
patient. I felt he should be emotionally prepared in case Sherman was
desperately ill (and also have the option not to go at all, if he so wished).

This would be the first time any of the three of us would see the face
of AIDS. Information in April 1985 was murky enough about how the
virus was transmitted that ahead of time we each paused to think about
where we were headed. Gary, the soul of easygoing affability, remembers thinking, "As long as I don't get too close, it'll be fine. It's a gig.
A sensitive gig, but still . . ." For Ellen, with her bright energy and
fearlessness in the face of most challenges, it was a test. "I was such an
egalitarian—thought everyone should be treated the same, no difference," she says today. "I wanted to see whether I would *really* feel that
way once I met her." My own anticipations were darker. I was reluctant
to see someone who was dying. I worried about exposure to the disease,
reminded myself not to accept a drink or use any of her utensils. Sonya
Sherman knew there was no danger in any of this. But I didn't know it,
and was fearful. A few days before the scheduled taping, my son got
strep throat. "We better call Sonya," I told Ellen, "to see if it's a
problem." "No problem," Sonya said. "Come along."

She swung open her apartment door and stood there smiling—a
small, very thin, tanned young woman. We would learn that the tan was
not from sunshine, but at first glance she looked as if she'd acquired her
color on some glamour slope in Aspen. The disease hadn't ravaged her.

Or didn't seem to have. Later, when her picture was published with her newspaper obituary, I saw the round-cheeked, beaming, and beautiful girl she had once been.

Sonya Sherman's apartment was furnished in cleanly finished woods and cheerful colors and there was a marmalade cat that would inadvertently become part of our story. After the interview was over and we said our good-byes, my first words to Ellen on our way back to NPR were "Leave in the part about the cat." It broke the tension at a crucial time.

Excuse me. I see that in writing about all this, I keep getting ahead of myself. But I knew the ending of Sonya Sherman's story then, as I know it now. Perhaps that sure conclusion propels this narration. I want to get to the end quickly because it's terrible, but it's terrible and I don't want to get there, so the story comes out pell-mell, rushing to finish and rushing *not* to finish.

We refused with thanks an offer of something to drink, and began to tape. At the beginning, in response to my questions, I noticed that Sonya Sherman had a common habit of the ill: She gave lengthy and detailed descriptions of her condition and her medications. Initially, that was all right—educational, in fact—as this was that early period of AIDS awareness—so early that on the air we were still translating the acronym. (It's always a watershed when an acronym becomes part of the language. With AIDS, that didn't happen until 1986.) So it was useful to hear her medical details. But I wanted to change the subject and listened for a way to do it.

The three of us—Ellen, Gary, and I—still remember how intense this conversation was. Sonya's voice was flattened, markedly unmusical—medication had damaged her hearing. Her mouth, dry from all the medicines, made smacking sounds when she talked. As she spoke, the awful details of her condition accumulated and became more and more graphic. But she was so matter-of-fact that the interview felt almost clinical. Which is why, after Ellen had edited our forty or so minutes of raw tape down to ten, I asked her to restore a section that had caught me by the throat when it happened—Sonya's description of crying over a Thanksgiving Day parade. I wanted some feeling on the air, something beyond a recitation of facts.

Please meet Sonya Sherman now, as I met her that April day in 1985.

STAMBERG: Sonya Sherman, you and I worried a little before we got together today. You worried that I might be allergic to your cat. And I worried because we've got strep in our house and I didn't want to bring those germs in here.

SHERMAN: I really thank you for that, too. I don't need a case of strep!

STAMBERG: Explain to listeners why that's so important.

SHERMAN: Well, I'm very susceptible to any type of infection that's floating around in the air. And unfortunately, most of the infections that I'm susceptible to are very hard to get rid of.

STAMBERG: (*Narrating*) Sonya Sherman has Acquired Immune Deficiency Syndrome—AIDS. She's tanned, blond, very attractive, about five foot five, thirty-four years old. She had been working as a legal secretary when her AIDS was diagnosed in October 1983. The Centers for Disease Control say there are 591 female AIDS cases out of a total of 9,405 cases nationwide. Since 1983, Sherman has been in and out of the hospital four times. She says she's been feeling well lately, has put on a few pounds, gained some strength. Sonya Sherman tries to lead a normal life, but her daily routine has changed greatly in the past year and a half.

SHERMAN: When I first get up in the morning, I give myself an insulin shot, because I developed diabetes from a reaction to a medication I was taking. And then I have breakfast, and if I don't have anything particular to do I usually stay in bed and rest up and save my energy. But if there's something that I want to do, I get up and go out and do shopping or go to the bank or I have a friend that comes over once or twice a week, and sometimes we go for rides out to Mount Vernon or something like that. But I get out and about. I go to the doctors once every three weeks out at NIH.

STAMBERG: Why?

SHERMAN: They do a blood workup on me every three weeks.

STAMBERG: Are you on any regular medication now other than insulin?

SHERMAN: I'm on two CDC-controlled drugs. They are not released through FDA yet. One is called clofazimine and the other one is called ansamycin. The clofazimine gives me my tan color. I'm not even allowed out in the sun, because the sun will react with the chemicals in the clofazimine. So, I take those every day.

I have a catheter inserted in my chest that was used for I.V.

feedings the last time I was in the hospital. You can leave it in indefinitely, as long as you take care of it properly.

STAMBERG: What does that do, what's that for?

SHERMAN: The catheter? Well, right now we're just keeping it in, in case I have to go on I.V.'s again, because my veins are very weak. They're hard to find. So they can hook up the I.V. to this. This goes through, I believe—I don't remember—one of the main veins in my heart. And now they draw blood off the catheter also, which is wonderful, because I don't have to get stuck.

STAMBERG: Fewer pinpricks!

SHERMAN: Yes. (*Laughs.*)

STAMBERG: Do you ever think in behalf of others about your disease? I mean, just as you worried that I might be allergic to your cat, do you consider the population in general? Do you go to restaurants or think about using utensils in a restaurant?

SHERMAN: I do go to restaurants a lot, as a matter of fact. I'm not worried about using utensils in a restaurant, because they go through the dishwasher and everything. I am more careful about washing my hands before I eat, or not eating from someone else's plate, or drinking out of the same glass. And that's more because I worry about what *I* might catch. I'm not worried about them catching AIDS, because you can't catch AIDS through casual contact. Can't catch it through saliva.

I don't kiss like I used to, I'll tell you that! I used to always say hello to friends and give them a kiss. If I do that now, it's on the cheek. Or I give them a hug.

STAMBERG: You know, that's an interesting thing you said about kissing. Feel free not to answer, but it makes me think you don't have sex like you used to, either. Do you?

SHERMAN: Oh, I haven't had sex for two years—over two years. It's something you get used to. I don't even date. It's a very difficult thing, because if you meet a new person—and I've had the situation come up—and they say, "Well, let's get together for a drink" or "Let's go out"—it suddenly hits you: "Well, I got to tell them I have AIDS, but when do I do it? When will they accept that?" Because you can't sort of say, "Well, gee, I'd love to go out with you but I have AIDS."

STAMBERG: When *do* you do it? When do you decide?

SHERMAN: Well, in *my* mind, if you're really going to start dating

---

INMATE 1: Say a particular man does have AIDS and he has contracted it from a woman, okay? So in that situation, as far as using a condom is concerned, sometimes they're probably doing that on a revenge-type thing, you know what I'm saying? Some of them think like that, you know—that they have to pay it back to so many other women, not just that particular one.

INMATE 2: That's true, that's true. Probably saying, "Since I got it, why not spread it?"

STAMBERG: Well, that's like committing murder.

INMATE 2: That's right. Yes, it is.

—*AIDS education class, D.C. Detention Center, August 1991*

somebody, you should let them know. Not that they should stay away from you, but they have to know that your relationship can only go so far. It's very unpredictable how you'll feel, too. Sometimes I won't even make plans. Right now, I've got plans to do something in June. That's pretty far in advance for me. But a lot of times people will say to me, "You want to go out for dinner next week?" And I'll say, "Call me next week, call the day that you want to go out, and I'll see how I feel."

STAMBERG: Do you get annoyed—you must have a lot of anger, as well—but annoyed at having to be so self-conscious, so aware of how you're feeling this morning, and whether it's different this afternoon? I mean, this interruption to normalcy that is your life.

SHERMAN: I'm not annoyed that I have to be aware of it, but I'm annoyed when I feel bad. Because there's nothing I can do about it. It takes me longer to take a shower, get dressed, put on my makeup. Sometimes I have to rest in between doing some of those things.

STAMBERG: Because it's an enormous effort? You're getting very tired from the most ordinary tasks?

SHERMAN: Even when it comes to crossing the street. I know I can't run on a yellow light anymore. (*Laughs*.) So, it takes more time for that, too.

STAMBERG: (*Laughs*.) It's probably safer! Stand on the curb for a while.

SHERMAN: (*Smiling*) Yeah, that's true.

STAMBERG: Will you tell us how you got AIDS?

SHERMAN: I contracted it sexually. We know that, because I did not use I.V. drugs and I am not Haitian and I had never had a blood transfusion or received any blood products prior to having AIDS. We're not sure who I contracted it from, because the bisexual males that I've had contact with are all okay. But there is a carrier effect. A person can carry the disease without being symptomatic.

STAMBERG: Are the men—however many there were—aware of your situation now, and are they supportive about it?

SHERMAN: The ones I've stayed in contact with are supportive. Of course, they were frightened when they heard it first. The person I think I contracted the disease from is somebody I was engaged to. And he calls me every once in a while to see how I'm doing. He lives in Texas now. So . . . but he calls me and . . . to check and see how I'm doing. And I think that he's as supportive as can be, being that far away. At least he didn't hang up the phone on me and run away!

(*Long pause.*)

STAMBERG: What's your cat's name?

SHERMAN: Nelson.

STAMBERG: He's about to pounce on our tape recorder. He's fascinated! Look at him, Sonya—he's sitting there watching those reels go around.

(*Laughter.*)

SHERMAN: Long as he doesn't tackle!

STAMBERG: He just may. We'll keep an eye out. If our listeners hear a very strange screech, it means that Nelson has lunged.

SHERMAN: That's right! Well, he doesn't have front claws, so it won't be too bad. (*Laughs.*)

STAMBERG: What about the idea that it's God's punishment?

SHERMAN: People have not actually said that to me, but they've asked me if I felt that way. My answer has been that I do believe there's a God—a superior being that has some control over our lives. But I don't look at disease as being a punishment from God. I don't blame things on God.

STAMBERG: But you're not blaming *anybody*. I find that extraordinary. You're not blaming former lovers. You're not blaming yourself. You're not placing blame anywhere.

SHERMAN: No, not really. I don't think that you can, especially if you've contracted the disease sexually.

STAMBERG: You're amazingly rational about this, though, amazingly sanguine. Is that hard won for you?

SHERMAN: No, it comes very easily. I have accepted what's going on. Yeah, I have my periods of time where I sit down and cry about it, or something like that. And the funny thing is, the smallest things set me off. Like last year, I was watching the Thanksgiving Day parade on TV and I started crying. But otherwise, I sort of have accepted the fact that I take things day to day. And I don't waste my energy on things that are unnecessary. Being angry about things you can't do anything about is a waste of energy.

STAMBERG: What was it about the parade that set you off, do you think?

SHERMAN: Oh, I think it kind of reminded me of my childhood and the past, and the fact that I don't know how many Thanksgiving Day parades I'm going to be able to watch.

STAMBERG: It's funny how a little thing like that will do it, isn't it?

SHERMAN: Yes.

STAMBERG: Especially when you spend so much time holding on and exerting restraint.

SHERMAN: It's funny. It really is. I was in the hospital at the time. So it was almost like . . . you know . . . I didn't get to spend Thanksgiving with my family. So, that's a little sad.

STAMBERG: Umm-hmm. (*Long pause.*) What's your prognosis, Sonya?

SHERMAN: Well, it's . . . my prognosis is the same as any other AIDS patient. It's very possible that within the next year or so, I'm going to die.

But as long as I'm aware of my health and I get in contact with my doctors at the beginning of symptoms, usually we can arrest what's going on. That's very important, because the more aware you are and the quicker you start treating it, the better chance you have of prolonging your life. But with the statistics that are out, I don't . . . I'm not sure now what the percentage of the mortality rate is. But I have heard that anybody who's been diagnosed with AIDS from 1980 on, the mortality rate is practically one hundred percent.

So . . . but I don't think that much of the dying. I'm afraid of the *process* of dying. I'm not afraid of death. But just the . . . the illness that will go along with it.

STAMBERG: You don't want to feel like hell.

SHERMAN: No. I'd like to just go to sleep and not wake up. Which is the ideal way. But with AIDS, it doesn't happen that way. It just gets to the point where it's better to die than to live the way you're living.

STAMBERG: Well, it's not only the loss of life, then, it's a loss of dignity.

SHERMAN: Oh, yes, yes. And I know some people who have . . . have taken their own lives before . . . before God has been prepared to take them. But it's only been a couple of weeks before.

STAMBERG: Would *you* consider doing that?

SHERMAN: I never thought I would, but if I were in the condition that these people were in, I probably . . . I might consider it, yes.

STAMBERG: (*Impulsively*) It's incredible to me that we're discussing all

241

this! We're sitting across this table. You and I could be having lunch in a terrific restaurant in Washington, D.C., and there's nothing in you that shows me in any way that we might not be talking four years from now.

SHERMAN: That's true.

STAMBERG: *Ten* years from now.

SHERMAN: That's true.

STAMBERG: That's the part I can't get my head around!

SHERMAN: But you could walk outside after you finish this interview and get hit by a car, and I wouldn't be talking to you a week from now.

But that's not what most people think of. And when I cross the street, it's funny now, I think, "Oh, God, please don't let me get hit by a car!"

(*Laughs.*)

I don't want to go that way.

───

Some are dead, and I understand that they died of AIDS, okay? One man died last year. We were together maybe about five or six years ago, okay? There was a female that died. They said she died of AIDS. We were together maybe about three years ago, okay? They said she contracted AIDS after the time we were together. I don't know. When I heard about it, it was like, you know, that feeling you get in the pit of your stomach. I mean it was just a great . . . It was a massive fear. All I could do was pray.

—Inmate, D.C. Detention Center, August 1991

A year after that broadcast, a journalism teacher at Virginia Tech in Blacksburg wrote that he'd been using a tape of this conversation in class to illustrate "various techniques for conducting an interview on a sensitive or difficult subject." He asked whether Sonya Sherman was alive. I phoned her apartment, and eventually ended up with a ladder of numbers, a line crossed through each row of them, signaling the series of moves she had made since we'd met. In search of care, Sonya Sherman had left that cheerful apartment on Sixteenth Street, the one I've passed so often in these intervening years. Finally, I reached Sunny's father, in Silver Spring, Maryland. He said she was living there with him and her mother and was doing well. Four months later, in August 1986, she died. She was thirty-five.

The day our interview was broadcast, in April 1985, we announced on *All Things Considered* that the Centers for Disease Control had removed Haitians from its list of groups with a known risk of contracting AIDS. And we reminded listeners that homosexual men and intravenous drug users remained on the high-risk list. Now, almost ten years later, nearly three hundred thousand cases of AIDS have been reported in this country. And the World Health Organization predicts that forty million people worldwide will be infected by the end of the century.

George Stevens, Jr. and Sr.

May 1985

STAMBERG: George Stevens, Junior, please list the movies your father directed—the major ones.

STEVENS: Well, he was a cameraman for Laurel and Hardy. And then *Swing Time* (Fred Astaire and Ginger Rogers), *Gunga Din, Woman of the Year* (the first Tracy/Hepburn picture), *Shane, A Place in the Sun, Giant* . . .

STAMBERG: (*Narrating*) And there was *The Diary of Anne Frank, The Greatest Story Ever Told.* . . . Forty years of filmmaking by George Stevens are reviewed and memorialized by his son in the new documentary *George Stevens: A Filmmaker's Journey.*

The father, who died in 1975, was a highly respected director from the thirties through fifties. But in those days, George Stevens, Junior, says, the focus was not on the director.

STEVENS: All you heard of were the stars and L. B. Mayer and Zanuck—the studio heads, the moguls.

STAMBERG: How come?

STEVENS: The stars were so luminous. They were bigger than life, the only people whose faces you saw (there was no television). The stars were so enormous that people weren't asking *how* those films got made. I looked at reviews of my father's films—important films of the late thirties and early forties—and sometimes in *The New York Times* his name wouldn't be mentioned.

STAMBERG: What were some of the Stevens signatures—things that would pop off the screen, which only your father would have put there?

STEVENS: I could sit in the dark and listen to the sound track of *A Place in the Sun* and hear things you would not hear in many other pictures.

STAMBERG: What would you hear?

STEVENS: Mood. The loon over a lake. After Montgomery Clift has drowned the girl, he comes back to Elizabeth Taylor, and they get in a motorboat to drive off. For the sound of the motorboat he used a recording of a Stuka dive-bomber. Somehow, viscerally, you feel it.

STAMBERG: Warren Beatty tells a story in your film about the sound in *Shane*.

STEVENS: My father was a mentor of Warren's, and when Warren made *Bonnie and Clyde,* they talked a lot. Warren learned how to shoot pistols into trash cans to get the loud noises that he wanted. He worked hard on the sound of the film. When it was finished, he went to London for a premiere in the big Warner Theater. He's sitting there, and it's all very quiet—the sound doesn't jump out at you, it doesn't surprise you. So Warren runs up four flights of stairs, bursts into the projection room, and the projectionist says, "Mr. Beatty, I really helped you out! I turned the sound down here, and I turned it up there." Then the projectionist said, "This is the worst-mixed picture we've had here since *Shane*!"

STAMBERG: *Shane* was a film against violence and guns. So your father was very meticulous and precise about getting those gunshot sounds as loud as he could, to make his point to the audience.

STEVENS: He wanted the same feeling of those sounds that he'd heard at war in Bastogne forty years ago.

STAMBERG: The footage he took when he was heading an army motion-picture unit during the Second World War is absolutely unique.

STEVENS: Yes. Army coverage was all thirty-five-millimeter black-and-white. General Eisenhower had asked my father to organize coverage for the D-Day invasion. He took along a sixteen-millimeter camera and shot his own diary of the war, in color. He sent all that film back home, put it in a storeroom, and it sat there for forty years. After he died, I looked at it and started to ask around. When I told people at the Imperial War Museum in London about it, it was like I was talking about the Dead Sea Scrolls! They thought there *was* no color film of D-Day or the liberation of Paris or Dachau. But this extraordinary record was there. It was beautifully shot and wonderfully preserved.

STAMBERG: I read a transcript of a conversation your father had over at the American Film Institute. He tells a wonderful story about the experience of sitting in a cutting room, running film over and over again and . . . please tell what happens.

STEVENS: Well, I'm going to go back a little. When he was a child—nine years old, in San Francisco—he used to sit under the stage waiting for his parents, who were actors, to finish a performance. When his father played *A Tale of Two Cities,* sitting there under the stage, he'd know when the end was coming. His father would speak the words of Sydney Carton, " 'Tis a far, far better thing that I do now than I have ever done. . . ." And he'd hear the audience go silent. Then he would hear the end of the speech, and then the crack of the guillotine coming down on Carton's neck. And then this breathlessness of the audience. And then another crack—the curtain hitting the floor of the stage. Then a beat, and then—as one—all of the hands in the audience hitting together in applause. So he had that instinct for the audience, and that's really what always guided him in his work.

    He used to sit in the afternoon editing a film—as he would do for months on end—trying to get it right. The pictures would be up there on the screen, but they didn't mean anything. Then the door in the back of the projection room would open a crack, and he'd feel another presence there. And all of a sudden, the screen would come to life.

STAMBERG: Because of the presence of that audience! It didn't matter who it was. Just the fact that there was another looking eye completed his creative circle.

STEVENS: Right. Ingmar Bergman said it another way. He said, "If I'm sitting running a picture and there's a cat on the other side of the projection room, I want something to come on screen that's going to amuse that cat."

———

Since the day George Stevens, Junior, told that story, I've often thought of it or repeated it, almost like a mantra. It gives voice to every broadcaster's experience—at typewriters, at computer keyboards, in editing booths—as we sit down to write copy, run audiotape, and then hunt for cuts, trying to get it all right and make it mean something. The piece may seem mostly fine, or it may have problems, but the moment you

JOHN IRVING: I never read to an audience something that, to my knowledge, is finished. I don't read from things once they're books.

STAMBERG: Why not?

IRVING: Well, what's in it for me? Then you really are wasting your time. You do get a certain fee when you give a reading, but the larger benefit is that you get to see which lines will make some people get up and walk out. You can sense the restlessness and the attention of an audience. You can sense the willingness to extend themselves, or go along, and you can see when you've lost a group.

—May 1979

read and play it for someone else, even before that person can offer suggestions, *the very fact of another human presence*—the presence of an audience—gives you the solution.

"Come be my cat," I'll invite producers and editors. "Just come and listen, so I can make it better."

Nairobi: The Women's Conference

July 1985

The summer of 1985 saw a desperate situation in the horn of Africa. A decade of drought in Ethiopia had already culminated, as of 1984, in one million deaths. And the misery continued. Famine and civil war drove Ethiopians into Somalia and Sudan, creating overcrowding, epidemics, more misery. In midsummer, a Live Aid rock concert raised seventy million dollars for African famine victims. In a more stable part of East Africa, a big United Nations conference was held, and *All Things Considered* went to cover it.

In the preface to her *African Stories*, Doris Lessing wrote that Africa "is not a place to visit unless one chooses to be an exile ever afterwards from an inexplicable majestic silence lying just over the border of memory or of thought."

In July 1985, eight of us—reporters, editors, producers, engineers—risked permanent exile by visiting Nairobi, Kenya, for the World Conference to Review and Appraise the Achievements of the United Nations Decade for Women, more handily known as the U.N. Women's Conference. Kenya captured our hearts as we tried to capture its spirit for *All Things Considered*.

Seventeen flying hours from New York, just below the equator in sub-Saharan Africa, we found Kenya a place in which to lose our shadows. The sun is directly overhead there, close enough so that even at four-thirty in the afternoon it burns sharp and hot. Nairobi, the capital, is six thousand feet up, higher than Denver. The altitude is such that U.S. diplomats posted there are advised to pack unpressurized

> There is no twilight here. The sun sets very fast, and it stays dark for twelve hours. What do you think happens when you lock a man and a woman inside a hut for twelve hours? You can't sleep that long. There's no electricity, so you can't read or work on projects. So you make babies.
>
> —*Ghanaian woman, July 1985*

On this twenty-fifth anniversary of its approval by the FDA, the Pill has introduced a degree of confidence we never had before. For the first time, women could plan their pregnancies with a real degree of certainty. That's been the single most important impact of the Pill.

—UCLA anthropologist Susan Scrimshaw, May 1985

tennis balls; otherwise the cans might explode. That high, the sky seems closer; the air is so thin it's like peering into space. Straight up, it's deep, deep cobalt. On the horizon, the color pales to robin's-egg blue. The skies are studded with cloud formations that cluster in ever-changing animal patterns—now a herd of buffalo, soon crocodiles, or rhinos.

Under those skies, some fifteen thousand women from 159 nations gathered to assess what had been accomplished as the U.N. Decade for Women came to an end. Some of the issues were at least as old as Eve: poverty, malnutrition, illiteracy, political power, property rights, violence against women, war and peace. And the biggest issue of all in the developing world: overpopulation (ironically, the conference was held the same year the birth-control pill had its twenty-fifth anniversary).

We learned a litany there, which I can still recite almost from memory: Women make up half the world's population, perform two thirds of the world's work, earn one tenth of its income, and own less than one one-hundredth of its property. Wherever you look, the poorest people are women.

After years spent tracking the women's movement at home, in Nairobi my microphone became an instrument of international social concern as I interviewed Third World women about their lives and hopes. Over and over they testified to women's double burden—responsibility for home *and* job. They dreamed of better lives for their children, especially their daughters. All women have such dreams. An underlying theme in Nairobi was how modernization might make those dreams come true. And an underlying question was: At what cost?

Grace Ogot, who was a delegate to the U.N. conference, is the Maya Angelou of Kenya. She began writing as a young village girl—reworking traditional folk stories, tales her grandmother had told her. As her life changed—she studied nursing in London, married, had four children, became (in 1983) an appointed member of Kenya's Parliament—Grace Ogot's stories changed. She began describing the collision between traditional values and new ideas in her country.

In Nairobi, I pried Grace Ogot away from one of the U.N. sessions to ask about her new story collection. *The Other Woman* told tales of urban people—a mother's terror when her child falls ill, the frightening train ride of a sophisticated author. . . .

STAMBERG: (*Narrating*) In "The Middle Door," a writer—a modern African woman with painted nails and a chic hairdo—reluctantly shares a train compartment with a peasant carrying bunches of unripe bananas and a red cock in her basket. The writer manages to get the village woman moved to a different car. Later, the writer's compartment is invaded by two policemen, who try to rape her.

OGOT: The policemen take the position that an ordinary, good woman would not have her nails painted and her hair done, so this writer must be a woman who expects them to *do* something. They felt she was too tempting.

STAMBERG: This misunderstanding between her and the police is interesting, because there you're writing the clash of the new Kenya and the old.

OGOT: It is very important. Remember also the village lady with the cock and the basket. She didn't see why a woman carrying no baby, who had nothing, wanted a compartment for herself. Everybody fought for independence, she thought. Why should she not share? Why would the modern woman want to be selfish?

STAMBERG: (*Reading*) "She regarded me," the modern woman says, "as a young woman who through luck or historical accident had managed to get education from the tax she paid. . . . I felt her eyes accusing me. 'Do you know who I am, you rich woman, eh? Where were you at the time when I and my kind nursed the wounded men during the struggle for independence? Where were you when we went without food and water? You rich woman, when we carried the little food we could steal to feed our men, where were you?' "

OGOT: And so you have a conflict between a lady who benefited from the independence, and the other lady, who also wants recognition.

STAMBERG: In this story, you're really criticizing modern life, criticizing the function of education, and saying someone who has these privileges—who can be a writer and have painted nails and afford a single compartment on the train—loses touch with her roots.

OGOT: They do! Modernization can bring a lot of joy, but it can also isolate. Even some of the stories that I myself have been able to write, I write because I have roots. And I should be able to pass on some of these roots to my children, so that they are Kenyans, and they are Africans. Because that is what will make him or her walk with the head high, as I did when I was studying abroad. I knew I was a Kenyan, I knew I was an African, and my country was beautiful and my people are lovely.

Poor women in the developing countries have always been very active. If you go and talk to poor women, they want income, they want to make it, they want their children to be educated. What had happened in the past, I think, is that the elite women, the educated women from developed countries, never thought of speaking to the poor women. So we never *knew* what they wanted. Now, thanks to these conferences, educated women in the developing and the developed world are realizing what the issues are. We are talking to our poor sisters. And the poor women have always been very liberated.

—Mayra Buvinic, International Center for Research on Women, U.N. Women's Conference, Copenhagen, July 1980

The Great White Hunter

July 1985

I had a farm in Africa, at the foot of the Ngong Hills. The Equator runs across these highlands, a hundred miles to the North, and the farm lay at an altitude of over six thousand feet. In the daytime you felt that you had got high up, near to the sun, but the early mornings and evenings were limpid and restful, and the nights were cold.

—Isak Dinesen, Out of Africa

Nairobi was abuzz, that summer of 1985, with talk of movies as well as women. Robert Redford and Meryl Streep had just finished shooting *Out of Africa* there—the story of Baroness Karen Blixen, who ran a coffee plantation in a Nairobi suburb before returning home to Denmark to write about it under the pen name Isak Dinesen. There were still people in town who had known Blixen, her husband, Bror—a Swedish aristocrat and great white hunter—and her lover Denys Finch Hatton— an English aristocrat and great white hunter. And there were people, descendants of the Kenya pioneers, who remembered the days when Kenya (the colonialists pronounced it "Keen-ya") was still British East Africa, a place of old ways and old manners.

I explored that long-ago world one evening at an extremely posh, extremely white, party in the suburb named after Baroness Blixen.

(*Party sounds, laughter, music, hubbub of many voices and clinking glasses.*)

WOMAN: Everybody who's anybody is here. You have a cross section of the young, the old, the rich, and the poor.

STAMBERG: Where are the poor? Show me one poor! This is *rich*!

(*Laughter.*)

STAMBERG: (*Narrating*) Very rich. They're the elite of Nairobi. About five hundred businesspeople, doctors, lawyers, original British settlers, diplomats, American-embassy types. Very few blacks, although there's a sizable wealthy black Kenyan community.

They all paid three hundred shillings—about nineteen dollars— to attend the Rhino Ball, a black-tie environmental charity event at Giraffe Manor in Karen—a suburb of Nairobi. There is beef Wellington on the buffet tables, disco music on the phonograph, and talk of endangered wildlife by people who *know* their wildlife.

(*Off-mike, to woman:*) Any luck on my great white hunter?

WOMAN: Oh, I saw one! That man over there with the gray hair. I don't know him well enough to introduce you.

STAMBERG: Where is he?

WOMAN: See over there? He was the president—his name is Tony Dyer.

STAMBERG: Tony Dyer. Great white hunter. Okay.

(*More party sounds as I cross the room to my quarry.*)

STAMBERG: Mr. Dyer, I'll tell you why I want to talk to you. You're the past president of . . . what was the organization?

DYER: The East African Professional Hunters Association.

STAMBERG: (*Narrating*) That's why I wanted to talk to him! Tall, white-haired, with the perfect number of weathered wrinkles circling his piercing blue eyes, and the first two joints of a finger on his left hand missing (his trigger finger?? his contribution to an attacking lion???), Tony Dyer is something out of Central Casting. If Hollywood ever remakes *Bhowani Junction,* Tony Dyer should play the Stewart Granger part. Born in Nairobi—his father settled from Britain in 1920 to farm—Dyer began going on safari fifty-two years ago. In those days, safaris were not the streamlined hot-shower-and-champagne-with-dinner affairs that they can be today.

DYER: No, they were totally different. It would be one very rough old vehicle, no roads. My first safaris were on foot. When I was about thirteen, I started going off on foot. We had wonderful hunting, right from the farm on.

STAMBERG: You mean you could just walk out your front door and find . . . what?

DYER: Elephant, rhino, buffalo, lion, leopard—the lot.

STAMBERG: Where was that farm?

DYER: The farm was actually eighteen miles from where we're standing here.

STAMBERG: On those safaris with your father, did you love it from the beginning, or were you frightened—as any child might be?

DYER: Oh, Lord, no! It was completely natural. A kid in New York—is

RONNIE BOY, SAFARI GUIDE: This park, Masai Mara, is six hundred—odd square miles, and we have in it eight rhino.

STAMBERG: Because of poaching?

BOY: Mostly because of poaching.

STAMBERG: We saw two of those eight yesterday.

BOY: Right. A male and female, and the female has lost her last two calves to lion. They're only susceptible, really, when they're young. Every one lost is a major disaster.

STAMBERG: What amazing creatures they are! They look like armored tanks from 8000 B.C.

BOY: In fact, wartime tanks are known in Swahili as *kifaro*, which is "rhino."

—*on safari, July 1985*

he frightened of the streets? Of course he isn't! It's his home. And the bush was *my* home.

STAMBERG: (*Narrating*) Tony Dyer got into the safari business after World War Two and was a professional hunter for fourteen years, on safari (the word means "journey" in Swahili) ten months out of each year. When he began, there were only twelve professionals. When he left the business, there were one hundred twenty.

DYER: I did two smart things in my life. One was to marry a very fine lady, and the other was to get out of hunting. (*Laughs*.)

STAMBERG: Why was it smart to get out of hunting?

DYER: It's such an intense life. If you do it well, there's no way for you to go on doing it forever.

STAMBERG: How long would an average safari last?

DYER: Well, in the early years, they were much longer. With one client, I did two five-month safaris.

STAMBERG: You stay out and move from one locale to another?

DYER: That's right. We used to hunt Kenya, Uganda, Tanganyika, Sudan. Even in the Congo. Thirty, forty different kinds of animals, one hunt.

STAMBERG: When you talk about the intensity of it, where did that tension come from? From needing to deliver? From having to produce for the people who were hiring you to take them out?

DYER: Well, it was almost like a ship at sea. You were the captain. But you didn't have any other officers to stand watches with you. You were on duty from, say, four o'clock in the morning until ten o'clock at night for maybe six weeks without a break. That's hard going!

STAMBERG: Why four o'clock in the morning?

DYER: Say you had two clients—one might sleep in and you'd hunt with the other. And when you came back, the other would be fresh and you'd go out again, and so on. It's rather like a relay race, but you're running all the laps.

And then it got too commercial. I think the worst thing that ever happened to the safari business is the four-wheel-drive car. Things like four-wheel drive and vitamin pills and all the rest of it—everybody was hopped up.

STAMBERG: How did it get too commercial?

DYER: Money got tighter. The old millionaires were more conscious of how much they were spending on a safari. The safari lost a lot of its grace under the modern conditions. I mean, I've had a person arrive off the plane carrying a pack on his back and say, "Okay, let's go!" I'd say, "Hang on—we've got to get licenses, we've got to decide where we're going and what you want." "Oh, I want to *go!* Let's *go, let's go!*" That's not the safari business I got into.

One example, from the days of the really old safaris: Alan Black—a name hardly known because he was such a secretive man—took a lot of royalty on safari in the early 1900s. And he insisted that his whereabouts remain secret. All sorts of government officials said, "Well, but we must know where that Very Important Person is!" And he'd say, "No way are you going to know where *my* Very Important Person is! Where I go is secret." But now safaris go out with radio telephones. They keep in touch with the stock market and all the rest of it. It's lost a lot of its old grace.

STAMBERG: Did the licenses you mentioned establish certain standards, rules and regulations, for what you could and couldn't do on safari?

DYER: Absolutely they did! In the classic tradition, if somebody did something wrong, he lost his license and that was it.

STAMBERG: What's "wrong"?

DYER: One hunter I knew well allowed a film company to pressure him into deliberately wounding a lion so that some champion rifle shot of America could shoot a charging lion. Well, the American missed. The lion actually killed him. And that professional hunter was broken for life. He was out of the business. He was only a youngster then, and he was finished.

STAMBERG: It's interesting that so much of your sympathy and concern goes to the hunters. Some of us might have more sympathy toward the animals. After all, you people were going out to kill them!

DYER: I've got a pretty good answer for that. The national parks of Kenya, Tanganyika, and Uganda were funded by the East Africa Professional Hunters Association.

STAMBERG: You mean you all feared the commercialization would endanger your animals? You felt you had to do something?

DYER: Absolutely.

STAMBERG: Hunting's been banned here since 1977.

DYER: Twentieth of May, 1977.

STAMBERG: You remember the date!

There is a plausible story that the term originated through Alan Black who, even in 1907, was much respected as a "white hunter." . . . Delamere needed two hunters to shoot game for his porters and employed Alan Black, whose skill at shooting with a bow and arrow was as great as that with a gun. But the second hunter was a Somali who also acted as *Neapara* or headman in camp. To differentiate between the two, on account of Black's surname, the Somali was referred to as "the black hunter" while Black was always called "the white hunter" and from this circumstance, the term caught on and stuck.

—*Errol Trzebinski,* **The Kenya Pioneers**

DYER: And on the twenty-sixth of August we closed down the Professional Hunters Association, because it was quite clear that our course was run.

STAMBERG: Did you grieve about it?

DYER: Of course we grieved. A lot of people felt it terribly keenly. But most of the good hunters were very tough, durable, adaptable men. They went and found other occupations.

STAMBERG: No office jobs?

DYER: No, no office jobs.

STAMBERG: Tell me a wonderful hunting story. Tell me the one that you found yourself telling most when you got back from a safari and sat around with the other hunters.

DYER: Well, rather than hunting stories, I'd prefer to speak of what safari life does to people. They'd never be completely content with life back home again. They would always want to come back to Africa. And quite a lot of the young ones would be immeasurably better people for it. More mature. I've seen youngsters completely turn their back on drugs, or biting their nails, or just generally mucking around. It's given them a complete new purpose in life.

STAMBERG: Why?

DYER: Well, I think for the first time in their lives many of them had found something that really had clear-cut values. Something where traditions had a meaning. Discipline or self-control all suddenly had a reason.

You can't go off, let's say, into the desert and drink all your water, or throw it away. You could die of thirst. You can't treat a person of another race as an inferior being, because you suddenly realize that some of these other races—so-called Bushmen or peasants—are quite possibly infinitely better people than you yourself.

STAMBERG: I appreciate your answer very much. What I can't help thinking, though, is that all of these values you're talking about, and all the revelations that came along with them, occurred in the pursuit, ultimately, of death. Of killing.

DYER: Yes, that's true. But not necessarily so. Some of the most famous safari clients who came back again and again and again were looking for the animal they hoped they'd never get. It wasn't the killing of an animal. I mean, anybody can kill an animal! It's the actual hunt—the being in the bush, the stalking, the tracking. Hunting is, literally, hunting. You're looking for something. You're not . . . I mean, if you

Animals in the wild are very wary of people on foot. When you get people in cars, you can approach very closely, not only to predators, but to large, dangerous animals—buffalo, hippo, elephant. To my mind, they obviously don't perceive people in cars as being the same thing that walks around on two legs and gives them such a fight.

—Zoologist Jonathan Scott, July 1985

want to go and murder something, well, you can go to a slaughter-house. But hunting is something else. Hunting is a very honorable business. You are looking for a trophy. When Jason hunted for the Golden Fleece, he spent many, many years looking for it and was never quite sure whether he found it or not. Hunting is very much the same.

STAMBERG: Tony Dyer, past president of the East African Professional Hunters Association. Today, he works for wildlife conservation.

I'm not against tourism. It's just that you have to control it. The drivers are quite unscrupulous, some of them. They will go right up to a cheetah that has baby cubs and disturb the mother so that, as happened on one occasion, a mother abandoned her cubs. In fact, she killed three of them herself. There was just too much pressure on her, too much harassment by drivers driving right up to these tiny cubs. And she was probably a first-time mother and very nervous.

—Kate Turner, Friends of the Masai Mara, July 1985

Photographing the Homeless

December 1985

In the early eighties, homelessness began creeping around the edges of American life. By January 1984, it was a newsmagazine cover story. Today, the homeless are part of every landscape.

Precise numbers are nearly impossible to pin down, but there may be more than four million homeless men, women, and children in the United States. In Washington, D.C., in 1992, the Center for Creative Nonviolence tallied fifteen thousand to twenty thousand citizens roaming the capital's streets, eating there, sleeping there—or in some three thousand beds in shelters.

In 1985, the year I interviewed some of Washington's homeless for this story, Madonna was bragging in song about being a "Material Girl." President Reagan signed the Gramm-Rudman Act, an attempt to control the burgeoning deficit. In the corporate world, takeover fever hit a record high—120 billion buyout dollars changed hands.

In 1985, Washington had about six thousand homeless, and a man named Jim Hubbard was trying to make us look at them in new ways. Hubbard was then the United Press International photographer at the White House. But more and more, he was leaving that citadel of power and crossing Pennsylvania Avenue to go into Lafayette Park, where he photographed the powerless—the Federal City's street people.

Jim Hubbard put together an exhibit of some of his black-and-white photographs. The people in them, wrapped in blankets, huddled against the cold, looked more like sacks, bags, something nonhuman.

HUBBARD: It's kind of a new phenomenon in America that they're out there with us now. They're not just in some Bowery or skid row, where they used to be years ago. We walk by them, and no one seems to know what to do. We just walk around them.

STAMBERG: In this picture, is this a woman or a man—I can't tell—so bundled up in the snow?

HUBBARD: That's a woman I watched for about an hour out on Pennsylvania Avenue, near the Capitol. It was the day before Inauguration Day in 1985. This woman had all of her belongings with her. She seemed a bit confused, like she was waiting for a bus, but no buses were running. And this woman was engaged in a very, very survival-based struggle on Pennsylvania Avenue—the same street President Reagan was to ride down the next day. The parade was canceled, you remember, because of the weather.

(*Outdoor city sounds: cars, sirens.*)

JONES: My name is Benjamin Franklin Jones.

STAMBERG: And you have these photographs that Jim Hubbard made of you. He gave them to you?

JONES: Yes, ma'am.

STAMBERG: (*Narrating*) Benjamin Franklin Jones is thirty-three years old. He sits on a large piece of cardboard spread out on Pennsylvania Avenue, just a block from the White House. He wears an old army jacket and wraps himself in a large piece of plastic against the cold. Mr. Jones has been on the streets of Washington since August 1984.

(*More traffic noise.*)

STAMBERG: How do you manage? How do you take care of yourself or find something to eat?

JONES: Basically from the good people that live and work here in the city of D.C.

STAMBERG: People on the street give you money?

JONES: Yes, ma'am.

STAMBERG: Do you get enough money so you can get food for yourself?

JONES: Sometimes, yes, ma'am. I had some cheese this morning. And last night . . . l-l-l-last night, I had some fish and some grapefruit juice.

STAMBERG: Tonight it might go down to ten degrees. Will you stay on the street or will you go to a shelter?

JONES: I stay on the street. I do better when I'm by myself and I'm thinking clearly and I'm not bothered with a lot of noise.

STAMBERG: It sounds like you really want to be on your own.

JONES: Yes, ma'am. L-l-l-like when I was at home in Kentucky, my biggest joy was, like, goin' huntin'. Before Bradley got hurt, me and him would go hunting together, right? Because, like, when we would . . . would be hunting, Bradley would be real quiet. And we'd be listenin' and watchin' and movin'. And . . . and . . . and we knew every stick that broke that wasn't our stick. Right. And . . . but . . . but, like . . . Bradley got hurt and I just go hunting by myself.

STAMBERG: Who's Bradley?

JONES: Bradley Holloway. He my blood brother, since I was real small.

STAMBERG: (*Narrating*) Benjamin Franklin Jones takes another look at Jim Hubbard's photographs, pictures that show Mr. Jones peering out from the sheet of plastic that he's draped over himself like a tent.

(*More traffic noise.*)

STAMBERG: Mr. Jones, if anybody in your family—folks you grew up with—saw this picture, would they know right away that was you?

JONES: Not hardly.

STAMBERG: What's different?

JONES: The conditions, I guess. (*Laughs.*) The total condition. 'Cause look like that, I'm just kind of, like, staring off, without having my mind completely focused on my next step. And back home, I was more or less an individual that moved in a more definite pattern. And right here, I don't have any control over my life. I can see that in the picture.

(*Traffic sounds out—cross-fade to studio ambience.*)

STAMBERG: Mr. Hubbard, you were careful to avoid the stereotypes in these photographs—no bums with pints of booze lying in the gutter.

HUBBARD: That's just an excuse for people to say, "Well, look—all they ever use their money for is to buy booze." That's simply not true. For some it is, but that's no different than mainline society. A lot of people in mainline society also use their money for booze and parties and drugs and whatever. So I feel, why feed into that? It's not necessary.

STAMBERG: This last picture—this could be anybody.

HUBBARD: Just shoes and a sidewalk—I shot it real tight. Both shoes

When you're a historian and get your name on the spine of a book, people think you know everything. Is mankind going to survive? Are we doomed? Well, all I can say is that so far as I know, things don't stop or come to an end. We have, after all, in our time done great things in social attitudes toward the masses, haven't we? We have really—in this country, and in Western developed countries on the whole—abolished basic misery and want that is not cared for. Social conscience is the great development of the nineteenth and twentieth centuries and, really, the period since the French Revolution, if you take that as a whole.

—*Barbara Tuchman, April 1980*

are split all across the bottom. They're totally worn out. They're wrapped with gauze and tape to keep them together. Shoes really take a beating from life on the street.

(*Outside again—traffic noise.*)

HOMELESS MAN: They were wrapped in rubber bands, all run-down, and I just made do until the Lord brought some new shoes to me. Lady works in a church gave me a pair . . . new pair of shoes. I left them outside. I went to a meeting in the church. I came back out and they had disappeared.

STAMBERG: But now you're wearing new shoes.

HOMELESS MAN: Well, these are from another source. The Lord provides! The Lord provides, you see.

(*Street sounds fade. Back to Hubbard in studio.*)

STAMBERG: What does it take for you to leave Lafayette Park, cross the street, and go back to an administration which many blame for exacerbating the problems the homeless are facing?

HUBBARD: That's a big problem for me. It's . . . it's also a big problem for me to go home at night, to my suburban middle-class home, to my middle-class job. It's becoming more of a problem for me. I agonize over it. But it's going to become an increasing problem for all of the people of the world, because the numbers of people who live in despair are growing. There's no doubt about it. And so we all have to agonize over it. Whether or not we admit it, it's there.

———

Jim Hubbard was studying for the ministry when we spoke in 1985. A year later, he quit UPI and founded the Shooting Back Education and Media Center in Washington. Homeless kids come there, learn how to work cameras, and go out and make photographs of their lives on the streets and in shelters. They develop their pictures, and Hubbard arranges shows of their work. He says he's giving young people tools and teaching them a craft they can use, as well as educating the public about their struggle.

In 1985, when producer Peter Breslow and I did this story, we had to trudge many long, wintry blocks before we found homeless people to interview. Today, all we have to do is go half a block from our office.

I interviewed one of the reporters who was with Bourke-White in India during the heartbreaking migrations of partition. She said at one point there was a family Margaret wanted to photograph, and she got them to pose, walking with all their belongings on their heads, and no money, and surely not enough food. Then she wasn't sure she had it, so she made them go back, and she made them go back again, and she made them go back again. The reporter was horrified. These people were dying! Margaret's feeling was that the picture would live forever to tell this story. I think in some peculiar way a photographer has to feel like that, or they don't get the story.

—biographer Vicki Goldberg, June 1986

Wish I'd Written That!

January 1986

> **I feel at this gathering that I am a literary tourist walking among the skyscrapers and tall buildings.**
>
> —John Barth, PEN Congress, January 1986

The forty-eighth International PEN Congress—a gathering of some of the most impressive authors in the world—grew so noisy and crowded that at one point, desperate for a quiet place in which to tape an interview, I led Poland's Ryszard Kapuściński into an empty elevator, hit the NO STOP button, and turned on my tape recorder. Kapuściński and I rode up and down in that elevator for six minutes.

A volume of writers, some seven hundred of them, spent several days at the beginning of 1986 on panels, in discussions, giving readings—all at the invitation of PEN, an organization of poets, playwrights, essayists, editors, novelists, and translators. It was like an assembly of the world's finest Faculty of Creative Writing—Saul Bellow was there, so were Nadine Gordimer, Mario Vargas Llosa, Grace Paley, Kōbō Abe, Isabel Allende, Breyten Breytenbach, Eugène Ionesco, Robertson Davies, Günter Grass, Czeslaw Milosz, Amos Oz, Tom Stoppard, Octavio Paz, Wole Soyinka—and that's just the unalphabetized list.

> **Writers have no tasks. That's for office workers. We have imaginations.**
>
> —Saul Bellow, PEN Congress, January 1986

The talk was alternately scintillating and long-winded ("This show wouldn't last on Broadway one hour," Arthur Miller whispered at the back of a meeting room). There were all sorts of flaps. Flaps about Secretary of State George Shultz being invited to address the assembly. Flaps about the underrepresentation of women on panels. (But Norman Mailer, president of the PEN American Center, smoothed that one over quickly by explaining that if more women were on panels, "All we'd be doing is lowering the level of discussion.") Some major writers signed a petition proclaiming their "acute distress at U.S. government intervention in Nicaragua," protesting U.S. subsidy of the *contras,* and urging that the Sandinista government be given "a real chance" to evolve toward democracy.

Rosario Murillo, a poet and the wife of Nicaragua's then leader, Daniel Ortega, arrived with her young children. "How do they like New York?" I asked. It was their first visit.

"They love it!" she smiled. "Especially the snow. My children have only seen pictures of snow covering the ground. They never realized it comes down from the sky."

At the PEN conference, I corralled writers to discuss a number of topics, political as well as literary, including that all-important initial plunge into text—the first sentence.

STAMBERG: Writers will tell you that the first sentence of a work is the most difficult sentence to write. James Joyce solved the problem in *Finnegans Wake* by not writing a first sentence at all. Or a last one. Joyce simply kept on writing in a circle.

MALE READING: "riverrun, past Eve and Adam's, from swerve of shore to bend of bay, brings us by a commodius vicus of recirculation back to Howth Castle and Environs."

STAMBERG: Most authors don't write the way James Joyce did. They begin with a first sentence and go on, sentence by sentence. I asked Arturo Arias of Guatemala to pick a first sentence he *wished* he'd written.

ARIAS: The first line of Gabriel García Márquez's *One Hundred Years of Solitude:* "Many years later, as he faced the firing squad, Colonel Aureliano Buendia was to remember that distant afternoon when his father took him to discover ice."

STAMBERG: Why do you like that so much?

ARIAS: Because it projects into the future—"Many years later." And it goes retrospectively back into the past, too. It's a very strong image—the firing squad—and the discovery of ice, which is something very conventional but, for a child, totally transforming in one's imagination. It immediately sets the tone for the whole novel in one line.

STAMBERG: And you *must* continue reading it!

ARIAS: Yeah, you cannot stop.

STAMBERG: Salman Rushdie, the first line of your novel *Midnight's Children* is "I was born in the city of Bombay . . . once upon a time."

The major theme of the Congress is the relation of the individual writer and the state. One of the things that's happening is that writers are being trapped into silly positions — maintaining, for instance, that art can't change anything; no books ever saved any lives. That, of course, is not true. But the reason otherwise sound and brilliant minds are caught in these assertions is because when you are writing, you argue all sides of a question. That's the nature of writing—especially good writing. But here, when you take a position, you take just one side of a question, so you're not being yourself. I think writers are writers only when they're writing. And when we're not writing, we're just as silly and foolish as everyone else!

—E. L. Doctorow, PEN Congress, January 1986

Is there a first line of somebody else's novel that you wish you had written?

RUSHDIE: I suppose I would like to have written the first line of *À la recherche du temps perdu*. I would like to have written *"Longtemps, je me suis couché de bonne heure."* And I would then have liked to go on to write the rest of the novel!

STAMBERG: You better translate the Proust for us, please. *Remembrance of Things Past,* and the first line?

RUSHDIE: The first sentence means, "For a long time, I used to go to bed early." That's not a particularly great line, except it then leads on to the best novel of the century!

STAMBERG: Gay Talese, pick a first line from a piece of your writing that you are most proud of.

TALESE: "New York is a city of things unnoticed"—no, that's not right. God! That's a dumb . . . I can't handle that! Look, I don't know what the hell . . . I've written so many long, long, long first sentences that to pick out *a* line . . . every line is a difficult line for me. We're not the king of the one-liners. If you want that, go to the Catskills and listen to Henny Youngman or someone like that!

KAPUŚCIŃSKI: First line for the author is a most difficult one.

STAMBERG: Ryszard Kapuściński of Poland.

KAPUŚCIŃSKI: You have something in your mind, some ideas, but they are vague ideas. And for myself, for example, once I have the first line, I have the book.

STAMBERG: Allen Ginsberg, *Howl* began, if I'm remembering correctly, "I saw the best minds of my generation destroyed by madness."

GINSBERG: Yes. Well, actually, the line completed "starving, hysterical, naked."

STAMBERG: I've been asking writers about first lines that they most appreciate.

GINSBERG: Their own writing?

STAMBERG: Yes, of your own.

GINSBERG: Well, let's see now. One line I like is "Bare skinned as my wrinkled sack when summer sun climbs up my back." But the best line is "Hey, father Death, I'm flying home."

STAMBERG: What about other people's writing? Are there first lines which you wish were yours?

GINSBERG: "I know, although when looks meet/I tremble to the bone,/ The more I leave the door unlatched/ The sooner love is gone." Yeats. And I also like "Can I see another's woe/ And not be in sorrow too?" Blake.

STAMBERG: Toni Morrison, of your own work, a first line that you're most proud of?

MORRISON: I was going to say, "He thought he was safe," which was the first line of *Tar Baby*. But just as I spoke it, I remembered the first line of *The Bluest Eye,* which now, I think, because it was the first line of *all* the books, is probably my favorite: "In the fall of 1941 there were no marigolds."

STAMBERG: And from somebody else's writing—the first sentence you wish you had written?

MORRISON: "Call me Ishmael."

GINSBERG: "The pure products of America go crazy." That's William Carlos Williams.

STAMBERG: Allen Ginsberg, you like this first-line business! Gay Talese just told me it was a trivial question.

GINSBERG: No. You know, any poetry is worth repeating.

Now We Are Five Billion

July 1986

STAMBERG: Werner Fornos, the Population Institute, which you direct, reports that as of today—July 7, 1986—there are five *billion* of us on earth. A milestone. The population has doubled in the last forty years. Do you have any idea where this all-important five billionth person is being born?

FORNOS: Probably in Africa, where today there are five hundred fifty million people. In the next thirty-five years, that population will triple.

STAMBERG: What about this child's religion?

FORNOS: In Africa, the chances probably are that he or she could be a Muslim. But more important, the child will almost inevitably have a very bleak chance for making its life work in any way that we might appreciate.

STAMBERG: Does five billion mean we are at our carrying capacity—that there are as many of us now on earth as can be fed and clothed and sheltered and employed?

FORNOS: It's interesting you ask that, because no one has ever done that study. We don't know what the carrying capacity of the planet is, or when it will break. Certainly, if we don't do anything about the problem, we are going to double the population of this planet one more time. Sometime, probably around 2100, we'll be at ten billion. What kind of life we'll have then heaven only knows, because no one has spent enough money to worry about the resource capability and how far we can stretch it.

STAMBERG: What's the pace of population growth?

FORNOS: We grew by eighty-five million last year—the largest annual increase we've ever experienced. And that pace may continue because the overall world population is so young. Almost half the Third World is under the age of fifteen. So by the turn of the century we will probably add an increment in population of about one hundred million a year, until it stabilizes. But it will stabilize.

———

By the spring of 1992, the Population Institute had revised its figures a bit. In 1986, Werner Fornos had predicted that there would be ten billion of us by the year 2100. Now the prediction is that we'll get bigger sooner. Despite the upsurge of family planning around the world, the population has already increased so rapidly that before a leveling-off can begin, a redoubling will already have occurred. That five-billion milestone we hit in 1986 is now expected to give way to the ten-billion mark by the year 2050.

This year, most of the baby boomers are turning thirty. The generation has delayed getting married for quite a few years, but the number of marriages right now is at a record high. So we're going to see increasing numbers of households with children. Then they'll be interested in making sure the schools are adequate for their children, making sure their communities do enough to protect their families from crime. You can see the growing concerns of a middle-aged America in the shifting attitudes towards drinking and driving—the raising of the drinking age in many states. You can see it in the growing concern about drugs, pornography. In fact, the girlie magazines are losing subscribers. This isn't just because some people in the Reagan administration are saying, "We don't like pornography." It's because people's interests are changing as they get older. Nobody's seen anything yet, as far as the baby boom's power. Economically and politically, it's all still to come.

**—Cheryl Russell,
American
Demographics,
August 1987**

The Incorrigible Racehoss

January 1986

When Emma reached a certain quota in her drinking her bitterness surged and I was the target. None of the gamblers dared to interfere, especially after that time Lakey spoke up, ''Emma, you ought not to whup 'em lak that.'' She flew into a rage and stabbed him in the shoulder with an ice pick and threw him out of the house for ''meddlin.''

—from Racehoss

ALBERT RACE SAMPLE: There was Ol' Cadlack, Ol' Florine, Ol' Black Gal, Sloped Eddie, High Pocket, Pile Driver, Dog, Mae Perl, Bix Six, Jack-Off, Choppin' Charlie, Li'l Chicken . . . (*Fade.*)

STAMBERG: They were his fellow inmates, four hundred in all, locked up in the Retrieve—a branch of the Texas state prison system reserved especially for them, the incorrigibles.

Albert Race Sample was one of them for seventeen years. In a way, he was born to be there. His mother, Emma, saw her mother murdered by her father when she was just a child. Emma ran away at fifteen, became a prostitute, had gambling and bootlegging operations in small Texas towns. Big Emma's son started hustling tricks for her when he was four. He bootlegged whiskey, watched for crooked dice, then ran away from home—from her beatings and abuse—and ended up in prison for robbery. Albert Race Sample describes his imprisonment and rehabilitation in the book *Racehoss: Big Emma's Boy*. The title comes from his nickname.

SAMPLE: Ol' Racehoss, that's what everybody called me in the prison system. I got that name chopping cotton. I was chopping cotton under Boss Band, and another convict in the number one hoe squad (which was the name of the work unit that I was assigned to), we were racing, chopping cotton. And when we got to the end of our rows, I was about twenty-five, thirty yards ahead of Old Railhead Shorty (that was the guy that I was racing with), and this Boss Band—who was a traveling executioner and had killed sixteen men in his prison career—he walked his horse over behind where I was working and he just sat there looking at me. I could feel his eyes burning into my back. He said, "You know what, ol' racehoss? I was watching your row, when you was racehorsing up and down through that field," he said, "and I ain't ever seen a nigguh clean a row like that before. And I think that's what I'm going to call you from now on—Ol' Racehoss. And when I call you that, nigguh, you better answer me. You hear me?" And I said, "Oh, Lawd!" And from then on, that's what everybody called me in the prison system—Ol' Racehoss.

STAMBERG: How much cotton did you pick that day to win that race?

SAMPLE: Eight hundred and fifty-five pounds, I believe.

STAMBERG: Boss Band was your supervisor, and one of the things he made you do—in addition to a whole lot of unmentionable, unforgivable, unbelievable things he made you do—was to address him every time as "Oh, Lawd."

SAMPLE: Yes, ma'am, that was Boss Band's commandments. He gave us those commandments when he first took over that squad. He told us, he says, "If any one of you nigguhs dispute my word, I'm going to kill you. If any one of you nigguhs don't do just exactly like I tell you, I'm going to kill you. And I don't want nar' one of you devils saying nar' a word to me unless you say, 'Oh, Lawd, speakin' to you, Boss,' first." And that's the way we had to start a conversation with him. If we wanted to get a drink of water, or to go pull it down, or whatever, we had to first say, "Speakin' to you, Boss, oh, Lawd," and then wait a while until he decided to answer.

STAMBERG: You were seven years under him. How many years under Big Devil—the warden, the one who ran the Retrieve?

SAMPLE: Thirteen years all total under him.

STAMBERG: And why was he called Big Devil?

SAMPLE: Because he was the warden in the burnin' hell, so how more appropriate? Big Devil. And he loved that name! He knew that the convicts called him that behind his back. We didn't dare say that to his face, but he knew we had a nickname for him, just like all of us had other names.

STAMBERG: You spent seventeen years in the Retrieve. You got out in 1972. And shortly after you got out, you heard that Big Devil had retired, and you found yourself driving on a road that led to his house. Tell what he said to you when he heard how well you were doing.

SAMPLE: (Laughs.)

What I am trying to do in everything I write is to make sure that I have absolutely irresistible characters, all of whom are black. I don't care that you can't relate. I will be giving no voice to white people. They have a lot of writers; they can write their own story.

But my family, and families like mine, families I've never seen that are black, are perfectly capable of having great drama. We have our own *Glass Menageries*. We have our own *Hamlets*. It *should* sound like a foreign language. White people don't live in my house.

—Ntozake Shange, October 1977

STAMBERG: Just describe that exchange. We'll see if we can put it on the radio, Mr. Sample!

SAMPLE: Yes, ma'am. Well, I was directing the Control Substance Act program in Texas. After they passed that law—possession of four ounces or less of marijuana is a misdemeanor—which was retroactive and effective immediately, it resulted in them having to release 476 convicts from the Texas prison system. I directed that program out of the governor's office, and I had gotten my last client and was on my way back to Austin, and some way I got on the wrong highway. The next time I noticed any signs, they said, "Lovelady—twenty miles." I had just seen ol' Big Devil's son at the prison camp, and he told me Big Devil had retired and was now living in Lovelady.

And I thought, "Well, what the heck, I'll just run on by here and holler at him, and see how is he doing." When I found his house, he came out, and we sat out on the front porch and talked about old times. His memory was still uncanny about all of us. He knew us by name, and he asked about a lot of convicts. And I told him, I said, "Well, I came by here really to . . . to ask you if you remember the last time that you put me in solitary confinement, when Mr. Meabs run me in?"

He says, "Yep. I remember it."

I said, "Well, God came to me while I was in there that time, Warden," I said. "My life hasn't been the same since, and I just wanted to tell you that."

He said, "Well, I'll tell you what, Ol' Racehoss," he says. "I'm sure glad I had something to do with helping to get your heart right."

I said, "I'm sorry, that's where you wrong, Warden. You didn't have shit to do with it." And sipped my lemonade.

That's the last line in the book.

STAMBERG: In reading that story, and thinking about it, I wonder how much somebody like Boss Band—"Kill-A-Band"—had to do with making you into the man that you are today. What do you think?

SAMPLE: Well, I'll tell you one thing, Susan, he sure drove me to reach down inside of me and find things that I didn't even know I had. I didn't know I could work as hard. I didn't know that I could endure the heat and as much physical abuse as he leveled against us.

STAMBERG: When you started picking cotton for him, you were having such a hard time, you couldn't keep up. Everybody else was hauling in two hundred pounds a day; you were lucky if you could pull forty.

SAMPLE: (*Laughs.*) That was really something! They had a rule: If you don't pick enough, you don't eat. The first cotton-picking season that I was at Retrieve, I nearly starved to death, because I never *could* pick enough. I'd pick fifty-five, sixty, seventy pounds per weighing, but that still wasn't enough, because my squad picked on a average, and there was some guys in my squad that could pick five, six hundred pounds of cotton. It sure looks bad when you step up there, some guy just hung up two hundred pounds, and you've got thirty-five. It don't look too good for you.

STAMBERG: Some of them found very clever ways to weigh down that cotton. They urinated on it, knowing that the liquid would make it heavier.

SAMPLE: That's right! (*Laughs.*) That's right!

STAMBERG: And you tried mud, too—got mud on some of it, to weigh it down.

SAMPLE: Sure. Do everything you can to make it back inside the building to lay down and get some rest and eat a little supper.

STAMBERG: It's so ironic, though, your saying you have to tip your hat to Boss Band. Because really, he dragged you down so that you ended up like an animal. But going through all that, you were able to drag yourself back up.

SAMPLE: Yes. He was instrumental in helping me be able to survive in that hell, because he drove me till I became the top hand. That was a position that almost ensured that I could get in the building and eat supper at night, and that I wouldn't have to hang on the cuffs no more and be put in solitary just because I couldn't work—because I couldn't keep up.

STAMBERG: Describe hanging on the cuffs.

SAMPLE: Well, that is a very painful, physical punishment. They have since outlawed that in the Texas prison system. But they put the handcuffs on your wrists and hang you up from the bars so's where your toes just barely touch the floor.

STAMBERG: Your hands are over your head, so you're really hanging by your wrists from those handcuffs.

SAMPLE: Yes, ma'am, just like Jesus.

STAMBERG: All night, too?

Along about hour six, one of the hangers began moaning louder and louder, violently jerking and pulling against his cuffs. He frantically wiggled and twisted his body around until he was facing the bars. Using his foot to push against them, he reared back, pitching and straining, and pulling as hard as he could. Realizing he couldn't get loose, he bit into his wrists as if they were two chocolate eclairs, growling and gnawing away like a coon with its foot caught in a steel trap.

—from Racehoss

SAMPLE: Yes, ma'am, and all day.

STAMBERG: And then solitary. The convicts called it The Pisser.

SAMPLE: Because it smelled so bad. You see, there's no commode, no face basin. It's just a little hole in the center of the floor that you do all your stuff in. And you in there buck naked, it's dark, you can't see that hole most of the time, so you miss it. And that's why they smell so bad. And then they airtight. That is one of the dreadful things about solitary is that the air . . . breathing in there is so difficult. It's almost like being entombed. You're behind three solid steel doors and it's pitch-black—you can't see nothing, you can't hear nothing. All you can do is lay in there and hurt.

STAMBERG: You were saying that some of the things, like hanging on the cuffs, they don't do anymore. But how much of that other stuff is still going on?

SAMPLE: Just about all of it, with the exception of that. Solitaries are still there. They still stink just like they did when I was there in them. And they still have them loaded with convicts. They put nine, ten, sometimes fifteen, twenty men in one cell, four-by-eight. There's still the brutality and the abuse. It still happens in—I'm ashamed to say—in my state, Texas.

STAMBERG: How unusual is *your* story, Mr. Sample? I mean, the fact that you got yourself rehabilitated and you've done a book. Are you one out of hundreds of thousands of people who—

SAMPLE: I feel that way! And I feel that way for this reason. When I went to prison, having grew up with Emma as a drill sergeant, I was prepared a whole lot better to survive in a place like that than most of the men that were there. Most of the men that were at that camp, they were classified as incorrigibles, true, but they still didn't quite have that toughness, that Teflon, on the outside. And Emma had already did that for me. When I walked through the gates of the Retrieve unit—the burnin' hell, if you will—I was already an incorrigible, a hard, callous, no-inside-feeling person. I didn't have to *learn* how to be that way. I was that way when I got there!

STAMBERG: Tell what she taught you—your mother, Big Emma— what she taught you to say when you were little, in case you had gotten into trouble with cops or something.

SAMPLE: Well, she taught me with a coat hanger about my birthday. And I remembered it. Right now, you can wake me up at four o'clock in the morning and ask me when I was born, and I can tell you (*speaking quickly, by rote, no space between the words*), "I was born on a Friday 3:20 the seventh day of February 1930 raining and snowing right behind the ol' jailhouse Gregg County Precinct number one and Mr. Hoot Garner was the sheriff." And that would get the police officer's attention long enough for Emma to hide the whiskey or something, and we wouldn't be taken down to the jail.

STAMBERG: But tell what she taught you to say at the very end of that recitation.

SAMPLE: "And I'm four years old."

STAMBERG: Albert Race Sample was released from prison in Texas in 1972. He got a full pardon in 1976. His book is called *Racehoss: Big Emma's Boy*.

———

Mr. Sample ("Call me Race," he insists on the telephone from Austin) has been out of jail for more than twenty years. "Not so much as a traffic ticket!" he brags. He's a full-time author these days. *Racehoss* is in its eighth printing in paperback, and Sample has written a screenplay adaptation. He has finished the manuscript for a second book. *Bitterfield, the Devil's Stomping Ground* is about the East Texas town where he grew up.

During the 1980s, America's prison population more than doubled. By the early 1990s, more than one million men and women were serving time in federal and state penitentiaries.

Kim Williams, R.I.P.

July 1986

If you're lost in the wilderness, head for a cattail swamp. That's a bit of advice I give to the students in my edible wild foods class. It's good advice. There's no excuse for starving if you can find cattails.

—*Kim Williams, July 1977*

A number of prominent people died in 1986: Jorge Luis Borges, Benny Goodman, Cary Grant, Georgia O'Keeffe, Kate Smith, Theodore H. White. Men and women who made outstanding contributions to society. But the death that touched NPR most that year was that of Kim Williams, who'd been part of our *All Things Considered* family for a decade.

A naturalist and writer, Kim's weekly exuberant, folksy commentaries on edible wild foods and most other things under the sun and rain brightened our spirits. She taught at the University of Montana in Missoula, wrote books, led hikes in the Rocky Mountains. We met her in 1976 through member station KUFM in Missoula when we were hunting around for new commentators. Kim was an instant hit on our air, even though our then president, Frank Mankiewicz (the Garrison Keillor kibosher), cringed every time he heard her. Frank was in the minority, though. Most listeners delighted in Kim Williams's sweetly bumpy voice (a cross between Edith Bunker's, Tiny Tim's, and Grandma Moses') and her innovative culinary suggestions.

"I have a pot boiling on my stove, but I don't know if I dare mention what's in it," Kim once confided on *All Things Considered*. "I'm designing a new recipe for a contest. The main ingredient has to be . . . well . . . here it is: Earthworms!"

A tamer suggestion was dandelions (this was in the seventies, before eating weeds got chic). "Dandelion greens are my spring tonic.

I can't start the year without a dandelion salad. You could call it a ritual. Well, we need rituals!"

We loved Kim's advice—aloe for burns; tobacco leaves to keep moths out of woolens; if the label shows more than ten ingredients, throw it out. We loved her spirit, her sunny presence, on our air.

In all her years on *All Things Considered*, I never met Kim Williams face-to-face. We'd talk by phone on various occasions, but the one time she came to Washington and visited NPR, in the spring of 1986, I was out of town, sorry to have missed her. That July, we learned she was dying. Knowing what she meant to our listeners, I wanted to say a public good-bye and asked Kim's family if I could phone her on the air. It is the most painful interview I've ever done.

STAMBERG: Kim Williams, what is it that you have heard from the doctor? Please tell us.

WILLIAMS: Well, the doctor says I have terminal cancer. It started out as ovarian cancer, and then I guess it turned into a general cancer of the abdomen. They took out some, and they left some in, and so I am getting ready to move on to new dimensions, you might say.

STAMBERG: Hmm. Have you been given some kind of time frame, Kim?

WILLIAMS: No, but I would say it's within a month.

    (*Pause.*)

STAMBERG: And is this something that's . . . that you've known for a long time, that's been going on for a long time?

WILLIAMS: No. It was sort of a surprise because . . . well, it . . . really, ovarian cancer is one of the ones, I guess, that don't give you many symptoms. I mean, I wasn't in pain. I was . . . it just happened that after a while I started looking as though I were seven months' pregnant, which is one of the signs. And all of a sudden I couldn't eat. I couldn't sleep. I couldn't breathe. So something had to be done quickly, and quickly it was done.

STAMBERG: Umm-hmm. How are you feeling right now, Kim?

WILLIAMS: Well, tired and . . . well, I guess I . . . what with all these medicines they give you nowadays, you don't feel too much of anything.

STAMBERG: And what are you saying to yourself these days, Kim?

WILLIAMS: Well, I am saying to myself that it is time to move on.

> You don't have to believe all this. What works for one person doesn't work for everyone. For a cold I believe in garlic, chili pepper, hats and white cotton socks.
>
> —Kim Williams, from Cookbook and Commentary

That's what it is. It is time to move on. And luckily, I wrote in my book a chapter on dying, so all I have to do is follow my own book. What it says is that most people know when they are going to die, and they evade it with this empire of medicine that we have around us.

In a primitive society, everybody knew when everybody was dying—unless they were eaten by a lion—and so it was something that people talked about and knew. But nowadays, people evade the whole subject. Instead of saying, "How are you dying? Are you coming along?," they all say, "What treatment are you getting now?" You see, that evades the whole thing. As long as you are getting a *treatment,* you can't be dying. So I think we are evading death, and it's all coming back to haunt us.

It seems to me some of the European countries are coming around to the idea that between you and your doctor, you can figure out whether you want to, as they say, *make a battleground* out of this illness, or whether you wish to die in peace.

STAMBERG: I have the book you were talking about in front of me, Kim. Your latest—*Book of Uncommon Sense*—and I have that chapter open—the chapter on death. You've called the first essay "I Wish to Die in Peace, Not in Pieces."

WILLIAMS: That's right! I want to die in peace, not in pieces. So what would be the point of going in for chemotherapy, and after that a little radiation, and then a little of this and then a little of that?

I was in the clinic yesterday. They have to remove a little fluid from my abdomen every once in a while because it just fills up so that you can't eat or breathe. And I was looking around there, and I said to the nurse, "You know, some of these people really look as though they're *enjoying* the whole thing."

They get all dressed up. Women get their hair done to go to the clinic. And the nurse said, "Yeah. Some people actually get so it's their life, at this point, to get dressed up and go have a treatment." You wouldn't believe that people are there being burned, and being poisoned, and the other things. They're there with their hair done, and their matching pantsuits, and everything is completely sanitized. You don't know that it's a matter of life and death.

STAMBERG: Yes. On the other hand, just as you are able to look directly at death and speak so openly with us, perhaps theirs is another way of dealing with it. There's a courage to that, too—their saying, "I am not going to let this get me down. I will do what I do."

I took off my girdle in 1965. Now I raise my right hand: "Women of the world, it's more than your bottom that you stuff into a girdle. It's your head."

—*from Kim Williams's Book of Uncommon Sense*

WILLIAMS: That's very true, and perhaps in a way that *does* take courage, and an ability to face life and death, also. It's a way of facing it by looking at it in the mirror.

STAMBERG: Umm-hmm. (*Pause.*) You have little epigrams at the beginning of the various chapters in your book, and the epigram for the death chapter is "Don't go ahead of time and don't go ignominiously." That's a larger word than you usually use, Kim Williams! But I like the thought very much.

WILLIAMS: Yes, many people allow themselves to be pushed around when it comes to life and death. They are pushed into treatments they don't want, or they are pushed aside when they shouldn't be pushed aside. There's a fight there. There is a fight for basic health care for everyone.

STAMBERG: Kim, are you . . . I take it you are turning down any sort of extraordinary means?

WILLIAMS: Yes. I belong to Hospice, and I do have a doctor, and he works with Hospice very closely, and so I have my medicines, and I have nurses and doctors, and . . . I have everything I need, I guess.

STAMBERG: Kim, how would we get in touch with you if we wanted to write?

WILLIAMS: You mean when I have passed on to the next dimension?

STAMBERG: No, ma'am! This minute!!

WILLIAMS: (*Laughs.*) Well, I would rather people did not send me too many cards, letters, and flowers and all that, because after a while it's like Grand Central Station around here, and I can't rest or do my thinking or my writing. Send your thoughts by another dimension.

STAMBERG: Kim, you . . . one of the pieces in (*turning pages*) this book is something quite wonderful you wrote about a friend who was dying, and this very strong sense you have that death is merely a change, and that at some point you say hello to a whole lot of people whom you've lost in this life.

WILLIAMS: Yes, and it is amazing how many letters I've already had— before I put out that call for no more letters—how many I have received from people who say they are going to climb a mountain or walk along a river or on a city street, and they will send their thoughts and energies, and they think that they will meet mine.

    (*Long silence.*)

STAMBERG: I believe that.

WILLIAMS: I do too.

STAMBERG: Kim, thank you very much.

WILLIAMS: Thank you, Susan.

STAMBERG: Good-bye.

WILLIAMS: Bye.

     (*Telephone clicks off.*)

━━━

The sound of that phone hanging up—it was producer Neenah Ellis's decision to leave it on the tape—was devastating. It was as if our lifeline with Kim had been cut, right then. For the first time in all my radio years, I cried on the air, and could barely get through our traditional sign-off ("And for this evening, that's *All Things Considered*") and the "Good evening" Noah Adams and I always said to our listeners at the end of the program. I scraped my way through the close credits, and when we were off the air I said to Noah, my dear friend and longtime broadcast partner, "It's too hard. It's too hard."

Letters about Kim Williams overran our mailboxes, and the next week Noah and I read many of them on the air—phoning Mel Williams, Kim's husband, out in Missoula to ask that he tune in so that Kim could hear them. Two weeks later, on August 6, Kim Williams died. She was sixty-two. The *New York Times* obituary included a photograph—Kim jamming a sailor's hat onto her head, grinning her life-loving grin.

It's painful, saying good-bye to a radio friend. Especially painful for me, then, because the week before I spoke with Kim, I had discovered a lump in my breast. My anxiety about it enshrouded our final conversation. At the end of July, I had a lumpectomy; after that, radiation. In early September 1986, deciding I had to get away from the stress of daily broadcasting, I said good-bye to my *All Things Considered* listeners and began planning *Weekend Edition*/Sunday, which would go on the air in January 1987.

I was fortunate. The prognosis was excellent. But cancer changed me, as it does everyone it invades. I got scrappier, more impatient, at times. And, in some ways, mellower, less driven, easier on myself. Experiencing cancer, I now find, has given me not exactly an *affinity* for sadness, but certainly an *empathy* I hadn't made room for before. I see it in my work. In the past, I spent a great deal of time asking extremely successful people how they did it, what it was like being at the top. In ensuing years, I've been talking more with people who hurt and manage to carry on.

I chose to confide about my health only to family and close friends. Not up to handling general sympathy, I also didn't want "She had cancer" to be the lead in my life. But I resolved to find a way to address cancer on the air, knowing it could help others. It took some years before I felt ready to do this. Then, in 1990, Nina Hyde of *The Washington Post* was speaking out about her battle with breast cancer, and her courage empowered me. Her story is some pages ahead.

I stood still and listened to the world coming awake. A woodpecker was thumping on a tree. Small birds were calling and chirping, greeting the day. The lake was placid as a millpond. Here and there I could see a spreading circle that a fish made as it rose to the surface, maybe for a May fly even though this was June. A chipmunk scurried around, a pine squirrel scolded. I walked on.

—*Kim Williams, from Cookbook and Commentary*

Jane Goodall on Chimpanzees

March 1987

Miss Goodall and the chimpanzees have been together almost as long as snow and Kilimanjaro. Jane Goodall's landmark studies of chimpanzee behavior are documented in *National Geographic* films and her several books. She's an invigorating combination of student and teacher, and she always has news to tell about her research in the forests of Tanzania. But one visit with Miss Goodall, in the late fall of 1986, posed problems of production and ethics.

That fall, I was preparing for the January debut of *Weekend Edition*/Sunday, stockpiling tapes to create a shelf of conversations that I could run once we were airborne. Tricky, because whatever you record in November needs to hold up for broadcast months later.

I decided to ask Jane Goodall to talk "ahead," to describe for us the rainy season in Gombe. We'd make tape we could use in March.

She was wonderful—even did some seriously uninhibited chimp imitations. But we ran out of studio time before I could ask any "Now let's sum it all up" questions. So I needed to find a way to end the piece.

Miss Goodall's newest book included a set of notes made in the field—raw data on chimp behavior. They gave a feel for what daily life in the forest was like—not just for the chimps, but for the observers, as well. Those notes could be my ending. Then I wanted to put in some sound. That's where the ethics came in.

At NPR, we have a library full of sound-effect records—hours of sounds captured by BBC microphones. But they can't be used in a news piece to create the impression that we're somewhere we are not. We have strict rules about the use of sound in our reports. You don't *manufacture* it; the sound must be authentic. I spent days, once, searching for a recording I had made in Kenya of insects buzzing in a field (this was for a profile of Isak Dinesen). The producer I was working with said he'd recorded some great buzzes in South America. "No," I said. "It has to be *African* insects. Dinesen lived in Africa!"

Now, for the Goodall piece I needed not only insect sounds, but rain, too—our subject was the rainy season, remember. I wanted to put listeners in Miss Goodall's environment, have them hear just what she heard, sitting and observing in that forest, hour after hour, day after day.

I decided to use the BBC sound-effect discs. But I had to write the introduction very carefully.

(Sound of rain.)
STAMBERG: The rain was recorded in England.
(Mix in sound of insects.)
The insects were recorded in Brazil. But if you close your eyes and do what radio lets you do best—imagine—you just might be able to put yourself in a forest in Africa, in the western part of Tanzania, where the behavior patterns of certain animals can be observed. In the forests of Gombe, now, it is the rainy season. And in one particular part of those forests, some seventy chimpanzees—a community of apes—climb and feed and travel and groom and are observed by a community of humans. The humans live nearby. In order to do their work, they endure the African seasons and the driving rain.
(Rain sound up again, then out.)
GOODALL: The rain will be absolutely pounding down on the roof of your house, and you lie there cozily and think of the poor chimps sitting out on their nests, huddled and shivering. By the time you get up and leave to go and see the chimps, it's stopped raining, but the vegetation is wet, clammy. You walk through the long grass, and you're soaked to the skin. Perhaps a cold wind springs up, so that even though the temperature may not be much lower than sixty, it feels very much colder.
STAMBERG: (*Narrating*) For the past twenty-six years, Jane Goodall has felt the wind in that part of Tanzania. She and her assistants at the Gombe Stream Research Center go into the forest daily to study chimpanzee behavior.

RICHARD LEAKEY: Some people have suggested that when humans lost their large canine teeth a million years ago, this led to the need for weapons and the need for adopting a more aggressive character, aggressive behavior. Because with the loss of our canine teeth, we lost our ability to be aggressive.

—November 1987

GOODALL: You get to the nest where the chimps are sitting, hunched and huddled. If it's a group, the adult males may perform some displays, which probably helps warm them up. The females and young ones will scream and rush up into the trees.

STAMBERG: What are displays, Dr. Goodall?

GOODALL: A charging display is a show of strength. It serves as the superb bluff, because when a male displays, he may walk upright, he may charge flat out across the ground, he may drag branches, haul rocks. His hair is bristling, and it makes him look much bigger and more dangerous than he may actually be.

STAMBERG: Does he make a lot of noise?

GOODALL: He stamps and slaps on the ground. He drums on the trees. He may utter a pant hoot as well. A pant hoot—*Whooh whooh whooh whooh whooh whooh*—I can't do it any louder because I'll blow out the mike, but . . . (*laughs*) . . . these displays enable a male to rise much higher in the hierarchy, if he does them in a very intimidating way. As I said, it's bluff. He doesn't have to actually fight.

STAMBERG: How else do they spend the day?

GOODALL: They'll travel for anything from ten minutes to half an hour or more, but then they'll come to a new food source—say, fruit, or some tasty leaf buds, or maybe some blossoms—and then they give these wonderful food calls—*Hmmph hmmph hah hah hah hmmph hmmph hmmph hmmph hah hah hah*—and climb up into the tree, and maybe give some of those pant hoots if it's a particularly delicious meal. They'll feed, perhaps for an hour, perhaps for slightly longer. Then they'll climb down, and if it's not actually raining, towards the middle of the day they may settle and groom one another in the branches.

STAMBERG: Describe the grooming. It has a lot of meaning within the chimp population.

GOODALL: Yes, it does. It's a way of ensuring that you maintain very relaxed and peaceful relationships within the chimpanzee community. It's basically you and your grooming partner, or there may be grooming clusters of anything up to twelve. Basically, you and your partner take turns looking through each other's hair to pick out little flakes of dry skin, to catch the odd chimpanzee louse that you spy in your companion's fur. They may groom at the same time, or they may take it in turns. High-ranked individuals tend to be groomed longer than your low-ranking ones.

STAMBERG: That's fascinating!

GOODALL: Grooming is used very often. A more dominant individual will come and reassure a subordinate who's nervous by grooming him. A mother will groom to calm her excited or frightened child.

STAMBERG: So it soothes stress?

GOODALL: It really does. It's like in humans: If you're a mother with a small child, you pat them, you stroke their hair. This is basically what they're doing, as well as its having a cleaning function. You have two types of maternal grooming. One is "Here's business." She just takes that kid, and she grooms the back, and she turns it over and grooms the tummy, and she holds it upside down and grooms the rump, and works her way down the legs and pokes into the ears. That's business. But then, other times, the child wants to run off, and the mother thinks it shouldn't because it's a frightening situation. So she grabs him, and he pulls, and she starts to groom him, and he relaxes.

STAMBERG: And so the day goes. Ultimately, they will sleep. For how long?

GOODALL: Well, they make their nests around dusk or seven o'clock in the evening, and they get up in the morning around first light—six-thirty to seven, depending on the time of year.

STAMBERG: Dr. Jane Goodall. Her most recent book, *The Chimpanzees of Gombe*, is a summary of findings gathered over the course of twenty-six years in Tanzania.

(*Sneak in insect and rain sounds, and hold under.*)

The book includes field reports—notes taken while an adult male chimp was followed. According to the notes, at 6:45 A.M., the chimp was in his nest. Five minutes later he left, climbed, fed on fruit. At 7:16, he wandered along, feeding on other fruits. An hour later, he stopped feeding, climbed, fed again. From 8:08 to 8:35, he traveled. At 8:40, he fed as he walked.

The account goes on: By 5:23 in the evening, the male chimp is building his nest. First, he grunted and climbed. By 5:30 at night, he is asleep, alone.

This kind of chimpanzee behavior is under way at this moment in the forests of Gombe, and Jane Goodall, or one of her assistants, is in the forest, making observations, taking notes.

(*Rain up full, and hold.*)

The working title for *House of Games* was *The Tell*.

A "tell" is an unconscious revelation. For example, you have a lot of politicians in your city. They're probably lying most of the time. But a common human "tell" is, if someone is lying, they have a tendency to touch their face, to pull their nose, or take off their glasses, or to wipe their forehead. I don't know why—I'm sure there's a real simple psychological explanation—but it's true. In gambling, a "tell" is something that another player is doing unconsciously when he or she bets, to reveal their hand. For example, if they have a weak hand, they might, as a "tell," fold their arms in front of their chest, to subconsciously protect themselves. If they have a strong hand, they might splay their fingers out, as if to say, "I'm hiding nothing." Everybody has "tells" of one kind or another. Body language is another term for a "tell."

—David Mamet,
March 1987

The Carters, Making the Most of It

June 1987

Journalist Stanley Karnow says the role of every modern president is to make his predecessor look good. We'll see what Bill Clinton does for George Bush. Certainly Bush and Ronald Reagan together made Jimmy Carter look terrific.

James Earl Carter, Jr., is surely our best ex-president. Busy as a mediator through his Carter Presidential Center in Atlanta, monitoring disputed elections in far-flung nations, working in a hard hat to rehabilitate inner-city houses, Jimmy Carter keeps his head down and attends to the business of improving things.

The Horatio Alger hero of politics, the peanut farmer who became president engineered the Panama Canal treaties and the historic Camp David peace conference between Israel's Menachem Begin and Egypt's Anwar Sadat. But he was blasted for being weak and ineffective. James Fallows, once chief speech writer in the Carter White House, called Carter's a "passionless" presidency and lamented the Georgian's "inclination to be a good man rather than an effective one." Fallows wrote that assessment *before* Jimmy Carter was hamstrung by the taking of American hostages in Tehran in 1979.

Our thirty-ninth president presided over an America of gas-station lines and shortages. He accused Americans of "malaise" and spoke of the need for morality in government. The country wanted more upbeat lessons and, in 1980, gave the White House to a man who knew how to communicate them.

In 1991, when the Reagan Presidential Library in Simi Valley, California, was dedicated, five presidents—Nixon, Ford, Carter, Reagan, and Bush—attended the ceremony. Jimmy Carter turned to the four Republicans and said, "At least all of you have met a Democratic president. I've never had that honor yet."

The Democrat and his wife, Rosalynn (called the Steel Magnolia in her White House years), came to NPR in the summer of 1987 as coauthors on a book tour. I greeted them with copies of the day's newspapers and asked Mr. Carter to spot stories on page 1 that had developed since he was president.

JIMMY CARTER: Well, the obvious thing that wasn't there when I was in the White House was illegalities by the CIA and violations of congressional mandates by the National Security Council.

STAMBERG: You get your news from the papers these days, just like the rest of us. As you read, is there anything you wouldn't like to be in a position to influence in some way?

JIMMY CARTER: Well, obviously, the number one person who can do something about issues in our country is the president. Since we've left the White House, we've had to find other means by which we could influence issues.

STAMBERG: Do the two of you, as you read the papers, have "if only" conversations—or "Why didn't they think?" or "How come?"

ROSALYNN CARTER: We do sometimes, but the fact is that we've been home for a long time, and you move on to other things. Sometimes I look at something—the situation in the Persian Gulf, for instance—and ask if we should have chosen sides in the Iran-Iraq war—which we obviously have, backing Iraq, sending them weapons to protect oil supplies. I'll ask him what he would have done. But you don't dwell on those things or say, "Oh, if we had been there, we could have done something differently." You don't do that.

STAMBERG: You write about going home in this book of yours. Mr. President, you tell what Harry Truman said when reporter Ray Scherer asked, "What's the first thing you did, Mr. Truman, when you went back home to Independence?"

JIMMY CARTER: Truman said, "I carried my grip up to the attic."
(*Laughter.*)
And we did a similar thing! Obviously, we had to tote our own

We are dealing here with a former frightened rabbit. Traces of it linger around the eyes, in the way the head is held, the beat before the answer comes. Those are the remnants of Rosalynn Smith, who at thirteen lost her father and became a second mother to her younger brothers and sister. Whom Plains, Georgia, knew as the painfully shy, quiet, very neat girl who became Rosalynn Carter, a timid wife. Who got physically ill before giving a speech for the first time in her husband's place, during the 1970 gubernatorial primaries. The woman who said, during the presidential primaries, when she spent eighteen months campaigning, that the hardest moment of the day was shaking that first hand at some steel mill in one of the thirty-four states she traveled, at six in the morning.

—from an S.S. essay, January 1977

luggage into the house, but we didn't have a place to put all the stuff
that we had accumulated during four years in the White House. So we
had to put a floor in our attic just to store things.

ROSALYNN CARTER: We had never had a floor.

JIMMY CARTER: So we did it ourselves. We carried all this lumber up
in the attic and did the hammering and nailing.

ROSALYNN CARTER: It was good to have those things to do when
we got home, because we didn't know what we were going to do
with the rest of our lives. All of a sudden, we had to get the house
in shape. We'd been gone for ten years. It was good for us not to
have to go home and have nothing to do and think about losing the
election.

STAMBERG: You looked for other useful work. Mrs. Carter, what do
you do with Habitat for Humanity?

ROSALYNN CARTER: We work a week every summer building
houses. This summer, we're going to be in Charlotte, North Caro-
lina. We're going to build fourteen houses in five days, with volun-
teers.

STAMBERG: President Carter, please tell us about that elderly woman
you met when you were working with Habitat in New York. She was
called the Russian Princess.

JIMMY CARTER: We were on the roof of an old dilapidated apartment
house that we were trying to renovate, and I looked over the edge
down in the little courtyard behind, and there was this older lady
there cooking her meal outdoors, on rocks, with an open fire. She was
boiling an ear of corn, and eggs. And you could look a little bit further
and see Wall Street, just a few hundred yards away.

So I went down to talk to her. She had on an old silk dress and
a long strand of pearls. She told us she lived in the abandoned
house next door. She didn't have running water. She didn't have
any heat. No electricity. And I said, "Well, that's a very beautiful
dress that you have on. Do you wear that all the time?" And she
said, "Oh, no! I heard that President Carter was next door, and I
thought I might see him." So I introduced myself, and she really
accepted me as though she was a true Russian princess, you know,
as though she was royalty.

ROSALYNN CARTER: And you learn so much in those situations. I
remember the day that Jimmy had a Coke can in his hand. He drank
the Coke, and he started to crush the can, and somebody said, "Mr.

President, don't bend that can." We found out that those people actually live on money they get from selling cans they pick up on the side of the road, and they don't get any money for them if they're bent. It's just a life that, so much of the time, we who are fortunate don't ever see.

STAMBERG: You're offering a Life Saver to your husband, and he's refusing it. Is that correct?

(*Laughter.*)

JIMMY CARTER: That's right.

STAMBERG: Would you prefer a different flavor?

JIMMY CARTER: No, that's fine.

(*Laughter.*)

STAMBERG: You write that doing this book together is the hardest thing you've ever done in forty years of marriage. Why? I mean, a woman who can offer her husband Life Savers in the middle of an interview . . .

(*Laughter.*)

JIMMY CARTER: We have different writing styles, first of all. I write very rapidly. I get up early in the morning. I am quite productive. Rosalynn writes very slowly. She likes to work at night. She'll spend a week or two honing down one paragraph; I might write a chapter in two days.

Then we had totally different memories of the same event. I would write a chapter and take it to Rosalynn, and she would read it, and she would come storming in. "This is not what happened!" And I would say, "Rosalynn, I was there. That's what happened." She'd say, "*I* was there. It did not happen that way." So once we argued and finally settled what happened, then the way I reacted to that incident was quite different from the way she reacted to it.

STAMBERG: Well, you've proven that there's life after the White House. Now, is there life after having written a book together?

(*Laughter.*)

Yes?

JIMMY CARTER: Sure.

STAMBERG: Jimmy and Rosalynn Carter. Their first—and last—literary collaboration is called *Everything to Gain: Making the Most of the Rest of Your Life.*

The Carters had a quick bite of lunch at NPR before going on to a book-signing session. They ate carryout tuna sandwiches and sipped soft drinks. And when they finished, the thirty-ninth president of the United States and his wife crumpled up their wax-paper sandwich wrappings and napkins, and Mrs. Carter began wiping off the table. We assured them that such housekeeping details could be taken care of here, and shooed them out of the room.

Traveling with M.F.K. Fisher

July 1987

STAMBERG: Was it very hard for you to get something published in the beginning?

FISHER: No, it was too easy. Much too easy! I never had any trouble at all, and I think that's too bad. Because I didn't even want to be a writer, really. It never occurred to me to be a writer. There I *was* one, before I knew it.

STAMBERG: (*Narrating*) W. H. Auden once called her "the best prose writer in America." Mary Frances Kennedy Fisher's first published work—*Serve It Forth,* which came out in 1937—was so different from what women were writing about food in the 1930s that many readers assumed M.F.K. Fisher must be a man. There were recipes, of course, but more important, there was history, sociology, art, humor, and careful, idiosyncratic observation. Her personal essays moved food off the women's pages, out of the kitchen, and into the realm of literature.

After *Serve It Forth,* Mrs. Fisher produced a pioneering translation of French gastronomer Brillat-Savarin's *The Physiology of Taste,* countless magazine articles (mostly for *The New Yorker*), and fourteen other books, including *How to Cook a Wolf* in 1942, *The Gastronomical Me* in 1943, various essay collections, *Among Friends* in 1970, *As They Were* in 1982—all revealing her keen eye and appreciation of what she says are the three essentials of life: love, shelter, and food.

M.F.K. Fisher is celebrating a half century as a published writer, and also celebrating her seventy-ninth birthday this Fourth of July weekend.

FISHER: I was born minutes before midnight of the third of July, and I was born that way because my mother was a very conservative woman who called children George and Henry and John, you know—things like that. And Father said, "It's nine minutes to midnight. If you don't hurry up, you are going to call this child Independencia." Mother was so horrified—probably thinking, "What will the nicknames be?" or something—that she gave a great heave and there I was!

STAMBERG: (*Narrating*) M.F.K. Fisher spent much of her life in Europe, and lives now in northern California's Sonoma Valley. But her earliest memories come from Whittier, California, where her father was owner and publisher of the local daily newspaper.

FISHER: We all wrote in my family, because I'm a fifth-generation newspaper person, and my father probably wrote two thousand words a day for sixty-five years of his life. I wrote my first novel when I was nine.

STAMBERG: Do you have any idea what happened to that novel?

FISHER: No, I don't. I don't think I finished it, because I suddenly realized that my father and mother were very amused by it, and I didn't write it to be amusing. They never did laugh at it, but every noon when father came home for lunch, they would say, "Now, what's happening today in that book?" And I told them, gleefully, my chapter of the day. Then I realized that I was amusing them, and I didn't want to amuse them *at all*!

STAMBERG: Do you remember what the book was about?

FISHER: Oh, yes, it was about all sorts of things I knew nothing about, like love and being older. It was during the war, of course—the First World War. So it was about a girl and a boy. The boy was a sailor, but he kept looking through his porthole window and sending her Morse code signals.

And she was a nurse, I think. I knew nothing about nursing or anything like that. But every day, she "hoped" into bed, and then she "hoped" out of bed. I didn't know how to spell, you know!

(*Laughter.*)

So, the whole novel, all she did was "hope." I didn't know what else to have her do, because I didn't know anything about anything then!

STAMBERG: Very often people will describe you as a "food writer." But you are not that, are you?

FISHER: Oh, no, I don't think I am, really. I think we are rather preoccupied—a little bit too much so, probably—with that aspect of living. It's not a sin to enjoy food, but these days it's become almost an obsession. I think we are overdoing it a bit, really, but it's just indicative to me of the fact that we don't want to face other, uglier things, so we face the kitchen stove, you know, or the parts thereof. It's an evasion, really.

STAMBERG: Mrs. Fisher, as fine as your writing about food is, I think of you as a travel writer. I've taken you along on some wonderful trips, and you've made a great difference to my traveling.

FISHER: Oh, gosh, that's nice to hear! Thank you.

STAMBERG: What about you? Are you still traveling?

FISHER: Well, I am not traveling right now, but I thank God I *have* traveled! I know what it's about, and I travel in my mind a lot.

STAMBERG: Do you miss the physical traveling?

FISHER: Oh, yes, I do, but I hate traveling now because, as I'm older, it's a bore to get to airports and stand around, you know, and I don't go dashing from place to place, either. My husband, once, in Paris, said that the best way to go to a place is to get off a train, head right for the nearest and best bar or pub in town—this is in Europe, of course, where you sat outdoors a lot—and just sit there until the sun goes down. By then, you know whether you want to stay or not. If you don't want to, you can get on the next train. But you usually stay. That's very true, you know! True for me, anyway.

STAMBERG: I discovered a wonderful place in a railway station in Paris, thanks to you. I was reading you at the time. Do you know what it is?

FISHER: I think I know. The Gare de Lyon.

STAMBERG: Can you describe that for us, the Gare de Lyon?

FISHER: Well, the station was built just about the turn of the century, and it was built for the Paris-Lyon-Mediterranean Railway. It's very garish and sort of grand. Long stairways and marble staircases. It's very imposing in a funny, outlandish, extravagant way—like a rather faded, beautiful old courtesan. It's sitting there, waiting.

(*Actress Elizabeth Ross, reading.*)

"As far as I can know or learn, no other railroad station in the world manages so mysteriously to cloak with compassion the anguish

People aren't adventurous enough. They stick within the confines of the usual trip. Getting lost is something unusual, even if it's something as crazy as taking the bus to the end of the line. There's always a way to get back. It allows for some of the serendipity in travel that people sometimes don't have because they're so programmed. Getting lost is a little bit of freedom that people wouldn't normally allow themselves.

—*travel consultant Deena Kaye, April 1982*

What most people think of as travel is actually lying on a beach. It's kind of horizontal, or sedentary. That's not travel. Travel's a fairly miserable business in which the journey is nothing but *self-discovery* is everything.

—Paul Theroux, March 1984

of departure and the dubious ecstasies of return and arrival. Any waiting room in the world is filled with all this, and I've sat in many of them and accepted it, and I know from deliberate acquaintance that the whole human experience is more bearable at the Gare de Lyon in Paris than anywhere else."

STAMBERG: You go up a flight of stairs at one end of that station.

FISHER: Yes. At the right-hand side, as you stand at the top of the staircase (which has always got palm trees on it—it's very elegant with brass rails and stuff), there is the Train Bleu, which was named for the famous train that comes over from London. So, once, most of the people there were English.

(Reading again.)

"It's one of the most amazing public dining rooms I've ever seen, or even imagined. The ceiling is very high and elaborate. The windows are tall, looking on one side upon a goodly part of Paris, and then to the right into and under the endless stretch of grey glass roof over all the tracks that come to a dead stop below . . . Switzerland, Italy, Spain, the Near East, all France to the south. . . ."

STAMBERG: If I remember properly, you were particularly struck by the rolls—the hard rolls.

FISHER: Well, it was the best bread in Paris by far, and it was the only bread that was any good after World War Two, when the bread was really pretty awful all through France. And then they have wonderful ham from Parma, which just smells like violets, you know, Parma violets. And they have beautiful little half bottles of champagnes that are made by small wineries in Reims—the champagne country. So that was my breakfast, always—bread and ham and champagne—before I started out.

STAMBERG: Mrs. Fisher, you say you travel so much now in your imagination. Now you've helped us to do that, too, I think!

FISHER: I hope so.

▬▬

M.F.K. Fisher was celebrating her seventy-ninth birthday the year we spoke. Two weeks before her eighty-fourth birthday, in late June 1992, Mary Frances Kennedy Fisher died at home in Glen Ellen, California.

Stars of *New York*

April 1988

STAMBERG: Twenty years ago this week, a new magazine appeared on newsstands—a snappy, well-written weekly devoted not to the news, not to recipes for housewives, but to life in one city: New York.

CLAY FELKER: We were all young and excited about living in the city, and we wanted a magazine to reflect our excitement and also to provide a road map, a guide, as to what the city ought to be.

STAMBERG: Clay Felker was the founder and editor in chief of *New York* magazine, which began as a Sunday supplement of the *New York Herald Tribune* and would eventually influence other magazines, newspapers, and create a new publishing form—the city magazine. In 1968, Felker's stable of contributing editors included a thirty-seven-year-old writer named Tom Wolfe.

WOLFE: I was a free-lance writer. The classification, I always felt, was a joke, until I became one, and then it was *more* of a joke!

(*Laughter.*)

I was kind of out on the beach, and Clay came along with *New York* magazine.

STAMBERG: Another member of Clay Felker's original staff was Gloria Steinem.

STEINEM: Well, I was also unemployed, but I thought it was just called being "a free-lancer" because I'd never *been* employed!

(*Laughter.*)

Actually, I've never had a job in my life, to tell you the truth! So I was a free-lance writer, writing very peculiar things, sometimes,

In Mr. Galbraith's own foreword to *Triumph*, he writes, "This is a story I have tried to tell before in articles and lectures." And, indeed, the handsome, witty, six-foot-three-economist-diplomatist has made notable contributions in the field of non-fiction and on the rostrum. But, by resorting to the novel form to convey his message, Galbraith has added little to his own stature or to the average reader's understanding of the limits of U.S. foreign policy and the limitations of U.S. policymakers.

—*Clare Boothe Luce, New York, April 8, 1968*

because it was all I could get the assignment for—like reviewing textured stockings for the Sunday *New York Times Magazine,* or something. All that time, I was working in political movements, but with no ability to bring my interests and my writing together. It was really Clay who brought the two things together for me; that is, what I cared about and what I could write about.

STAMBERG: Just taking a look at this first issue of *New York* magazine, the writers make up a pantheon of young men and women who would become the American greats—Jimmy Breslin, Gail Sheehy. Avery Corman was writing the society page—he went on to become a best-selling novelist. Clare Boothe Luce—who'd had a minor career, right? In the first issue, she reviewed a novel by John Kenneth Galbraith. Stephen Sondheim was writing about crossword puzzles and creating them for *New York* magazine.

STEINEM: That was one of *my* great coups for the magazine, getting Steve, who is a puzzle/game nut, to do a double acrostic. He's just enormously expert—you can see from his lyrics how good he is at words. Then he in turn got Mary Ann Madden, who is still doing the competitions in the back of the magazine.

STAMBERG: We are holding a small reunion here of founders of *New York* magazine, which turns twenty this week. I want to say hello now to a later hire. Aaron Latham came to the magazine in 1972, hired as . . . ?

LATHAM: As an editor and a writer.

STAMBERG: How were you hired?

LATHAM: I was assigned by *The New York Times Magazine* to do a story about *New York* magazine. So I went to interview Clay Felker. We spoke for an hour or two—a very long interview—and then *The New York Times Magazine* never ran the story. It finally occurred to them that if they ran it, they were giving *New York* magazine free advertising! (*Laughs.*)

So all that work was for nothing, except I met Clay, and several months later he got back in touch with me and asked if I'd like to come to work for him.

STAMBERG: So Aaron came to *New York* having tried to write an article about it for another publication. Tom Wolfe, you, for *New York*, wrote about *The New Yorker* magazine, which was probably *New York*'s heaviest competition. Could you please tell that story?

WOLFE: Yes. I should begin at the end by saying that after that piece was published—not that I expect magazines to mention me—but I became a nonperson at *The New Yorker*. They never mentioned my name. That rule was broken only two months ago, when they relented to give an extremely bad review to *The Bonfire of the Vanities*.

(*Laughter.*)

Anyway, we were at the *Herald Tribune* when I wrote that in 1965—*New York* magazine was then the new Sunday supplement of the *Herald Tribune*—and all these puff pieces started appearing, celebrating the fortieth anniversary of *The New Yorker*. I'll never forget it. Each piece seemed to outdo the one before in saying what a great American institution this was. But everybody knew—even the people writing the articles—that nobody was reading *The New Yorker* anymore. It had become so dull!

So I wrote a two-part profile of the editor, William Shawn, in which I tried to present him as the world's most colorful minimal maniac.

STAMBERG: The first part of your profile was called "Tiny Mummies! The True Story of The Ruler of 43d Street's Land of The Walking Dead!"

WOLFE: I thought that the piece was all good fun. Apparently, *he* didn't. Someone, I think it was the *Herald Tribune* editor Jim Bellows, decided he'd just send Shawn an advance copy as soon as it came off the press. Well, this was soon followed by a protest letter to Jock Whitney, the owner of the *Herald Tribune,* in which Mr. Shawn—he's Mr. Shawn to everybody; I find *myself* calling him Mr. Shawn—said not only was the piece slanderous and libelous and a lot of other things, but *murderous*! I gather Jock Whitney was actually quite shocked to get this letter. He said to Bellows, "What do we do about this, Jim?" Bellows said, "Well, I'll show you." And he picked up the telephone and called up *Time* and *Newsweek* and read them the letter.

FELKER: I was in the office when that happened.

WOLFE: Oh, you were there?

FELKER: And as I watched, I really got a lesson in how tough newspapers can be. And it was the making of *New York* magazine!

STAMBERG: Really?

FELKER: Absolutely! Up until that time, we were averaging less than ten pages of advertising an issue. After that, it went to thirty pages of advertising an issue, and it was a great success because the whole

Omerta! Sealed lips! Sealed lips, ladies and gentlemen! Our thing! We are editing *The New Yorker* magazine. Harold Ross' New Yorker. We are not running a panopticon. Not exactly! For weeks the editors of *The New Yorker* have been circulating a warning among their employees saying that someone is out to write an article about *The New Yorker*. This warning tells them, remember: *Omerta.* Your vow of silence . . .

—Tom Wolfe, "Tiny Mummies!" New York Herald Tribune, April 1965 world, except for the people who were actually paid by *The New York,* agreed with Tom's point of view. It also taught me another lesson, which was that there's nothing more involving and better publicity for something than a fight.

(*Laughter.*)

STAMBERG: Gloria Steinem, there's a story about you that Aaron Latham remembers.

LATHAM: Back when I was doing my research for the piece that never came out about *New York* magazine, I was told, Gloria, that when you brought in your story and handed it to Clay for that first issue, he just took it and handed it to somebody and said, "Take this to the printer." As I heard the story, you said, "Well, what the . . . aren't you going to read it? What if you don't like it?" And Clay said, "How could I not like it? It's *here*!"

(*Laughter.*)

STEINEM: That's absolutely true! It's completely true. And if you were accustomed to the editorial process of other kinds of publications, you were staggered by this.

STAMBERG: Issue number three came out a bit after Lyndon Johnson announced he would not run for re-election. It was the heart of the worst days of Vietnam. Then Martin Luther King was assassinated. The country was having a nervous breakdown. There were riots in many cities, and Clay sent you, Gloria, to cover what was happening in Harlem.

STEINEM: That was a change for me, as well, to do that kind of story, because I had always been a journalist in monthly publications, so I was not accustomed to newspaper thinking. After hearing about Martin Luther King's murder, I was just walking around in my apartment feeling terrible, wondering what would happen. I was just totally absorbed in what I was feeling and thinking. And Clay called up and said, "You call yourself a *reporter*?! What are you doing at home? Get up there to Harlem and see what's going on!"

It turned out to be an odd advantage, being a white woman in that setting. A white man had more trouble, because men were viewed as bringing the culture with them. Somehow I, as a woman, wasn't seen that way. And if things got rough, I could always go stand with the women, anyway! I remember staying out for at least one night, maybe several nights.

Also, I was not accustomed to newspaper writing at all. I mean *literally*—in terms of how you structure a story. I actually tried to rhetorically connect my paragraphs. Well, Clay took out a large scissors and started to cut the paragraphs apart to rearrange them to accommodate some other reporter's stuff. I almost had a heart attack! (*Laughs.*) I said, "Clay! I *connect* my paragraphs! This isn't going to work this way!"

STAMBERG: Tom Wolfe, did *your* work change in the course of writing for *New York* magazine? Or were you doing what you'd done all along, just doing it more?

WOLFE: This was a period in which I was doing the first long pieces I'd ever done. So I was having the luxury of experimenting every week, because there were really no rules for a magazine like this. There was no canon. There were no standards that you were violating if you tried some ridiculous experiment, and I tried quite a few. It was the greatest time of my life in terms of creating a style, creating an approach to writing. The things I learned at that time—the things that worked—I've used ever since.

STAMBERG: The New Journalism wasn't born at *New York* magazine—but it certainly grew into its toddling stages there.

FELKER: Well, that's right. When print journalism was under attack by television, and we could no longer be the first to bring you news—the way that newspapers had traditionally done—we had to do something else. It was called thinking and writing! So what we did as a group was to return to the basic techniques of English literature.

STAMBERG: Using the tools of fiction—scenes, dialogue—to tell news.

STEINEM: What Clay is saying is very important, because the *old* journalism—the who-what-where-why-when pyramidal journalism —was being treated as sacred, and it wasn't. It was a function entirely of the telegraph machine.

FELKER: Exactly!

STEINEM: And *The New York Times* and everybody behaved as if we were doing something—

WOLFE: Oh, they were shocked! They were shocked!

FELKER: Which was part of the fun, too!

STEINEM: Yeah, right!

     (*Laughter.*)

WOLFE: I was acutely conscious of the need to make the reader turn the first page. I thought if you could make the reader turn the first page, you might have him. I can remember just sitting down and thinking,

"What is some new way to start a story?" And in one of the pieces I did for *New York,* it suddenly dawned on me that no narrator had ever started a story by screaming angrily at his characters.

I was doing a piece about this crazy intersection down at Greenwich Avenue, Sixth Avenue, Waverly Place. They all come together where the old Women's House of Detention was. So I started the piece with me, the narrator, screaming at the central figure in the story. It was a boy named Harry, and I started saying, "Haaaaaaarrrrryyyy. Yes, you standing there with your wide-wale corduroy pants bought lately in the tissue-paper mail-order edition of *The Manchester Guardian.*"

(*Laughter.*)

"Yeah, you with the bulky-knit Norwegian sweater that you think knocks all the girls dead. Yeah, you're the one. . . ." And just going on, raving like a maniac. And I kept it up. I actually counted the number of characters on the page to make sure that in the normal layout this screaming wouldn't stop until you turned the page. I figured the reader would at least go far enough to find out what the screaming was about!

LATHAM: One of the things that Clay would often do—which was just so embarrassing to a writer—you'd come in and you'd hand in your piece and he would say, "What's the point of the story?"

(*Laughter.*)

Which was usually the first time that question had crossed your mind!

(*Laughter.*)

STEINEM: It's true! Usually when you came in and talked to an editor about an idea, it just sort of lay there like a lox in the middle of the table. But with Clay, it took form. You knew what kind of fish it was! It had a point, and it got to be bigger, not smaller. I am not sure I have ever worked with an editor before or since who can do that in the same way.

WOLFE: I found out later that Clay had told the managing editor that when my stories came in, if they needed to be shortened, not to let me do it. He said, "Tom will always cut the point out first."

(*Laughter.*)

STAMBERG: Clay, you had to have learned as you published. What were some of the biggest changes you made along the way? For instance, the first pages of the first issue are filled with gossip—Jackie

Preparations are already under way for the Yippie Festival this summer, planned to coincide with the Democratic National Convention. Sleeping in the streets, love-ins, street-corner theater and folk-song marathons may begin a month or more in advance. The idea is to exhaust all the forces of the Establishment before the Convention begins, so demonstrations can take place more freely during it. "Ours is a festival of life," say the Yips, some of whom will come all the way from California. "We see the Convention as a festival of death."

—from gossip section,
New York,
April 8, 1968

Kennedy reportedly asking David Lean to produce a film for her
... President Johnson wearing makeup all the time to appear healthy.
That up-front gossip changed pretty fast, didn't it?

FELKER: Yeah, we made some big mistakes in the first issue. We saw
that we didn't know how to do gossip. (*Laughs.*)

One day, I got a call from a man who was an idol of mine, Bill
Bernbach, one of the great creative geniuses of American advertising
and communication, the founder of Doyle, Dane, and Bernbach, the
great advertising agency. He said, "Do you mind having lunch?" So
we had lunch, and he asked me, "Why are you opening up your
magazine like this? When you start a symphony, you hit the big chord.
You really know the symphony is beginning. What you are doing is
kind of noodling around. We don't really know that you're getting to
something important."

Now, normally for a lesson like that, somebody like the Sara Lee
Bakery Company would mail him a ten-million-dollar check!

(*Laughter.*)

I went back to the office and said, "That's it! From now on, we
get rid of all this stuff."

STEINEM: We also had some publicity that was hard because it lost
advertising. Remember the great Viva debacle?

FELKER: Yeah, I'll say!

STEINEM: Viva was an Andy Warhol star, a very beautiful, ethereal
woman. In a series of photographs, she appeared nude—not shock-
ingly nude—but I think she was lying in a tub, and then she was
sitting on a stool, something like that. It wasn't so much the nudity
that was shocking, but that her armpits were not shaven. Well, the
department stores in this town went crazy, pulling their advertising!

WOLFE: That was one of the incidents that made me realize that *New
York* was going to be a great magazine. Because I remember before you
ran that piece, Clay, I was up in the office and you said, "Tom, would
you read this and look at these photographs and tell me if you think we
ought to run it? Our advertising people are telling us that it's suicide to
run this piece." I read the article. It was by Barbara Goldsmith. It was
a brilliant piece, and I said, "I don't see how you can *not* run it." Clay
was obviously waiting to hear something like that. My head wasn't on
the block. Clay's was. And it ran, and the results were just horrible.

FELKER: They were devastating! We lost a half a million dollars' worth
of advertising because of that. It almost put us out of business.

Viva stretched, rubbed
her eyes and yawned.
"I'm tired out from that
Tucson location trip for the
movie. I didn't get any
sleep. The first two nights I
slept with John Chamber-
lain, who is an old lover of
mine. I slept with him for
security reasons. Well,
then it was a different one
every night. One night
Allen Midgette and what's
his name, Tom Hompertz,
both made it with me."

—*Barbara L.
Goldsmith, "La Dolce
Viva," New York,
spring 1968*

STAMBERG: Thank goodness it didn't! Lady and gentlemen, thank you so much for helping us to observe this twentieth anniversary of a truly remarkable magazine. Clay Felker, founder and very first editor of *New York* magazine. Early members of the masthead—Gloria Steinem, Tom Wolfe. And a later arrival, Aaron Latham, who was writer and editor for the magazine. Thanks to all of you.

EVERYONE: Thanks, Susan! . . . It was nice talking to you. . . . Thanks! . . . Bye!

Elia Kazan, Director

May 1988

This is a long conversation—seventeen and a half minutes on the air—
so I'll keep the introduction short. Two things you should know: In the
early 1950s, thousands of lives—countless careers—were destroyed
when the House Un-American Activities Committee (HUAC) investi-
gated communism in the entertainment world. Second, far less important, I am an only child. As such, I never learned to fight easily or
effectively. This can be a handicap in broadcasting, as in life.

STAMBERG: This is *Weekend Edition*. I'm Susan Stamberg. Mr.
Kazan, you are a director, so would you direct me, please, in the
pronunciation of your first name?

KAZAN: Il-*lee*-ya. Il-*lee*-ya. See, American people don't have that
sound—"ya." Il-*lee*-ya. It comes from the Bible, "Elijah."

STAMBERG: Well, thank you very much for that guidance. And for this
book, *Elia Kazan: A Life*. Seventy-eight years—there's lots for us to
talk about. I would like to get the HUAC business out of the way first.

KAZAN: Oh, no, let's not start with that!

STAMBERG: I'd like to.

KAZAN: (*Annoyed, loud*) There are forty pages—that's all there is of
HUAC in the book. In every interview it comes out that that's the
most important thing, and I'm *tired* of it!

STAMBERG: I *don't* think it's the most important thing, and it's why—

KAZAN: Then start with something else.

STAMBERG: No, I'd like to start with it, to get it out of the way.

KAZAN: No, you're not going to get me . . . you're not going to get me to talk!

STAMBERG: (*Softly*) So reluctant to discuss this?

KAZAN: No, I'm not a bit reluctant, but I want it in the scale of everything else. There are forty pages in the book, and soon as you start with it, it makes it the most important thing. It's not the most important thing in *my* life.

STAMBERG: I'll tell you something. I came to your autobiography thinking actually that that *was* going to be the most important thing to read. In fact, it was not at all the most interesting thing.

KAZAN: Yes, so talk about what's interesting!

STAMBERG: You really are a director, Mr. Kazan. You're directing this conversation.

KAZAN: (*Big laugh*.) Good for you! That's very nice, Susan. Don't get mad. It's just that, you know, there are two sides to an interview, right? And I'm not a victim, naturally, in life.

STAMBERG: (*Narrating*) Scrappy and tough, Elia Kazan has survived all kinds of difficulties and challenges, including the turbulence of the 1950s, when actors, directors, writers, artists of all kinds, were called before HUAC, the House Un-American Activities Committee. When it came time for Elia Kazan to testify in 1952, he chose to tell the committee of his 1930s involvement in the Communist party *and* to give the names of eight others—all members of the Group Theatre in New York—who had also been party members. It is an action for which he is still criticized. He *will* talk about it. But he wants to begin with his life as an artist.

Elia Kazan is one of stage and film's greatest directors. He helped shape the major theatrical events of the 1950s and '60s—Arthur Miller's *All My Sons* and *Death of a Salesman*, the films *Gentleman's Agreement, East of Eden, Viva Zapata!,* and Tennessee Williams's plays *Cat on a Hot Tin Roof, Sweet Bird of Youth,* and, before them, *A Streetcar Named Desire,* which he directed for both stage and screen.

Kazan cast Marlon Brando as *Streetcar*'s Stanley Kowalski—a choice that electrified theatre audiences.

KAZAN: I had produced a play called *Truckline Café,* and he played a part in it. I got to know him, and I called Tennessee Williams—he was up in the Cape—and I said, "I want to send somebody to you just to meet as a possibility for Stanley." And he said, "Okay." I gave

Brando twenty bucks and said, "Now you take the bus and go up to the Cape."

I called Williams a couple of days later, and he said, "Nobody showed up." I said, "Well, I don't know what happened." I started looking at other actors. All of a sudden I found out that Brando, in order to save the twenty bucks to eat on, had hitchhiked up to the Cape. When he finally showed up, Williams was just completely taken with him.

(*Sound clip from* A Streetcar Named Desire—*Brando: "I never met a woman yet that didn't know if she was good-lookin' or not without bein' told . . ."*)

STAMBERG: Talk about Marlon Brando as an actor.

KAZAN: Well, he was rather miraculous. He always did things, Susan, that surpassed your direction. I'd start talking to him about what a certain moment should be like, and right in the middle of what I was saying he'd turn around and walk away. I got mad at first—*What the hell's he doing?* Then I realized that he'd heard enough, and he wanted to *build* on what I said and add his own feeling to it.

STAMBERG: You worked so often with Brando, in theatre, then in film—in addition to the film version of *Streetcar* you did *On the Waterfront* and *Viva Zapata!* together. You write about little things he does in a role that make it special. The scene in *On the Waterfront* where he's walking with Eva Marie Saint and gets her glove.

KAZAN: They were walking together, and she was shy with him, uneasy with him. Putting a glove on . . . accidentally, she dropped it. And Marlon picked it up, but he didn't give it back to her right away. He held the glove, and they walked along, talking. She kept reaching for it, but he wouldn't give it to her. Finally he put his hand in it, which I suppose has some sort of sexual overtone, and then she finally took it out of his hand. But that subconscious gesture illustrated what he felt about her. I got credit for a lot of direction with Brando which I shouldn't get credit for. He did things that made me look good.

STAMBERG: How old was he when you met him?

KAZAN: Twenty-four or -five.

STAMBERG: I know an eighteen-year-old actor, someone in my neighborhood (*smiling to myself because I'm referring to my son*), who has been told he's a young Brando—not bad! I told him I was talking to you, and he has a question he wants me to ask you.

KAZAN: Fire away.

He could make each actor think he was his closest friend. I think his method, if it can be given so self-conscious a name, was to let the actors talk themselves into a performance. Far more by insinuation than by command, he allowed the actors to excite themselves with their own discoveries, which they would carry back to him like children offering some found object to a parent.

—from Timebends, Arthur Miller

STAMBERG: Okay. What do you believe is the most important characteristic in a young actor?

KAZAN: Well, one simple thing is that he have great emotional depths in him that he's not embarrassed by. That he's ready to experience anything. And with that, he has to have tremendous concentration on what he's doing—what he wants of his partner, what he wants in the scene. So that the scene is motivated by that.

STAMBERG: Hmmm. He has to be submerged in it? Is that what you are saying?

KAZAN: Well, yes, "submerged" is pretty good, too. I say "need." An actor should *need* something out of the scene. Otherwise he's just there, saying lines.

STAMBERG: I don't understand what you mean by needing something.

KAZAN: If he's with another person, he'll either want to defeat them, or win them over, or seduce them, or whatever, and he has a *need* for that, that comes out of something in him. The actions he takes in the scene fulfill that need. Is that clear now?

STAMBERG: Hmmm. Yes, thank you.

KAZAN: (*Laughs.*) I'm giving lessons in acting!

STAMBERG: Umm-hmm. And thanks. (*Pause.*) Now we get to HUAC.

KAZAN: All right.

STAMBERG: In the 1930s, a number of artists and others in this country became members of the Communist party. Years went by. Many such people became disaffected. They didn't like things that were happening within the party cells here. They didn't like what they saw Stalin doing in the Soviet Union. Ultimately, they resigned. 1950s—I'm telescoping all of this—the House Un-American Activities Committee begins hearings. The committee calls on various artists, you among them.

You and everybody else had a range of choices at that point. You could choose *not* to appear. You could choose *to* appear and refuse to speak on the grounds that it might incriminate you. You could choose to appear and speak only about yourself. Or you could name names. Your choice was the last. Why?

KAZAN: (*Takes a long pause, then noticeable change in speaking style. Says each word as if it were a separate sentence.*) When I faced that choice, I wavered. I went one way or another. Something not nice about naming names. (*Picks up speed.*) I also felt that the other people in our little unit—eight, nine people—should also do the same thing, and at that time I felt truly that if they were still Communists, I had less sympathy for them. I also felt that there's no use ruining my career for something I didn't believe in at all. I not only didn't believe it, but I had violent antipathy towards it. Do you understand?

STAMBERG: Hmmm. (*Hesitantly*) Yes.

KAZAN: Well, that's it! So that when it got down to it, wavering back and forth . . . there was something about it that was distasteful, of course, as there would be to any man. I spoke to some of them. I spoke to Clifford, and he agreed with me.

STAMBERG: Clifford Odets.

KAZAN: Yeah. I spoke to Lee Strasberg and Paula Strasberg. She was a member; he was not.

STAMBERG: You went around to everyone and said, "I am going to name you"?

KAZAN: No, I did not go around to everyone. I just went to those two. By the time I did that, they were the two that I thought represented the sort of clearest thought about the whole thing. Lee Strasberg and his wife felt as I did, and I thought, "Well, I am going to do it." And I did.

(*Pause.*)

STAMBERG: Essentially—

KAZAN: You ask me if I *liked* doing it? I did not.

STAMBERG: Basically, you wanted to keep working in film, and you thought that your film career would be jeopardized if you kept quiet.

KAZAN: I *assure* you that had very little to do with it, because I had a good career in the theatre. I could just . . . I could have worked in the theatre from then on, and I was getting plays of all kinds. I also could have worked in Europe, in films and so on. That wasn't the main thing. It's easy for people to say that, but it simply is not the truth of my experience.

STAMBERG: The thing is, the party was so *weak*. I mean, at that . . . at that point the Communist party in this country was *nothing*. It was a pitiful nothing.

KAZAN: Dear girl, I don't believe that. I don't believe it was nothing. It wasn't *much*, but it influenced many young intellectuals and many, many young people in colleges. There were many movements that were guided by that.

STAMBERG: Mr. Kazan, I can understand not liking what the Communists were doing in the United States. The hard part is understanding

There were days when I'd long to be forgiven, when I yearned to return to my old innocence, those harmonious times of long ago. Other days I became rambunctious, and what I longed for was a fight. I felt myself toughening. I enjoyed the apartness, had to. If I was a wolf, I'd be a lone wolf, not a herd animal. I thought about it and believed then—and I'm afraid I do still—that what's best is to be half liked, half disliked. It's a more trustworthy relationship for an artist.

—from **Elia Kazan:**
A Life

how that dislike can translate into action which then can ruin the lives of others.

KAZAN: It didn't ruin their lives at all. I don't think it *helped* them. I think it hurt them some, but it didn't ruin their lives, because they all had the same choice I did.

STAMBERG: How long, after you testified, did it take before you got a good night's sleep? I am not doing a guilt trip on you, Mr. Kazan. I am asking you a simple question.

KAZAN: Two nights later! I got over it quickly, because I thought I was right. When you're right, you don't have a problem with sleep. I felt great! I was being snubbed and so forth, but I began to be defiant.

STAMBERG: Hmmm. You were widely criticized at the time by some people who'd been members of your inner circle. The playwright Arthur Miller, for example, who when his turn came appeared in front of the committee but refused to name names. And yet, years later you worked together.

KAZAN: Well, he asked me to direct a play of his, so I did. Miller has a perfect right to what he did. That's the way he felt about it. I have a right to what I did. That's the way I felt about it. Perhaps you are blessed by having nothing but a series of decisions that didn't have an opposite side to them, but very often in life you make a decision that is difficult. So I felt bad about one aspect of that thing, but I . . . I . . . talk about sleep, I always sleep well.

STAMBERG: I don't know. . . . I just stop and think about you, and think about how I organized myself to come to this interview, and it was a funny . . . a strange balance. On the one hand was Kazan, the director of the most extraordinary performance pieces that have been around in my lifetime. On the other hand was Kazan, namer of names.

KAZAN: Well, don't you think there might be some connection between the two?

STAMBERG: What *is* the connection?

KAZAN: The connection is that I always do things that I feel strongly about, and I feel honestly about.

(*Very long pause.*)

STAMBERG: That's a good answer, Mr. Kazan.

KAZAN: (*Loudly*) It's TRUE, that's why it's good! (*Softer*) It's a true answer. That's why it's good, Susan. And your preparation, I think . . . I don't know . . . sort of led you into a trap about this thing.

STAMBERG: Hmmm.

KAZAN: There goes that—(*laughs*)—"hmmm" again. Forgive me, I am enjoying the interview!

    (*Laughter.*)

STAMBERG: Me, too. Me, too.

KAZAN: Okay.

STAMBERG: I think I'll say good-bye to you now.

KAZAN: Okay.

STAMBERG: (*Half-beat pause.*) I'll call it a draw. (*Laughs.*) Thank you.

KAZAN: Right.

STAMBERG: Elia Kazan calls his autobiography *A Life*. It's the director's seventh book.

———

Jules Feiffer gave me hell for that interview. The political cartoonist, playwright, and screenwriter was *Weekend Edition*/Sunday's movie reviewer, and a careful listener. To Feiffer, Kazan represented morality in the eighties—charming, manipulative, unapologetic, treacherous. He thought I let Kazan get away with too much. Jules may be right. In the end—edgy though I still feel about it—Kazan charmed me, too.

Facts no longer interest us. See the *Today* show if you want facts; wait for the seven o'clock news. But theatre as an event of the free fancy, one that involves its audience totally in a flight of the imagination, will exist always and I believe become less "realistic," and so, like painting and dance, more of an art. Wonder is our need today, not information.

**—*from* Elia Kazan:
A Life**

The Empress of Art

November 1988

Helen Frankenthaler was exasperating. At least twice. And it ended up being absolutely worth it.

Sometime in the early eighties, I clipped a magazine article about her—Frankenthaler is an American painter who began making her mark in the fifties—and scribbled a note along the top margin: "try 4 intv." After a series of phone calls, my assistant, Dee Clarke, came back, frazzled, to report that Ms. Frankenthaler would consider an interview, but only if I sent a list of the questions. Most unusual. Heads of state don't ask for questions in advance. The pope surely doesn't ask for questions in advance. Frankenthaler asks.

I dislike such requests—I don't want to be limited to a list, and I don't want my guest to start rehearsing answers. I can certainly understand a guest's wish to do research, look up dates, call his or her brain trust or mother (often one and the same), get prepared. But an interview is not a test, and I'm not especially interested in "right" answers. I'm after the process of thought, the stroll up to whatever the answer turns out to be.

There are those, however—CEOs, politicians, prosecuting attorneys—who have utterly no interest in revealing their thought processes, who in fact guard against that possibility. They only want to get their side out. A most breathtaking example of that sort was Zbigniew Brzezinski, to whom I occasionally spoke when he was President Jimmy Carter's adviser on national security affairs. Brzezinski set ground rules for an interview. "I do not want to be edited," he said. So he insisted on speaking to us live or, if he was to be pre-recorded, being informed precisely how long the conversation would air. Then he would set his watch, tape for exactly the amount of time we'd told him, and insist we run the tape just as it was recorded, no deletions. I am pained to report that there were times we acceded, however reluctantly, to his conditions because his perspective was needed.

Zbigniew Brzezinski was a savvy media manipulator whose words, at the time, had policy-setting weight. But the glowing, paint-stained canvases of Helen Frankenthaler were from a different, less dire, world, and her request for questions, in a very busy week, was an annoyance. So I pulled back. "See if you can gently withdraw the invitation," I asked Dee. And moved on to other matters. (Maybe Brzezinski was coming in.)

A few years later, a publisher's pamphlet arrived, one of those slick, hyperbolically written catalogs (". . . groundbreaking contribution . . . destined to become a classic . . . piercing shrewdness") publishing houses put out to announce forthcoming wares. This particular publisher—Harry N. Abrams—was announcing the arrival of a book on Frankenthaler to coincide with her sixtieth birthday and a retrospective exhibition in New York. Clearly, it was time to re-extend the request for an interview.

Now Connie Drummer was my assistant. Same response when she called: "Send a letter with a list of questions you want to ask." By this time (1988) I was off the daily program and hosting *Weekend Edition/ Sunday*. There was now more time to do the research I'd need before writing a letter. I read through files, watched an old PBS documentary on Frankenthaler, then wrote.

Dear Ms. Frankenthaler,

Thanks so much for agreeing to the interview. I'm looking forward to meeting you, and promise to keep to a thirty-minute schedule. I know you'll be busy that day.

Here's what I hope we can cram into our allotted thirty:

1. Some biography. When you first saw real works of art. How was it to see/meet Pollock. The first picture you sold. Where is it today?

2. How you work. Why staining? What does it let you do that you can't do with brush alone?

And so on.

A week later, another assistant-to-assistant conversation. Ms.

Frankenthaler would be interviewed, but wanted to talk with me first. "Fine!" I said. Connie arranged a phone date. Frankenthaler said she'd be extremely busy on the day I'd asked to come (I would fly from Washington to New York to do the interview) and could see me only in the morning. Would I arrange for a car to come to her studio when we concluded our interview—"at exactly eleven-thirty"—to take her downtown to her publishers?

"Of course!" I assured her, as if providing cars in Manhattan was something we did every day. It's something we *never* do. This is a beer-budget operation, National Public Radio. *Coke* is closer to our budget line. Make it tap water. At NPR, "sending a car" usually means asking the intern to ask her boyfriend if he might be free sometime in the morning a week from Thursday unless something else comes up.

But there I was, telling Helen Frankenthaler that a car would certainly be available, and then entreating my producer to let me make arrangements with a town-car service (suggested by an Ultimate Consumer friend of mine in Manhattan) that charged maybe twenty-five dollars an hour and was allegedly extremely reliable.

Looking down the already pricey barrel of round-trip airfare and a day's expenses in New York (I'd stay free at this town-car-tipster friend's apartment, so no hotel fee, at least) *plus,* now, the cost of a car for an hour in that crowded, costly city, the producer responded with a grimace.

"Well . . . okay." (I know he was thinking, "This better be worth it!")

The appointed day arrives. Manoli Wetherell, an audio technician at our New York bureau, meets me at ten-thirty—a half hour before taping time—at Frankenthaler's East Side studio. Manoli is an all-time favorite of mine. About my height (walking together, we are Amazon Women on the March), she has carrot-red hair and a round, fun-filled face, wears funky earrings and purple-rimmed eyeglasses, and is easygoing, thoughtful, and a sharp, sharp observer. Post-interview conversations with Manoli—in rented cars, in taxis, on buses, on airplanes going home—always produce insights that enrich my scripts.

"Hi! How ya doing?"

"Yes! Good! Glad to see you!"

So here we are, Manoli and I, on a fine September New York morning, happily reconvening at Helen Frankenthaler's studio. An assistant lets us in. Ms. Frankenthaler hasn't arrived.

"Okay. We'll just get set up and tape some ambient sound while we're waiting."

There's outside traffic, staple guns snapping in a back room where several men are stretching huge sheets of unprimed canvas across slim wooden frames for the artist. Manoli pokes around with her mike. I jot notes in a skinny reporter's pad—"Chevy Caprice Classic eggplant (black) station wagon parked inside studio . . . one of her paintings on wall . . . floor of studio splashed with a streak of green—ran over the edge of a canvas she was working on . . . photo—Monet. WHY?"—visual details that strike me and may end up in my script.

By now it's eleven o'clock—time for Frankenthaler's arrival. Then it's time plus ten minutes. Another ten. My bequeathed half hour is now cut to ten minutes, and there is no famous artist to be seen. In ten minutes, the town car will arrive, meter ticking (and ticking), and ticking into double time—the public radio equivalent of hell.

"Where's Frankenthaler!!??"

At twenty minutes of twelve—a full *forty* minutes after we were to have begun, a full *ten* minutes past the time we were to have concluded, I've had it.

"Manoli, let's go!" I jump up from the couch where I've been tapping my pen against the notepad and start pacing. "This is unspeakably rude. We've been waiting here almost three quarters of an hour after she was so fussy about our showing up on time. Now there's *no* time left. That *car's* gonna cost the world. Let's get out of here!"

Manoli sits up straight, blinks a few times behind her purple frames, then relaxes back into her chair.

"Susan," she says. "Let's wait just a little more. Look—we're here! She could show up any minute. Let's see."

She is such a pool of tranquillity, that Manoli, sitting there with her fish-pole mike and headsets. Clearly, she has no place else to be at this particular moment, which reminds me that *I* don't either. I sit back down, take out another pen, and practice drum paradiddles on my pad in an effort to stabilize my dwindling reservoir of goodwill . . . until . . . Frankenthaler walks in.

Small and imperious, with the kind of well-bred New York accent I'd grown up overhearing on buses in the days when wealthy people used public transportation in Manhattan, Helen Frankenthaler barely says hello, certainly doesn't apologize for being late, and strides past us to inspect the stapling work of the muscular young canvas men in the back room.

More waiting.

More.

I go outside and discover the town-car company to be indeed as reliable as my Ultimate Consumer friend (okay, her name is Debra Allee, and she's my "longest" friend—we've solved each other's problems and celebrated each other's achievements since the tenth grade) had predicted. I explain our situation to the pleasant young driver and ask him to go around the block 112 or so times. "We're in Wonderland," I'm thinking. "There's no telling what the Red Queen has in mind."

Back inside, after issuing a series of precisely articulated orders, the artist finally finishes with the staple-gun men. Then she greets us, sits down, and rummages through her purse, eventually producing the letter I had sent. Unfolding it, she glances down the page, and, noticing Manoli sitting there holding a mike, she reads what I've written aloud: "Some biography. When you first saw real works of art." Then she begins her response.

"No, no, Ms. Frankenthaler," I hasten to interrupt. "Excuse me, that's not the way we're going to do this. You don't need to run through answers to each of my written questions. This is to be a *conversation*! Let's just talk with each other. Some of the subjects in the letter will come up as we go along, but I know there'll be other things, too. So let's just *talk*. Okay?"

Helen Frankenthaler hems and haws, wonders whether she'll remember dates, frets over this and that, says she wants to hear the tape before it's broadcast. *God!*

All of a sudden, exasperated as I am, I find the whole scene absolutely hilarious and—in the seam between anger and humor—discover understanding. I realize that she is extremely *nervous* about this interview, insecure as to how she will sound. That's why she's so rarely spoken to reporters. Maybe that's why she made so many demands and showed up so late? I try to reassure her, but I also *have* to get on with my work (tick-tick-tick).

"This is *tape,* Ms. Frankenthaler. If you're not happy with the way an answer is coming out, you can just stop, and start the answer again. We will edit this. It will be fine!"

She looks relieved. Perhaps she's pleased that someone has stepped

into the middle of her fretting with calming words. Perhaps her apparent
need to control is simply a search for control from somewhere outside
herself. Who knows? Anyway, Manoli starts the Nagra, hands me a
microphone, moves a second mike under the painter's rather patrician
nose, and we begin.

She spends an *hour* talking with us and never once looks at her
watch. When we finish, she insists we share the waiting car, and as the
still-pleasant driver creeps through the crowded city streets, Helen
Frankenthaler laughs and jokes as if we were all headed for a Bennington class reunion. Relief that it's over? Anticipation of a delicious lunch
at her publishers? Genuine pleasure in our company? Which, Ms. F? We
part with smiles and promises of tape in the mail—edited tape, a copy
of the finished report.

Manoli says—another twenty-five dollars on the transportation tab
later—"Gee. It was rough there for a while. But she turned out to be all
right."

STAMBERG: In 1978, Perry Miller Adato made a film for public television about the painter Helen Frankenthaler. The film ends this way:
(*Sixteen seconds of ambient sound, primarily silence—occasional footsteps, a squeegee swooping paint across canvas, but,
mostly, silence. Fade and hold under for:*)
The cameras have recorded Helen Frankenthaler at work in her
studio. There are no easels. An immense canvas is spread across the
floor. The artist, in jeans and a white lab coat, approaches the canvas
carrying a pail of coral-colored paint and a wide bristle brush. She
pauses, kneels on the blank canvas in silence—it's almost like a
prayer—and then brushes, pours, sponges, *rubs* the paint across the
center of the massive white space.
(*More film ambience briefly, then out.*)
Helen Frankenthaler uses a variety of implements: small sable
brushes, rollers, wipers, her fingers, and some tools we use to clean
house: mops, sponges on long poles, squeegees, buckets, and pails.
Her colors are yellows, pinks, mauves, cobalt, and royal blue. Her
shapes can be calligraphic or bulky. A thin red line divides one
matte-brown canvas vertically and plummets into a blob of red, the
paint daubed on with the fingertips.
By diluting her paint and applying it like watercolor—soaking
and staining her unstretched, unprimed cotton-duck canvas—in the

1950s, Helen Frankenthaler took modern painting a step beyond the Abstract Expressionism of Jackson Pollock, one of her mentors.

(New, today sounds. Frankenthaler, off-mike, giving instructions. Then staple gun, workers' low voices. Hold under.)

On the day we visited Frankenthaler's New York studio, she was back in the city after four months, extremely busy, giving orders, supervising workers as they stapled a recent canvas onto a large wooden frame. It took a while before she could sit down and talk . . . carefully . . . deliberately . . . *emphatically*—to begin with about where she had gone to look at art, growing up in New York.

FRANKENTHALER: I went to the Museum of Modern Art, which was then referred to as "The Museum," because there were no other museums! I mean, to this *day* I still call MOMA "The Museum." And there are *scores* of wonderful museums now in New York. But if you were brought up with the Museum of Modern Art—even though the Met was full of treasures then—"The Museum" meant Fifty-third Street between Fifth and Sixth.

STAMBERG: Helen Frankenthaler will be sixty next month. She's a small woman, spare, high-strung, beautiful, with immense dark eyes. Married for a time to the painter Robert Motherwell, she is something of a diva of art, treated with utmost respect, *demanding* utmost attention. Her paintings from the 1950s—those pioneering years— can sell for three hundred thousand dollars. Newer work goes for between sixty and ninety thousand.

One of her paintings hangs on a wall of her studio along with an autographed photo of Al Jolson and various mementos including the framed notice, dated 1951, announcing an exhibit of work by "the New Generation, the most advanced and most solid of the younger generation of abstract painters in New York City." Frankenthaler's name is on that list.

I notice something else on a ledge in the studio where we sit talking—a wonderful photograph of Claude Monet in *his* studio, holding his palette.

FRANKENTHALER: I love that picture!

STAMBERG: He's working on one of the "Water Lilies" paintings. Why is that photograph here?

FRANKENTHALER: A good friend gave it to me, and it's very touching to me. Because clearly, this is where the man really *lived,* in the true sense of the word. I think most artists feel that their real selves and lives exist in relation to their work and the environment they work in—that's where they are really living, no matter what other life situation they might be involved in. But one is closest to one's self when one is closest to one's work, and dreams, and hopes, and . . . making your own magic.

STAMBERG: I was surprised that you permitted public television cameras into your studio.

FRANKENTHALER: I was, too! And I have had many second thoughts about it. The making of a picture is one of the most private things a person can do, and *must* be done alone. One *has* to feel not exposed at those moments but totally free and private to be as inventive, crazy, brooding—whatever—by one's self.

Painting is not theatre, and I think more and more people confuse one with the other. The act of painting is not entertainment. The *result* of good painting—you hope—is growing pleasure.

STAMBERG: Describe how you work. You unroll the canvas onto the floor of your studio, and it's *big*! You approach it with buckets of highly diluted acrylic paint. And you pour pools of paint onto the canvas. What determines what you do? Is it that you've got green in that bucket? Or that the canvas is this size, so you'll try the upper left-hand corner?

FRANKENTHALER: It's a combination of things. It's never the same twice, like anything else that's full of feeling—cooking, or love, or anything else. It isn't a hit-or-miss thing, but the very careful drawing, painting, coloring, of creating a picture.

STAMBERG: What about the pouring and staining? Did you invent these techniques? You've certainly developed them to their fullest point.

FRANKENTHALER: Well, working on the floor I had learned, in a sense, knowing and watching Jackson Pollock in the very early fifties.

STAMBERG: (*Narrating*) She liked watching Pollock dip wooden sticks into cans of enamel paint and then bend his arms and shoulders into the canvas to create carefully composed ropes and lassos of paint. He made movement important . . . improvisation . . . *how* the painting is made.

Helen Frankenthaler says Jackson Pollock changed our ideas about surfaces that work, in abstract pictures. He removed art from the easel. Its edges became limitless.

FRANKENTHALER: I think what I took from him was the gesture and the attitude and the floor working. But I wanted to work with *shapes* in a very different way. What evolved for me out of *my* needs and invention had to do with pouring paint, and staining paint.

STAMBERG: When you work with highly diluted paint, you can see the weave of the canvas through it.

FRANKENTHALER: Well, it's a kind of marrying the paint into the woof and weave of the canvas itself, so that they become one and the same.

STAMBERG: (*Narrating*) An early triumph of stain painting, inspired by Pollock, was Frankenthaler's radiant nine-foot-wide 1952 canvas, "Mountains and Sea." Now at the National Gallery, it was her breakthrough picture; so influential that the young artists Morris Louis and Kenneth Noland scraped together whatever money they could to travel from Washington to New York just to see it. It launched a new artistic movement—Color Field painting.

I asked Frankenthaler about her earliest works—the first works she'd sold.

FRANKENTHALER: The first painting I sold, I sold for fourteen dollars in 1949. And I was *flabbergasted* that anybody wanted it! It's a wonderful little picture that is a dead ringer for a Braque-Picasso analytic-cubist 1912 study. Obviously a real pastiche of another style, because I was a student and had been trained within that tradition during my college years at Bennington—trying to see what it was that Braque and Picasso did with such magic and knowledge. I would look and look and look and draw and draw and draw!

I showed this painting in fear and trepidation; yet I knew it was good! A composer named Lionel Novak loved it and bought it. He called me a couple of years ago, because there was a show of my small, small canvases that the U.S.I.S. sent around the world, and that was one of the major pictures in it. And he said, "What's the insurance on this now?" He didn't like the answer at all. (*Laughs.*)

STAMBERG: I guess it was more than fourteen dollars.

FRANKENTHALER: (*Smiling*) It was!

STAMBERG: And if you see the painting now, do you look at it and say, "The girl has promise"?

FRANKENTHALER: I am very moved by it and very proud of it. I understand perfectly how I developed from there and why I had to proceed from there and make what I made.

314

STAMBERG: That must be so rewarding, to see your own continuity—
to see where you came from.

FRANKENTHALER: It is! Because I don't feel—*ever*—phony about it.
I feel I recognize with such truth, step by step, how I became what I
am—for good or bad. But it's what I am. Yes.

STAMBERG: Helen Frankenthaler. The artist is having a very big year.
In January, an exhibit at the Andre Emmerich Gallery in Manhattan,
plus a large, lavishly illustrated book on her work. In May, a retrospective at "The Museum" (of Modern Art). And before any of that,
on December twelfth, a major birthday. "If," as Frankenthaler put it,
"being *thirty* is major!"

———

Days after this profile ran, a picture postcard arrived from Frankenthaler (a reproduction of her "Renaissance," 1971) scrawled with hand-
written thanks—"It sounded like me! Real."—and hearty good wishes.

A few months later, I encountered Helen Frankenthaler again, at a
White House ceremony honoring the winners of the National Medal of
Arts. Ms. Frankenthaler is a member of the President's National Council on the Arts. Her ex-husband, Robert Motherwell, was one of the
day's honorees.

She smiled warmly and asked me to sit with her during the ceremony. John Frohnmayer had recently become head of the National
Endowment for the Arts, and controversy swirled about government
funding. I asked Frankenthaler about it and, as she began responding,
pulled out my small tape recorder and mike. Frankenthaler frowned.
"Oh, put that thing away!" she said. I did, wanting to avoid a scene
(and, also, because I wasn't really working the ceremony). But later,
thinking about my persistent impulse to ask questions and capture the
answers on audiotape, it occurred to me that I could no more put away
my tape recorder than she could put away her cans of paint. And I think
if I explained that to her, she would understand.

Ms. F?

Going Home

October 1989

You can observe people. You can hear people without entering into their lives. You can always evaluate people just by their actions, their expressions, what they say or the way they look, the way they act, or what they do, what their pastime is, what their job is, and the way they live and the kind of house they live in and what they do for a living. All these things add up to a person's character. You don't have to go out and ask them questions. They reveal themselves as they are.

—*Erskine Caldwell, November 1976*

In 1989, the world as we'd known it for nearly half a century began coming apart. Régimes tumbled in Eastern and Central Europe. Poland was first. There, Solidarity was legalized, then voted into power. Next, Hungary cut the barbed-wire fence along its Austrian border, opening a passage for East Germans; thousands and thousands fled west. Hungary then elected a new parliament and prime minister. East Germany cracked down on emigration, then opened and ultimately demolished the Berlin Wall. In Bulgaria, there were rallies. Czechoslovakia had a "Velvet Revolution" (its first anniversary is observed some pages forward). Romania toppled Nicolae Ceaușescu.

Nineteen eighty-nine took our breath away.

In the fall of that year, perhaps in some subconscious search for stability, I made a reporting trip home, to Manhattan. We were doing a series on *Weekend Edition*/Sunday. We'd sent several reporters back to their hometowns to find out what had changed since they'd left. The last visit in the series was mine, and it let me do my favorite kind of reporting—hit the streets, microphone in hand, and talk to strangers. You can feel the energy on the block, grab chunks of its sounds, walk and talk into the mike, describing what you see.

I decided to walk backward through my life in New York. Other than that, I had no preconceived plan, no interviews lined up, no experts to meet. Producer Deborah George (who's helped me do some of my best work), engineer Manoli Wetherell (yes, marvelous Manoli again!), and I just went onto the street to see what we would find.

STAMBERG: The big city consists of countless neighborhoods that act like small towns. Tall apartment buildings are vertical neighborhoods—your doctor is on 4, your best friend on 17. The streets are so jammed with stores and schools and services that an entire lifetime can be spent on just a handful of city blocks. I spent forty percent of my life in a one-mile stretch of Manhattan—the Upper West Side, between 96th and Central Park West (where I grew up), and 116th and Broadway (where I went to college).

(*Sneak in street ambience, up, then fade for:*)

Barnard was my last stop in New York. I left the city after graduation, but Barnard College is where this story starts. There, on its leafy and sheltered campus across the street from Columbia University, a professor emeritus of social work addressed the question at the heart of our series.

(*Speaking to professor:*) What's changed? I went to school here thirty years ago. What's happened in these thirty years? Catch me up.

PROFESSOR: Same and different.

STAMBERG: How different?

PROFESSOR: Same and different. Young people probably are more accepting of reality—I mean, accepting the world with all its shortcomings a little bit better.

STAMBERG: (*Narrating*) Thirty years ago, this was a Woody Allen kind of neighborhood. His Manhattan—where Gershwin tunes were always playing somewhere in the background—was the Manhattan I knew. Barnard and Columbia students peaceably strolled the brick walks of campus or walked along Broadway toward a beer or a bookstore.

(*More street sounds, low traffic, conversation.*)

Now, just two blocks from Barnard, some of the realities the professor spoke about are already evident. Eighty men, shabbily dressed, line up at a soup kitchen. They come from other parts of the city for free food.

(*Ambience changes. Bookstore. In background, salesman helps a customer. Hold under next section.*)

PHILIPPE CHENG: These guys come constantly into our store and try to rip us off, and we're chasing them all the time.

STAMBERG: At the Barnard Book Forum, the young manager, Philippe Cheng, complains about the soup-kitchen people and others.

CHENG: The same problems that's all around New York. It's just probably more prevalent here, because of the student population. There are a lot more bums and a lot more panhandlers because they get money from the students. Well, the students don't see them year-round, or they don't see them as much as *we* see them because they are always camped out in front of our stores.

STAMBERG: You live in this neighborhood?

CHENG: My whole life! I grew up here my whole life. And I feel like I am being forced to make a decision that I don't want to make, maybe to leave the city. Because the quality of my life is important to me, and I want to be able to walk out my door and have a clean street and not see all these guys selling clothing and all. I feel for them. But you know, you think that someday you're going to walk out and see *your* things out there.

(*Out on Broadway again.*)

WOMAN: (*With a thick European accent*) Terrible! Indescribable!

STAMBERG: (*Narrating*) A Jewish refugee from France, she's lived up here for thirty-five years and hates how the area has changed.

WOMAN: The neighborhood was Irish, German, and Jewish, and they all escaped.

STAMBERG: Yes. There was a period of "white flight"—a great exodus of the middle class. In the early fifties, Puerto Ricans filled the vacuum.

WOMAN: Puerto Rican was terrible! There used to be five generations in one apartment—*you* know that.

STAMBERG: They were very poor. They had no money, and that's how they had to live.

WOMAN: No, but the landlords used to make a lot of money from welfare. And then, later, Columbia University started—thank God—to buy them out, and it was wonderful.

STAMBERG: (*Narrating*) Now Columbia is the major landlord here. In the sixties and seventies, the rents went up. By the eighties, single-room-occupancy buildings, where you could live inexpensively, turned into costly apartments. Some thirty thousand rooms were lost, and the homeless came out.

WOMAN: They sleep on the benches. (*whispers*) It's indescribable. I want you to go to 110th Street and see what's going on behind the corner. See it, what is going . . . it's indescribable. Pretty please, go and see!

(*Siren, police-radio sounds.*)

STAMBERG: Some blocks before 110th, on the corner at 113th, a policeman is on duty—for this day only. The city found that most robberies occur on Wednesdays. So they sent office workers from the police station out on the street on Wednesdays. The crime rate dropped.

While he talks to me, this cop keeps looking over my shoulder, his eyes constantly moving.

COP: That teller machine directly behind you, that's what I am trying to look at. Because people will go get money, and somebody might jump out of a car, grab their money, jump back in the car, and take off. They will have to come this way. That's why I am staying on this side of the street.

STAMBERG: How has this Wednesday been for you so far?

COP: It's been relatively quiet out here today—hot, but quiet. Very nice.

STAMBERG: Thanks, Officer.

COP: You're welcome.

(*More siren sound, getting softer.*)

STAMBERG: Now to 110th. A street vendor, black, in her mid-thirties, sips wine from a goblet as she sells books, magazines, some furniture.

VENDOR: The cops give us an hour to pack up. We have a time frame in which to move.

STAMBERG: What do you do on rainy days?

VENDOR: We don't sell anything.

STAMBERG: And what about drugs and stuff in this neighborhood— and the homeless?

VENDOR: Well, we *are* homeless. This is my house right here.

STAMBERG: I see. That card table. So you live—

VENDOR: Out here.

STAMBERG: —on the street, and you set up what you can.

VENDOR: I set up everything I can. It's not the best, you know. I miss my apartment on Riverside, but—

STAMBERG: You had an apartment up here?

VENDOR: Yeah, over on Riverside Drive.

STAMBERG: (*Narrating*) For five years, she lived in subsidized housing. Then, she says, she got a promotion at work. Her rent went from two hundred thirty-eight dollars to seven hundred sixteen dollars. She got sick, lost her job, couldn't meet the rent, and has been on the street for a year.

STAMBERG: What are your plans?

VENDOR: Yah. (*Winces, lowers her head.*) You sound like my mother! What are my *plans?* . . . (*voice breaks*) I don't know.

STAMBERG: Her pain and confusion are clear. So is her spirit. At 110th Street, despite those warnings from the Frenchwoman, we are not hassled or badgered or followed. On this sunny and hot Wednesday afternoon, we have found a subtler sadness—private problems made public by the Manhattan realities: inflation, poverty, bad luck.

(*Portable radio, playing pop music.*)

At 107th and Broadway, Columbia University academia gives way to some yuppification. A young woman in an easy cotton dress pushes a stroller through the aisles of a Korean grocery store, her toddler blissfully asleep in his Osh-Kosh overalls. She says her eleven-year-old goes to a neighborhood public school, she's well aware of the bums and drugs, but she's committed to living in a place she finds vibrant and exciting.

YOUNG WOMAN: I want to live in New York, and so I am willing to put up with the costs, and to train my kid—who seems like a little midwesterner, even though he grew up on the streets—how to handle the city.

STAMBERG: What is the toughest lesson you had to teach him—the one where, as the words came out of your mouth, you said to yourself, "I don't believe I am telling this to my child"? Have you had that experience?

YOUNG WOMAN: Oh, sure! All the time. The toughest thing for me, having grown up in the Midwest, is having to teach him to be distrustful of people, and to not smile at people, to not be friendly with somebody who very well might *be* friendly—and how to make distinctions. That's been the hardest lesson.

(*Another scene shift. Sound of man screaming in Spanish.*)

STAMBERG: On 104th Street, Broadway grows suddenly Latin. The professor's lesson about new realities is taught in a language I can't understand.

(*More Spanish screaming. A woman joins in.*)

STAMBERG: I lived on 104th, a block off Broadway, and went to fourth grade in a public school a few streets away. An umbrella-covered Sabrett hot-dog cart was probably on the corner then, too, and people had fights. But never until this day have I seen a man crazed with drugs standing on one leg in the middle of the street, crowing like a rooster.

These blocks were always complicated. Drugs weren't so prevalent years ago; the poverty was more contained and transitory. But we moved from 104th down to 96th, in the nice, stable, neighborly 1950s, because we were robbed twice here. The burglar climbed up a fire escape and through my bedroom window.

(*Kids playing, chanting, jumping rope.*)

I used to sit at that window and stare across the street at a huge, crumbling old dark Victorian building with a sign carved over its door: Association for the Relief of Respectable Aged Indigent Females. I was too young to understand. I thought "indigent" meant "indignant." I kept wondering what they were so *mad* about.

(*Ad libbing, on the street.*) I see now that the building is still standing, and it may be coming on better days. It's going to be the New York International Youth Hostel, so it's changing from older women to younger people now, and it's under reconstruction, improving. And this neighborhood doesn't look that different, really. It just depends so much on which corner you stand.

One corner away, a guy was screaming his lungs out, maddened by drugs, but here's a corner—another corner, a block away—full of school kids with book bags, holding their mothers' hands and asking for some after-school candy, please. And guys just sort of lounging outside an insurance office, and women going in and out of the dry cleaners.

New York is as varied and complicated and confusing, I suppose, as it ever was—just less *consistent,* maybe, or . . . or . . . or more confusion packed in fewer blocks and fewer square inches than it used to be.

(*Cars starting off at green light.*)

Off Broadway at 100th Street, heading toward Amsterdam Avenue—and it's still there! (*beaming*) I can barely believe it! New York Free Circulating Library. It's the first library that I ever belonged to.

PASSERBY: Oh, it's the Ukrainian Institute now, I think.

STAMBERG: It's not the library?

PASSERBY: It hasn't been a library for a long time.

STAMBERG: (*Sadly*) Oh.

ALFRED KNOPF: I liked going behind the stacks in the public library as a child and picking out books. As I got older, I never borrowed a book. I don't like to read borrowed books, other people's books. I like to mark up a book if I feel like it.

STAMBERG: Do you underline passages that you especially like?

KNOPF: Chiefly that. Once in a great while I'll write in comments that I'll later wish I hadn't.

STAMBERG: Like "Bah, humbug"?

KNOPF: Yeah, or "Nonsense!" or "Terrible!"

—September 1982

PASSERBY: But the building has just been put up for landmarking, and we've been involved in it.

STAMBERG: Good for you! Thank you very much for landmarking it, because my first library card came from there.

PASSERBY: And George Gershwin wrote "Concerto in F" in a little suite over in that hotel. You've just bumped into a neighbor and an amateur city historian!

(*Busier traffic sounds.*)

STAMBERG: Big, broad 96th Street, and my old building, just off the park—number 12 West. (*Sound changes—indoors, very echoey.*) Inside the lobby here . . . is it inevitable that places where you've grown up always look smaller when you come back? Because it does. The marble floor is still handsome—white with black trim. And the old brass fittings around the elevators are the same. The dial that tells what floor the elevator is on. I think there's still an elevator man in this building!

(*Elevator door clangs open.*)

Hi! We're doing a story for radio. I used to live here, and I thought there wouldn't still be an elevator man.

ELEVATOR MAN: (*With a Spanish accent*) *Sure* there is!

STAMBERG: When I lived here, there was a man named Oscar.

ELEVATOR MAN: Don't know him.

STAMBERG: No, it was a long time ago. You have a bench there, where I can remember sitting more times than—

ELEVATOR MAN: Same bench?

STAMBERG: Probably. (*Laughs.*)

ELEVATOR MAN: It looks like it's been re-covered a few times, but beneath, it's the same bench. I think they are gonna change the elevator, if I am not mistaken.

STAMBERG: Oh, no, to what?

ELEVATOR MAN: No, it will still be the same cabin, but they'll put a new motor inside.

STAMBERG: But there'll still be somebody operating it? It won't be an automatic elevator?

ELEVATOR MAN: No.

(*Elevator gate clanks shut; motor starts.*)

STAMBERG: (*Narrating*) Riding up in the elevator again, wrapped in sounds that were part of my days until I was twenty-one years old, I see that Thomas Wolfe was wrong. You *can* go home again, to the sounds and smells of your childhood . . . in certain places . . . and for certain individual and very fleeting moments.

(*Elevator door opens.*)

STAMBERG: We stop on 12 (my floor was 9), and a girl and her mother get on. It is not a scene from *This Is Your Life*. I was chubby and dark. She is slim, with straight blond hair. As we ride, I think about *her* neighborhood—and mine.

(*Music sneaks in, "Concerto in F."*)

On floors of this building, in apartments that are co-op now and sell for more than three hundred thousand dollars, they play Gershwin CDs and rent *Annie Hall* or *Manhattan*. But when they leave the wood-paneled quiet of the elevator, the city that greets them is a rougher, harsher place. The fantasy New York is available to fewer and fewer of its citizens. The professor's "new reality" translates, ultimately, as the struggle to *preserve its graces.*

For my part, despite the professor's lesson—or maybe *because* of it—I find myself wishing, briefly, that I could stay on this elevator forever.

(*Music continues. Elevator stops. Door opens. "Watch your step, watch your step!" Door closes. Gershwin full to end.*)

STAMBERG: In all your years of thinking and talking about and visiting cities, have you found for yourself, Jane Jacobs, the perfect city in which to live?

JACOBS: That would be a negation of life. It would be a cemetery, and that's not my idea of the perfect place to live. Things change. New problems keep arising. Perfection is impossible, you always have to be chasing it.

—September 1980

Barbara Bush in the White House

October 1989

STAMBERG: Mrs. Bush, good morning. Millie, good morning.

BUSH: (*Giggles.*) That's my shadow!

STAMBERG: I think we've bored her already. She's lying down on the floor and not paying any attention.

BUSH: Well, she's not allowed to speak. She's been told that this morning.

———

Millie arrived in the Diplomatic Reception Room first—no leash, no verbal commands—a busy English springer spaniel prancing two inches in front of Barbara Bush's feet. The president's wife, in the kind of serviceable gray wool skirt, navy sweater, and pearls New England women wear for volunteer work at the hospital, smiled greetings and apologies for a twenty-second lateness. "I was getting pinned up," she said with a roll of her eyes. "All morning. Standing around having skirts shortened."

Mrs. Bush was my fourth first lady. My first was Betty Ford, who came to the White House in 1974 under the cloud of Richard Nixon's resignation. A month after that resignation (and four days before Gerald Ford's controversial pardon of Nixon), the new president's wife held a news conference. I got to cover it, which was unusual (the White House correspondent covers White House news conferences, not hosts), exciting (it was my first White House news conference), and probably sexist (it was the *wife's* news conference, so let a woman cover it). I didn't

care. I got to go. Although I could as easily have stayed home. Betty
Bloomer Warren Ford made absolutely no news that day. But the press
sat on little gold chairs under shimmering chandeliers in the State Dining Room and took notes, anyway. It was, after all, a White House news
conference. You take notes.

In general, I dislike news conferences. By definition they're pack
encounters at which few questions can be probing, and no answer can
be exclusive.

In my earliest radio days, I was so puzzled by such gatherings and
so unsure of what was important to report that I'd watch to see when
other reporters made notes or instructed their cameramen to roll, then
I'd put a note on my own pad to use that same clip because it was
obviously news! I suspect most rookie reporters do the same thing—a
skill learned in sociology classes in freshman-year college. For more
on-the-job news training, I'd rush home at night to see what the television reporter who'd been sitting across the aisle ran on the air, or check
my reporting against the next day's newspaper version. At some point
in a reporter's life comes the realization that her own reaction to what
she is observing is the valid reaction, that what she believes to be the
news is, in fact, the news. But that doesn't happen right away. And even
the most seasoned reporters can walk away from a news conference,
turn to one another, and shrug, "What's the lead?" Seasoning just
makes them less self-conscious about asking.

After many a season, in 1989, nine months into the Bush administration, I was at the White House for a one-on-one conversation with
Presidential Wife Number Four.

If Nancy Reagan is champagne without the bubbles, Barbara Bush
is a solid cream sherry. No nonsense, no frills. A woman who has raised
lots of children, loved them, and gotten love back, Barbara Bush was
sixty-four when we met, handsome with her garland of white hair. She
has the direct self-confidence of someone accustomed to position and
money. In conversation, discussing the issue of family values years
before Vice President Quayle made it a political flash point, I found that
Mrs. Bush's position and money seemed to make for certain blind spots.

At the time, she was involved with improving literacy—a decade-
long concern of hers. I asked what had sparked her interest.

BUSH: Someone spoke to me about it a hundred years ago when George
    was in the Congress, and I thought, "Literacy. That's so boring." I

Betty Ford said today
she is "very happy" in the
White House, would cam-
paign for the Equal Rights
Amendment for women,
and takes a moderate
stand on abortion.

At her first full-scale
news conference she re-
fused to say whether she
would like her husband to
run for a full term in the
presidency. But when
asked if she would cam-
paign in 1976, she re-
plied, "I'll be happy to
campaign—and for guess
who!"

—UPI,
September 5, 1974

was very busy. I had five children and lots of action, back and forth to Texas. But when George started to run for higher office, I realized I ought to come up with a project, and, anyway, it was time for me to shift.

I am one who believes that every ten years you ought to shift your emphasis and try something new, get excited in things. So, I spent the summer jogging (*rolls her eyes and smiles*)—I was considerably younger—and thinking about what I could do that would really be a good project. At that time we didn't have AIDS, nor did we have hunger in this immense amount. But we had other problems. We had teenage pregnancy. We had crime. We had inner-city problems. We had all those single mothers who are locked into welfare. And it suddenly occurred to me that every single one of those problems—drugs, unemployment, *everything*—would be better if people could read, write, and comprehend.

STAMBERG: I've heard you talk about illiteracy as a kind of bondage.

BUSH: It is. You can't get off welfare! You cannot get out of public housing unless you get into a literacy program that networks. It isn't just teaching you to read, write, and comprehend. They have to teach you how to get through this *maze*. Because if you give up your welfare, you're out of public housing. You don't get food stamps. You've got children, you don't have day care.

STAMBERG: Educated women have those stresses, too. Do you ever look at today's women and think, "Good Lord, I couldn't do that" or "How do they live with that degree of—"

BUSH: Yes, I do. How do they cope? How do they cope! I *do* look at that, and of course I have daughters-in-law and a daughter who work, and it's very hard for them. But it's not *all* your life, you know. It's such a short period. You think at the time, it will never end. You have to have priorities, and if you opt to work, then you've got to make an added effort. It's hard on you, but you have to put your children first. And I think your boss has to accommodate a little bit. I mean, if you need to go to school to see your child in a school situation, they should make accommodations for it. You'll have to make it up, but that's just a fact of life.

STAMBERG: You've said that women can't really have it all. You can't be a bank president and a mother.

BUSH: You can't! Well, you can *do* it, but are you going to give the

On-site day care would help. So would job flexibility, job sharing. I also think after maternity leave, bosses should allow their valued employees to phase into the job—not to come back full-time at the beginning, but maybe to come back three days a week, then four, rather than expecting this woman to return a few months after having a baby and jump in full-stream, working ten or twelve hours a day the way she was working before.

—journalist Julia Kagan, March 1985

children the time they need? Now, I am assuming a bank president has to work like a president of the United States—fourteen hours a day. That just isn't fair when you've had children.

STAMBERG: Such an old-fashioned idea, though!

(*Mrs. Bush sits up straighter, raises an eyebrow.*)

The working women of America—

BUSH: What are you going to do about these children? Why do we have these crises in the schools? Now, if there's also a father at home, that's different, but we're talking about the single parent—mother *or* father.

STAMBERG: You're saying that if a *married* couple has children, the woman of that family can be a bank president?

BUSH: Yes. It's the single parent we are talking about. You chose to have those children. They didn't ask to come. You *chose*. You have a responsibility to spend time with them.

I never spent my time better, and I've never been more grateful for the fact that I was *lucky* enough and *fortunate* enough to be able to stay home with my children.

STAMBERG: That *was* luck. And so few now, given inflation and what prices are like—

BUSH: Well, no. Given what we want! We don't want one TV set—*two!* I mean, I am not talking about the single mother who *has* to work. I am talking about the woman who *chooses* to work.

STAMBERG: Most families I hear about, where both people work, do it because they *must*—simply to pay the rent in a *not* extravagant house with just *one* television set.

BUSH: Yes.

STAMBERG: I mean, just to cover the bare necessities!

BUSH: And that I would say you have to do. But I know a lot of young women who are very successful who opt to work, too.

STAMBERG: Your job, for the last nine months, has been as first lady. Eleanor Roosevelt once said, "Any woman who goes into public life has to have a hide like a rhinoceros." How's *your* hide, Mrs. Bush?

BUSH: Like a rhinoceros. (*Laughs.*) No, no. She's right. But let me tell you what Lady Bird Johnson said—I like this even better. Lady Bird Johnson said, "Being the wife of the president gives you a bully pulpit." And if it gives you a chance to talk about causes you are interested in, and things you really want to help with, get involved in, that's *wonderful*. "If you don't take advantage of it," she said, "you

> **The whole idea of having to say "I'm *just* a homemaker." A homemaker has a very valuable profession, and there are different types of homemakers as there are different types of professionals outside the home.**
>
> **Another problem is how homemakers are portrayed in the media. Usually, it's as if their entire life revolves around getting the ring out of somebody's collar. Homemaking involves much more than that.**
>
> **—Barbara Resnick, at a homemakers' conference, September 1975**

sort of fritter your time away." She also said, "If by chance it reflects
well on your husband, well, that's what it's all about." Now, I know
that's not modern—but that's not bad!

STAMBERG: Thank you very much, Mrs. Bush.

BUSH: Thank *you* very much.

———

Barbara Bush did not like being called old-fashioned. And she didn't
seem to understand a family's need for two salaries, not to accumulate
luxuries but simply to pay for basic necessities. The shelter of privilege
kept her from understanding. But you *do* sense that this woman, whose
millionaire husband got excited when he discovered supermarket scan-
ners, could, if she had to, load a shopping cart with food for an army
and then go home and cook it with very little complaint.

In early 1993 Barbara Bush ceded her White House tenure to
Hillary Rodham Clinton. A thoroughly modern woman, Mrs. (her
choice, not Ms.) Clinton works outside the home (in the politically
correct parlance of the seventies), thinks, strategizes. More first partner
than first lady, Hillary Clinton has positioned the role for the twenty-
first century, a period that will doubtless see a first man moving into the
White House with his wife, the president.

**I suddenly was some-
body. I wasn't just the
suburban housewife who
was taking care of the
children and being the
backup to this man who
was out front. Not only
that, but he was there! He
was there every night. His
office was only hundreds
of yards away, as com-
pared to when we lived in
Virginia and he went all
the way in to the Capitol.
So, I felt a part of it. He
was no longer traveling.
That was a very fulfilling
time.**

**—Betty Ford,
March 1987**

Nina Hyde and Breast Cancer

April 1990

The last decade of the twentieth century began with brio. A half million celebrants set off firecrackers and popped open champagne bottles on New Year's Eve at the Brandenburg Gate in what would soon no longer be *East* Berlin. Nine months into the new year, the Germanys were unified.

In Washington, George Bush began his second year in office buoyed by public support, calling in his State of the Union Message for big reductions in U.S. and Soviet troops in Europe. Iraq's invasion of Kuwait and the marshaling of more than a quarter million American troops to Saudi Arabia would come later in the year.

In 1990, I followed these events as NPR Special Correspondent. I'd left *Weekend Edition*/Sunday in October 1989, eager to go back to weekdays, reporting for the various news programs and sitting in as guest host on *Morning Edition* and *Weekend Edition*/Saturday. It was for that Saturday program, anchored by Scott Simon, that I fulfilled a difficult promise I'd made to myself four years earlier.

SIMON: On Friday, the thirteenth of April, Nina Hyde entered Georgetown University Hospital in Washington, D.C., with complications from breast cancer. Miss Hyde is fifty-seven years old. Her name is familiar to many people in Washington and those in the fashion industry. She is the fashion editor of *The Washington Post*. Miss Hyde has chosen to spend much of her time in recent months speaking out about the illness that has consumed her. NPR Special Correspondent Susan Stamberg went to visit Nina Hyde at home last month.

STAMBERG: In her three decades in the fashion business, Nina Hyde covered all the collections, complained about the high cost of fashion, and never told women what they had to wear. Nina Hyde also made her name—in Washington circles, anyway—for the annual list of "Ins" and "Outs" she published every January first on page one of *The Washington Post* "Style" section. I first spoke with her about that list in 1983.

(*Archive tape. Hyde's voice is vibrant, lively.*)

HYDE: Pants that are cropped short are in, and too-long pants are out. White sheets—in. Designer sheets—out. New rock, new wave—in. Disco—out. Crew necks—in. Cowl necks—out. All purple tones—in. All orange shades—out. Diaphragms—in. The Pill—out. Marriage is in. Living together is out. Quality is in. Lists are out!

STAMBERG: And there sits Nina Hyde, maker of this list, in a purple crew-neck sweater. How *in* can you get?

(*Laughter.*)

How do you know? How do you know what's in and what's out?

HYDE: Well, should I tell you that I surveyed three thousand people, very scientifically—or should I tell you more honestly?

(*Archive tape fades out.*)

STAMBERG: She knew the yearly "Ins and Outs" list was silly, superficial—elitist, even. She also knew it was terrific fun and something that readers looked forward to and talked about at the start of each year.

(*Sneak in outdoor sounds, birds, cars passing.*)

So, when I went to see Nina Hyde last month at her home in a graceful tree-lined Washington neighborhood called Cleveland Park, I had to bring up the list again.

(*To Hyde:*) Did you . . . forgive me, I missed it because I wasn't in town then. . . . did you do your "Ins and Outs" column this year?

HYDE: (*Weak-sounding*) Yes.

STAMBERG: Well?

HYDE: You're always in.

STAMBERG: Am I in good company?

HYDE: And you're in very good company. (*Laughs.*) God, that is so far . . . I mean, three months back is so far away from what's on my mind at the moment!

STAMBERG: (*Narrating*) Nina Hyde's mind—a mind slowed but not dulled by medication—is on the cancer she's been dealing with for the last five years. In 1982, at age fifty, Nina Hyde had her first mammogram. It was misread. She put off having another mammogram until 1985. That one showed she had had breast cancer for at least three years. Despite a lumpectomy, radiation, a year of remission, and five rounds of massive chemotherapy, the cancer moved to her spine. So, the woman who'd bounced into our studios in 1983—her eyes bright, her black hair a lustrous, thick crown around her head—was, on the day we last met, sitting carefully, with a discomfort she fought to disguise.

She chose a straight-backed chair to support her now-frail body, and her voice was thinner. Her handshake, when we arrived, had been like an encounter with feathers. You eased up, touching her hand—knowing that your ordinary strength would be too much for her. But there was spirit, still, in her eyes. That same spirit had led her, three years ago, to ask the fashion industry for help—money for breast-cancer research. The industry only had to look around, she said, to see the problem.

HYDE: Donna Karan, you know, had to think about Anne Klein, her mentor . . .

STAMBERG: . . . who died of cancer?

HYDE: Who died of breast cancer. Oscar de la Renta had to think about Françoise, his wife, who died of breast cancer. It's an industry in which women make the clothes. Women are the manufacturers. Women run the sewing machines. Women sell the clothes. Women wear the clothes. It wasn't very hard to convince the industry to help.

STAMBERG: (*Narrating*) Nina Hyde was able to raise more than a million dollars from designers all over the world—men and women who knew her, respected her work, and understood the need.

Ralph Lauren started the money ball rolling. Bill Blass, Yves Saint Laurent, the House of Chanel, made donations.

(*Sneak in hospital sounds, low-volume lab machinery.*)

A year ago January, the Nina Hyde Center for Breast Cancer Research was established at Georgetown University Hospital. In a cluster of immaculate, brightly lit rooms, scientists in lab coats run complicated equipment and conduct tests. The head of the center— Nina Hyde's physician, Marc Lippman—speaks of his patient.

LIPPMAN: Well, she's been a tremendous pal. She's spoken out publicly on any number of panels concerning these issues, and that's always beneficial.

STAMBERG: Marc Lippman says the number of women who have come to the center has increased ninefold in the past twenty months, in part because of Nina Hyde's work. Dr. Lippman says he is sure that cancer researchers are on the edge of a breakthrough. The money Nina Hyde was able to raise helps bring that breakthrough closer.

LIPPMAN: We have a great deal of understanding of the fundamental things that make normal cells different from cancer cells, and we have substantial numbers of ideas that are already working in the test tube, in experimental animals, that can cure human cancers. Many of these things will be entering clinical trial in the next several years, and I'm very optimistic about some of them working.

(*Neighborhood sounds again—street, birds.*)

STAMBERG: At home in Cleveland Park last month, in a back room converted into a makeshift bedroom, Nina Hyde told of her illness, her treatment, and the decision to get psychological support. Every now and then, she touched her hair—gray, now, and thin, clearly growing out for the second or third time after all the chemotherapy.

HYDE: I knew I was in deep trouble when I finally went to NIH and saw Dr. Lippman. He said to me, "We've got a lot of work to do." And I decided, I can't spend my time spinning wheels worrying about whether or not this was picked up before. Now there's a major lump. I also knew that I had lost three very important years. Instead of a ninety-percent chance of recovery, I had a ten-percent chance of living five years. So I just moved on, and decided to keep on working and try not to disturb other people with it.

Finally Dr. Lippman said to me, "Why don't you get some help? If there was ever a time in your life that you deserved some kind of a support system, this is it!" He recommended a couple of people, and *boy!*—they just weren't my kind of people. I just remembered the vinyl chairs and the . . . you know, the shoes without socks, and the . . . (*Fade.*)

STAMBERG: (*Narrating*) Trust an award-winning fashion editor to notice the upholstery and footwear! (Although it should be pointed out that Nina Hyde was never a fashion victim. She always looked good—in simple, well-cut clothes, no jewelry, no bright colors. But she never *led* with her clothes.) Anyway, she finally found a psychoanalyst she could work with, and twice-weekly therapy sessions helped her to reach for help—to family, friends, the fashion people who gave money for research. She also decided she had to take charge of her health.

HYDE: I realized that I was spending more time looking at the fibers in socks than I was looking into my own medical care, and with breast cancer there are so many choices.

STAMBERG: Lumpectomy versus mastectomy, radiation and/or radiation implants, the degree of aggressiveness of the chemical or hormonal therapies. Decisions a patient must weigh *with* the doctors, after doing a good deal of research.

Nina Hyde, an outgoing but very private woman, decided to go public about her disease and what she had learned. At conferences, luncheons, dinners, on radio and TV talk shows, she urged women to have regular mammograms, to do self-examinations, to be responsible for their health. As a result of these appearances, she started getting phone calls from women she had never met.

HYDE: Total strangers. Total strangers. A woman called me the other day from Little River, New Hampshire, a two-hour drive from Boston, saying she'd had a mammogram and the doctor said there was something on the chest wall, but "Let's wait till we take a mammogram again next year and look at it again." And I said, "No! You have to take that mammogram tomorrow, and get another opinion on it." I'd take a phone call from a woman who calls me about that before I'd take one from Calvin Klein.

(*Off-mike chatting, up briefly, then under.*)

STAMBERG: As we spoke, the gray Washington afternoon deepened the shadows in Nina Hyde's house. A big old dog—a mutt with black-and-gray whiskers—lapped water from a dish on the kitchen floor. Next to the hospital bed that had been installed in the room, brown plastic pill bottles were arranged on the table—more bottles than you could count with your eyes. On another table, framed photographs: Nina Hyde, her husband, their two daughters. Her voice grew more and more faint as we kept talking. She was expending an enormous amount of energy on this conversation, speaking more from sheer will and self-discipline than strength.

(*Brief off-mike chatting again.*)

What was striking about Nina Hyde that afternoon—and it still is—was her total absence of anger. The circumstance of her illness is infuriating: a mammogram misread. Yet she had no rage, no bitterness or self-pity.

People are often described as "battling" cancer. Sometimes it's true. But there are others who give in to the disease—are overwhelmed by it. Nina Hyde *battled* cancer. She chose the most aggressive treatments, and spoke out in the midst of her illness to keep other women from—in her words—"getting into the same lousy state that I'm in."

(*To Hyde:*) What about the business of bravery, Nina—bravery in the face of serious illness? Why shouldn't we be able *not* to be brave?

HYDE: There's no reason. Absolutely no reason to be brave. I don't consider myself as being brave. Susan, you would do exactly . . . I'm convinced you would do exactly the same thing that I've done, if you were in the same position. I've never said, "Why me?" because I've always been very strong, and I've always really thought, maybe, "Thank *God* me, and not my kids or somebody who is less strong than I am." I've been able to withstand the chemotherapy pretty well. That's being *strong*—that's not being *brave*. I don't consider myself brave, not for a minute.

(*Quiet house ambience up briefly, then out.*)

STAMBERG: Nina Hyde's last byline appeared in *The Washington Post* on Sunday, April eighth. Her "Fashion Notes" column described a new Perry Ellis collection—clothes designed to wear in the fall. I'm Susan Stamberg.

———

Less than a week after that report was broadcast, Nina Hyde died. I sent her daughters, Andrea and Jennifer, a cassette of the complete conversation from that spring afternoon in Cleveland Park. They played a portion of it at the memorial service—rather, the "celebration" of Nina, held in June.

One of the letters I received in response to my report came from a Maryland woman who said that she had sat listening in her car in a parking lot, weeping "for Nina Hyde, for myself, and for all women.

"What keeps us going," she went on, "is that most of us live, scarred and never quite the same, but *alive,* usually well, often stronger than before. We are a very large club, we survivors, and we hang tough together."

The letter was signed Carolyn C. Finegar. Underneath the signature she wrote, "(mastectomy, 1987)."

The club gets larger by the day. In 1992 in this country, there were 180,000 new cases of breast cancer and 46,000 breast-cancer deaths. One out of eight women alive today will develop breast cancer in her lifetime; by the year 2000 it will likely be one in seven. The mortality rate has barely changed in half a century. There is a breast-cancer epidemic here. Nina Hyde's work to get funding for research is a fragment of what *must* be done. For all of us.

Walk tenderly in the first snowfall. Later on you can shovel and storm and cuss and bemoan. But the first snow is like a newborn baby—so clean and soft. It makes the world newborn. Walk gently into that first snow.

—from Kim Williams's Book of Uncommon Sense

The First Lady of the American Theatre

May 1990

When I can, I like to make something happen in an interview. Something unexpected. It's fresh for the guest—especially if I'm stop number 437 on the publicity tour—and it's good radio.

When Tony Bennett came in, I tested out a friend's theory that the true measure of a singer's voice is how it sounds when you play back a 33 rpm recording of it at 45 rpm (this was in 1987, when there were still non-CDs in record stores). Together, we listened to some singers at the wrong speed. Bennett sounded great. So did Tormé and Sinatra. Robert Goulet fell apart.

"I know this is a nervy request," I said on tape to longtime *Vogue* editor Grace Mirabella at her Manhattan town house, just days after she'd been fired from the magazine, "but could I see your closet?"

"That *is* a nervy question! Come on upstairs."

The fashion editor's closet was spare—no overdose of clothes—just a few perfect garments hanging in dry cleaner's plastic, waiting for wearing.

In 1990, Helen Hayes wrote a memoir. When I paid a call on her for *Morning Edition,* her book helped me make something sweet happen on tape.

(*Birds, carpenters sawing wood in distance, busy, comfortable nature sounds.*)

STAMBERG: Helen Hayes does not disappoint. Almost ninety now, her eyes are as twinkling in person as they are on screen. Her skin is a soft nest of wrinkles. She's thrilled with a small gift, prompted by a chocolate habit she reveals in her book.

HAYES: Oh, M&M's! I adore them!! (*Sound of candy wrapper crinkling as it's opened.*) Oh, bless your heart! Aren't you sweet! (*More paper crinkles.*) M&M's, my blessed things. Do you know when I like to eat these? At night, sitting up in bed reading.

(*More outdoor sounds.*)

STAMBERG: Miss Hayes lives in a big white Victorian house in Nyack, New York, twenty-seven miles north of Broadway. She and her late husband, Charles MacArthur, bought it in the thirties. A deep porch runs along the back, where the actress can sit and listen to the birds and watch the flow of the Hudson River some yards away, down a series of broad, terraced steps.

This is clearly a home that has welcomed friends. The living room glows with light from big windows. There's lots of flowered chintz on the chairs and sofas. The room is comfortable and unpretentious, much like its owner. Helen Hayes is the same age as this century, but you only know that by her occasional loss of a word.

HAYES: (*Lively and upbeat*) I think that's the secret of success in the theatre, is the . . . total . . . um . . . uhh . . . (*gropes for the word, then whispers:*) Oh, God!

STAMBERG: The way she *recovers* the word shows her skill as a performer.

HAYES: What is the word I am trying to say . . . ?

STAMBERG: Is it "push"?

HAYES: (*Quickly, with relief*) Dedication!

STAMBERG: Yes, say it again?

HAYES: (*Firmly again*) I think that is the secret of success in the theatre—that total dedication to perfection. (*Smiles.*)

STAMBERG: (*Narrating*) Helen Hayes has won every major award in theatre and film. She's been on radio, TV. But Miss Hayes never *chose* to be an actress. She was pushed on stage as a child. By twenty, she was a star.

HAYES: I never got the opportunity, which I am sure is very good for an actress, to *yearn* to perform. I was on at the age of six, and my career was really a vicarious one for my mother, who wanted very

337

much to be in the theatre. I think it was an ebullience of youth that carried me along for a long time. Then I had to stop and learn my profession.

STAMBERG: She took every kind of lesson: dancing, body movement.

HAYES: I took tap dancing to use my feet well, and to know how to keep them flat on the floor when you're not walking. (*Grins.*) I took boxing lessons!

STAMBERG: Again, for the footwork. She studied enunciation, and practiced by sticking out her tongue. Those lessons are audible today. When she speaks, Helen Hayes doesn't just cross her *t*'s, she dots her *i*'s! And of course she took acting lessons—but never Method acting, in which performers are taught to work from inspiration and emotional memory. Miss Hayes thinks Method acting hurt a whole generation encouraged to think of acting as an art.

HAYES: I *don't* think of it as my art. I think of it as my craft. And if I once or twice in life reach the point where it becomes an art—a moment of pure art—I thank God for it, and I don't expect it to be there every performance. But I have the craft to simulate it on the nights that I can't make it come true.

STAMBERG: Helen Hayes had such a moment in 1933 as Mary Stuart of Scotland. The "moment" extended to her entire performance.

HAYES: After the first act, the actors backstage didn't address me at all. I went to the dressing room and changed my costume. The dresser didn't talk to me. And when the curtain fell on the last act, leaving Mary alone in the cell waiting for her beheading, there wasn't a sound from the audience. No applause at all.

I changed into my street clothes and went out the back door of the theatre. That long alley on a drizzly night was filled with people—the audience had moved back there. And as I went out and down the little steps from the door to the ground and walked through the crowd, they applauded. *That's* when they applauded.

It was just a wonderful and incredible experience, and I never told anyone, because I thought, "They'll think I'm crazy. They'll think I dreamed this, or am boasting."

Years later, I was on a set in Hollywood, and a woman came up—one of the extras—and she said, "I want to tell you that you are the reason I am here today. I saw you one night in Columbus, Ohio, in *Mary of Scotland*." She said, "I went away from that alley. I walked home in the rain, and said to myself, 'I have to go to New York or to California. I *have* to live in that world.' "

Then I dared tell it—(*laughs*)—because I had a witness!

STAMBERG: Miss Hayes's greatest acclaim came in 1935, playing Britain's Queen Victoria. That's when she was dubbed the First Lady of the American Theatre. After *Victoria Regina,* other stage performances and films—*Anastasia, Airport* (her 1969 Oscar winner)—countless roles in countless productions.

HAYES: Well, it's a great way of life, and, you know, whenever young people come up to me and say they hope that they get into the theatre, they're studying and so on, I never feel like discouraging them. I've heard actors and actresses say, "Ohhhh, it's a hard profession. Ohhhh, it's difficult to succeed." Well, if they're not really for it, they'll find out, and they'll lose heart—they really will. They won't stay with it long if it isn't for them. But if it *is* for them, they will go through starvation and fire and disasters, all to get to that point of being an actor.

STAMBERG: Miss Hayes, how do you want to be remembered?

HAYES: (*Groans.*) Oh! (*Laughs.*) I don't know. I have chosen for my epitaph the last line of Victoria's great speech, after she comes back from her Diamond Jubilee. She's then crowding ninety, as I am now, and at one point some rough-looking men get through the police and troops guarding the route and run along beside the carriage, shouting and cheering her. She hears one of them say, "*Go* it, old girl! You've done it well!" Well—(*laughs*)—I want that on my tombstone. I hope that the world will say, maybe, that I did it well.

STAMBERG: Helen Hayes. Her memoir, written with Katherine Hatch, is called *My Life in Three Acts.* I'm Susan Stamberg.

——

There's always at least one precious moment you have to leave out of a profile like that—some piece of tape that gets cut just before airtime so that the report will fit. With Helen Hayes, I kept those twenty-five seconds of audiotape in my files, liking what it revealed about her and (yes, ghoulishly) thinking it might be useful for an obituary.

Miss Hayes told of touring in *Twelfth Night* and, after many weeks on the road, phoning her husband, Charles MacArthur, from Pittsburgh.

"Charlie!" she exulted. "Tonight I played Viola *just* the right way! I did it! I found it tonight!"

Her husband replied, "Helen, you're *closing* tomorrow night."

"Yes," Helen Hayes said. "But I have two more goes at it—matinée and evening!"

The Velvet Revolution Plus One

November 1990

The young people of Czechoslovakia helped reclaim their country in the Velvet Revolution of 1989. Their story got lost in the tumult of dramatic changes in Eastern and Central Europe that year. A year later, I got a chance to tell it.

Visiting Prague for a television project in the fall of 1990, I kept my tape recorder handy as tales of Czechoslovakia's youngest citizens spilled out—with pride, tears, euphoria—from everyone I encountered. On the eve of the Czech revolution's first anniversary, I put the stories together—a report on how the rebellion began.

STAMBERG: In Prague, when they talk about what happened to them in the last extraordinary year, one date keeps coming up again and again. They remember it the way we remember the Kennedy assassination—remember where they were, what they were doing, when everything changed in Czechoslovakia.

(Outdoor sounds, guitar playing, singing.)

On a soft, clear evening last month—and maybe today, too—on a cobbled street near Wenceslas Square, two young men in their twenties entertained after-dinner strollers.

(Music up again.)

For centuries, Prague has been home to artists—musicians, painters, playwrights. (The city is located in that part of Czechoslovakia called Bohemia, as in "bohemian," *La Bohème*—people who are free, easy, unconventional.) But a year ago, the young singers would have been forced from their street corner by the Communist government's police. There is music on the streets of Prague today because of what happened one year ago tomorrow.

(*On street, talking to a high-school student.*)

Where were you on 17 November?

YOUNG MAN: I was in the place when the policemans did the police action against the students. And that was really terrible.

STAMBERG: Why were you there in the first place?

YOUNG MAN: I hate the Communists and all the régime. It's a dirty policy, and my family had many problems with Communists. . . .

(*Cross-fade—shouting, chanting, demonstration.*)

STAMBERG: There had been demonstrations before, small protests. But dissent, in cautious Czechoslovakia, had mostly been in the hands of a few artists, intellectuals, journalists. On 17 November, it was the turn of the young.

Born after 1968, when Soviet tanks crushed the spirit of freedom in Prague's streets, raised in a totalitarian system—their textbooks and teachers controlled—they were a generation of which nothing had been expected. "The children are apathetic," their parents said. "All they care about is rock music and blue jeans!"

The children changed everything.

PAVLA EBLOVA: I am really very proud of my daughter. My oldest daughter, you know.

STAMBERG: High-school English teacher Pavla Eblova.

EBLOVA: I have four children, and she is twenty-two. She was in the first line facing the policemen when it all happened. Fortunately, she was only arrested.

STAMBERG: University students had gotten permission to observe the fiftieth anniversary of the death of a young Czech boy shot by the Nazis. It was the first official student march in twenty years. Some saw it as a chance to push for reform at their universities. Others thought to protest against the government. Word was out that this march was important, bigger than anything that they'd had before, and that there might be trouble.

(*BBC documentary tape: Students singing* "Gaudeamus igitur.")

They gathered in the afternoon of 17 November—a Friday—with banners and posters and lighted candles. It was four o'clock. Dusk comes early in Prague in November. Pollution helps to darken the sky. At first there were a few, then thousands—ten to twenty thousand (numbers are hard to pin down, but it was immense for Czechoslovakia)—young people mostly, from local colleges and high schools.

(*Singing continues. Man reads from posters: "Abolish the monopoly of the Communist party of Czechoslovakia."*)

They carried their banners into a national cemetery, where they were supposed to hold their memorial.

(*Shouting, soft at first, then growing louder.*)

Then someone, or several of them, began shouting political slogans and urging the crowd to leave the cemetery and march to Wenceslas Square, where an equestrian statue of the sainted Czech king is a symbol of statehood. This would be a defiance. The students had permission to assemble only at the cemetery.

(*Loud shouting now.*)

They went. Or tried to. They never got to Wenceslas Square.

YOUNG MAN: We went into the National Street, Národní Třída. We were singing our national songs. And then the policemans close the street, they told us all the time to go out. But there wasn't any way to leave.

WOMAN: Then the policemen started to beat people, and the people just showed their hands. "We have empty hands," they said. "We can't do anything. We can't do any harm. Please, let us go."

SECOND YOUNG MAN: It was terrible.

STAMBERG: Felicity Goodey, a reporter for the BBC, was in National Street that night.

GOODEY: (*From BBC documentary*) Another demonstrator is being marched away by the police now. He's being held with his arm up his back, and his hair . . . being pulled along by his hair. I saw him being kicked—oh, my goodness! (*Getting agitated.*) The demonstrators are having to run the gantlets of the *police*!! The police are beating them as they come through. (*Shocked and angry.*) Beating and kicking them!

(*People screaming and shouting.*)

The policeman are running after demonstrators now, beating them, beating them heavily with truncheons. Another one's been arrested.

(*Sounds of beating, shouting.*)

Now they are running past me. Most of them are limping. Awhhhh! (*Gasps.*) You can hear the men beating them.

(*More beating, slow fade, go to black for brief silence.*)

STAMBERG: There were no deaths, although there were rumors. State radio said thirty people were beaten. Official records show doctors treated four hundred fifty demonstrators, some so seriously injured that they are crippled for life.

PAVLA EBLOVA: That was really too much, even for adults. Because the children are . . . you know, it's too emotional for me. . . . the children cried there, "Parents, where are you? Fathers, mothers, where are you? *We* are here. Where are you?" Well, I cried then, you know, I couldn't help myself. And I decided to do everything to help our children to know that it was not in vain.

STAMBERG: Today, in the arcade where police had trapped and then beaten the young people, there is a memorial on the wall. A large, flat, black granite rectangle. In the center of the rectangle, sculpted hands thrust out at the viewer—hands making a V sign, hands held up flat to show that they are empty. Beneath the hands, a simple horizontal bar with this inscription: 17. 11. 1989. And beneath the inscription, a shelf, where flowers and candles are left and lit.

(*Czech national anthem plays.*)

STAMBERG: On the eighteenth of November, the students went on strike. In film and TV classrooms, they began editing videos and printing photographs taken the day before. Young people—the Minutemen of the Czech revolution—showed the videos in shop windows so people could see what had been done to them.

They invited to their campuses intellectuals prevented from teaching for forty years. Ten to fifteen people a day presented lectures. One philosopher, who had been jailed and sentenced to forced labor by the Communists, found the students didn't ask political questions. They asked philosophical ones. They asked the meaning of Czech existence.

(*Czech anthem again.*)

Theatres joined the strike. Instead of performances, there were town meetings, where one ordinary person after another stood and spoke of abuses by their government.

Civic Forum was formed by Václav Havel to represent the voices of opposition, and each day in cautious Czechoslovakia, thousands, then hundreds of thousands, gathered in Wenceslas Square, urged on by the students, shouting for freedom and a change in government. Young people took their bloody photographs to factories and plants and coal mines across the country, and called for a two-hour nation-wide strike. Unlike the Solidarity trade union in Poland, Czech workers were not part of the opposition. The students knew they had to have the support of the workers or nothing would change.

(*Sound from Czech student documentary film: man trying to make a speech, being shouted down by crowd.*)

At CKD, Prague's biggest industrial plant, the Communist boss, trying to rally workers, told them, "No country allows fifteen-year-olds to decide when a president should go, and who he should be." The workers began a chant: "We're no children," they said. "We're no children." And then, "Resign! *Resign!*"

(*Workers chanting. Cross-fade to radio beeps, beginning of newscast.*)

On November twenty-fourth, a week after the students held their march, an announcement on the radio: The entire leadership of the Czechoslovak Communist party resigned.

(*Newscast ends. Then cheers, joyful screams.*)

Pavla Eblova, what difference did that day make? What difference did 17 November make to Czechoslovakia?

EBLOVA: Well . . . (*Sighs. Smiles.*) Everything is different. If I am to say what is the most different in my life, that's the feeling of hope. Because before, it was hopeless to live. I very often asked myself why I gave life to so many children. I have four children—the youngest is seven—and I just didn't know what world they were brought into.

You know, the country is in terrible mess. There are many things which are much worse now—economy and so on. We know that the situation is really very bad. But we can breathe. And that's really the most important thing in life.

STAMBERG: In Czechoslovakia, on 17 November, 1989, ordinary people began doing extraordinary things, fueled by the energy of children. They were the catalysts—so young, they hadn't been traumatized when freedom was crushed in 1968. They hadn't collaborated—as most everyone had—simply to get along, to make a life. They were new.

(*Soft guitar music and singing, street sounds in background.*)

And so, last month—and, maybe, even today—on a soft autumn evening on Prague's Charles Bridge, two young men sang of the brevity of life, and all there is to learn. As they sang, twenty or so

The capacities of mankind, the human species, are very great and very wonderful and have shown themselves in very wonderful accomplishments throughout the ages. For the moment we tend to forget that, because we see things going so badly, so out of control, and, in a sense, so badly managed. You see Ford and General Motors shutting down when they could very well have had a little sense and produced small cars to begin with. I mean, it's just damn stupid!

I feel tired of writing about the tragedy of history, about wars and things turning out badly. I want to remind myself that our species does have other capacities and I don't think they've changed. I think they're latent at the moment, or suppressed. In abeyance, you could say.

—Barbara Tuchman,
April 1980

other young people surrounded them. All, except for one couple kissing at the edge of the crowd, listened with great and serious concentration, as the words floated out into the lavender-colored air.

(*Music up briefly.*)
I'm Susan Stamberg.
(*Music to end.*)

Her Life with Picasso

January 1991

Françoise Gilot is history's witness. She watched Pablo Picasso creating. She saw him work, then rework, ideas and materials. With her artist's eyes, Gilot watched.

We're back on the Picasso beat, in pursuit of genius with someone who knew him well. In 1983, art historian Rosamond Bernier described her friend Picasso. After Bernier, I met a woman whose relationship with Picasso was more intimate.

Françoise Gilot lived with the Spanish artist from 1946 to 1954. They met when she was twenty-one and he sixty-two. She's the mother of two of his children, Paloma and Claude. And she's the only woman who ever loved *and* left Pablo Picasso. Herself a painter, in her 1964 book, *Life with Picasso,* Gilot chronicled their turbulent, difficult relationship. In her early seventies now, with pale gray-green eyes and no makeup, Mademoiselle Gilot is a beautiful woman. Her sweet smile has mischief in it. A devilish laugh erupts out of her, quite unexpectedly, in the middle of a sentence. We spoke twice.

In 1991, I invited Françoise Gilot to join me in inspecting some paintings at the National Gallery of Art. Walking into a room full of art, she was like an animal in the forest—on the alert, looking piercingly from one canvas to another, deciding where to . . . not *rest,* exactly, but where to pay serious attention. That high-heeled stroll from gallery to gallery was a walk through the history of twentieth-century art. A shrewd visual analyst, Gilot pointed out a shape Picasso used over and over again:

"Here, in this very famous 'Family of Saltimbanques,' " she told me, "he depicts himself as Harlequin—the quintessential Harlequin—masked, mischievous, the buffoon. And for me, the diamond shape of his costume here is almost the logo of his entire work. The diamond shape is the form that defines Picasso before anything else. Look, for example, at the paintings of the cubist period. In 'Desmoiselles d'Avignon,' for example, the diamond shape is used for the muscles of all the women in that painting. I think it's his signature. Even if the piece had not been signed, those triangles and diamond shapes are really the mark of Picasso himself, or his own presence in his paintings."

Another observation from Gilot (it's affected the way I look at pictures now) was about how paint is applied to a canvas. We were standing in front of a Matisse. "The brushstroke is like the artist's fingerprint," she said. "No two artists use a brush in the same way." Before I could make a closer inspection, she strode off into another room, stalking art once again.

Our first encounter, in 1985, had been easier on the feet. In Studio Six, we sat with a book of Picasso reproductions open on the table in front of us. Leafing through the book, I searched for her face.

STAMBERG: Is this you?

GILOT: Yes, that's a painting by Pablo Picasso called *"La Femme-Fleur"*—"The Woman-Flower." It's of 1946.

STAMBERG: Is this you?

GILOT: Yes. That's a self-portrait that I made in 1945.

STAMBERG: Is *this* you?

GILOT: Yes, that's also a painting called "The Painters of 1952" that I made—it includes Picasso, myself, and two other painters.

STAMBERG: So, we have two of yours and one of his of you, but how *many* of his are there of you, do you think?

GILOT: Well, you know, during the ten, eleven years when we were together, most of the paintings were modeled after me, even though they were never what you might call actual portraits. I didn't have to sit for them. I did sit once, but he was not painting. He was looking. And I was not sitting, I was standing! (*Laughs.*)

And so, you know, we always use words but they mean something else!

STAMBERG: Tell that story, please.

GILOT: That was in 1946. I had made some paintings or sketches of Pablo Picasso—from memory, mostly, because painters do not like to ask another painter to sit—it's so boring! We cannot trouble each other with that. And fortunately, we develop such visual memory that we usually don't need a sitting, especially when the features of another person's face and body are strangely familiar, in the sense that they belong to your own inner world.

Now, of course, there is another way to treat a portrait, which is to have the person sit or stand in front of you, and then draw what you see. In fact, that is *not* what Pablo did for "The Woman-Flower." He just asked me to stand in front of him one afternoon, because he wanted to compare what I really looked like with things he had in his mind.

STAMBERG: So he was not painting you at the time?

GILOT: No! After that, the next day, he started. I was intrigued to see what he would do. Usually, we worked in the same house but not in the same studio so we couldn't see what the other was doing. But I decided I would stay and look at what was happening. And it was very interesting, because at first the portrait was in a more realistic fashion. He painted me sitting on an African stool. After the first day, he decided that these were details that had nothing to do with me.

There are many ways to do a portrait. You can imitate nature—*describe* a person. Or you can *evoke* a person. That's what twentieth-century art has wanted to do—to evoke—to give a strong symbol. (You know, the meaning of "symbol" is "coming together.") So, what are the features or the forms that can *evoke* a person best?

If you want to see what people look like most, they look many times like an animal. Sometimes a compliment, sometimes a criticism! (*Laughs*.) If you look like a horse—(*great whooping laugh*)—long face! If you look like a bull, well then, you know you look a little bit like a beast! For myself, as he went on he thought that what I became was "The Woman-Flower." A flower, isn't that nice? So little by little,

I told him I had often thought he was the devil and now I knew it. His eyes narrowed.

"And you—you're an angel," he said scornfully, "but an angel from the hot place. Since I'm the devil, that makes you one of my subjects. I think I'll brand you."

He took the cigarette he was smoking and touched it to my right cheek and held it there. He must have expected me to pull away, but I was determined not to give him the satisfaction. After what seemed a long time, he took it away. "No," he said, "that's not a very good idea. After all, I may still want to look at you."

We started back to Paris the next day.

—from Life with Picasso

the body that was more realistically designed at the beginning became stemlike, and the African stool disappeared. Then the arms were no longer arms but looked more like appendages. My hair became like the leaves.

By the way, it was interesting that in February of '46, when we were still keeping our relationship secret, he took me to meet Matisse. As soon as Matisse saw me, he said to Pablo, "Oh, how nice of you to bring Miss Gilot here. I think I'd like to make a portrait!" That was a bit of a joke, because they were great friends, also a bit of rivalry between them. Picasso was very possessive—(*loud, explosive laugh: "HA!"*)—of *my* image that he had not even painted as yet. So, that was really a blow! But Matisse was undaunted and went on to say, "Yes, I see exactly how I would do a portrait, by having your hair olive-green and your complexion light-blue." (*Laughs.*)

As we came back from that visit, Pablo said, "What *nerve*! Why should *he* do your portrait? I didn't even do it myself as yet! Would I do portraits of Lydia?" (She was Matisse's model and mistress—a very strong presence in his paintings then.) I said, "Well, if you would do something of Lydia, you would tread on Matisse's territory. But since you did almost nothing of me, why should not Matisse try first?"

(*General laughter. She whoops the hardest.*)

He didn't like that idea at all, and I think that was the reason why he started "The Woman-Flower."

STAMBERG: But he took Matisse's idea. In fact, your skin *is* blue and your hair is green in Picasso's picture.

GILOT: Yah! That's very interesting, isn't it?

STAMBERG: Yes. Something else interesting—he painted you *before* he painted you! There are early works of his in which your face appears before he ever met you!

GILOT: Yes. In fact, the earliest portrait of my son, Claude, even pre-dates portraits of me in his work. In 1906, which was the end of the Pink Period, there is a portrait of a woman and a child. The woman looks very scared of something—doesn't look like me at all. But the portrait of the child is astonishing, because it was painted in 1906 and Claude was born in 1947! *Ha!* Forty-one years later, and it's really the face of that child—you can't mistake it! So, perhaps it took

STAMBERG: You went to his funeral, Matisse?

FRANÇOISE GILOT: No, I was in Paris at that time. And, you know . . . Matisse . . . one of his last words was "Et surtout, il ne faut jamais mourir"— "Above all, one must never die." So the idea of going to Matisse's funeral . . . I think he's still alive in his work. That's the most important!

—January 1991

him all that time to go from art into life, and have a human being looking exactly like that portrait.

With me, it was mostly the series of one hundred engravings called "The Vollard Suite." Some of the faces look exactly like my face when he met me. Which is what he said: "You are the person in my own inner world, come to life." But when he made that in the 1930s, I was only a child, and didn't even look like that!

STAMBERG: How do you explain that?

GILOT: Well, I think it's something mysterious that can hardly *be* explained. But if we want to explain it, we can say that nature follows art, and not art nature.

STAMBERG: Do you find—I'm doing this at this moment and I wonder whether the rest of the world does it, too—that people look at you with a particular kind of intensity because we've seen your face so often in his work?

GILOT: I don't notice that, because they also notice me for many other reasons. One being that I'm a writer, and another one, I'm a painter. So, I'm . . . in my own right, I'm somebody.

STAMBERG: I think you may be misunderstanding me, Miss Gilot. What I mean is, knowing all of that about you—or not knowing it—we look at the shape of your eyebrow and think, "Yes, we've seen that on a canvas somewhere."

GILOT: No, I don't think it's . . . that would be a little bit annoying for me.

STAMBERG: I'll bet!

GILOT: I have a book that I wrote recently called *Interface: The Painter and the Mask*. I say the painter is somebody who looks—either in his inner world or the outer world. And painting is a mask. So, for me, the recognition of some of Picasso's work in my face is just a mask. It's not me.

———

Françoise Gilot rushed to point out that she was her own woman—not defined through the extraordinary men she has been with. Since 1970, Miss Gilot has been the wife of Jonas Salk, developer of the Salk polio vaccine. Eighteen years into that marriage, she dedicated *An Artist's Journey,* a book about her work, "to Jonas, who possesses the art of science."

"Paloma" means "dove." I was named at the time that he drew the peace dove for the peace movement. I think it was the best gift that I was ever given. My father was always very prejudiced about calling his sons by *his* name, like they do in Spain. He *always* wanted to name his sons Pablo. And because he changed women, it was always the first son. So he said to my mother, "We will call our son Pablo"—Paul. And my mother said, "You already have one. I mean, let's not be ridiculous! It won't work every time." But somehow, when it got to be girls, he never wanted to play with the Spanish rule. He would always put a different name on the girls. So I'm called Paloma.

—*Paloma Picasso, December 1984*

Gilot speaks and writes of Picasso infrequently—in addition to *Life with Picasso* in 1964, there was *Matisse and Picasso: A Friendship in Art* in 1990. In connection with that book, she lectured on the two artists to a standing-room-only audience in Washington. But she limits such appearances. "If I spoke all the time about Pablo Picasso," Françoise Gilot says, "I would have time for nothing else."

The Man Who Made Us Modern

January 1991

Halfway through the twentieth century, John Bardeen, a theoretical physicist, made a discovery that would transform the rest of the century everywhere in the world. And it's likely you've never heard of him. I certainly hadn't until the start of 1991, when Dr. Bardeen died and I was asked to write his obituary for *Morning Edition*. That obituary follows, but first (as we keep saying in radio), some notes on *Morning Edition*.

It is strange, reporting for that program—"the O.P." ("Other Program"), I used to call it, in a healthy spirit of competitiveness—after all those years on *All Things Considered*. It is even stranger sitting in as host of *Morning Edition* when Bob Edwards is away. Bob left *ATC* in 1979 and has anchored *Morning Edition* ever since. Once I began substituting for him, I understood what the nature of Bob's life has been all these years.

It's AWFUL!

Morning Edition goes on the air at 6:00 A.M. But you don't just stroll in five minutes before airtime. The host arrives at 2:30. In the morning (the middle of the night, actually). To read the wires, write introductions, pre-record overseas interviews, prepare for live interviews or conversations to be taped later in the day.

RRRRRRrrrrrring.

The alarm goes off at 1:30, but it's absolutely unnecessary. I never really get to sleep when I'm subbing on *Morning Edition*. I've gone to bed at seven in the evening, right after supper. It's like being bad and getting sent upstairs. Not to sleep or to dream. To lie awake in the semi-darkness, waiting for sleep. *Hoping* for sleep. PRAYING for sleep.

"If I don't get to sleep right *now,* I'll never be able to make it on the air."

Awake.

"If I don't get to sleep *this minute,* I'll mess up. My brain will stick. I won't be able to think."

Awake.

"If I don't—"

RRRRRRinggggg.

Thank God! Time to get up. I can stop worrying about not sleeping.

Tiptoe out of the house. Drive in the pitch-dark straight down Connecticut Avenue—by day, a car-choked city strip; by night, as slick and empty as a bowling lane. If I time it right—going exactly thirty-one miles per hour—I can cruise downtown without hitting a single red light. I never time it right.

Sharing the streets with me at that hour: one desultorily patrolling cop car, a bread truck, some sloppy drunks, and, in summer, college kids who party all night.

Get to M Street. The parking garage's Early Bird Special is laughably irrelevant. At this hour, even the bird's asleep. Walk a wide circle around the big planter in front of the NPR building. A giant rat was spotted prowling near that planter six years ago. I don't want to meet him.

Upstairs, relying on just a single functioning brain cell, I feel slightly sick, and sway unsteadily from sleep deprivation. I've come to the right place. In the middle of the night, the *Morning Edition* production area feels exactly like an intensive-care unit. The patient is a two-hour radio program. America's strongest coffee is the transfusion.

Office lights are dim. There's almost no sound except for the electronic clicking of computer keyboards. The few members of the overnight staff are huddled in front of terminals or tape machines, reading the wires, writing copy, editing tape, talking softly by phone to reporters overseas.

" 'Morning," I groan to Carl Kassell, the program's veteran newscaster, who hasn't missed a story or a time post since he joined *Morning Edition* in 1979.

"Well, Mrs. Stamberg!!" Carl's never too busy to look up from writing his headlines and eight-and-a-half-minute hourly 'casts to smile a greeting and give a reassuring hug.

Six o'clock arrives more quickly in the early-morning hours. *Morning Edition* goes on the air hitched to several million radio–alarm clocks—the waking sound of listeners' days. Johnny Carson put America to sleep for thirty years. Bob Edwards wakes them up. Or I do, when I sit in. I love the idea of being the first voice people will hear that day.

(*Opening theme.*)

"Good morning. Czechoslovakia begins voting today—a general election on whether the federation survives or splits. I'm Susan Stamberg. Today is Friday, June fifth, and this is NPR's *Morning Edition.*"

(*Theme up, then down again.*)

For two hours, we move the news into bedrooms, bathrooms, commuter cars, joggers' headsets. The program glides out like a well-oiled machine, with few crises and many chances to fix mistakes before a tape of the live East Coast version rolls over, first to the middle of the country, later, to the West Coast. At eight, it's over. I gather up scripts, pens, and an empty coffee cup and leave the studio. While we were on the air, the sun has come up. The day has begun.

"Nice job."

"Good piece."

"You were wrong on the socialist-versus-free-market business."

"We fixed it for the next feed."

"Putting music into the middle of that copy really didn't work!"

There's always much reaction in the halls—everyone at NPR has awakened to the program, listened on the way in. That's different from *All Things Considered.* You have to remember an evening ATC piece all the way through the night and into the next morning in order to compliment or criticize. So it has to be *some piece,* to get reaction inside the building.

Hang around from eight to noon, when *Morning Edition* goes off the air out West, taping and writing and planning for the next day, standing by in case news breaks and there's a need for updates. If that *does* happen, after consultation with an armada of editors and producers, there's a dash into the studio, and we cut into the program, replacing something on tape with something live. ("This just in," I may get to say. Always a thrill. When Prince Charles and Lady Diana's first child was born, I said, "This just *out.*") A live cut-in is always tricky. It has to be precisely the length of the tape it's replacing. The director and I stare at the countdown clock, willing ourselves and the guest to be finished when the clock says 00:00. This particular day, no updates are necessary.

At nine o'clock, after more than twenty-four sleepless hours, rigor mortis begins to set in. Ten. Eleven. Twelve!

"Bye! Checking out. Just wanted you to know."

"Bye, Susan. Thanks." Ellen McDonnell, *Morning Edition*'s producer, grins her farewells as I stagger off. She's chirpily cheerful *always*—by nature and because she's arrived at work just three hours ago. Because of its early start time, and because most news happens during the day, *Morning Edition* is staffed around the clock, with daytime, swing-shift, and overnight crews. The producer works days. A nice advantage. Another advantage: With a twenty-four-hour crew, the *Morning Edition* host rarely encounters the crash-and-burn panic that afflicts *All Things Considered* from time to time as the *ATC* crew scrambles to broadcast a news-jammed program at five o'clock that they've been working on only since nine that morning. McDonnell and the day bunch settle in with their story lists, planning for the next program.

"Bob Edwards returns Monday," I've said on the air. With immense relief. On Monday, *he* can get up in the middle of the night and announce *my* reports.

EDWARDS: Scientist John Bardeen died yesterday. His name is not especially well known, but his work will have an effect on just about everything you do today. NPR Special Correspondent Susan Stamberg reports on the two-time Nobel Prize winner.

STAMBERG: In 1947, at the Bell Laboratories in New Jersey, John Bardeen, along with William Shockley and W. H. Brattain, did work that would earn the 1956 Nobel Prize for Physics and revolutionize our lives. John Bardeen and his colleagues invented the transistor. What difference did it make? Here is Nick Holonyak, professor of electrical engineering at the University of Illinois, where John Bardeen was professor emeritus.

HOLONYAK: You wouldn't have the computer. You wouldn't have your little watch on your wrist. You wouldn't have this telephone system that we're talking on.

STAMBERG: You wouldn't have avionics . . . or rheostats . . . or power drills . . . or pacemakers. You wouldn't have the Sony Corporation. In short, without the transistor, you wouldn't have modern life as we know it.

Nick Holonyak remembers the day in 1951 when John Bardeen brought his brand-new invention into class. Holonyak was Bardeen's first graduate student at Illinois. The professor arrived with a plastic box.

HOLONYAK: About ten inches long, about eight inches high, and four inches thick, and it had a little loudspeaker on the front of it, and two of these point-contact transistors sitting in some sockets, and a battery. As soon as he flipped the switch on, the thing started to play! I almost fell out of my seat. As a grad student, I knew how to build things out of *vacuum tubes*. You turn it on and you wait for the filaments to warm up. You wait for a considerable time before the thing does anything. This thing, whatever it was doing—the magic— went on immediately, soon as the power was turned on. I knew right away: Uh-oh! This man has got something different sitting here in our face!

STAMBERG: The day of the bulky vacuum tube was over. The era of electronics had begun. And John Bardeen was its father. Considered by colleagues to be in the same brilliant league as Enrico Fermi and Albert Einstein, it's curious that his name is not familiar. Perhaps it's because quiet, deliberative John Bardeen—some students called him "Whispering John," he lectured so softly—never sought publicity. And Professor Nick Holonyak says there's something else.

HOLONYAK: It's just the kind of culture we are. Just a couple of days ago, Red Grange, the legendary football player, died. Now, there's no doubt that he was an interesting man who did various things. But you know what? Red Grange did not change this planet the way John Bardeen changed it! I got a Russian friend coming in a couple of weeks, and when I say to him, "You know Red Grange died?," he's going to say, "What?" But when I tell him John Bardeen died, he's going to cry.

STAMBERG: Nick Holonyak of the University of Illinois Center for Advanced Study remembering his teacher, colleague, and friend, John Bardeen, co-inventor of the transistor. Mr. Bardeen died yesterday at the age of eighty-two.

John Bardeen was also co-developer of the theory of superconductivity, work which led to his second Nobel Physics Prize, in 1972. He was the first to explain how electricity could be transmitted without wasting any energy. And who knows? Superconductivity could create the *next* revolution for us. In Washington, I'm Susan Stamberg.

The Grace of Andre Dubus

July 1991

I'd known Andre Dubus, the stories he wrote, and the terrible story he was living, for years before we met. He's someone I kept talking with on the air. Our first conversation was in 1980. Andre sat in our Boston studio, I was in Washington, and we spoke about his writing—unvarnished tales of hardscrabble New Englanders, working-class people who know about grief and fight to find love. Powerful, luminous (John Updike's word for Dubus) stories, the writing stayed with me. Years later, when I learned of the accident that put him in a wheelchair, I got in touch again by telephone, and again . . . and again. Finally, on a high summer day in 1991, when Dubus published a new book—his first nonfiction—I went to see him.

Andre Dubus was a magnet for me and, I felt, for listeners. The unlikely combination of deep religious faith, powerful art, and long-ago military discipline create in him a man of indomitable spirit who is loving, funny, and totally lacking in self-pity. He's a touchstone for strength in the face of everything that can go wrong. In Haverhill, Massachusetts, I met a man of grace.

STAMBERG: In 1988, two years after he stopped at the scene of an accident and got hit by a runaway car . . . two years after his left leg was amputated and his right leg became useless . . . Andre Dubus got a MacArthur Fellowship.

(*Electric motor, chain grinding—sound up, then down and hold under.*)

> There are advantages. In the chair, my natural field of vision now . . . If you were standing here in my room and I were looking at you, it would be from the top of your breasts to just about the top of your thighs. That's my field of vision.
>
> —*Andre Dubus, July 1988*

He spent two thousand dollars of that money to install, on the roof of his car, a high-tech chain-and-pulley device that, at the push of a button, reaches down, grabs his wheelchair, folds and hoists it atop the car, and tucks the chair under a protective covering so he can drive off—into the sunset, if he so wishes!

(*Car door slams shut.*)

Andre Dubus has been on *All Things Considered* before. In 1980, six years before he got hurt, we talked about his story collection *Finding a Girl in America*. We talked about love.

DUBUS: (*Archive tape*) I'm really more concerned, in a woman I love, with how she will treat me when she feels bad . . . (*laughs*) . . . when her life is going badly, when she has the flu. What I really want to see people do, and want to do myself, is to be able to decide what should happen in a relationship, and then to use *will* to make it happen. Or else, you know, love can't ever last.

STAMBERG: Now, eleven years, three wives, and two new children later, and five years after *his* life began going badly—the accident— Andre Dubus is willing himself back to well-being. These days, he talks about getting around in a wheelchair. He's just back home from a trip to New York. It was rough.

DUBUS: The Hilton was not great. The bellman brought us up. (*Laughs.*) I said, "You call this a big bathroom?" He says, "It's got a wide door." I said, "That's like calling a man with a big mouth a big man. I got to *turn* the chair!" I had two showers there. They were scary. I didn't like the feeling. I thought, "For this . . . for this I want four hundred dollars an hour or revenge!" (*Deep laugh.*) I stay angry a lot.

STAMBERG: He's a big-chested man, fifty-five, an ex-Marine—red-faced and sun-loving, with a gray beard and dark hair combed back off a high forehead. He's tied a pink bandanna around his stump. Dubus is utterly straightforward, uncomplaining, but furious about the lack of facilities for—his word—*cripples*. He says being in a wheelchair is like being black in America in the 1930s.

We talk about being crippled. And writing.

DUBUS: Since I got run over in '86, I've only written four stories, and that constantly bothers me. Because, you know, I'm afraid that something is gone besides parts of my body. I have a notebook from before I got hurt, and I used to say I had enough ideas for stories to last me all my life, 'cause I'm a very slow writer. I still have the notebook, and the ideas for stories seem to be in someone else's notebook that I found.

STAMBERG: Do you think fiction just comes from someplace that's not healed yet in you—that you've been too busy surviving physically?

DUBUS: I don't know. I don't ever know where fiction comes from. I've never known a writer who knew where it came from. And I've never intimately known a writer who wasn't afraid that the well would dry up someday.

(*Car sounds, driving.*)

STAMBERG: But his storyteller's impulse is very much intact. Driving through town, Andre Dubus spots a woman walking a small collie, an audiocassette in her hand. "Where is she going?" he wonders aloud. "Why is she carrying that tape? How come no tape machine? Think she's going to play it for a friend? A lover, maybe?" A story maker, waiting for a red light he asks the basic question of art (of life, really): What's going on here?

(*Scene change. Horses' hooves; off-mike talk.*)

STAMBERG: After nearly an hour on narrow, winding, hilly Massachusetts roads (his car is fitted with hand controls for gas and brakes), we're in Boxford, at Windrush Farm. Marjorie Kittredge runs the place. She gives riding lessons to para- and quadriplegics, and others with problems. It's physical therapy. Andre asked to go to her a year after his accident—said he wanted to "do something brave." His physical therapist told him to wait another year, to let his bones heal. He waited. They healed.

KITTREDGE: So, he came. We had two side walkers and a leader, and put him on a horse. What'd you think?

DUBUS: The first thing I said was, "This is freedom!" As soon as I said, "Walk," Banjo started walking. First time in two years I'd looked *down* at anybody, for one thing!

STAMBERG: Riding, for Andre, is pleasure; it's also enormous effort. So are most things he does. He's had to make extraordinary physical and emotional adjustments. Sixteen months after his accident, his third wife left him. She took their two little daughters. His four other children are grown and live nearby. Marjorie Kittredge says there have been many times when all the difficulties got him terribly down.

KITTREDGE: Things were so frustrating he quit riding, he quit writing.

> It's not enough for a story to flow. It has to kind of trickle and glint as it crosses over the stones of the bare facts.
>
> —*John Updike,*
> *June 1983*

> My wife left in November of '87, and took my little girls. So actually, this year was worse than the first year, because losing children is worse than losing a leg. I see them, but I don't see them as much as a father should.
>
> —*Andre Dubus,*
> *July 1988*

His whole energy level dropped way down, and he simply couldn't cope. I said, "Look, you gotta quit all this nonsense of staying in bed. Come on out and ride!"

(*Touch-tone dialing on car phone; Dubus talking off-mike: "Yes, I'm out in Boxford at the farm now. We'll swing by and pick up the book. See ya later!"*)

STAMBERG: Who were you talking to?

DUBUS: The bookstore. I told him I'd bring you by, because I pick up curb-service books there.

STAMBERG: Oh, wonderful!

DUBUS: See, that'll be a dramatic handicap experience for ya! (*Laughs.*)

STAMBERG: (*Narrating*) It's not *that* dramatic. When we get back to Haverhill, his friend at the bookstore brings Dubus's new book out to the car for Andre to sign. He buys several books to add to the buckling shelves in his semi-tidy house. There's already lots of Chekhov, a Bible with the binding falling off, a well-thumbed, slightly dusty copy of *Introduction to the Devout Life* by Saint Francis de Sales (Dubus is Roman Catholic. He goes to Mass every morning he can). And there's a shelf filled with various editions of his own nine books—*Adultery and Other Choices, The Times Are Never So Bad, The Last Worthless Evening,* other collections of stories. Tacked to the edge of one shelf, the jacket of *Broken Vessels,* the new essay collection.

There's a piece written just before his accident, about stopping to help a fifteen-year-old girl who was being beaten by a punk. And there's an essay about pushing a woman to safety on Route 93, before he was hit in the accident that took his legs. He has this impulse to help.

DUBUS: That's the way I was always taught to do. I have always wanted to do. I don't think it's extraordinary. I think it's what we should do.

STAMBERG: Do you know how many people would have just driven by?

DUBUS: I *don't* think that most people go home and say, "Oh, there was a mugging. I didn't care." I don't think that's the way it is. We're not confident, really, most of us. And to suddenly go into a crowd and say, "Step aside, give this person some air, I'm taking over, you do this!" takes some kind of instinct which I think should be trained into

There is such a thing as moral imagination in a writer. And I think Andre feels with great pain the things that the rest of us fly past on the evening news on television or read in the tabloid pages of the newspapers. Andre feels you have to step in when you're there. If you see it, it's your duty to do so.

—*William Goodman, Dubus's editor, November 1988*

people from preschool on. I don't think most human beings just don't care about somebody being hurt. I really don't.

(*Long pause.*)

STAMBERG: I hope you're right.

DUBUS: I hope so.

STAMBERG: Because that's really . . . it's an important view of humanity you've got there.

DUBUS: Every one of my grown children would have done the same, I know that. None of them would have driven by. They don't let things happen within their range of vision. Be a better place, if nobody let things happen within their range of vision.

I have a friend who was taught by nuns, and the nuns told the little girls, every time they heard a siren, to bow their heads and pray for the person who was in trouble. And my friend said, "You know, it was a wonderful thing. It made us *aware* of someone else's suffering." This woman said she would like to teach a course to little children about caring. Say, go to a party and find a shy one, and play with the shy one. And you would therefore get out of your self, which is a good thing to do—(*laughs*)—for most of us, I think—get out of ourselves.

STAMBERG: There's an essay in Andre Dubus's new book about baseball. He wrote it in 1989, three years after his accident. He remembers an instruction manual for boys by Joe DiMaggio, who said, "If you stay in Class D or C ball for more than one season, unless you've been injured, you should get out of professional baseball." DiMaggio was wrong, Dubus says. His advice deprives.

DUBUS: I think it deprives most of us of fulfilling our dreams, since most of us are minor leaguers, right? It was very good practical advice for an excellent athlete who would be a major leaguer. But what I saw, as a grown older man writing the essay, was . . . very few people make it to the major leagues; they don't even know what the major leagues are. You have to keep playing the game you play, because one day you might do something you could never have done before.

STAMBERG: At the end of this essay, which is called "Under the Lights," Andre Dubus remembers a summer evening in 1948 in Louisiana, where he grew up. He was eleven, a ball boy for the Class C Lafayette Brahmin Bulls. And how it was when a first baseman—an unspectacular hitter—distinguished himself on the ball field. Andre Dubus writes:

"I see Billy Joe Barrett on the night when his whole body and his whole mind and his whole heart were for one moment in absolute harmony with a speeding baseball and he hit it harder and farther than he could at any other instant in his life.

"We never saw the ball start its descent, its downward arc to earth. For me, it never has. It is rising white over the lights high above the right field fence, a bright and vanishing sphere of human possibility soaring into the darkness beyond our vision."

——

If your eyes are sound, your whole body will be full of light.

—Saint Luke
(epigraph to a Dubus story collection)

Andre Dubus was finishing a new short story a year after our meeting. Nicole, his social-worker daughter, had suggested he try writing about people in chairs. "Write from where you are," she said. The hero of Dubus's story has two broken legs. Andre says ideas for stories have started to come again. Enough for another collection, maybe.

Picturing Annie Leibovitz

April 1991

Certain people, in certain societies, won't allow their pictures to be taken. They believe it steals their souls. Susan Sontag wrote about photography as an act of aggression. To George Bernard Shaw, it was less lethal, more hit-and-miss. "A photographer," Shaw said, "is like a codfish who lays a million eggs in the hope that one may hatch."

The portrait photography of Annie Leibovitz is neither random nor rapacious. Her pictures are badges for fame in America. Chief photographer for *Rolling Stone* magazine in the 1970s, since 1984 she has been principal portrait photographer for *Vanity Fair*. When eighty Leibovitz pictures—twenty years' worth of work—went on display at the National Portrait Gallery, I went over to meet the photographer. Producer Melissa Block and engineer Suzanne Mesnick were with me, and I asked Suzanne to bring along her camera—to see if we could make something happen for my report. I began this taping just as I had my interview with Lord Snowdon twelve years earlier. With very different results.

(*Echoey gallery ambience; off-mike talk between Leibovitz and me: "Take a picture." "Absolutely! Now, first I have to figure out how to open it. Wait. Sometimes . . ."*)

STAMBERG: (*Voice-over narration*) Annie Leibovitz looks great with a camera.

(*More off-mike Leibovitz: "No, it must be this. There you go. Okay, so . . . hold it. . . ."*)

Margaret Bourke-White was twenty-three years old and had just graduated from college and moved to Cleveland in an effort to become an architectural photographer. One day when she was walking her portfolio across Cleveland, she came to a public square and found a black preacher preaching to a flock of pigeons. There were no people in the square. She thought to herself, "Ahhhh! A photograph, a veritable photograph!" But she didn't have a camera with her. So she dashed to the nearest camera store and said to the clerk, "I *must* have a camera!" He looked somewhat askance at her, but she must have been a very convincing person because he loaned her a large camera. She went back and found the preacher still preaching, although the pigeons had gotten bored and moved off. So she bought some peanuts, put them in the hands of some little boys who were hanging around, and asked them please to feed the pigeons. She took this picture of a preacher, standing on a soapbox preaching to a flock of birds. It was the first picture she ever sold, to the Cleveland Chamber of Commerce.

—*biographer Vicki
Goldberg,
February 1988*

She looks great, even with the dumb point-and-shoot Japanese model we brought along to the interview.

(*Whir of camera motor. "Ooops! Wait, I have to put the flash on. I don't see any flash!"*)

She is tall and slim—New York chic in her brown suit with the miniskirt, her long, straight, dark blond hair. And glasses. A photographer with glasses. I will forget to ask whether that is a problem. It's too exciting that she's taking our picture.

(*"Oh, you have to lean back. Lean back now. We'll just . . . much better . . . okay." More camera-motor whirs and clicks.*)

Relaxed and open, Annie Leibovitz is a straight shooter. And for a woman who has photographed some of the best-known people of our times—people recognized by just one name: Ella . . . Mick . . . Wilt . . . Clint—she is more serious than you might expect. And thrilled to have her pictures in a museum.

LEIBOVITZ: I walked in here yesterday morning and saw it lit for the first time, and it was . . . I was . . . I was speechless. I . . . it just suddenly . . . I am going to cry again. (*Laughs.*) Suddenly I realized what all the work was about.

STAMBERG: At the age of forty-one, Annie Leibovitz is the second living American photographer to have a solo show at the National Portrait Gallery. The first was Irving Penn, who was seventy-two at the time of his exhibit. Like Penn, Leibovitz captures famous people on film, but hers are mostly pictures of popular-culture celebrities. And one picture in particular—because of who is in it and when it was taken—has become an icon.

LEIBOVITZ: It turned out to be a photograph that had many more meanings. Several hours after it was photographed, John Lennon was murdered.

STAMBERG: How did it come to be taken this way? How was the decision made that he would be naked, and that he would wrap himself around Yoko Ono like that?

LEIBOVITZ: Well, the story for me—and working for magazines, I always look for a way to tell a little story—the story for me was that they were still together after all these years. I really wanted to photograph them in an embrace. I was hoping that she would also be naked. At the last minute, she decided she wanted to leave her clothes on. Which turned out to make the photograph even more poignant, looking back at it now. He's in a very fragile fetal position, and he's clinging to her, and it's almost as if he's kissing her good-bye.

STAMBERG: Did you have any trouble taking pictures after that, for a while?

LEIBOVITZ: I actually did. Yeah. Every photograph after that, for about a six-month period, I felt had to be really special—and of course, it's hard. Today, if I take five photographs a year that I really, really like, you know, I . . . I . . . I'm . . . I say I'm . . . I'm . . . that's great!

STAMBERG: (*Narrating*) Although not a photojournalist, Annie Leibovitz has an uncanny ability to be where the action is. If the seventies were about rock and counterculture, the place to be was *Rolling Stone*. So, pictures of a cadaverous-looking Mick Jagger in a bathrobe in Buffalo, and Belushi and Aykroyd blue-faced in Hollywood. In the greedy eighties, *Vanity Fair* fed the fame frenzy. Leibovitz's photo of the Trumps before plastic surgery and Marla Maples—seated and formal in a sea of gilded furniture—is the ultimate eighties image.

There is more. Whoopi Goldberg, before she was famous, lying back in a bathtub filled with milk. Lauren Hutton, the model, topless, slathered in mud. Diver Greg Louganis, like a Greek god, arcing underwater. Annie Leibovitz calls these "atmospheric photos." She puts people in places she thinks are appropriate, and has them *do* something.

LEIBOVITZ: The things I ask people to do are really . . . you know, they really are *about* the person. They come from somewhere. They come from my research. They come from an idea that I worked with the person on. My work originated with reportage, and I was always sitting in the back watching something go on and waiting for a good moment. When I started to do the covers for *Rolling Stone,* a specific appointment time was set up, and people were coming to *me.* I felt very uncomfortable just doing a straight-on, one-to-one portrait. And I must have been thinking, "I have to invent an activity," or something that I could use to bring myself back to what I feel comfortable with—which is recording something going on.

STAMBERG: In 1980, Annie Leibovitz took a series of photos of major American poets for *Life* magazine. Before meeting Robert Penn Warren, she read his poems about death and finding peace with his own mortality.

LEIBOVITZ: I went to photograph him, and I shot all these sort of very

STAMBERG: Have you ever taken your own photograph—a formal portrait?

YOUSUF KARSH: I have, yes.

STAMBERG: Were you pleased with it?

KARSH: No, because I couldn't get myself to be as interested in me as I am interested in others.

—*October 1981*

A poem isn't about . . . it somehow . . . it's an itch first. Really, I mean, it's something . . . an impulse. It doesn't quite have a focus. Something is nagging you and you don't know what it is. When I get that feeling, I just go off and lock myself up in my study in my barn, and sit there and stare . . . stare at the ceiling.

—*Robert Penn Warren, February 1986*

normal "poet" photographs—him lying on the ground under a tree, him sitting in his library. When I finished, I pulled out of the driveway and looked up at the window of his bedroom, and there he was, looking out the window at me. He was staring at me in this kind of . . . this stare. As I drove away, I said, "I've got to get back. I gotta go back," you know. "I don't have it," you know. "I don't have it."

STAMBERG: She asked if she could come again. This time they went to the bedroom.

LEIBOVITZ: He sat down, and he said, "What would you like me to do? I'll do anything you want me to do." And I just . . . we were . . . it was sort of in a trance. I just started to . . . I asked him to take his shirt off. He had a T-shirt on underneath, just a tank-top sort of T-shirt, and . . . I was just trying to get to his *eyes*. I was just trying to peel away . . . I . . . I . . . you know, and I did it in a . . . I guess in a graphic way. Then I asked him to take off his tank top, and . . . (*laughs, then gets very serious*) . . . it's a strange photograph. And when I pulled out of the driveway, he was still in the window looking out. (*Laughs*.)

I don't know. You enter some pretty dark chambers when you go into this business—I mean, into this world.

STAMBERG: In the picture, Robert Penn Warren, three-time Pulitzer Prize winner, America's first official poet laureate, stares fiercely at the camera, body tense, brow furrowed, lips set in a thin line. His skin hugs the muscles in his upper arms, but under his arms, around the breasts and at the waist, it sags from his bones with the weight of seventy-five years. It is indeed a strange photograph.

But in a way, they *all* are—these pictures by Annie Leibovitz. Strange and idiosyncratic and revealing. Each with a point of view, a take. A story. The walls of the National Portrait Gallery are filled with twenty years' worth of stories.

LEIBOVITZ: The work feels established now, and I can just continue to do my work. It has a support. It has a backing now which I think can only make the work stronger. I mean, it's really exciting-exciting-*exciting*! (*Grins*.)

STAMBERG: What a lovely time in your life!

LEIBOVITZ: It's pretty *great*! It's pretty great. Now I just have to keep *working*, you know. Working-working!

———

Her seventies and eighties pictures grandly installed at the National Portrait Gallery, Annie Leibovitz produced the ultimate image for the nineties four months after our meeting. The August 1991 cover of *Vanity Fair* carried her photograph of actress Demi Moore—very beautiful, very naked, very pregnant.

The pictures Annie Leibovitz took of fully clothed Melissa, Suzanne, and me that day are propped on a shelf near my desk. There are three of them, snaps shot in forty-five seconds, using available light. They're not great. But in them, you can see the photographer at work, just as you heard her at work on the air.

The first picture shows me in a chair, holding my mike. For picture number two, Leibovitz moves back to include Suzanne, perched with all her recording gear on a big bench in the middle of the gallery room. Melissa sits on the floor just behind Suzanne. Before she takes the next shot, Leibovitz asks me to swing my chair sideways and lean back in it. She backs off again, and moves some three feet over to our right. The photographer is starting to design her picture. Photo number three has the beginnings of composition. The graceful curved line of my chair arm at the left is carried across the picture by some tape-recorder cable spilled along the bench. Suzanne's leg makes a frame on the right. The fish-pole mike she holds creates a rectangle that outlines Melissa's face. By picture number three, we're all smiling. Having a wonderful time as Annie Leibovitz takes our photograph.

Looking for Mr. Poetry

May 1991

May 15, 1991. Floods in Bangladesh trap more than a million people. The prime minister of France resigns. Yugoslavia faces a constitutional crisis. Kuwait announces it will hold trials for those accused of collaborating with Iraqi occupying forces during the Persian Gulf War. Queen Elizabeth goes to a baseball game in Baltimore.

And for *All Things Considered,* on that fairly business-as-usual news day, I am pursuing poetry. I spend some nine radio minutes at the Library of Congress, visiting a literary official before his year-long term comes to an end.

(*Off-mike voices, sound bouncing off marble walls.*)

STAMBERG: I'm here to see the poet laureate. Mark Strand.

RECEPTIONIST: Do you have an appointment with him?

STAMBERG: Yes, I do.

RECEPTIONIST: Okay, uhhh . . . probably the best way to get there would be . . . (*fade and hold under*)

STAMBERG: (*Voice-over narration*) I am in search of the most important poet in America—or, at least, the most *official* one. The search is not easy.

RECEPTIONIST: . . . to the control room, you have to walk all the way through that control room . . .

STAMBERG: The control room?

(*Squawks from walkie-talkie.*)

GUARD: She got to come through his . . . to his office.

RECEPTIONIST: Okay. He's on the third floor.

STAMBERG: He's up in the attic!

RECEPTIONIST: Yeah.

GUARD: Oh, you talking about . . . is she talking about that—?

RECEPTIONIST: The poet! (*Fade again for voice-over.*)

STAMBERG: I want to see him because *The New York Times* just quoted him lamenting the lack of intellectualism in Washington, and criticizing the White House guest list. Such outspokenness is rare in this city. Hard to find.

SECOND GUARD: Yes, ma'am?

STAMBERG: Well . . . (*beginning to sound discouraged*) I hope you can help me. I see elevators. I'm trying to get to the poet laureate's office.

SECOND GUARD: Poet laureate?

STAMBERG: Yeah, up in the—

SECOND GUARD: The poetry office?

STAMBERG: No. (*Wearily.*) It's the poet *laureate.*

(*Fade for voice-over:*)

Like bad poetry, the library is a maze of corridors . . . corridors . . . *more* corridors!

(*Door slides open.*)

STAMBERG: Elevator.

(*Elevator bell. Door closes.*)

STAMBERG: "Attic!" The button says so, right there.

(*Elevator door opens. My footsteps down corridor.*)

SECOND RECEPTIONIST: Ms. Stamberg is here.

STAMBERG: Eureka!

STRAND: Hi.

STAMBERG: (*Narrating*) The poet laureate's office is tucked in a corner, a nice bright lemon-painted room with a non-view—just the roof of the rest of the library. Mark Strand is certainly above everything here.

(*To Strand*) When I called to ask if I could come and hear your views on the shortage of intellectualism in this city, I told you I thought I'd found Diogenes—the last honest man on Capitol Hill. *Is* that you, do you think?

ROBERT PENN WARREN: Archibald MacLeish didn't want to be Librarian of Congress. He wanted to write poetry. The President, Franklin Roosevelt, said, "Oh, Archie, don't bother about it. You can get all the library work done in the time you can shave. Then you can spend the rest of the day writing poetry." And Archie said, "Great God! He thinks that poetry comes just like that." He said it was a grinding, miserable job of administration, running a big library.

STAMBERG: Sure. But poets often say that's grinding miserable work, too—writing poetry.

WARREN: Oh, yes, but the poet chooses that. Nobody takes it as a job. It's a very poor paying job, I can tell you!

—*MacLeish obituary, April 1982*

STRAND: (*Smiling; deep, soft voice*) No, I don't think so. I mean, I'm just a visitor, you know. I'm really passing through town. I've made some terrific friends here, and I stare at the seat of power over there—the Capitol.

STAMBERG: (*Narrating*) Strand says he's found some really brainy people here. Washington is full of them. *But*—

STRAND: I'm just astonished at the White House, that they choose to have businessmen and movie actors to dinner. I mean, there's a whole constituency out there of intelligent people that don't seem to make their way into the halls of power. Perhaps President Bush is afraid of them. (*Smiles*.)

STAMBERG: Have you been invited to dine or lunch at the White House?

STRAND: No.

STAMBERG: But you're the poet laureate!

STRAND: Oh . . . Yeah . . . but it doesn't mean anything at the White House. Poetry does not matter in the White House.

STAMBERG: (*Narrating*) Mr. Strand would grace any dinner table. He is very tall and very handsome. Gray hair, plaid shirt, well-worn jeans. At fifty-six, his wise eyes have good lines around them. Although he hasn't written any poems in his year here, and has had to read too much bad poetry, he says he's enjoyed being in the capital. Even our weather has been fascinating to him, after nine years in Salt Lake City. And when the poet laureate of the United States talks about the weather, you really listen.

STRAND: It's not only the light here that's different. The air in the West seems much more delicate—at least in the high desert of Utah. It's very caressing. It has a light touch. The air is thicker here. You feel it. Especially on hot days, you can feel the weight of the air. Its dampness. It seems palpable. You can almost bite it, and chew it.

STAMBERG: Here is one of Mark Strand's poems. It touches on most of his themes: leaving, and staying, and being alive. The poem was written twenty-two years ago. He remembers this exactly, although the date is not in the book. It's called "The Guardian."

STRAND: *The sun setting. The lawns on fire.*
The lost day, the lost light.
Why do I love what fades?

You who left, who were leaving,
what dark rooms do you inhabit?
Guardian of my death,

preserve my absence. I am alive.

STAMBERG: Mark Strand says he's received a lot of poetry in the mail this year—writers asking for his opinion, his encouragement. During Operation Desert Shield/Desert Storm, parents of soldiers forwarded poems they were getting from the Persian Gulf.

STRAND: These soldiers in the desert were afraid of never returning home, and of perhaps dying. And they turned to poetry in this period of trial—they took the most important experience or event in their lives and chose poetry to represent it. I find that moving.

What's sad is that many of the people who find the occasion and the need for poetry have not found it more often. I mean, it has to be that prospect of death that brings it out of them.

STAMBERG: Well, but look at all the people who turn to religion when they think they're dying or have a terrible disease. Maybe it's that sort of place of last resort, the place for ultimate understanding.

STRAND: There's a big difference. I think poetry is the shape *we* give to our inner lives. Religion is the shape that an *institution* gives to our inner lives. In some ways, religion is easier. Religion tells us what we feel and what we believe. And poetry encourages us to make up our own belief. A poem speaks to *one* individual on behalf of *another* individual. It doesn't speak on behalf of an institution. And it doesn't say, "You have to believe me, or else you're damned." It's not that kind of bullying urgency that I find repulsive in religion.

STAMBERG: (*Narrating*) Mark Strand is not a man to shirk tilting at institutions. In fact, another early work is set in an institution somewhat like the one he's now about to vacate. This is one of Strand's best-known poems. It gets anthologized. It's called "Eating Poetry."

STRAND: *Ink runs from the corners of my mouth.*
There is no happiness like mine.
I have been eating poetry.

The librarian does not believe what she sees.
Her eyes are sad
and she walks with her hands in her dress.

> **Almost everybody is a writer in some sense. Anybody who can dream can write, except that most people don't do it. And the difference between me and a lot of people I went to school with who are also talented . . . is simply that I kept doing the actual labor of the writing.**
>
> **—Judith Rossner,**
> **August 1976**

The poems are gone.
The light is dim.
The dogs are on the basement stairs and coming up.

Their eyeballs roll,
their blond legs burn like brush.
The poor librarian begins to stamp her feet and weep.

She does not understand.
When I get on my knees and lick her hand,
she screams.

I am a new man.
I snarl at her and bark.
I romp with joy in the bookish dark.

I get a certain amount of post from students and schoolchildren and so on. The ones that are hopeless are the ones that look simplest. "Dear Mr. Golding, how did you do it . . . ?" I've had explications of *Lord of the Flies* sent to me by students from one place or another. I suppose they're all right, I don't know. I've really rather abandoned the position I once had of thinking that an author actually does know what his books are about. I've come to the conclusion that he doesn't at all—not altogether.

—William Golding, October 1983

Recently, I got a bunch of letters from a high school in Los Angeles. They were studying this poem and they didn't understand it, although some of them had gotten close to an idea of what the poem is about. They asked me to explain it, which I did.

STAMBERG: What did you tell them?

STRAND: I said that the dogs represent something wild and emotional and basic in my nature. And the librarian represents something perhaps repressive. And I'm making a choice in this poem to "romp with joy in the bookish dark"—to be fabulously involved with poetry but at the same time ignorant. And not put too much weight on conscious learning.

STAMBERG: And isn't it also about the need to free poetry from the libraries, get it out of the library, get it off the shelves?

STRAND: Well, I don't . . . I hadn't that in mind, but if you see it in the poem—(*smiles*)—it's there. It's poss . . . I'd have to read the poem over again to . . . umm . . . it doesn't speak well for libraries, I'll say that! So, maybe poetry does belong elsewhere. But for the time being, I'm happy it's *somewhere.* A library is better than *no*where.

STAMBERG: (*Narrating*) Poet laureate Mark Strand leaves his remote office in the attic in the Library of Congress at the end of the month to return to teaching at the University of Utah. The new poet laureate, Joseph Brodsky, takes over—same office, same attic—in September. In Washington, I'm Susan Stamberg.

———

It was as difficult finding my way out of the poet laureate's office that afternoon as it had been to get in. Finally, when I'd retraced my steps and located the exit on the ground floor, a Library of Congress security guard asked to inspect my purse. People pinch volumes from the nation's biggest library. I did have a book in there. My son's marked-up, beat-up paperback copy of *Mark Strand Selected Poems*.

Out on the sidewalk now, I'll say good bye to you before catching a cab back to NPR. It seems a fitting place to stop—after a funny, frustrating, and ultimately satisfying hunt for the poet laureate of the United States. The search, in a way, is emblematic of my work in radio. Trying to find art, insight, connections, in the middle of the news of the day. Working to make those connections—ideas and interactions that lift us beyond the day's "events"—become an intrinsic part of the news we tell. Searching for things that last.

My microphone is right here. So is a fresh audiocassette and my ear, shaped like a question mark.

Let's talk.

Acknowledgments

Talk is neither cheap nor solitary. Hundreds and hundreds of people have helped with the decades of work represented here, moving it first out over the airwaves, then onto the printed page.

Of the radio people, Don Quayle, National Public Radio's first president—yes, Don; Dan Quayle was learning to spell *potato* when Don Quayle ran our shop—and Bill Siemering, our first director of programming, hired me when the network began, launching me on this grand, airborne adventure. Jack Mitchell was the producer who decided that *All Things Considered* should have cohosts—a man and a woman—and that I should be the woman. Today, NPR president Doug Bennet and our vice president for news and information, Bill Buzenberg, guide an ever-growing, often-changing team of producers, reporters, editors, audio engineers, and others (many of their names are scattered throughout these pages) who have forged the work of the NPR pioneers into an institution. Member stations keep the institution strong, building the bonds between our studios and your radios.

NPR is like a good university. Wander the halls, and you'll encounter an array of expertise. *Talk* has benefited from the wisdom of Noah Adams, Art Silverman, Michele DuBach, Maury Schlesinger, Laura Ziegler, Melissa Block, Tom Cole, Steve Tripoli, Andy Trudeau, Brooke Gladstone, Sean Collins, Rob Robinson, Margot McGann, and Richard Harris. Sue's Girls—my affectionate rubric for Claire Etheridge Dimsdale, Terrell Lamb, Dee Clarke Welles, Connie Drummer, Laura Taylor, Deidre Berger, and Debbie Dane—are the intrepid editorial assistants who over the years have got me into and out of broadcast studios, interviews, assignments, and assorted pickles. The following NPR computerniks F10-ed me almost daily: Max Cacas, Anthony Harris, Marshall Peterson, Miles Oliver, and Rick Jarrett. Thanks also to Corinne Hauser, Deborah Johnson, Benjamin Dreyer, Linda Kline, Ira Berlin, Adela Karliner, Maryanna Manfred, Karen Steineg, and Marlene Sanders.

Amy Schenkenberg sunnily plowed through twenty years' worth of archive tapes and, when that was finished, researched the mountain of questions I'd accumulated. Janice "The Goddess of Transcriptions" Verrey put all the talk onto perforied paper for the first time, transcribing an exhausting forty-plus hours of tape. Jonathon Lazear, my agent, arranged it all in the first place so that we'd have this work to do. As I assembled the twenty-year time line, my sieve-shaped memory got a boost from Lois Gordon and Alan Gordon's *American Chronicle: Seven Decades in American Life, 1920–1989.*

Joni Evans of Turtle Bay Books proves that publishing still has great editors. Joni's spirited, wise, anxiety-ridding guidance never wavered (plus we had some great laughs and at least one good meal).

My mother, Anne Roslyn Rosenberg Levitt, read aloud to me in her lilting voice when I was young. Just one of countless sweet ministrations, it shaped my love for sound. In 1975, Clea Larrosa came from Uruguay to help take care of Josh and ended up a member of our family. Without her, the intervening years would have been sans soccer, sanity, and supper.

Louis Collins Stamberg is my husband. He has been that since 1962. The worlds implied by those two sentences could never be written down, erased, or appreciated enough, ever.

Permissions Acknowledgments

Index